ETHICAL ISSUES IN DEATH AND DYING

MCCARQUDALE

Ethical Issues in Death and Dying

ROBERT F. WEIR, Editor

Second Edition

COLUMBIA UNIVERSITY PRESS
New York

Columbia University Press
New York   Guildford, Surrey
Copyright © 1986 Columbia University Press
All rights reserved
Printed in the United States of America

Library of Congress Cataloging-in-Publication Data

Ethical issues in death and dying.

   Includes bibliographies and index.
   1. Medical ethics.   2. Terminal care—Moral and
ethical aspects.   3. Death—Proof and certification.
4. Euthanasia—Moral and ethical aspects. 5. Suicide—
Moral and ethical aspects.   I. Weir, Robert F.,
1943–   .   [DNLM: 1. Attitude to Death.   Death.
3. Ethics, Medical.   4. Euthanasia.   5. Suicide.
W 50 3824]
R726.377   1986   174'.2   86-4191
ISBN 0-231-06222-2
ISBN 0-231-06223-0 (pbk.)
p 10 9 8 7 6 5 4 3 2
c 10 9 8 7 6 5 4 3 2 1

Contents

Preface

The first edition of this book was published in 1977. At that time the field of thanatology, the study of death and dying, was still reasonably new and was dominated by research done by psychiatrists and social scientists. The most notable person in the field at that time was Elisabeth Kübler-Ross, who was widely credited with having brought thanatology into public view with the 1969 publication of her book *On Death and Dying*. Two research centers on death and dying were gaining national reputations: the Foundation of Thanatology in New York (Austin Kutscher, director), and the Center for Death Education and Research (Robert Fulton, director) at the University of Minnesota.

The interdisciplinary field of biomedical ethics was also reasonably new when the first edition of this book came out. Among the ethical issues receiving considerable attention from philosophers, religious ethicists, and other concerned professionals were several issues connected with death and dying: truthtelling with terminally ill patients, the technological prolongation of dying, decisions about treatment termination, the proper use of cadaver organs, and the meaning of death itself. An increasing amount of analytical and normative work on these issues was coming forth from scholars located in universities, research centers, and a variety of clinical settings. Much of this work was done at two research centers: the Institute of Society, Ethics, and the Life Sciences in New York (Daniel Callahan, director), and the Kennedy Center for Bioethics (LeRoy Walters, director) at Georgetown University.

By 1977, ethical issues in death and dying were already overlapping with legal developments, a trend that has accelerated in the years since that time. The legislature in Kansas had enacted a new statutory definition of death (1970), Alexander Capron and Leon Kass had proposed a statutory definition of the standards for determining death (1972), Vincent Montemarano had been prosecuted and acquitted for committing euthanasia with one of his patients (1974), John Robertson had pointed out the criminal penalties that might be brought against parents and physicians who withheld treatment from handicapped newborns (1975), the New Jersey Supreme Court had written its opinion in the Karen Ann Quinlan case (1976), most states had repealed their laws making suicide a criminal offense, California had become the first state to pass a Natural Death Act (1976), and the Supreme Judicial Court of Massachusetts had decided the Joseph Saikewicz case (1977).

Now, nine years after the first edition, the second edition of this book is intended to provide a contemporary discussion of the ethical issues in death and dying as they confront us in the practice of medicine, in legislative statutes and judicial decisions, and in our personal lives. The ethical issues selected for discussion comprise the six sections of the book. By including articles by physicians and legal scholars, extended discussions by ethicists, and important legal cases (at the end of each section), I have tried to present readers with some of the best informed thinking about death and dying available today. It is my hope that, as a consequence of reading these selections, you will be stimulated to do serious thinking yourself about some of these vital issues that confront us all.

Three persons played important roles in helping me put together this collection of readings. Richard O'Neil gave me advice and suggestions that revised my initial selection of readings to the ones that now appear in the book. Fenella Rouse provided me with a copy of the disposition in the Montemarano case. Marilyn Verhalen did most of the typing of the final manuscript. To each of these persons, my sincere thanks.

ETHICAL ISSUES IN DEATH AND DYING

ONE
Truthtelling

Truthtelling is one of the fundamental ethical issues in the practice of medicine. Cutting across all medical specialities, questions related to truthtelling arise whenever physicians choose to mislead patients regarding the severity of medical conditions, recommend unnecessary surgery, use placebos for research or experimental purposes, misrepresent the features of a randomized clinical trial, misuse informed consent documents, or "protect" patients from clinical findings deemed too technical or too harmful for them to know.

As the authority figures in the physician-patient relationship, physicians may fail to carry out either or both of the dimensions of truthtelling: they may fail to *tell the truth* by imparting inaccurate information, or they may fail *to be truthful* by choosing to deceive their patients. Of course, patients may also fail to tell the truth or be truthful with their physicians, thereby possibly making their own treatment or restoration to health more difficult.

Of all the clinical contexts in which physicians have some choice in controlling the information and advice patients receive, none is more controversial than the regularly occurring situation of terminally ill patients who do not yet know their prognosis. For many persons, their situation represents the paradigm case for discussing the issue of truthtelling in medicine. Does a patient—any patient—have the right to receive accurate information and honest counsel in this situation? Does a physician have the right—or privilege—of conveying, withholding, or distorting information in this situation to serve therapeutic goals?

Until fairly recently, the answers given to these questions often differed significantly, with patients generally indicating a desire to be told about a fatal illness and physicians frequently claiming a "therapeutic privilege" to withhold such information whenever they judge patients to be unable to handle such damaging news. The interest of patients in being informed can easily be illustrated. William Kelly and Stanley Friesen did a survey years ago of patients' views on truthtelling. Published in 1950, the survey consisted of questions addressed to cancer patients, patients without cancer, and patients participating in a cancer detection program. The great majority of the cancer patients (89 percent) indicated that they preferred knowing about their medical condition, 82 percent of the noncancer patients expressed a desire to be told if they should be diagnosed as having cancer, and 98 percent of the patients in the cancer detection center wanted to be told the medical findings (*Surgery*, June 1950). A Gallup poll done almost three decades later came up with essentially the same results. The 1978 Gallup poll indicated that in response to a variety of questions, 82–92 percent of the population expressed a preference for being told if they had a terminal condition.

By contrast, the medical profession has traditionally refused to acknowledge an obligation to engage in truthtelling with terminal patients, preferring instead to interpret truthtelling within the context of physician discretion. Codes of medical ethics (such as the Hippocratic Oath, the World Medical Association's Declaration of Geneva in 1948, and pre-1980 versions of the American Medical Association's Principles of Medical Ethics) simply did not include truthtelling as part of a physician's responsibility. Physicians writing on the subject of truthtelling were sometimes inclined to declare that "deception is completely moral when it is used for the welfare of the patient," and "every physician should cultivate lying as a fine art" (see chapter 6 in James Childress, *Who Should Decide?*). A survey published in 1961 suggested how widespread such attitudes were among physicians. Conducted in Chicago by Donald Oken, the survey indicated that almost 90 percent of the physicians questioned had a policy, depending upon the factors in a case, of withholding the truth and being less than truthful with patients who had cancer (*Journal of the American Medical Association*, April 1961).

In recent years this disparity of views regarding truthtelling with dying patients has lessened somewhat. Because of the patients' rights movement, the increase in malpractice suits, greater public awareness of the causes of death (especially heart disease and cancer), the hospice movement, and a heightened awareness of the need for patient cooperation and informed participation in combating chronic diseases, physicians as a group seem to be more inclined to engage in truthtelling with terminal patients than in earlier years. The report by Dennis Novack and colleagues, included in this section of readings, is indicative of this apparent change in attitude on the part of some physicians. The change is also evident in the 1980 version of the AMA Principles of Medical Ethics, which call upon physicians to "deal honestly with patients and colleagues." A survey in *The Journal of Family Practice* in 1983 suggests this same change in attitude, at least to some degree. The family physicians seem more willing to tell their patients the truth about prognosis than physicians in earlier years were inclined to do (78 percent said they "usually give information to the patient regarding prognosis"), yet they demonstrate a continued willingness to use deception and coercion with patients (thus violating the requirements of truthfulness).

The readings in this section indicate that even with a changed attitude on the part of some physicians, debate continues regarding the extent to which physicians are obligated to engage in truthtelling with terminally ill patients. The survey by Novack and his colleagues indicates that physicians may agree that patients have a right to know and may often be inclined to tell patients the truth, but still occasionally withhold the truth for a variety of reasons. Mack Lipkin, a retired professor of family practice and psychiatry, states that "simplistic assertions about telling the truth" are misplaced because "transmittal of accurate information to patients is often impossible." Saul Radovsky, a physician in private practice, disagrees, arguing that "if you take time to talk with people . . . your story will be heard." The article by Weir suggests parallels in truthtelling in two different clinical contexts, and offers three reasons for regarding truthtelling as a prima facie moral obligation for physicians.

The legal case that concludes this section focuses on the unlimited discretion that physicians sometimes claim to have to withhold information from their patients, whether or not those patients are terminally ill. Ralph Cobbs, having had two operations and numerous serious medical problems following surgery on a duodenal ulcer, sued his surgeon for malpractice for having failed to disclose that serious bodily harm and death were known risks of the surgery. The Supreme Court of California, in addressing the legal obligation that physicians have to inform patients of the possibility of death when securing informed consent, ruled that "the patient's right of self-decision is the measure of the physician's duty to reveal" the truth. This case has obvious implications for cases involving patients with terminal conditions.

Changes in Physicians' Attitudes Toward Telling the Cancer Patient

Dennis H. Novack, M.D., Robin Plumer,
Raymond L. Smith, Herbert Ochitill, M.D.,
Gary R. Morrow, Ph.D., and John M. Bennett, M.D.

A number of surveys since 1953 have investigated the physician's approach to the cancer patient regarding the issue of disclosing the diagnosis.

Of 442 physicians surveyed through the mail in 1953, 31 percent said they always or usually tell the patient, while 69 percent said they usually do not or never tell the patient. Of those who generally did not make the diagnosis known, exception occurred when the patient refused treatment or needed to plan. Of those inclined to share the diagnosis, reluctance arose when they were discouraged by the family or afraid of the patient's response.[1] In 1960, of 5,000 physicians, 16 percent said that they always told the patient, and 22 percent responded that they never told the patient. The rest sometimes told the patient. Their decisions were influenced by such factors as the stability of the patient, the insistence by the patient or family, the necessity

Reprinted from the *Journal of the American Medical Association* (March 2, 1979), 241:897–900, with the permission of the authors and publisher. Copyright © 1979 by the American Medical Association.

for the patient to put affairs in order, and the unavailability of anyone else who could be told.[2]

In Oken's survey of 219 physicians at Michael Reese Hospital, based on questionnaires and personal interviews, 90 percent generally did not inform the patient.[3] Although more than three fourths of the group cited clinical experience as the major determinant of their policies, the data bore no relationship to length of experience or age. Many showed inconsistencies in attitudes, personal bias, and resistance to change and to further research, suggesting that emotion-laden a priori personal judgments were the real determinants of policy. Underlying were feelings of pessimism and futility about cancer.

By 1970 a questionnaire survey responded to by 178 physicians showed that 66 percent sometimes inform the patient, 25 percent always tell the patient, and only 9 percent never tell the patient.[4] This suggests a modification of previous practice. To assess whether this represents a genuine change, the present survey was undertaken.

Methods

The survey population consisted of 699 physicians whose names appeared in the *Physician Staff Directory* of Strong Memorial Hospital. Only pathologists and psychiatrists were excluded.

All subjects received an 18-item structured questionnaire through the mail almost identical to Oken's questionnaire in 1961, which covered physicians' attitude and practice toward the cancer patient.

Results

Two hundred seventy-eight, or 40 percent usable responses, were returned from a single mailing. Nine specialties were represented: internal medicine represented 35 percent of the total returns; pediatrics, 7.5 percent; obstetrics and gynecology, 2.5 percent; surgery and neurosurgery, 10 percent; oncology, 11.7 percent; family practice, 2.1 percent; radiology, 2.1 percent; subspecialty, 18.7 percent; others, 7.9 percent; and specialty not indicated, 2.5 percent. The sample appeared to represent a cross section of specialties within the hospital's physician population, with the exceptions that oncology was slightly overrepresented, and surgery and obstetrics and gynecology were slightly underrepresented.

In comparing the 1977 and 1961 populations, the present sample had a mean age of 37 years and was 91 percent men, while the 1961 sample had a mean age of 50 years and was 97 percent men. Oken reported that the great bulk of physicians in the sample were in active private practice in addition to taking a regular part in the teaching program. Two thirds of our respondents were older than 31 years and were involved in the practice of their specialties. Many took an active role in the hospital's teaching program.

As shown in table 1.1, 98 percent reported that their general policy is to tell the patient. Two thirds of this group say that they never or very rarely make exceptions to this rule. This stands in sharp contrast with Oken's 1961 data, which showed that 88 percent generally did not tell the patient, with 56 percent saying that they never or very rarely made exceptions to this rule.

No differences between specialties were found, with the exception that the pediatricians, while reporting that their usual policy is to tell the patient, make exceptions to this rule more frequently than other physicians. With minor exceptions this lack

Table 1.1. PHYSICIANS' POLICIES ABOUT TELLING CANCER PATIENTS

	Do Not Tell, No. (%)		Tell, No. (%)	
Exceptions	*1977*	*1961*[a]	*1977*	*1961*
Never	1(0.4)	18(9)	17(7)	0(0)
Very rarely	2(0.8)	90(47)	152(61)	6(3)
Occasionally	1(0.4)	56(29)	71(28)	10(5)
Often	2(0.8)	5(3)	5(2)	8(4)
Usual policy	6(2)	169(88)	245(98)	24(12)

[a]1961 data from Oken.

of speciality difference was a consistent finding for all question-naire items.

The results seem to indicate that the many factors that went into the decision to tell the patient influenced not only whether a physician would tell the patient but also the manner in which he made the diagnosis known, perhaps influencing the timing or wording of the communication.

The four most frequent factors considered in the decision to tell the patient were age (56 percent), intelligence (44 percent), relative's wish about telling the patient (51 percent), and emotional stability (47 percent).

Four factors most frequently believed to be of special importance were the patient's expressed wish to be told (52 percent), emotional stability (21 percent), age (11 percent), and intelligence (10 percent).

Eighteen percent of the sample reported they were less likely to tell a child, while approximately 10 percent were inclined to tell a patient who was old or who had poor comprehension. Fourteen percent said that they would tell the patient less frequently or might delay telling if they thought the patient was prone to depression or suicide. Approximately 12 percent would tell the patient somewhat more frequently if personal affairs needed to be put in order.

The bases for policies in 1977 and 1961 are tabulated in table 1.2.

The topic of communication with the cancer patient

Table 1.2. SOURCES FROM WHICH POLICIES WERE ACQUIRED

	Every Source, No. (%)		Major Source, No. (%)	
Source	*1977*	*1961*	*1977*	*1961*
Medical school teaching	59(24)	14(7)	7(3)	0(0)
Hospital training	128(53)	72(35)	33(15)	10(5)
Clinical experience	222(92)	191(94)	153(70)	146(77)
Illness in friends or family	89(37)	61(30)	15(7)	15(8)
Other	22(9)	24(12)	10(5)	17(9)
Total	520[a]	362[a]	218(100)[b]	188(100)[b]

[a]More than one answer can be given by respondent

[b]Figures rounded to nearest percent.

seems to be more frequently discussed now in medical schools and hospital training programs. Twenty-four percent of the 1977 sample vs. 7 percent in the 1961 sample mention medical school teaching, and 53 percent of our sample vs. 35 percent in 1961 mention hospital training as sources from which policies are acquired.

As before, clinical experience was given the major credit in both studies, with more than 90 percent citing it as a source and more than 70 percent citing it as a major source. As in Oken's data, analysis of the age of respondents citing clinical experience as a major policy determinant showed that younger physicians were just as likely to cite clinical experience as their seniors. Seventy-four percent of our group (and 86 percent of Oken's group) said that their policy had not changed in the past.

Thus, as in 1961, it appears that personal and emotional factors are of major importance in shaping policy, perhaps even more so in the present study. Subsequent to the general inquiry, "How did you acquire your policy?" it was specifically asked if personal issues were determinants. Seventy-one percent of the 1961 survey and 92 percent of the current survey reported that personal elements were involved. Again, as in 1961, these respondents were about equally divided as to whether these factors were most important. The physicians specializing in oncology (12 percent of total respondents) indicated that personal factors were less important in shaping their policies, suggesting that they believed there was some objective policy to be followed that was independent of personal considerations.

There is further evidence of the continuing importance of personal and emotional factors in shaping policy. Our sample evidences an even greater resistance to change and opposition to further research. Questioned about the likelihood of policy change in the future, our respondents show significantly less likelihood that they would change their policy in the future (P < .01). Five percent said that there was no possibility of change, 48 percent said that change was very unlikely, and 34 percent said that change was unlikely, although they were not sure. Only 9 percent said that change was probable, and 4 percent said that it was certain.

This resistance to change was also evident with 28 percent

responding that their policy would not be swayed by research as opposed to 16 percent of Oken's sampling. Only 15 percent of our sample said that perhaps their policy would be changed; 29 percent responded this way in 1961. One of the comments seemed to sum up the general feeling: "I would not be swayed by research (but I think my opinion is correct)."

Responses to the last two survey questions are perhaps indicative of the conviction with which the present policies are held. One hundred percent (vs. 60 percent of the 1961 sample) indicated a preference for being told if they themselves had cancer. One hundred percent thought that the patient has the right to know.

Comment

There appears to have been a major change in physicians' attitudes concerning telling patients their diagnosis of cancer. Even if only those physicians who believed strongly about telling the patient responded to our survey, there has still been a significant change since Oken's study. Indeed, there is some evidence that our results may be representative of more widely held views. In a recent study in which 50 patients undergoing radiotherapy were interviewed, 94 percent used the word "cancer" or "malignant tumor" to describe the reason for being treated. All patients were told their diagnosis by the physician who referred them for therapy.[5] How might we account for this change in attitude? Our respondents' written replies and additional comments suggest several explanations.

Therapy for many forms of cancer has notably improved in recent years. Oken's data suggested that the great majority of physicians believed that cancer connoted certain death. As many patients shared this pessimism, this common belief was often an effective deterrent to free communication. Today advances in therapy have brought longer survival, improved quality of life, and, in many cases, permanent cure. Physicians believe they can offer their cancer patients more hope.

There has been an increase in public awareness of cancer at

many levels. The media are constantly presenting evidence of the ubiquity of carcinogens. Public figures such as Betty Ford and Happy Rockefeller spoke openly about their malignant neoplasms. The American Cancer Society publicizes the "Seven Danger Signals of Cancer." Perhaps all of this has led to a lesser stigmatization of cancer, a greater ease in talking about its reality, and a greater awareness of its signs and symptoms.

Oken suggested that most physicians thought that the diagnosis of cancer, with its expectation of death, deprived the patient of hope, and hence they were reluctant to tell cancer patients the diagnosis. Our data suggest that this attitude has also changed. Even when death is expected from the disease, physicians are nevertheless telling their patients the diagnosis. Perhaps improved therapy allows physicians to be overly optimistic with their patients. Perhaps some physicians feel more comfortable in relating to dying patients. At least, many understand better the dying process. This is certainly due, in part, to the recent upsurge of interest in death and dying. Good empirical studies have been done, and many authors have made important contributions to our knowledge in this field.[6] This knowledge may have led to more effective communication with dying patients, a reduction in the fear that the dying process necessarily engenders loss of hope, and a greater understanding of the concerns and needs of dying patients. Our data show that these issues are more frequently discussed in medical schools and hospital training programs.

Perhaps more patients are being told because more need to know. Many university hospitals are major clinical research centers, and patients who agree to participate in research protocols must be told their diagnosis to satisfy the legal requirements of informed consent. At the University of Rochester, in 1975, 15 percent of patients with all newly diagnosed cancer participated in national protocols.

It is impossible to know to what extent the literature on telling the cancer patient has shaped attitudes. If it has had any effect, however, it would be in the direction of encouraging frankness. Koenig systematically reviewed 51 articles appearing in the professional journals between 1946 and 1966 that discussed the treatment of fatally ill patients.[7] He concluded that the tendency of authors appears to be strongly in favor of informing fatally ill patients of their conditions. This has been more recently reaffirmed by Cassem and Stewart, who, in suggesting a general policy of frankness, cite two sets of empirical studies.[8] The first set includes those studies in which patients were asked whether or not they should be told. These indicate overwhelming positive favor for telling. The second set looks at the effects of telling on patients and their families. These studies dispelled the myth of the harm that telling the patient might engender.

The comments of some of our respondents indicate that the reason for the present reversal in attitude is due, in part, to more sweeping social changes. The rise in the consumerism movement and increasing public scrutiny of the medical profession have altered the physician–patient relationship. In this era of "patients' rights," an attitude of frankness feels right and, indeed, given the current disputatious atmosphere of medical practice, may be the safest one to adopt.

Many questions remain. Do physicians tell patients they have "cancer," or are euphemisms such as "tumor" or "growth" still widely used, and if so what does that mean for the communication process? Are changing attitudes on telling the patient accompanied by the emotional support that a patient's knowledge of his diagnosis may demand of a physician? Saunders wrote, "The real question is not 'What do you tell your patients?' but rather, 'What do you let your patients tell you?' "[9] Now that we tell our patients more, are we also listening more? Unfortunately one survey cannot answer these questions.

Is the present policy of telling the patient the best policy? The majority of our respondents cite clinical experience as shaping their present policy, even though most of them have never had experience with another policy. The majority of Oken's respondents also cited clinical experience in shaping the exact opposite policy. While not discounting the value of clinical experience, its use as a determinant of policy must be called into question.

Our data suggest that, as in Oken's study, the present policy is supported by strong belief and emotional investment in its being right. One hundred percent of our respondents stated that patients have a right to know. Yet in asserting this in a blanket manner, are physicians sometimes abdicating a responsibility to make subtle judgments in individual cases? Do patients also have a right not to know?

Is it possible to determine who should be told what, when, and how? What are the criteria by which we judge if telling is right? Patient evaluation in future studies on telling might include assessments of compliance with the medical regimen, quality of communication with physician and family members, ratings of adjustment to illness, or psychological tests of depression and anxiety.

Our respondents' written comments seem to indicate that the current policy of telling the patient is accompanied by increased sensitivity to patients' emotional needs. There is some evidence that telling is the best policy.[10] Yet how rational is the process of deciding what to tell the patient with cancer? Even though the policies have reversed, many physicians are still basing their communication with cancer patients on emotion-laden personal convictions. They are relying on honesty, sensitivity, and patients' rights rather than focusing on the following relevant scientific psychological question: Does telling the diagnosis of cancer help or harm (which) patients and how? Only further systematic research can answer these questions.

Notes

1. W. T. Fitts, Jr., and I. S. Ravdin, "What Philadelphia Physicians Tell Patients with Cancer," *Journal of the American Medical Association* (1953), 153:901–904.

2. D. Rennick, ed., "What Should Physicians Tell Cancer Patients?" *New Medical Material* (1960), 2:51–53.

3. D. Oken, "What to Tell Cancer Patients: A Study of Medical Attitudes," *Journal of the American Medical Association* (1961), 175:1120–1128.

4. H. S. Friedman, "Physician Management of Dying Patients: An Exploration," *Psychiatry Medicine* (1970), 1:295–305.

5. G. W. Mitchell and A. S. Glicksman, "Cancer Patients: Knowledge and Attitudes," *Cancer* (1977), 40:61–66.

6. H. Feifel, ed, *The Meaning of Death* (New York: McGraw-Hill, 1959); C. Saunders, "Care of the Dying," *Nursing Times* (1959), 55:960–961, 994–995, 1031–1032, 1067–1069, 1091–1092, 1129–1130; J. M. Hinton, *Dying* (Baltimore: Penguin Books, 1967); B. G. Glaser and A. C. Strauss, *Awareness of Dying* (Chicago: Aldine, 1965); E. Kübler-Ross, *On Death and Dying* (New York: Macmillan, 1969); G. L. Engel, "Psychological Responses to Major Environmental Stress," in *Psychological Development in Health and Disease* (Philadelphia: Saunders, 1962), pp. 272–305; and W. A. Greene, "The Physician and His Dying Patient," in S. B. Troupe and W. C. Greene, eds, *The Patient, Death and the Family* (New York: Scribner's, 1974), pp. 85–99.

7. R. R. Koenig, "Anticipating Death from Cancer—Physician and Patient Attitudes." *Michigan Medicine* (1969), 68:899–905.

8. N. H. Cassem and R. S. Stewart, "Management and Care of the Dying Patient," *International Journal of Psychiatry in Medicine* (1975), 6:293–304.

9. C. Saunders, "The Moment of Truth: Care of the Dying Person," in L. Pearson, ed., *Death and Dying* (Cleveland: Case Western Reserve University Press, 1969), pp. 49–78.

10. B. Gerle, G. Landen, and P. Sandblom, "The Patient with Inoperable Cancer from the Psychiatric and Social Standpoint," *Cancer* (1960), 13:1206–1217.

On Telling Patients the Truth

MACK LIPKIN, M.D.

Should a doctor always tell his patients the truth? In recent years there has been an extraordinary increase in public discussion of the ethical problems involved in this question. But little has been heard from physicians themselves. I believe that gaps in understanding the complex interactions between doctors and patients have led many laymen astray in this debate.

It is easy to make an attractive case for always telling patients the truth. But as L. J. Henderson, the great Harvard physiologist-philosopher of decades ago, commented:

To speak of telling the truth, the whole truth and nothing but the truth to a patient is absurd. Like absurdity in mathematics, it is absurd simply because it is impossible. . . . The notion that the truth, the whole truth, and nothing but the truth can be conveyed to the patient is a good specimen of that class of fallacies called by Whitehead "the fallacy of misplaced concreteness." It results from neglecting factors that cannot be excluded from the concrete situation and that are of an order of magnitude and relevancy that make it imperative to consider them. Of course, another fallacy is also often involved, the belief that diagnosis and prognosis are more certain than they are. But that is another question.

Words, especially medical terms, inevitably carry different implications for different people. When these words are said in the presence of anxiety-laden illness, there is a strong tendency to hear selectively and with emphases not intended by the doctor. Thus, what the doctor means to convey is obscured.

Indeed, thoughtful physicians know that transmittal of accurate information to patients is often impossible. Patients rarely know how the body functions in health and disease, but instead have inaccurate ideas of what is going on; this hampers the attempts to "tell the truth."

Take cancer, for example, Patients seldom know that while some cancers are rapidly fatal, others never amount to much; some have a cure rate of 99 percent, others less than 1 percent; a cancer may grow rapidly for months and then stop growing for years; may remain localized for years or spread all over the body almost from the beginning; some can be arrested for long periods of time, others not. Thus, one patient thinks of cancer as curable, the next thinks it means certain death.

How many patients understand that "heart trouble" may refer to literally hundreds of different abnormalities ranging in severity from the trivial to the instantly fatal? How many know that the term "arthritis" may refer to dozens of different types of joint involvement? "Arthritis" may raise a vision of the appalling disease that made Aunt Eulalee a helpless invalid until her death years later; the next patient remembers Grandpa grumbling about the damned arthritis as he got up from his chair. Unfortunately but understandably, most people's ideas about the implications of medical terms are based on what they have heard about a few cases.

The news of serious illness drives some patients to irrational and destructive behavior; others handle it sensibly. A distinguished philosopher forestalled my telling him about his cancer by saying, "I want to know the truth. The only thing I couldn't take and wouldn't want to know about is cancer." For two years he had watched his mother die slowly of a painful form of cancer. Several of my physician patients have indicated they would not want to know if they had a fatal illness.

Most patients should be told "the truth" to the extent that they can comprehend it. Indeed, most doctors, like most other people, are uncomfortable with lies. Good physicians, aware that some may be badly damaged by being told more than they want or need to know, can usually ascertain the patient's preferences and needs.

Discussions about lying often center about the use of placebos. In medical usage, a "placebo" is a treatment that has no specific physical or chemical action on the condition being treated, but is given to affect symptoms by a psychologic mechanism, rather than a purely physical one. Ethicists believe that placebos necessarily involve a partial or complete deception by the doctor, since the patient is allowed to believe that the treatment has a specific effect. They seem unaware that placebos, far from being inert (except in the rigid pharmacological sense), are among the most powerful agents known to medicine.

Placebos are a form of suggestion, which is a direct or indirect presentation of an idea, followed by an uncritical, i.e., not thoughtout, acceptance. Those who have studied suggestion or looked at medical history know its almost unbelievable potency; it is involved to a greater or lesser extent in the treatment of every conscious patient. It can induce or remove almost any kind of feeling or thought. It can strengthen the weak or paralyze the strong; transform sleeping, feeding, or sexual patterns; remove or induce a vast array of symptoms; mimic or abolish the effect of very powerful drugs. It can alter the function of most organs. It can cause illness or a great sense of well-being. It can kill. In fact, doctors often add a measure of suggestion when they prescribe even potent medications for those who also need psychologic support. Like all potent agents, its proper use requires judgment based on experience and skill.

Communication between physician and the apprehensive and often confused patient is delicate and uncertain. Honesty should be evaluated not only in terms of a slavish devotion to language often misinterpreted by the patient, but also in terms of intent. *The crucial question is whether the deception was intended to benefit the patient or the doctor.*

Physicians, like most people, hope to see good results and are disappointed when patients do poorly. Their reputations and their livelihood depend on doing effective work; purely selfish reasons would dictate they do their best for their patients. Most important, all good physicians have a deep sense of responsibility toward those who have entrusted their welfare to them.

As I have explained, it is usually a practical impossibility to tell patients "the whole truth." Moreover, often enough, the ethics of the situation, the true moral responsibility, may demand that the naked facts not be revealed. The now popular complaint that doctors are too authoritarian is misguided more often than not. Some patients who insist on exercising their right to know may be doing themselves a disservice.

Judgment is often difficult and uncertain. Simplistic assertions about telling the truth may not be helpful to patients or physicians in times of trouble.

Bearing the News

SAUL S. RADOVSKY, M.D.

According to surveys, at least 70 percent of doctors now believe in telling people the truth about their cancers, as compared with 82 percent who practiced oppositely only twenty-four years ago.

Surveys often show quick turnabouts of public opinion, especially toward issues and leaders, but the attitudes of physicians in this area changed little in the 160 years before the past twenty. Thomas Percival, in his *Medical Ethics,* first published in 1803, argues that "to a patient . . . who makes inquires which, if faithfully answered, might prove fatal to him, it would be a gross and unfeeling wrong to tell the truth."[1] He died the following year, and we do not know whether he saw the end approach or was glad or sorry for any foreknowledge. A fair man, he quotes clerical and lay opinions at variance with his, notably the views of the Reverend Thomas Gisborne and the redoubtable Samuel Johnson.

Reprinted from *The New England Journal of Medicine* (August 29, 1985), 313:586–588, with the permission of the publisher. Copyright © 1985 by the Massachusetts Medical Society.

Nearly fifty years later, Worthington Hooker, a Connecticut practitioner, took issue with Percival in *Physician and Patient,* but his arguments apparently had little impact on the profession. Similar pleas by practitioner-writers D. W. Cathell, in 1885, and Austin Flint, in 1898, were also largely ignored.[2]

In the mid-1930s the Reverend Russell Dicks wrote a chapter entitled "The Dying" for *The Art of Ministering to the Sick,*[3] a collaboration with Dr. Richard Cabot. Dicks, who used a case-by-case approach, admits to having learned openness from the seriously ill and makes reference to the heroism of the dying and to the privilege of sharing in their extremity.

Also in the mid-1930s, Lawrence Henderson, a physician who practiced brilliant chemistry instead of medicine, gave a Harvard address titled "Physician and Patient as a Social System." Toward its end, he says, "Try . . . to modify [the patient's] sentiments to his own advantage, and remember that . . . nothing is more effective than arousing . . . the belief that you are concerned wholeheartedly and exclusively for *his* welfare."[4] It is a worthy goal, but set by Henderson ahead of truth rather than as a means to it.

In 1950 Dean Willard Sperry of the Harvard Divinity School found space close to Percival. Cautioning against errors in diagnosis and prognosis and deploring the outspokenness of his physician colleagues, he concludes, "Whether a doctor is to tell the truth depends primarily on his knowledge of the patient and his frame of mind."[7] Written when most doctors were still withholding the truth, it suggests that he had a skewed acquaintanceship.

My own passage in this area began badly. While I was in training at Boston City Hospital, an angry and demanding woman, apparently without relatives, came in short of breath, with a hard lymph node under her arm next to the site where a breast had been removed for cancer some years before. Throughout her workup she insisted on knowing the truth, whatever it might turn out to be. Like King Lear unaware of the more said the less intended, I took her at her word; when the tissue report came back I told her what it showed. Her shrieking and tearing at herself went on for days, unnerving her sick neighbors and deeply affecting me, a party to its induction. We house officers, among ourselves, along with pity expressed anger at her wild exhibition of feeling. At the time, people were more authoritarian toward themselves as well as one another.

Had I been neutral, the episode might have turned me against a policy of disclosure, but I persevered, at first with misgivings. In thirty years I have not seen another such reaction. Two new patients, both with abdominal masses, went back to doctors they had known before, and a lonely widower with a shadow on his chest film vanished for several months and died within a year, frightened, unaccepting, and delirious. Everyone else took the news of serious trouble in the spirit in which it was given, as useful information to be dealt with according to its demands. If surgery, then surgery; if chemicals or radiation, their pros and cons and then a decision, often shared in by husband, wife, or child; sometimes the hardest course, waiting and taking care of complications as they arose. Family members, if possible, never knew more than the patient wished, as part of a policy of the patient's remaining in charge. Like the Reverend Dicks, I have been impressed with the heroism of the incurably ill and the dying, since it has seemed almost invariable. In fact, all save the man I mentioned died courageously.

Reversing apparent logic, I wish to discuss the method of openness ahead of its reasons, since this is the way I arrived at it.

To begin, if you take the time to talk with people, not at them, your story will be heard. Informed consent is not analogous. It's usually a one-time affair with an operation pending, with its abrupt change of circumstance, usually general anesthesia, and usually several days of pain and medication afterward, all ideally suited to resist easy imprinting and to erase any imprinting that may occur. One session may not be enough. Doctors who wish to retain more than 5 percent of a lecture's content must go over its material more than once—preferably soon, and again after a delay—so why not patients?

There is no need to feel nervous when talking about cancer. People with symptoms are rarely surprised that they have it or that it has returned. When they cough up blood or see it in a bowel movement, have a new pain after cancer surgery or cannot get rid of a headache, they think of cancer. We doctors, because we find it in so few such instances, are more often surprised. Besides, most people have an extraordinary self-protective capacity to absorb bad medical news about themselves.

Labels are not helpful. They might be called "disinformation," if there is such a word. You should tell all you know, but with a minimum of labels and an absence of jargon, and with a conscious effort at transparency, to encourage a response in kind.

You should not tell more than you know. Admissions of ignorance serve to confirm your knowledge. A patient or family member may ask you to peer into the future, and if they have a good reason, you may wish to guess, extrapolate from what has gone on or invoke prior experience, or accept the challenge of Dr. So-and-so, who in the case of another family member, hit right on the mark. Resist if you can, at least until your patient has reached the narrow place near the end. Trouble can come from more directions than can be predicted, and its timing is its own.

People generally have more trouble dealing with the possibility of cancer than with its discovery or return. The woman I described would seem to have been an exception, but she was alone and a stranger. She could have had a brain metastasis or an underlying psychosis, but mainly she had poor relationships, including the one with me. I did not care about her as I should have, only about her disease. The definition of disease had been the focus of my training until then, and I was still caught up in it.

Matter-of-factness is crucial. Pity and sympathy are distancing; they separate giver from receiver by emphasizing the differences in their lots. People in desperate trouble need sharing instead, which they get from the acknowledgment in your words of what they are up against, the promise in your attentiveness that you'll be there, and the declaration in your attitude that you and they are fellow wayfarers on a road beset by fate and ending always in the betrayal of the physical self.

Most important, keep people in charge. People with incurable cancer are entering a mysterious land that they must cross in travail in order to reach an enigma. Each ends the trip alone and should be in command all the way. His or her qualities of leadership nearly always suffice, with a minimum of flagging. To usurp the role is tempting for either a physician or family member, but it will be one of a physician's less noble acts.

The alternative to the approach of sharing the burden while promoting independence is to decide for oneself or with the family what to do. It often means complicated lying. Sometimes it means deciding to forgo treatment for someone entitled to make that decision. Worse, it means arrogating to oneself or a family member the decision about how someone will face death, and in the process making him or her subordinate and childlike. And it means saying things that inevitably will be contradicted by events, bringing an increasing portion of isolation and mistrust to someone who, more and more, will need their opposites. It must be especially hard to decline while everyone, including oneself, pretends it is not happening, or that it is for reasons too dreadful to be discussed.

As for the reasons for being open, some are implicit or explicit in what has been said. One may argue, however, that I have been insensitive to the signals of people who really do not wish to know, or that my experience has been biased. There is a sorting process, as every practitioner knows. Although the majority of doctors have gone from not telling to telling, are there a certain number of people for whom the truth would be unbearable? And if so, should we try to identify and shield them?

I would make four points. The first is that we doctors are not wise enough to tell in advance who should not be told. We sense who will be difficult to tell, but that is a different matter, having as much to do with ourselves as with our patients. Families, who should know their members far better than we can, have regularly been wrong in my experience, as they have been in the matter of whether to continue life support for someone who can make that decision.

The second point is that shielding is ultimately impossible and that the price of its temporary achievement is an enduring sense of betrayal. Once lied to, even supposedly in their own interest, people will not trust fully again. And the lie is inevitably discovered, laid bare by the powerful truths of growing weakness, steady weight loss, worsening pain, and so on.

The third is that even if we knew whom to shield and could carry it off, we still should not. Not only is lying wrong in an abstract sense, though one may argue over possible exceptions, but in this instance it is especially so. Dying is a condition of living, an implicit consequence of our aliveness, and is unpredictable in its occurrence. I, though seemingly well, might not have lived to finish this essay, and you, though the same, may not live to read it through. (We are almost there, however.) Not only as physicians but as human beings we have no right to deny someone the chance to survey his or her life in the context of the beginning definition of its end. If people have a right to this knowledge, we should offer it. We regularly offer medicines and surgery despite the risk of adverse reactions, because we believe in the correctness of our offerings. May we not say the same of honesty?

Finally, we physicians need to look further into ourselves, and to ask, when we falter at telling bad news or manage its consequences badly, how often it is a blinking at our own mortality, a reluctance to admit the failure of what we have done for prevention or cure, or an unworthy desire to control. Perhaps, just as we refer patients whose symptoms or diseases are beyond our competence, we should also refer those whose incurability and dying are beyond it.

Notes

1. C. D. Leake, ed., *Percival's Medical Ethics* (Baltimore: Williams and Wilkins, 1927), pp. 186–196.

2. Worthington Hooker, *Physician and Patient* (New York: Baker and Scribner, 1849), pp. 360–382.

3. D. W. Cathell, *The Physician Himself and What He Should Add to His Scientific Acquirements in Order to Secure Success,* 4th ed. (Baltimore: Cushings and Bailey, 1885), p. 113.

4. Austin Flint, *Medical Ethics and Etiquette* (New York: D. Appleton, 1898), p. 24.

5. Richard C. Cabot and Russell L. Dicks, *The Art of Ministering to the Sick* (New York: Macmillan, 1936), p. 34.

6. Lawrence J. Henderson, "Physician and Patient as a Social System," *New England Journal of Medicine* (1935), 212:819–823.

7. Willard L. Sperry, *The Ethical Basis of Medical Practice* (New York: Paul B. Hoeber, 1950), pp. 120–122.

Truthtelling in Medicine

ROBERT F. WEIR, Ph.D.

"To tell or not to tell" is a moral problem central to physician-patient relationships. How much "truth" is necessary—or advisable—in communicating a diagnosis to a patient? When and what should a physician communicate to a patient known to be dying? How much information is necessary for a patient to be "informed"—and thus give informed consent—prior to going to surgery? What are the defining limits of informed consent for randomized clinical trials which may or may not prove beneficial for a particular patient? What are the advantages and disadvantages of informing patients about the possible use of placebos? How much deception with parents is morally permissible in communicating the prognosis—or cause of death—of a handicapped neonate?

Because of its centrality in a number of clinical contexts, truthtelling in medicine is one of the recurring themes in the field of biomedical ethics. Two problems exist, however, in the

Reprinted from *Perspectives in Biology and Medicine* (Autumn 1980), 23:95–112, with the permission of the University of Chicago Press. Copyright © 1980 by the University of Chicago.

interpretations of truthtelling in the bioethical literature. First, the classic case of truthtelling—the case of the dying patient—dominates the scene to the point that many discussions of truthtelling in medicine rarely get beyond an analysis of conversations with terminal patients. Second, much of the literature on truthtelling in other medical contexts (e.g., those requiring informed consent) tends to be contextually isolated, suggesting that the moral requirements of truthtelling in one clinical situation have no application to other clinical situations.

I intend to discuss the issue of truthtelling by focusing on its two dimensions of truth and truthfulness, showing how the requirement of truthtelling applies to two different clinical contexts, and putting forth reasons for regarding truthtelling as a moral obligation applicable to all medical fields. The clinical contexts are those involving dying patients and genetic counselees, the former chosen because it is the traditional "paradigm case" of truthtelling and the latter because genetic counseling is representative of a number of medical fields in which physicians regularly confront the issue of truthtelling with patients who are not dying. My purpose will be to demonstrate, using genetic counseling as a comparative context, that the issue of truthtelling in medicine is richer, more complex, and more central to the entire medical enterprise than it seems when limited to the traditional context of dying patients or when analyzed solely in one of the new clinical contexts requiring informed consent. The perspective from which I will be working is an understanding that the pivotal thinkers of Western philosophical and religious traditions have been in general agreement that (in Sissela Bok's words) "truthful statements are preferable to lies in the absence of special considerations."[1]

The Physician as Truth-Controlling Authority

There can be little question that physicians are regarded as authority figures in their relationships with patients, nurses, and virtually everyone else in a hospital setting who has not received a medical degree. The precise reasons for this status as authority figures are varied and include their roles as restorers of health, masters of a

technical knowledge, decision makers in crisis situations, comba-
tants against disease and death, dispensers of powerful drugs, and
choreographers of a vast array of technological procedures and
equipment. In a nutshell, physicians possess a highly specialized
knowledge and perform a number of highly specialized tasks
which are valued by persons who are dependent on them.

It is the possession of a specialized knowledge which is
relevant to the issue of truthtelling in medicine. Dying patients
seeking information—and persons seeking genetic counseling—
are caught up in a dependency relationship in which a medical
expert controls highly significant or risk-laden knowledge which
is not generally accessible to nonmedical persons. Certain parts of
this knowledge may be sought (and sometimes secured) from
nonmedical sources, but in order to secure the most accurate and
complete knowledge relevant to their medical conditions, both
dying patients and persons seeking genetic counseling are dependent on an authority figure whose training gives him or her
special access to the knowledge—or truth—being sought.

This relationship of dependency—and the role of the physician as a truth-controlling authority—is illustrated by an exchange of comments between two highly respected geneticists at
a conference sponsored by the Hastings Center. D. J. H. Brock,
professor of human genetics at the University of Edinburgh, and
Arno Motulsky, professor of medical genetics at the University
of Washington, compared notes on the issue of truthtelling in the
following manner:

BROCK: Take the example of myotonic dystrophy. A man in his early
thirties just contracting the disease comes in for counseling. *In the interest of efficiency,* surely the genetic counselor *should describe in very real
terms what is going to happen to him,* what the prognosis is. If he doesn't
do it, this man who is minimally affected at the time simply cannot see
the need to curtail his reproduction. He can't see that there is any point
in doing this, unless it is spelled out to him in very clear terms what the
eventual outcome of the disease is going to be. *And yet this would seem to
me to be totally inhumane.*
MOTULSKY: You have an alternative to what you can tell this man.
You can tell him, "Your case is rather mild. Many people with the
disease have a mild case. However, the disease can be very bad." Then
proceed to tell him about severely affected cases.

You don't have to take the props out from under a man. I try to give the patients some hope. *Giving the patient the truth and all the unadorned facts is erring against the ethos of medicine* by which we try to help the patient. Sometimes, withholding of all information is in *the best interest of the patient.* If I think it is better that a man not be told that he has cancer, I will not tell him. As a physician, I have to make this decision myself. It is hard. I can share and discuss with my colleagues, but ultimately it is my decision. *To give the whole truth to every patient is not humane.*[2]

As suggested by these comments, physicians often understand themselves to have the right of controlling (or at least managing) the truth, whether the immediate context is a dying patient's room, a counseling room in a genetics clinic, or some other clinical setting. Working out of the perspective of medical paternalism, physicians sometimes think they know more about a patient's needs, interests, and emotional stability than the patient does and withhold potentially damaging information to protect the patient from possibly undergoing an emotional catastrophe. As controllers of vital information, they conclude that the withholding of all (or at least a significant part) of such information is often in "the best interest of the patient."

Because this accepted role is common in the medical profession, there are numerous clinical situations in which a physician may choose to control the truth a patient receives simply by withholding all or part of the relevant information. Two such situations involve dying patients who seek information about their medical conditions and persons genetically at risk who seek scientific and mathematical information about a particular genetic disease. The two geneticists quoted above obviously think there are close parallels between the two situations and appear to agree that in both kinds of situations the "withholding of all information" or at least the withholding of some of the "truth and all the unadorned facts" is a proper part of the physician-patient relationship because such practices are in the patient's best interests.

Is the physician-patient relationship generally understood by both parties to include the right of physicians to control the truth by withholding some or all of the relevant medical information? Are the situations of dying patients and persons genetically at risk sufficiently alike in moral terms that to answer the questions of truthtelling in one situation is also to answer them in the other? What, in fact, does it mean to engage in truthtelling in these situations?

What Constitutes the Truth in These Medical Contexts?

In much of the medical literature that addresses the issue of truthtelling with dying patients, the actual nature of "the truth" is taken to be self-evident. The question, "Should dying patients be told the truth?" is taken to be a question in reference to the correctness or incorrectness (e.g., inaccurate euphemisms) of what a patient may be told about her medical condition. When understood in this manner, the truth rather obviously means logical truth or verbal accuracy—the correspondence of verbal statements to reality. Thus, years ago, when William Kelly and Stanley Friesen did a survey of cancer patients, and when Donald Oken did a survey of physicians who treat cancer patients, portions of the questions regarding truthtelling were left unstated: "Do you want to be told (the medical evidence)?" or "What is your usual policy about telling patients (what the medical data are)?"[3]

Understood in this way—with no reference to the veracity of the speaker—the truth for dying patients means nothing more or less than an accurate representation of the medical facts: an accurate diagnosis (e.g., stage IV cancer of the cervix) followed by an accurate prognosis (it is terminal), backed up with evidence accumulated through biopsies, lab tests, and surgery. Put another way, the truth for dying patients is frequently interpreted to mean a Cronkite-like statement of the medical findings: "And that's the way it is. . . ."

In a similar manner, the truth for persons genetically at risk is generally understood to mean nothing more or less than an accurate representation of the genetic evidence: an accurate diagnosis (e.g., Duchenne muscular dystrophy), accompanied by an accurate family history, interpretation of the inheritance pattern (X-linked recessive), recurrence risks, prognosis (rapid deterioration, likely terminal during the teenage years), and possibilities of treatment if any exist. Depending upon the particular disease, the truth communicated during a counseling session can often be backed up with clinical evidence: chromosome studies, biochemical tests on blood and urine, skin biopsies, and so forth.

The problem that confronts genetic counselors at this point, however, is that the truth in terms of scientific accuracy is often difficult to determine and, at times, simply impossible to know because of the comparatively elementary state of the science. It was, after all, as recently as 1956 that the normal chromosomal number in humans was determined to be 46 and only in 1959 that a genetic disease (Down's syndrome) was traced to a chromosomal aberration.[4] The extent of scientific knowledge yet to be discovered in human genetics can only be estimated by observing the number of incomplete tables in medical genetics textbooks, or by noting the extraordinary recent gains in genetic knowledge (as reflected in the five editions of Victor McKusick's *Mendelian Inheritance in Man*) and surmising that much more is yet to come.[5]

An additional problem is the complexity of the genetic evidence already known. If, for example, all that a genetic counselor had to do to tell the truth was to identify genetic conditions caused by alleles at a single chromosomal locus and then interpret the etiology of the condition in terms of autosomal dominant, autosomal recessive, or X-linked inheritance patterns, the relation between verbal accuracy and scientific evidence could be drawn fairly easily. When, however, an unusual genetic condition is present and the affected individual's pedigree shows no readily identifiable pattern, a counselor must consider a variety of factors which can affect gene expression: penetrance, expressivity, pleiotrophy, sex-limited traits, variable onset age, polygenic inheritance, and so forth.[6] The truth—in terms of accuracy—can in these circumstances be very elusive.

What About Truthfulness with Patients and Counselees?

There is another dimension to truthtelling in medicine that we have not yet covered. The first dimension is an objective one: the accuracy of what a patient or counselee is told about the medical facts. The second and morally more important dimension is a subjective one: the intended result of what is said to a patient or counselee. As Bok correctly observes, the moral question "of whether you are lying or not is not *settled* by establishing the truth or falsity of what you say. In order to settle this question, we must know whether you *intend your statement to mislead*."[7]

Truth and truthfulness are obviously closely related, and, up to a point, each is indispensable to the other. Fortunately for all of us, the two frequently come together in the written and verbal communications we have with other people. If this were not the case, there would be little possibility for any of us ever to participate in intelligent, truthworthy conversations with other persons. We would be constantly alert lest we be confused by someone who was not reporting factual information correctly, or lest we be misled by someone who was deliberately trying to deceive us.

On those occasions when, in retrospect, we become convinced that meaningful communication has broken down, our reaction usually varies depending upon our assessment of why the communication has broken down. If we find out that the information we were given was wrong, we are likely to have second thoughts about going to that person again for the same kind of information. When we need factual data of the same sort the next time, we will probably consult another person who we hope will be more competent and will be able to "get the facts straight." If, however, we become convinced that communication has broken down because the person lied to us or in some other manner tried to deceive us, our reaction is likely to be much different and much more intense. The excuse we might make for the person in the first case ("everybody makes mistakes") simply does not fit the person in the second case. Rather than offering excuses for the person or perhaps questioning the person's competence in a certain area of knowledge, we are apt to be resentful, disappointed, and suspicious in any further dealings we have with that individual.

What the truth/truthfulness distinction points to, therefore, is the difference between epistemological certainty and moral choice.[8] For a person to be able to "speak the truth" depends upon that person's knowledge of a certain sphere of information and ability to give an accurate representation of that knowledge. In medicine, as in any other field, communication sometimes breaks down for the undeniable reasons of human ignorance and fallibility: a physician may tell a patient something that the physician thinks is correct, whereas in reality the physician has made a mistake and given the wrong diagnosis or prognosis. For a person to be able to "speak truthfully" depends, in contrast, not on that person's knowledge or professional competence in some field, but on the person's moral choice to be honest and straightforward in speech. In medicine, again as in any other field, communication breaks down for the simple reason of moral choice: a physician may give a patient factually correct information and nevertheless intend to mislead the patient through a deceitful use of that information.

Physicians sometimes depart from truthfulness with dying patients by engaging in what Robert Veatch describes as "the big lie": a rationalization of lying by which a physician engages in self-deception as well as deception of a patient.[9] Two particular forms of the big lie described by Veatch are deliberate decisions not to be honest with patients. In the "truthful lie" (or, more correctly, the technically true lie), physicians attempt to fulfill the obligations of telling the truth by spewing medical jargon, while at the same time avoiding any communication of the medical evidence which the patient can understand. A physician's words to a patient may be technically true (e.g., "You have a neoplasm with the characteristics of a leimyosarcoma with possible secondary metastatic growth"), but the physician intentionally deceives the patient by using a highly specialized language that few nonmedical persons understand. In "indirect communication," physicians rationalize that "direct, immediate, blunt talk" is harmful to a patient and should be replaced by communication that can be handled by the patient because it is suggestive only. Again, the physician's words to a patient may be technically correct, but the physician is dishonest because he communicates through intentionally ambiguous terminology and evasive responses to questions. When either of these forms of the big lie occurs, physicians are blameworthy not because they give inaccurate information or withhold some of the medical facts, but because they are less than truthful with patients who trust them and expect them to be honest.

The same sort of problems often characterize the communications between genetic counselors and their counselees. In fact, counselors who want to avoid being truthful can find any number of alternatives that are personally and professionally satisfactory. For instance, a counselor who anticipates that the genetic information to be communicated will have a serious impact on an individual's life or marriage may give an accurate diagnosis and then modify the actual prognosis with overly optimistic statements and false assurances. Thus counselors working with members of choreic families do on occasion, after having accurately diagnosed Huntington's disease, engage in false reassurances along the line that "medical science will find a cure" in the next two or three decades or that "lightning never strikes twice in the same place."[10] Or, alternatively, a counselor may correctly identify a general category of genetic disease (chromosomal aberration, inborn error of metabolism, etc.), but decide to deceive counselees regarding which disease in the category is at issue. Thus, in the "unexpected chromosome" case in which a pregnant woman had amniocentesis performed for the purpose of detecting Trisomy 21, the counselor could have chosen to give the woman a technically true statement (e.g., the amniocentesis "confirmed the presence of an extra chromosome"), yet intentionally deceive her by not telling her that the extra chromosome detected was a Y chromosome (giving the fetus the XYY sex chromosome configuration) rather than the extra twenty-first chromosome, which would be present if the fetus had Trisomy 21.[11] In either of these instances, one of the results of not being honest with counselees is that they may, because they have been misled by the counselor, make decisions about procreation or abortion or some other important matter which they would not have made if the counselor had been truthful with them.

What Constitutes the Problem of Truthtelling in These Situations?

As illustrated by the Kelly-Friesen and Oken studies cited previously, the problem of telling dying patients the truth often hangs on the moral conflict between the patient's right to know the truth and the patient's welfare if the truth cannot be handled. The Kelly-Friesen study indicates that the overwhelming majority of patients with cancer (89 percent), as well as patients without known cancer (82 percent), want to be told that they have an irreversibly terminal condition if that is what the medical evidence indicates. The Oken study, in sharp contrast, shows that 88 percent of the physicians in one major hospital have a personal policy of not telling patients that they have cancer even if that is clearly indicated by the medical evidence. A more recent study of physicians' attitudes in another hospital shows that, while the responding physicians indicate unanimous agreement that cancer patients have "the right to know" and 98 percent of the group report an unspecified policy of telling the patients the truth, the majority of the physicians (91 percent) sometimes do not tell patients the truth because of "personal and emotional factors" (such as possible patient depression or undefined suicidal tendencies).[12] Thus physicians, as controllers of a specialized knowledge, sometimes decide on paternalistic grounds to withhold information which they agree patients have a right to know.

Put in a alternate way, the moral conflict in telling dying patients is between advocates who argue along deontological lines (the physician has a duty to tell the patient the truth) and others who argue along consequentialist lines (to hear the truth might harm the patient). Even though utilitarian arguments are occasionally put forth for telling patients the truth, the utilitarian arguments that surface most often in this debate are similar to Motulsky's statement quoted earlier: "Withholding of all information is in the best interest of the patient." Thus euphemisms, circumlocutions, and lies are sometimes regarded by physicians as justifiable means of achieving the desirable ends of maintaining a patient's hope, preventing the patient from getting depressed, and avoiding the possibility that some patients who cannot cope with medical reality will attempt suicide.

As to the failure to be truthful with dying patients, a physician's personal attitudes toward death and toward dying patients may be colored by a tendency to deny the reality of death and to postpone having to admit that, despite his specialized knowledge and skills, another patient is irretrievably dying.

As suggested by the Oken study and backed up by the research of Herman Feifel et al., physicians do have a problem confronting the reality of death and admitting their technical limitations before that inevitable fact.[13] The result is that it is psychologically easier for some physicians to be dishonest and deceptive with dying patients than to confront—personally and with the patient—the unpleasant tasks imposed by a policy of honesty.

It is obvious from the Brock-Motulsky comments quoted earlier that the same kind of moral conflict regarding truth and truthfulness exists among medical geneticists. Brock suggests (for the wrong reason) that a genetic counselor is obligated to describe "in very real terms what is going to happen" to the man with myotonic dystrophy. Namely, the condition the man has inherited is a progressive myotonia, accompanied by expressionless facial muscles, cataracts, decreased functional activity of the gonads, frontal baldness (in males), mental deterioration, abnormal heart activity, and death between the ages of 40 and 60 due to congestive heart failure.[14] Motulsky's response is to give a consequentialist argument regarding truth and truthfulness: out of concern for the man's welfare (possible loss of hope), either (a) withhold some of the relevant medical facts from the patient (do not tell him the truth), or (b) give an overly optimistic diagnosis and prognosis (do not be truthful with him).

Other factors add to the problem of truthtelling with counselees. One of these factors is the rapidity with which new genetic information is being accumulated. Hymie Gordon observes that "scarcely a week passes without a new syndrome being delineated, a new diagnostic procedure being proposed or additional statistical insights being provided."[15] When a field of science is expanding this rapidly, it is difficult for a genetic counselor to keep abreast of new developments. Consequently, a counselor's knowledge (or lack of it) regarding the diagnosis and possible treatment of "new" genetic diseases sometimes imposes a practical limit to the truth that can be told a counselee.

Another factor that contributes to the problem of truthtelling in medical genetics is the extraordinary ease with which risk figures can be manipulated to fit the value system of the counselor. A simple shift in wording—from telling a woman she has a 50 percent chance of having a defective child to telling her she has a 50 percent chance of having a normal child—"colors" the accuracy of the statement. Or, to illustrate the problem further, suppose that a woman has some reason to think she may be a carrier of Niemann-Pick disease and comes to see a genetic counselor. The truth (accuracy of information) and truthfulness (honesty) she receives may well be influenced by a counselor's moral judgments regarding amniocentesis, abortion, the actual effects of this disease in young children, the importance of this woman having children, and the possible transmission of a genetic condition which is characterized by neurological degeneration and death around the age of 5 years. If a counselor wishes to deter the woman from having a child, he may emphasize the risk (25 percent) of producing a genetically affected child. If the counselor chooses to be optimistic, he may downplay the risk by indicating that there is a 75 percent chance of producing a normal child. If, in addition, the counselor thinks that amniocentesis is a safe diagnostic procedure and selective abortion a morally justifiable operation should Niemann-Pick disease be detected prenatally, he may emphasize that the chance of producing a normal child is drastically improved once amniocentesis and abortion are part of the picture.

Still another factor that complicates the issue of truthtelling in medical genetics—in contrast to truthtelling in dying patients—is the frequent failure of counselees to understand genetic information. As Elisabeth Kübler-Ross and Avery Weisman have demonstrated, dying patients often have predictable psychological reactions when told the truth about their dying.[16] The immediate reaction is denial of the truth, followed in many instances in a rather unsystematic fashion by anger, bargaining, depression, and, sometimes, acceptance of the truth that he has an irreversible medical condition and is dying. Yet a dying patient—when no longer going through denial—does not have to understand the specifics of the case (e.g., the particular form of sarcoma) to know intuitively that the truth communicated by the physician is a prediction of irreversible decline and death. Because there is no known therapy that will alter the medical condition, a dying patient's understanding of the medical facts is irrelevant to the ultimate outcome.

In contrast, a person receiving information that she has or carries a genetic disease needs to have at least a minimal understanding of the etiology of the disease, the severity of the disease, and the probabilities of the disease's recurrence—if that person is to use the truth in making decisions about the future. A counselee undoubtedly undergoes some of the same initial psychological reactions to the truth that a dying patient does, but in order to accept the framework of reality imposed by the truth communicated by the counselor, a counselee must understand the implications that truth has on her own individual health picture, marriage plans, and possibilities of procreation. And the difficulty many counselees have in understanding genetic information and mathematical risk figures is a significant reason why truthtelling in genetic counseling is a problematic enterprise.

Truthtelling as a Moral Obligation in Medicine

We now arrive at the heart of the issue. Numerous variables involved in physician-patient relationships have direct bearing on the issue of truthtelling: the power imbalance between physician and patient, the specialized knowledge possessed by the physician, legal requirements and potential legal liabilities for the physician, occasional uncertainty as to whether a patient wants or can handle troubling information, decisions on the part of the patient that are dependent upon accurate information honestly rendered, the physician's interest in not harming the patient, and so forth.

Given these variables, truthtelling in the physician-patient relationship can be—and is—interpreted in three ways. Telling patients the truth and being truthful with them can be regarded as a legal requirement imposed on the traditional physician-patient relationship by recent court decisions. Telling the truth and being truthful with patients can be considered, as evidenced by the Brock-Motulsky exchange, a contextually limited privilege granted by physicians when they consider it appropriate and withheld when they judge it not in the best interests of a particular patient. Or telling the truth and being truthful with patients can be interpreted as a moral obligation on the part of physicians that must be carried out in all but the most exceptional circumstances.

When truthtelling is interpreted as a legal requirement with little or no additional moral significance, physicians easily become defensive about this unnecessary intrusion of the law into the traditional physician-patient relationship. Brought about by the patients' rights movement, malpractice suits, and laws mandating freedom of information, the requirement of truthtelling represents a legal obstacle course which must be successfully maneuvered by physicians in all branches of medicine.

The practical implications of this view are several, and together they represent a troubling perspective on the practice of medicine—and on the relationship between medicine, law, and ethics.

1. Virtually all of the obstacles in this course have to do with the sort of information giving that will satisfactorily fulfill the requirements of the law and protect physicians from malpractice suits. The result is a minimalist understanding of truthtelling that equates the truth with legally protective documents (e.g., informed consent documents) and disregards any particular responsibility for truthfulness in speech because verbal deception is not likely to bring about legal problems.

2. Because the legal instruments now used in medicine are regarded as primarily serving the purpose of protecting physicians from legal liability, they easily come to represent for some physicians unnecessary paperwork that merely complicates the physician-patient relationship. If a physician chooses to do so, he or she can react to this paperwork burden by making sarcastic comments to patients about the legal forms ("I think these are silly, but our lawyers tell us we have to use them"), thus suggesting to patients that they really need not take the forms seriously because, after all, doctors are "good guys" who do not need lawyers telling them how to conduct their business.

3. By equating the truth with legally required forms, and by making derogatory remarks about the forms, some physicians end up practicing defensive medicine: patients are given information about their conditions and about recommended medical procedures because the law requires it, not because patients have

a right to the information and may benefit from knowing it. In this defensive approach to medicine, the truth (e.g., information about surgical risks) is reluctantly told out of professional self-interest, and truthfulness with patients can easily suffer through the deceptive use of legal forms.

Illustrative of this defensive approach to truthtelling are the practices of some physicians with dying patients and with persons who may be genetically at risk. An internist who has a legalistic and self-protective understanding of truthtelling may attempt to forestall future legal problems by informing the relatives of a dying patient that the patient is irretrievably dying, but never get around to telling the patient or being truthful with that particular patient. An obstetrician may give genetic counseling to a woman or couple at risk merely to avoid the possibility of being sued for negligence in a "wrongful life" suit, while being very critical of the courts because of the time and effort required to do an accurate family medical history.[17] Or, alternatively, a genetic counselor in a prenatal genetic counseling session may, for similar legalistic and self-protective reasons, make informed consent documents (e.g., for amniocentesis, for a national chromosomal registry) the focal point of the counseling session by giving a detailed reading of the documents, but never inform the counselees that they give up the right to confidentiality when they sign one of the forms.

When truthtelling is interpreted as a contextually limited privilege, it can be granted or withheld at the discretion of any physician in any clinical context. Accurate information and candid communication can be withheld any time the physician in charge of a patient decides the truth and truthfulness are not "in the patient's best intersts"—regardless of the patient's physical, mental, or emotional status. As long as the physician stays within the boundaries of the law, there is no compelling reason to engage in truthtelling with any given patient or to have a consistent policy of truthtelling that carries over from one patient (or clinical context) to another.

As with the legalistic perspective on truthtelling, there are several practical implications of this view.

1. This interpretation clearly subsumes the responsibility of telling the truth and being truthful with patients under the

paternalistic model of the medical profession. Even when, as in the study by Dennis Novack and his colleagues, physicians acknowledge that patients have a right to the truth, that "right" is ignored when the physician judges that telling a particular patient the truth would do harm to the patient. In other words, a physician, because of presumed greater wisdom and acknowledged greater power in this context, decides to interfere with the patient's freedom by withholding information and/or intentionally engaging in deception.

2. Physicians who determine that truthtelling would bring harm to a patient are often thereby making psychiatric and moral judgments for which they have no special qualifications. Having the knowledge and skill to make an accurate diagnosis in a particular case in no way gives a physician special qualifications to know that telling *this* patient the truth will bring about greater harm to the patient than withholding the truth; or that *this* patient, upon hearing accurate information honestly rendered, will immediately lose all hope and go into suicidal depression; or that *this* patient's "best interests" are limited to whatever the physician happens to know about the patient through limited contact in a clinical setting.

3. By making truthtelling a context-limited privilege, physicians who function under the paternalistic model frequently set up a list of criteria by which only certain patients qualify for the privilege. The study by Novack and colleagues is again illustrative. When asked about their policy of telling cancer patients (who may or may not have a terminal form of the disease) the truth about their conditions, approximately half of the responding physicians listed the patient's age, the patient's intelligence, the patient's emotional stability, the patient's expressed wish to be told, and the wishes of the patient's relatives as "frequent factors" in determining whether or not to tell patients the truth about their cancer.

4. The decision "to tell or not to tell" in this paternalistic model is thus dependent on isolated factors in a particular clinical context that are frequently nonmedical in nature and, more important, the physician's perception of these factors. Telling the truth and being truthful depend not so much on the status of the law or on acknowledged patient rights as on a physician's belief

that a particular patient "qualifies" for the privilege. Therefore, one patient may be given accurate information and honest counsel by a physician, whereas in the next room another patient whose medical condition, psychological status, and personal interests are roughly the same as the first patient's may be denied the truth and given evasive answers by the same physician because, for any number of fleeting variables, the physician believes that this patient does not qualify for the privilege.

It is not necessary at this point to give additional examples of this approach to truthtelling in medicine because of the prominence of the paternalistic model in virtually all medical fields. Suffice it to say that, as we have seen, physicians with dying patients and genetic counselors with counselees sometimes do not engage in truthtelling because they believe that some patients/counselees cannot understand the information and/or will be harmed by the information and its impact on their lives. In either case, the patients and counselees are denied a "privilege" that could be granted them: an accurate diagnosis and a straightforward assessment of what the diagnosis means.

When truthtelling is interpreted as a moral obligation in medicine, it cannot be restricted to the use of legally required documents or the occasional granting of a privilege to patients who qualify. Its status is different from and more extensive than codes of law or moral rules of thumb (e.g., "Tell patients the truth when they qualify for it") that have limited application to physician-patient relationships in differing clinical contexts. Rather, as a moral obligation or duty, it applies generally to all physician-patient relationships involving mentally competent patients—including those relationships in which there is no usage of legal forms and in which there is wide disparity of patient age, intelligence, ability to articulate, emotional stability, socioeconomic status, marital status, and so forth.

The claim need not and should not be made that truthtelling is an absolute duty that obligates all physicians in all clinical contexts always to tell the truth and be truthful with their patients. To do so would be to take away the freedom of physicians as responsible moral agents. Instead, the claim that can and should be made is that truthtelling is a prima facie duty that obligates all physicians in all clinical contexts to tell the truth and be truthful with their patients unless there is a conflicting and stronger duty that takes precedence in a particular clinical context. The "unless" clause does not weaken the claim that truthtelling with patients is a moral obligation applicable to all physicians. It merely acknowledges that there could be exceptional circumstances (e.g., a clear, indisputable indication that truthtelling would lead to an attempted suicide by the patient) in which another obligation to a particular patient would override the physician's truthtelling responsibility.

If truthtelling is a moral obligation in medicine, why is this the case? Why should truthtelling in medicine be regarded as a moral obligation rather than merely a legal requirement or physician-controlled privilege? There are, in my judgment, three persuasive reasons.

First, the most common arguments against truthtelling with patients—those coming from the perspective of medical paternalism—do not stand up to examination. Granted that the ancient moral principle of nonmaleficence ("above all, do no harm") continues as a vital part of morally responsible medical practice, there are serious reasons for questioning the frequency with which it is used as a rationalization for not telling patients the truth and being truthful with them. How, for instance, can a physician after very limited contact with a patient know that truthtelling with that patient would be more harmful than withholding relevant information and being dishonest with the patient? Even when the issue at hand is as vital as a patient's emotional health, or the restoration of the patient's physical health, or the prolongation of the patient's life, how can a physician know that this particular patient—in the absence of relevant medical information and an honest assessment of alternatives—"agrees" with the decision that has been made in his behalf?

The limitations of this paternalistic model—sometimes referred to as "benevolent deception"—can rather easily be demonstrated. Suppose that an internist decides to withhold diagnostic information from a dying patient because she believes the truth will be more harmful to the patient than not knowing the diagnosis. In other words, she determines that it will be better for this patient to live out the remaining days of his life in ignorance and deception than in knowledge and truthfulness—and presumes that the patient would agree with that judgment. To make an accurate judgment along these lines would require intimate knowledge of the patient's life history, the ways in which he copes with personal crises, his feelings of obligation to family and career and friends, the sorts of things he would want to do to "put his house in order," and the hierarchy of values by which he governs his life.[18]

Given the highly specialized and impersonal character of modern medicine, it is exceedingly unlikely that any physician could plausibly claim to have access to such personal information or would feel confident in making other highly invasive decisions in this particular patient's behalf. In fact, it is unlikely that the physician could confidently claim such predictive and evaluative capabilities even if the decision were being made in behalf of one of her close friends.

The same problem exists in genetic counseling. Take, for example, the case of myotonic dystrophy mentioned earlier. A man in his early thirties comes in for genetic counseling and is diagnosed as being in the early stage of a progressively degenerating disease that will increasingly affect his hands, eyes, facial muscles, reproductive organs, and heart function and will cause his death, possibly within 10 years. For a counselor in this situation to withhold relevant information and to deceive the man about his genetic future is to make the predictive and evaluative judgment for the counselee himself that it would be better to live out the remaining years in ignorance than in knowledge. In order to presume accuracy in such a judgment, the counselor would need to know all of the things mentioned above in the case of the dying patient, plus highly personal information about the man's reproductive plans, his feelings of responsibility in running a 50/50 risk of passing on the disease, his long-range personal and professional goals, and other highly valued aspects of his life that are dependent upon normal eyesight and muscle performance. Given the limited contact genetic counselors have with counselees, the possession of this kind of knowledge about any particular counselee would be highly improbable.

Second, truthtelling is a moral obligation in medicine because patients and counselees are autonomous persons. Even though they are in a dependency relationship with a medical authority who possesses specialized knowledge about their bodies, they in no way can be said—short of being defined as prisoners—to have given up their personal autonomy when they entered that medical context. As persons, they have the right to autonomy shared by all persons: namely, the right to choose a life plan and make decisions relative to that life plan. The life plan may be well conceived or poorly thought out, praiseworthy or blameworthy, consistently followed or rarely achieved in fact. The point is that all persons, within certain legal constraints, have a moral right to determine the course of action they intend to follow in their lives, to make specific plans that are likely to bring that desired course of action into reality, and to make independent decisions along life's way which have direct bearing on that chosen course of action.

In order to make the right decisions relative to a chosen life plan, autonomous persons—inside and outside of medical contexts—need to have accurate information and honest advice at crucial points along the way. No person is likely to come close to realizing his or her life plan if critical decisions are made in the absence of important factual data or under deception. The relative achievement of a life plan is even less likely if critical decisions are made by someone else on an individual's behalf, especially if that someone else has only a limited knowledge of the individual based on minimal interpersonal contact.

Given their status as autonomous persons, patients in medical contexts have a legitimate claim to accurate information about their medical conditions and to an honest interpretation of the ramifications of that information by the physician. They do not need nor should they lay claim to "the whole truth": surely patients and counselees need not be told all of the myriad scientific details known by the physician in a specific case. But in order to make correct decisions relative to their chosen life plan, they do have a right to the truth which may be relevant to that life plan and to the sort of truthfulness which will provide them with an honest assessment of alternatives available to them. With dying patients, that means an accurate diagnosis of the disease and a candid appraisal of the disease's probable trajectory, the possibilities and limitations of available therapy programs, and the advisability of choosing a social context other than the hospital (e.g., home, hospice) for dying. With counselees, it means an accurate diagnosis of the genetic disease the person has or carries (if a diagnosis can be made) and honest judgments regarding the severity of the disease, the inheritance risks, the usual effects of the disease on a family unit, the benefits of available therapies, the "track records" of health care institutions in the area, and so forth. Only when such truth and truthfulness are provided by the physician can patients or counselees make responsible decisions about the future that awaits them.

Third, truthtelling is a moral obligation in medicine because of the fiduciary relationship between physician and patient. As in other professional relationships built on confidence and trust (e.g., lawyer-client, priest-confessor) the physician-patient relationship has a number of unstated expectations at its center: the physician will not inflict unnecessary pain on the patient, the physician will not divulge confidential information about the patient, the patient will follow the physician's medical recommendations, and so on. While any physician who departs significantly from some of these expectations might be legally liable, the expectations are only implicitly contractual in nature, and in many physician-patient relationships the expectations have no basis other than the confidence and trust engendered by the relationship itself.

One of the expectations vital to the physician-patient relationship concerns truth and truthfulness in communication. When physicians ask patients questions about their personal medical history and current physical problems, they expect true and nondeceptive responses and proceed in their task as physicians trusting that the answers they have been given are accurate and trustworthy. Should later lab results or other evidence prove that they have been misled or deceived, the physicians will undoubtedly judge that important time and energy has been wasted and will have serious reservations about continuing to see these particular patients.

In the same way, because a fiduciary relationship is a two-way street, patients also expect the truth and nondeceptive communication from their physicians (should evidence prove this point wrong, physician-patient relationships are worse off than I imagine). By entering into a relationship in which specialized knowledge and vitally important personal information can best be secured when communicated by the physician, patients proceed through periods of anxiety and uncertainty trusting that they are being given accurate information about their conditions and honest responses to their questions. Should a dying patient later find out that she has been the victim of a conspiracy of silence, or a counselee later discover that he has been given misleading statements or false reassurances about a genetic disease, these patients will undoubtedly feel betrayed by persons whom they had trusted. If such feelings of betrayal occur in a significant percentage of patients, the resulting damage to the foundation of trust on which physician-patient relationships are based would be monumental.

One final comment. Sometimes discussions of truthtelling in medicine focus on the manner of communicating with patients, with physicians arguing that it is emotionally harmful for patients to be confronted with "the brutal truth." Having given three reasons for telling patients the truth and being truthful with them, I do not intend to suggest that truthtelling has to be done or should be done in a blunt, brutal, insensitive, or sadistic manner. Obviously, the factors of timing and communication dynamics need to be adapted to the circumstances of particular patients. The point is that patients have a right to the truth and truthfulness—communicated with compassion, understandable language, empathy, and respect.

Notes

1. S. Bok, *Lying: Moral Choice in Public and Private Life* (New York: Pantheon, 1978), p. 30.

2. Discussion section. In B. Hilton, D. Callahan, M. Harris, et al., eds., *Ethical Issues in Human Genetics* (New York: Plenum, 1973), p. 98 (emphasis added).

3. W. D. Kelly and S. R. Friesen, "Do Cancer Patients Want To Be Told?" *Surgery* (1950), 27:322–326; and D. Oken, "What to Tell Cancer Patients," *Journal of the American Medical Association* (1961), 175:86–94.

4. V. A. McKusick, *Human Genetics,* 2d ed. (Englewood Cliffs, N.J.: Prentice-Hall, 1969).

5. V. A. McKusick, *Mendelian Inheritance in Man,* 5th ed. (Baltimore: Johns Hopkins University Press, 1978).

6. J. S. Thompson and M. W. Thompson, *Genetics in Medicine,* 2d ed. (Philadelphia: Saunders, 1973), pp. 73–80.

7. Bok, p. 23.

8. Bok, pp. 6–31.

9. R. M. Veatch, *Death, Dying, and the Biological Revolution* (New Haven, Conn.: Yale University Press, 1976), pp. 222–29.

10. J. S. Pearson, *H. D. Handbook for Health Professionals* (New York: Committee to Combat Huntington's Disease, n. d.), p. 4.

11. R. M. Veatch, *Case Studies in Medical Ethics* (Cambridge, Mass.: Harvard University Press, 1977), pp. 137–39.

12. D. H. Novack, R. Plumber, R. L. Smith et al., "Changes in Physicians' Attitudes Toward Telling the Cancer Patient." *Journal of the American Medical Association* (1979), 241:897–900.

13. H. Feifel, S. Hanson, R. Jones, et al., "Physicians Consider Death." *Proceedings of the American Psychological Association Convention* (1967), pp. 201–202.

14. J. J. Nora and F. C. Fraser, *Medical Genetics: Principles and Practice* (Philadelphia: Lea & Febiger, 1974).

15. H. Gordon, "Genetic Counseling: Considerations for Talking to Parents and Prospective Parents." *Journal of the American Medical Association* (1971), 217:1215–1225.

16. E. Kübler-Ross, *On Death and Dying* (New York: Macmillan, 1969); and A. Weisman, *On Dying and Denying* (New York: Behavioral Publications, 1972).

17. W. J. Curran, "Genetic Counseling and Wrongful Life," *American Journal of Public Health* (1978), 68:501–502.

18. A. Buchanan, "Medical Paternalism," *Philosophy and Public Affairs* (1978), 7:370–390.

Cobbs v. Grant

Supreme Court of California,
8 Cal.3d 229, 502 P.2d 1 (1972)

MOSK, Justice:
This medical malpractice case involves two issues: first, whether there was sufficient evidence of negligence in the performing of surgery to sustain a jury verdict for plaintiff; second, whether, under plaintiff's alternative theory, the instructions to the jury adequately set forth the nature of a medical doctor's duty to obtain the informed consent of a patient before undertaking treatment. We conclude there was insufficient evidence to support the jury's verdict under the theory that defendant was negligent during the operation. Since there was a general verdict and we are unable to ascertain upon which of the two concepts the jury relied, we must reverse the judgment and remand for a new trial. To assist the trial court upon remand we analyze the doctor's duty to obtain the patient's informed consent and suggest principles for guidance in drafting new instructions on this question. . . .

    Since this is an appropriate case for the application of a negligence theory, it remains for us to determine if the standard of care described in the jury instruction on this subject properly delineates defendant's duty to inform plaintiff of the inherent risks of the surgery. In pertinent part, the court gave the following instruction: "A physician's duty to disclose is not governed by the standard practice in the community; rather it is a duty imposed by law. A physician violates his duty to his patient and subjects himself to liability if he withholds any facts which are necessary to form the basis of an intelligent consent by the patient to the proposed treatment."

Defendant raises two objections to the foregoing instruction. First, he points out that the majority of the California cases have measured the duty to disclose not in terms of an absolute, but as a duty to reveal such information as would be disclosed by a doctor in good standing within the medical community. . . . Moreover, with one state and one federal exception every jurisdiction that has considered this question has adopted the community standard as the applicable test. Defendant's second contention is that this near unanimity reflects strong policy reasons for vesting in the medical community the unquestioned discretion to determine if the withholding of information by a doctor from his patient is justified at the time the patient weighs the risks of the treatment against the risks of refusing treatment.

The thesis that medical doctors are invested with discretion to withhold information from their patients has been frequently ventilated in both legal and medical literature. . . . Despite what defendant characterizes as the prevailing rule, it has never been unequivocally adopted by an authoritative source. Therefore we probe anew into the rationale which purportedly justifies, in accordance with medical rather than legal standards, the withholding of information from a patient.

Preliminarily we employ several postulates. The first is that patients are generally persons unlearned in the medical sciences and therefore, except in rare cases, courts may safely assume the knowledge of patient and physician are not in parity. The second is that a person of adult years and in sound mind has the right, in the exercise of control over his own body, to determine whether or not to submit to lawful medical treatment. The third is that the patient's consent to treatment, to be effective, must be an informed consent. And the fourth is that the patient, being unlearned in medical sciences, has an abject dependence upon and trust in his physician for the information upon which he relies during the decisional process, thus raising an obligation in the physician that transcends arms-length transactions.

From the foregoing axiomatic ingredients emerges a necessity, and a resultant requirement, for divulgence by the physician to his patient of all information relevant to a meaningful decisional process. In many instances, to the physician . . . the particular treatment which should be undertaken may seem evident, but it is the prerogative of the patient, not the physician, to determine for himself the direction in which he believes his interests lie. To enable the patient to chart his course knowledgeably, reasonable familiarity with the therapeutic alternatives and their hazards becomes essential.

Therefore, we hold, as an integral part of the physician's overall obligation to the patient there is a duty of reasonable disclosure of the available choices with respect to proposed therapy and of the dangers inherently and potentially involved in each.

A concomitant issue is the yardstick to be applied in determining reasonableness of disclosure. This defendant and the majority of courts have related the duty to the custom of physicians practicing in the community. . . . The majority rule is needlessly overbroad. Even if there can be said to be a medical community standard as to the disclosure requirement for any prescribed treatment, it appears so nebulous that doctors become, in effect, vested with virtual absolute discretion. . . .

The scope of the disclosure required of physicians defies simple definition. Some courts have spoken of "full disclosure" . . . and others refer to "full and complete" disclosure . . . , but such facile expressions obscure common practicalities. Two qualifications to a requirement of "full disclosure" need little explication. First, the patient's interest in information does not extend to a lengthy polysyllabic discourse on all possible complications. A mini-course in medical science is not required; the patient is concerned with the risk of death or bodily harm, and problems of recuperation. Second, there is no physician's duty to discuss the relatively minor risks inherent in common procedures. . . .

However, . . . when a given procedure inherently involves a known risk of death or serious bodily harm, a medical doctor has a duty to disclose to his patient the potential of death or serious harm, and to explain in lay terms the complications that might possibly occur. . . .

In sum, the patient's right of self-decision is the measure of the physician's duty to reveal. That right can be effectively exercised only if the patient possesses adequate information to enable an intelligent choice. The scope of the physician's communications to the patient, then, must be measured by the patient's need, and that need is whatever information is material to the decision. Thus the test for determining whether a potential peril must be divulged is its materiality to the patient's decision.

TWO
The Definition and Determination of Death

For centuries, death was understood to mean the irreversible cessation of spontaneous cardiac and respiratory activity. Quite simply, when a person's heart stopped beating and lungs stopped pumping air, that person was considered dead. Without cardiopulmonary activity, human life was deemed impossible. Just as simply, the ways of distinguishing between a dead body and a body still alive, though unconscious, consisted of a variety of tests: determining the warmth or coolness of the flesh, listening for a heartbeat, detecting movement by the chest, or possibly using a mirror or feather to check for exhalation.

The majority of persons who die this year will die in the traditional manner: their hearts and lungs will cease to function, spontaneous circulation and respiration will stop, and their bodies as a consequence will be alive no more. For the persons in this group who die outside of medical centers, their deaths may well be determined in ways virtually identical to the practices of people in earlier centuries. If you, for instance, should be on a lonely country road (or similarly isolated location) some night and come across an unconscious human body lying on the ground, how would you determine if it is alive or dead? The chances are very great, unless you happen to travel with a stethoscope in your possession, that you would do the same sorts of things that people have done in similar situations over the centuries. Assuming that you do not run or drive away from the scene, you would probably do several empirical tests on the body to check on body temperature, pulse, and breathing.

If, instead, that body were being maintained by medical technology in a hospital, the determination of whether the body is alive or dead might be no simpler than if you happened across the body miles away from a hospital. Of course physicians at the hospital would have a number of sophisticated ways of checking out the body's functions: electrocardiograms, electroencephalograms (EEGs), drug screening, angiography, lab tests on blood, tests on reflexes, and so forth. But the task of determining if the body is that of a patient or that of an unburied corpse might be complicated by three factors. First, the use of a respirator and other artificial means of life support may blur clinical determination that spontaneous cardiopulmonary functions have ceased. At the very least, the use of respirators, heart-lung machines, pacemakers, and artificial hearts raises questions about traditional understandings of cardiac activity. Second, depending upon the physicians in a particular case, there may be some disagreement regarding the concept and exact locus of death. Is death to be interpreted in all cases as the irreversible cessation of spontaneous cardiopulmonary function? In cases of technological intervention, is death to be interpreted as the irreversible cessation of neocortical function *only* (thus allowing for brainstem activity), or is it to be understood as the irreversible cessation of *all* brain functions? Third, the bodies of brain-dead patients sustained on respirators still manifest some functions normally found in living bodies. Such brain-dead patients, with proper maintenance, can breathe, circulate blood, digest food, filter wastes, and even (in a few cases of brain-dead, pregnant women) nurture a fetus for several weeks.

Attempts to arrive at the correct way of defining and clinically determining death in these cases of technological intervention have been going on since the 1960s. In fact, two events in 1968 can now be seen as harbingers of a long, involved debate among physicians, attorneys, state legislators, and ethicists that is still not completely resolved. The first of these events was the death of a Richmond man named Bruce Tucker. Tucker was a patient at the Medical College of Virginia after suffering a massive head injury. Following emergency brain surgery and a tracheostomy, he was attached to a respirator, fed intravenously, administered medication—but given little chance to live even though the respirator kept him "mechanically alive." Hours later the respirator was turned off, Tucker was pronounced dead on the basis of a single flat EEG reading, and his heart was transplanted into another patient's body. Tucker's brother subsequently brought suit against the surgeons for wrongfully ending Bruce's life (*Tucker v. Lower*, May 1972). The case now represents one example among many of judicial attempts to reconcile rapidly evolving medical practices with legal standards of death written years earlier.

The second event involved the report of an ad hoc committee at the Harvard Medical School (*Journal of the American Medical Association*, August 1968). Concerned about the increasing number of patients in irreversible coma who can be kept "alive" indefinitely with the aid of respirators, the committee recommended four clinical tests that could be used to determine the deaths of such patients. These clinical tests are to be used to demonstrate that an unconscious patient (a) lacks awareness of externally applied stimuli, (b) lacks ability to breathe spontaneously (apart from the respirator), (c) lacks reflex responses, and (d) lacks brain activity as measured by an EEG. These tests have subsequently been widely adopted in American hospitals, although some physicians regard the committee's recommended 24-hour delay before repeating the tests and declaring the patient dead as being unnecessarily conservative.

Following these events, numerous proposals were made in the 1970s concerning the definition and determination of death. Many of these proposals were attempts to change state laws and, with Kansas having taken the lead in 1970, twenty-five states subsequently updated their definition-of-death statutes in an effort to make the law consistent with contemporary medical practice. By 1980, the pattern of new laws had taken the following form:

1. three states had followed Kansas and enacted statutes patterned on the Kansas model;
2. seven states had enacted a model statute proposed in 1972 by Alexander Capron and Leon Kass;
3. five states had enacted a model statute proposed in 1975 by the American Bar Association (ABA);
4. two states had adopted the "Uniform Brain Death Act" proposed in 1978 by the National Conference of Commissions on Uniform State Laws (NCCUSL);
5. seven states had passed idiosyncratic statutes;
6. and some other states were considering various model statutes, including one proposed in 1979 by the American Medical Association (AMA).

The readings in this section indicate that the debate continues regarding the medical, legal, and philosophical aspects of defining and determining death. Robert Veatch, an ethicist at the Kennedy Center for Bioethics, was concerned in the mid-1970s that much of the debate over the definition and determination of death was philosophically sloppy. Although his comments are obviously directed at the debate at that time (including criticism of the Harvard ad hoc committee), many of his observations continue to be applicable to the debate in its contemporary form. The second selection is taken from a report by the President's Commission for the Study of Ethical Problems in Medicine (1980–1983). In its 1981 report the Commission discussed the major earlier proposals for updating death statutes, compared these proposals with one made earlier in 1981 by the Law Reform Commission of Canada, and then presented its own Uniform Determination of Death Act (UDDA). This model law had the approval of the ABA, the AMA, and the Uniform Law Commissioners as a substitute for their previous proposals; the proposed UDDA has subsequently become law in seventeen states and the District of Columbia, and it is pending in several others.

The third selection consists of medical guidelines for the

determination of death, in the form of a report to the President's Commission by fifty-six medical consultants attempting to update the "Harvard criteria" for the clinical determination of death. The fourth selection indicates that the work of the President's Commission, while highly regarded, did not end the debate over the definition and determination of death. James Bernat, Charles Culver, and Bernard Gert, all faculty members at Dartmouth University, propose a model statute they believe to be preferable to the one recommended by the President's Commission.

The legal case in this section shows how important a clear, updated understanding of death can be. In this homicide case the Supreme Judicial Court of Massachusetts upheld the ruling that the defendant was guilty of murder, because the victim had experienced "brain death" (according to the Harvard criteria) prior to being removed from the respirator sustaining his organ functions.

Defining Death Anew: Technical and Ethical Problems

ROBERT M. VEATCH, Ph.D.

F our separate levels in the definition of death debate must be distinguished. First, there is the purely formal analysis of the term *death,* an analysis that gives the structure and specifies the framework that must be filled in with content. Second, the *concept* of death is considered, attempting to fill the content of the formal definition. At this level the question is, What is so essentially significant about life that its loss is termed *death?* Third, there is the question of the locus of death: where in the organism ought one to look to determine whether death has occurred? Fourth, one must ask the question of the criteria of death: what technical tests must be applied at the locus to determine if an individual is living or dead?

Serious mistakes have been made in slipping from one level of the debate to another and in presuming that expertise on one level necessarily implies expertise on another. For instance, the Report of the Ad Hoc Committee of the Harvard Medical School

Reprinted from *Death, Dying and the Biological Revolution,* pp. 24–26, 29–33, 36–51, with the permission of the author and Yale University Press. Copyright © 1976 by Robert Veatch.

to Examine the Definition of Brain Death is titled "A Definition of Irreversible Coma."[1] The report makes clear that the committee members are simply reporting empirical measures which are criteria for predicting an irreversible coma. (I shall explore later the possiblity that they made an important mistake even at this level.) Yet the name of the committee seems to point more to the question of locus, where to look for measurement of death. The committee was established to examine the death of the brain. The implication is that the empirical indications of irreversible coma are also indications of "brain death." But by the first sentence of the report the committee claims that "Our primary purpose is to define irreversible coma as a new criterion for death." They have now shifted so that they are interested in "death." They must be presuming a philosophical concept of death—that a person in irreversible coma should be considered dead—but they nowhere argue this or even state it as a presumption.

Even the composition of the Harvard committee membership signals some uncertainty of purpose. If empirical criteria were their concern, the inclusion of nonscientists on the panel was strange. If the philosophical concept of death was their concern, medically trained people were overrepresented. As it happened, the committee did not deal at all with conceptual matters. The committee and its interpreters have confused the questions at different levels. The remainder of this [essay] will discuss the meaning of death at these four levels.

The Formal Definition of Death

A strictly formal definition of death might be the following: "Death means a complete change in the status of a living entity characterized by the irreversible loss of those characteristics that are essentially significant to it." Such a definition would apply equally well to a human being, a nonhuman animal, a plant, an organ, a cell, or even metaphorically to a social phenomenon like a society or to any temporally limited entity like a research project, a sports event, or a language. To define the death of a human being, we must recognize the characteristics that are essential to humanness. It is quite inadequate to limit the discussion to the death of the heart or the brain.

Henry Beecher, the distinguished physician who chaired the Harvard committee that proposed a "definition of irreversible coma," has said that "at whatever level we *choose* . . . , it is an arbitrary decision" [italics added].[2] But he goes on, "It is *best* to choose a level where although the brain is dead, usefulness of other organs is still present" [italics added]. Now, clearly he is not making an "arbitrary decision" any longer. He recognizes that there are policy payoffs. He, like the rest of us, realizes that death already has a well-established meaning. It is the task of the current debate to clarify that meaning for a few rare and difficult cases. We use the term *death* to mean the loss of what is essentially significant to an entity—in the case of man, the loss of humanness. The direct link of a word *death* to what is "essentially significant" means that the task of defining it in this sense is first and foremost a philosophical, theological, ethical task.

. . . .

The Concept of Death

To ask what is essentially significant to a human being is a philosophical question—a question of ethical and other values. Many elements make human beings unique—their opposing thumbs, their possession of rational souls, their ability to form cultures and manipulate symbol systems, their upright postures, their being created in the image of God, and so on. Any concept of death will depend directly upon how one evaluates these qualities. Four choices seem to me to cover the most plausible approaches.

IRREVERSIBLE LOSS OF FLOW OF VITAL FLUIDS

At first it would appear that the irreversible cessation of heart and lung activity would represent a simple and straightforward statement of the traditional understanding of the concept of death in Western culture. Yet upon reflection this proves otherwise. If patients simply lose control of their lungs and have to be permanently supported by a mechanical respirator, they are still living persons as long as they continue to get oxygen. If modern technology produces an efficient, compact heart-lung machine capable of being carried on the back or in a pocket, people using such devices would not be considered dead, even though both heart and lungs were permanently nonfunctioning. Some might consider such a technological man an affront to human dignity; some might argue that such a device should never be connected to a human; but even they would, in all likelihood, agree that such people are alive.

What the traditional concept of death centered on was not the heart and lungs as such, but the flow of vital fluids, that is, the breath and the blood. It is not without reason that these fluids are commonly referred to as "vital." The nature of man is seen as related to this vitality—or vital activity of fluid flow—which man shares with other animals. This fluidity, the movement of liquids and gases at the cellular and organismic level, is a remarkable biological fact. High school biology students are taught that the distinguishing characteristics of "living" things include respiration, circulation of fluids, movement of fluids out of the organism, and the like. According to this view the human organism, like other living organisms, dies when there is an irreversible cessation of the flow of these fluids.

IRREVERSIBLE LOSS OF THE SOUL FROM THE BODY

There is a longstanding tradition, sometimes called vitalism, that holds the essence of man to be independent of the chemical reactions and electrical forces that account for the flow of the bodily fluids. Aristotle and the Greeks spoke of the soul as the animating principle of life. The human being, according to Aristotle, differs from other living creatures in possessing a rational soul as well as vegetative and animal souls. This idea later became especially pronounced in the dualistic philosophy of gnosticism, where salvation was seen as the escape of the enslaved soul from the body. Christianity in its Pauline and later Western forms shares the view that the soul is an essential element in the living man. While Paul and some later theologian-scholars including Erasmus and Luther sometimes held a triparite anthropology that included spirit as well as body and soul, a central element in all their thought seems to be animation of the body by a noncorporeal force. In Christianity, however, contrasting to the gnostic tradition, the body is a crucial element—not a prison from which the soul escapes, but a significant part of the person. This will become important later in this discussion. The soul remains a central element in the concept of man in most folk religion today.

The departure of the soul might be seen by believers as occurring at about the time that the fluids stop flowing. But it would be a mistake to equate these two concepts of death, as according to the first fluid stops from natural, if unexplained, causes, and death means nothing more than that stopping of the flow which is essential to life. According to the second view, the fluid stops flowing at the time the soul departs, and it stops because the soul is no longer present. Here the essential thing is the loss of the soul, not the loss of the fluid flow.

THE IRREVERSIBLE LOSS OF THE CAPACITY FOR BODILY INTEGRATION

In the debate between those who held a traditional religious notion of the animating force of the soul and those who had the more naturalistic concept of the irreversible loss of the flow of bodily fluids, the trend to secularism and empiricism made the loss of fluid flow more and more the operative concept of death in society. But man's intervention in the dying process through cardiac pacemakers, respirators, intravenous medication and feeding, and extravenous purification of blood has forced a sharper examination of the naturalistic concept of death. It is now possible to manipulate the dying process so that some parts of the body cease to function while other parts are maintained indefinitely. This has given rise to disagreements within the naturalistic camp itself. In its report, published in 1968, the interdisciplinary Harvard Ad Hoc Committee to Examine the Definition of Brain Death gave two reasons for their undertaking. First, they argued that improvements in resuscitative and supportive measures had sometimes had only partial success, putting a great burden on "patients who suffer permanent loss of intellect, on their families, on the hospitals, and on those in need of hospital beds already occupied by these comatose patients." Second, they argued that "obsolete criteria for the definition of death can lead to controversy in obtaining organs for transplantation."

These points have proved more controversial than they may have seemed at the time. In the first place, the only consideration of the patient among the reasons given for changing the definition of death was the suggestion that a comatose patient can feel a "great burden." If the committee is right, however, in holding that the person is in fact dead despite continued respiration and circulation, then all the benefits of the change in definition will come to other individuals or to society at large. For those who hold that the primary ethical consideration in the care of the patient should be the patient's own interest, this is cause for concern.

In the second place, the introduction of transplant concerns into the discussion has attracted particular criticism. Paul Ramsey, among others, has argued against making the issue of transplant a reason for updating the definition of death: "If no person's death should *for this purpose* be hastened, then the definition of death should not *for this purpose* be updated, or the procedures for stating that a man has died be revised as a means of affording easier access to organs."[3]

. . . .

At first it would appear that the irreversible loss of brain activity is the concept of death held by those no longer satisfied with the vitalistic concept of the departure of the soul or the animalistic concept of the irreversible cessation of fluid flow. This is why the name *brain death* is frequently given to the new proposals, but the term is unfortunate for two reasons.

First, as we have seen, it is not the heart and lungs as such that are essentially significant but rather the vital functions—the flow of fluids—which we believe according to the best empirical human physiology to be associated with these organs. An "artificial brain" is not a present-day possibility but a walking, talking, thinking individual who had one would certainly be considered living. It is not the collection of physical tissues called the brain, but rather their functions—consciousness; motor control; sensory feeling; ability to reason; control over bodily functions including respiration and circulation; major integrating reflexes controlling blood pressure, ion levels, and pupil size; and so forth—which are given essential significance by those who advocate adoption of a new concept of death or clarification of the old one. In short they see the body's capacity for integrating its functions as the essentially significant indication of life.

Second, as suggested earlier, we are not interested in the death of particular cells, organs, or organ systems but in the death of the person as a whole—the point at which the person as a whole undergoes a quantum change through the loss of characteristics held to be essentially significant, the point at which "death behavior" becomes appropriate. Terms such as *brain death* or *heart death* should be avoided because they tend to obscure the fact that we are searching for the meaning of the death of the person as a whole. At the public policy level, this has very practical consequences. A statute adopted in Kansas specifically refers to "alternative definitions of death" and says that they are "to be used for all purposes in this state. . . ." According to this language, which has resulted from talking of brain and heart death, a person in Kansas may be simultaneously dead according to one definition and alive according to another. When a distinction must be made, it should be made directly on the basis of the philosophical significance of the functions mentioned above rather than on the importance of the tissue collection called the brain. For purposes of simplicity we shall use the phrase *the capacity for bodily integration* to refer to the total list of integrating mechanisms possessed by the body. The case for these mechanisms being the ones that are essential to humanness can indeed be made. Man is more than the flowing of fluids. He is a complex, integrated organism with capacities for internal regulation. With and only with these integrating mechanisms is *Homo sapiens* really a human person.

There appear to be two general aspects to this concept of what is essentially significant: first, a capacity for integrating one's internal bodily environment (which is done for the most part unconsciously through highly complex homeostatic, feedback mechanisms) and, secondly, a capacity for integrating one's self, including one's body, with the social environment through consciousness, which permits interaction with other persons. Clearly these taken together offer a more profound understanding of the nature of man than does the simple flow of bodily fluids. Whether or not it is more a profound concept of man than that which focuses simply on the presence or absence of the soul, it is clearly a very different one. The ultimate test between the two is that of meaningfulness and plausibility. For many in the modern secular society, the concept of loss of capacity for bodily integration seems much more meaningful and plausible, that is, we see it as a much more accurate description of the essential significance of man and of what is lost at the time of death. According to this view, when individuals lose all of these "truly vital" capacities we should call them dead and behave accordingly.

At this point the debate may just about have been won by the defenders of the neurologically oriented concept. For the most part the public sees the main dispute as being between partisans of the heart and the brain. Even court cases like the Tucker suit and the major articles in the scientific and philosophical journals have for the most part confined themselves to contrasting these two rather crudely defined positions. If these were the only alternatives, the discussion probably would be nearing an end. There are, however, some critical questions that are just beginning to be asked. This new round of discussion was provoked by the recognition that it may be possible in rare cases for a person to have the higher brain centers destroyed but still retain lower brain functions, including spontaneous respiration.[4] This has led to the question of just what brain functions are essentially significant to man's nature. A fourth major concept of death thus emerges.

THE IRREVERSIBLE LOSS OF THE CAPACITY
FOR SOCIAL INTERACTION

The fourth major alternative for a concept of death draws on the characteristics of the third concept and has often been confused with it. Henry Beecher offers a summary of what he considers to be essential to man's nature: "the individual's personality, his conscious life, his uniqueness, his capacity for remembering, judging, reasoning, acting, enjoying, worrying, and so on. . . ."[5]

Beecher goes on immediately to ask the anatomical question of locus. He concludes that these functions reside in the brain and that when the brain no longer functions, the individual is dead. We shall take up the locus question later in this [essay]. What is remarkable is that Beecher's list, with the possible exception of "uniqueness," is composed entirely of functions explicitly related to consciousness and the capacity to relate to one's social environment through interaction with others. All the functions which give the capacity to integrate one's internal bodily environment through unconscious, complex, homeostatic reflex mechanisms—respiration, circulation, and major integrating reflexes—are omitted. In fact, when asked what was essentially significant to man's living, Beecher replied simply, "Consciousness."

Thus a fourth concept of death is the irreversible loss of the capacity for consciousness or social integration. This view of the nature of man places even more emphasis on social character. Even, given a hypothetical human being with the full capacity for integration of bodily function, if he had irreversibly lost the capacity for consciousness and social interaction, he would have lost the essential character of humanness and, according to this definition, the person would be dead.

Even if one moves to the so-called higher functions and away from the mere capacity to integrate bodily functions through reflex mechanisms, it is still not clear precisely what is ultimately valued. We must have a more careful specification of "consciousness or the capacity for social integration." Are these two capacities synonymous and, if not, what is the relationship between them? Before taking up that question, we must first make clear what is meant by capacity.

Holders of this concept of death and related concepts of the essence of man specifically do not say that individuals must be valued by others in order to be human. This would place life at the mercy of other human beings who may well be cruel or insensitive. Nor does this concept imply that the essence of man is the fact of social interaction with others, as this would also place a person at the mercy of others. The infant raised in complete isolation from other human contact would still be human, provided that the child retained the mere capacity for some form of social interaction. This view of what is essentially significant to the nature of man makes no quantitative or qualitative judgments. It need not, and for me could not, lead to the view that those who have more capacity for social integration are more human. The concepts of life and death are essentially bipolar, threshold concepts. Either one has life or one does not. Either a particular type of death behavior is called for or it is not. One does not pronounce death half-way or read a will half-way or become elevated from the vice presidency to the presidency half-way.

One of the real dangers of shifting from the third concept of death to the fourth is that the fourth, in focusing exclusively on the capacity for consciousness or social interaction, lends itself much more readily to quantitative and qualitative considerations. When the focus is on the complete capacity for bodily integration, including the ability of the body to carry out spontaneous respiratory activity and major reflexes, it is quite easy to maintain that if any such integrating function is present the person is alive. But when the question begins to be, "What kinds of integrating capacity are really significant?" one finds oneself on the slippery slope of evaluating kinds of consciousness or social interaction. If consciousness is what counts, it might be asked if a long-term catatonic schizophrenic or a patient with extreme senile dementia really has the capacity for consciousness. To position oneself for such a slide down the slope of evaluating the degree of capacity for social interaction is extremely dangerous. It seems to me morally obligatory to stay off the slopes.

Precisely what are the functions considered to be ultimately significant to human life according to this concept? There are several possibilities.

The capacity for rationality is one candidate. *Homo sapiens* is a rational animal, as suggested by the name. The human capacity for reasoning is so unique and so important that some would suggest that it is the critical element in man's nature. But certainly infants lack any such capacity and they are considered living human beings. Nor is possession of the potential for reasoning what is important. Including potential might resolve the problem of infants, but does not explain why those who have no potential for rationality (such as the apparently permanent back ward psychotic or the senile individual) are considered to be humanly living in a real if not full sense and to be entitled to the protection of civil and moral law.

Consciousness is a second candidate that dominates much

of the medical and biological literature. If the rationalist tradition is reflected in the previous notion, then the empiricalist philosophical tradition seems to be represented in the emphasis on consciousness. What may be of central significance is the capacity for experience. This would include the infant and the individual who lacks the capacity for rationality, and focuses attention on the ability for sensory activity summarized as consciousness. Yet, this is a very individualistic understanding of man's nature. It describes what is essentially significant to the human life without any reference to other human beings.

Social interaction is a third candidate. At least in the Western tradition, man is seen as an essentially social animal. Perhaps it is man's capacity or potential for social interaction that has such ultimate significance that its loss is considered death. Is this in any sense different from the capacity for experience? Certainly it is conceptually different and places a very different emphasis on man's essential role. Yet it may well be that the two functions, experience and social interaction, are completely coterminous. It is difficult to conceive a case where the two could be separated, at least if social interaction is understood in its most elementary form. While it may be important for a philosophical understanding of man's nature to distinguish between these two functions, it may not be necessary for deciding when a person has died. Thus, for our purposes we can say that the fourth concept of death is one in which the essential element that is lost is the capacity for consciousness or social interaction or both.

The concept presents one further problem. The Western tradition which emphasizes social interaction also emphasizes, as we have seen, the importance of the body. Consider the admittedly remote possibility that the electrical impulses of the brain could be transferred by recording devices onto magnetic computer tape. Would that tape together with some kind of minimum sensory device be a living human being and would erasure of the tape be considered murder? If the body is really essential to man, then we might well decide that such a creature would not be a living human being.

Where does this leave us? The alternatives are summarized in the table at the end of the [essay]. The earlier concepts of death—the irreversible loss of the soul and the irreversible stopping of the flow of vital body fluids—strike me as quite implausible. The soul as an independent nonphysical entity that is necessary and sufficient for a person to be considered alive is a relic from the era of dichotomized anthropologies. Animalistic fluid flow is simply too base a function to be the human essence. The capacity for bodily integration is more plausible, but I suspect it is attractive primarily because it includes those higher functions that we normally take to be central—consciousness, the ability to think and feel and relate to others. When the reflex networks that regulate such things as blood pressure and respiration are separated from the higher functions, I am led to conclude that it is the higher functions which are so essential that their loss ought to be taken as the death of the person. While consciousness is certainly important, man's social nature and embodiment seem to me to be the truly essential characteristics. I therefore believe that death is most appropriately thought of as the irreversible loss of the embodied capacity for social interaction.

The Locus of Death

Thus far I have completely avoided dealing with anatomy. Whenever the temptation arose to formulate a concept of death by referring to organs or tissues such as the heart, lungs, brain, or cerebral cortex, I have carefully resisted. Now finally I must ask, "Where does one look if one wants to know whether a person is dead or alive?" This question at last leads into the field of anatomy and physiology. Each concept of death formulated in the previous section (by asking what is of essential significance to the nature of man) raises a corresponding question of where to look to see if death has occurred. This level of the definitional problem may be called the locus of death.

The term *locus* must be used carefully. I have stressed that we are concerned about the death of the individual as a whole, not a specific part. Nevertheless, differing concepts of death will lead us to look at different body functions and structures in order to diagnose the death of the person as a whole. This task can be undertaken only after the conceptual question is resolved, if what we really want to know is where to look to determine if a person is dead rather than where to look to determine simply if the person has irreversibly lost the capacity for vital fluid flow or bodily integration or social interaction. What then are the different loci corresponding to the different concepts?

The *loci* corresponding to the irreversible loss of vital fluid flow are clearly the heart and blood vessels, the lungs and respiratory tract. At least according to our contemporary empirical knowledge of physiology and anatomy, in which we have good reason to have confidence, these are the vital organs and organ systems to which the tests should have applied to determine if a person has died. Should a new Harvey reveal evidence to the contrary, those who hold to the concept of the irreversible loss of vital fluid flow would probably be willing to change the site of their observations in diagnosing death.

The locus, or the "seat," of the soul has not been dealt with definitively since the day of Descartes. In his essay "The Passions of the Soul," Descartes pursues the question of the soul's dwelling place in the body. He argues that the soul is united to all the portions of the body conjointly, but, nevertheless, he concludes:

There is yet . . . a certain part in which it exercises its functions more particularly than in all the others; and it is usually believed that this part is the brain, or possibly the heart: the brain, because it is with it that the organs of sense are connected, and the heart because it is apparently in it that we experience the passions. But in examining the matter with care, it seems as though I had clearly ascertained that the part of the body in which the soul exercises its functions immediately is in no wise the heart, not the whole of the brain, but merely the most inward of all its parts, to wit, a certain very small gland which is situated in the middle of its substance. . . .[6]

Descartes is clearly asking the question of locus. His anatomical knowledge is apparently sound, but his conclusion that the soul resides primarily and directly in the pineal body raises physiological and theological problems which most of us are unable to comprehend today. What is significant is that he seemed to hold that the irreversible loss of the soul is the critical factor in determining death, and he was asking the right kind of question about where to look to determine whether a man is dead.

The fact that the Greek term *pneuma* has the dual meaning of both breath and soul or spirit could be interpreted to imply that the presence of this animating force is closely related to (perhaps synonymous with) breath. This gives us another clue about where holders of the irreversible loss of the soul concept of death might look to determine the presence or absence of life.

The locus for loss of capacity for bodily integration is a more familiar concept today. The anatomist and physiologist would be sure that the locus of the integrating capacity is the central nervous system, as Sherrington has ingrained into the biomedical tradition. Neurophysiologists asked to find this locus might reasonably request a more specific concept, however. They are aware that the autonomic nervous system and spinal cord play a role in the integrating capacity, both as transmitters of nervous impulses and as the central analyzers for certain simple acts of integration (for example, a withdrawal reflex mediated through the spinal cord); they would have to know whether one was interested in such simple reflexes.

Beecher gives us the answer quite specifically for his personal concept of death: he says spinal reflexes are to be omitted.[7] This leaves the brain as essentially the place to look to determine whether a man is dead according to the third concept of death. The brain's highly complex circuitry provides the minimal essentials for the body's real integrating capacity. This third concept quite specifically includes unconscious homeostatic and higher reflex mechanisms such as spontaneous respiration and pupil reflexes. Thus, anatomically, according to our reading of neurophysiology, we are dealing with the whole brain, including the cerebellum, medulla, and brainstem. This is the basis for calling the third concept of death *brain death,* and we already discussed objections to this term.

Where to seek the locus for irreversible loss of the capacity for social interaction, the fourth conception of death, is quite another matter. We have eliminated unconscious reflex mechanisms. The answer is clearly not the whole brain—it is much too massive. Determining the locus of consciousness and social interaction certainly requires greater scientific understanding, but evidence points strongly to the neocortex or outer surface of the brain as the site.[8] Indeed, if this is the locus of consciousness, the presence or absence of activity in the rest of the brain will be immaterial to the holder of this view.

The Criteria of Death

Having determined a concept of death, which is rooted in a philosophical analysis of the nature of man, and a locus of death, which links this philosophical understanding to the anatomy and physiology of the human body, we are finally ready to ask the operational question, What tests or measurements should be applied to determine if an individual is living or dead? At this point we have moved into a more technical realm in which the answer will depend primarily on the data gathered from the biomedical sciences.

Beginning with the first concept of death, irreversible loss of vital fluid flow, what criteria can be used to measure the activity of the heart and lungs, the blood vessels and respiratory track? The methods are simple: visual observation of respiration, perhaps by the use of the classic mirror held at the nostrils; feeling the pulse; and listening for the heartbeat. More technical measures are also now available to the trained clinician: the electrocardiogram and direct measures of oxygen and carbon dioxide levels in the blood.

If Descartes' conclusion is correct that the locus of the soul is in the pineal body, the logical question would be "How does one know when the pineal body has irreversibly ceased to function?" or more precisely "How does one know when the soul has irreversibly departed from the gland?" This matter remains baffling for the modern neurophysiologist. If, however, holders of the soul-departing concept of death associate the soul with the breath, as suggested by the word *pneuma,* this might give us another clue. If respiration and specifically breath are the locus of the soul, then the techniques discussed above as applying to respiration might also be the appropriate criteria for determining the loss of the soul.

We have identified the (whole) brain as the locus associated with the third concept of death, the irreversible loss of the capacity for bodily integration. The empirical task of identifying criteria in this case is to develop accurate predictions of the complete and irreversible loss of brain activity. This search for criteria was the real task carried out by the Ad Hoc Committee to Examine the Definition of Brain Death of Harvard Medical School; the simple criteria they proposed have become the most widely recognized in the United States:

1. Unreceptivity and unresponsitivity
2. No movements or breathing
3. No reflexes
4. Flat electroencephalogram

The report states that the fourth criterion is "of great confirmatory value." It also calls for the repetition of these tests twenty-four hours later. Two types of cases are specifically excluded: hypothermia (body temperature below 90° F) and the presence of central nervous system depressants such as barbiturates.[9]

Other criteria have been proposed to diagnose the condition of irreversible loss of brain function. James Toole, a neurologist at the Bowman Gray School of Medicine, has suggested that metabolic criteria such as oxygen consumption of the brain or the measure of metabolic products in the blood or cerebrospinal fluid could possibly be developed as well.[10]

European observers seem to place more emphasis on demonstrating the absence of circulation in the brain. This is measured by angiography, radioisotopes, or sonic techniques.[11] In Europe sets of criteria analogous to the Harvard criteria have been proposed. G. P. J. Alexandre, a surgeon who heads a Belgian renal transplant department, reports that in addition to absence of reflexes as criteria of irreversible destruction of the brain, he uses lack of spontaneous respiration, a flat EEG, complete bilateral mydriasis, and falling blood pressure necessitating increasing amounts of vasopressive drugs.[12] J. P. Revillard, a Frenchman, reportedly uses these plus angiography and absence of reaction to atropine.[13] Even among those who agree on the types of measure, there may still be disagreement on the levels of measurement. This is especially true for the electroencephalogram, which can be recorded at varying sensitivities and for different time periods. The Harvard-proposed twenty-four-hour period is now being questioned as too conservative.

While these alternate sets of criteria are normally described as applicable to measuring loss of brain function (or "brain death" as in the name of the Harvard committee), it appears that many of these authors, especially the earlier ones, have not necessarily meant to distinguish them from criteria for measuring the narrower loss of cerebral function.

The criteria for irreversible loss of the capacity for social interaction are far more selective. It should be clear from the above criteria that they measure loss of all brain activity, including spontaneous respiration and higher reflexes and not simply loss of consciousness. This raises a serious problem about whether the Harvard criteria really measure "irreversible coma" as the report title indicates. Exactly what is measured is an entirely empirical matter. In any case, convincing evidence has been cited by the committee and more recently by a committee of the Institute of Society, Ethics and the Life Sciences that no one will falsely be pronounced in irreversible coma. In 128 patients who underwent autopsy, the brain was found to be "obviously destroyed" in each case.[14] Of 2,650 patients with isoelectric EEGs of twenty-four hours' duration, not one patient recovered ("excepting three who had received anesthetic doses of CNS depressants, and who were, therefore, outside the class of patients covered by the report").[15]

What then is the relationship between the more inclusive Harvard criteria and the simple use of electrocerebral silence as measured by an isoelectric or flat electroencephalogram? The former might be appropriate for those who associate death with the disappearance of any neurological function of the brain. For those who hold the narrower concept based simply on consciousness or capacity for social interaction, however, the Harvard criteria may suffer from exactly the same problem as the old heart- and lung-oriented criteria. With those criteria, every patient whose circulatory and respiratory function had ceased was indeed dead, but the criteria might be too conservative, in that some patients dead according to the "loss of bodily integrating capacity" concept of death (for which the brain is the corresponding locus) would be found alive according to heart- and lung-oriented criteria. It might also happen that some patients who should be declared dead according to the irreversible loss of consciousness and social interaction concept would be found to be alive according to the Harvard criteria.[16] All discussions of the neurological criteria fail to consider that the criteria might be too inclusive, too conservative. The criteria might, therefore, give rise to classifying patients as dead according to the consciousness or social interaction conception, but as alive according to the full Harvard criteria.

A report in *Lancet* by the British physician J. B. Brierley and his colleagues implies this may indeed be the case.[17] In two cases in which patients had undergone cardiac arrest resulting in brain damage, they report, "the electroencephalogram (strictly defined) was isoelectric throughout. Spontaneous respiration was resumed almost at once in case 2, but not until day 21 in case 1."[18] They report that the first patient did not "die" until five months later. For the second patient they report, "The patient died on day 153." Presumably in both cases they were using the traditional heart and lung locus and correlated criteria for death as they pronounced it. They report that subsequent detailed neuropathological analysis confirmed that the "neocortex was dead while certain brainstem and spinal centers remained intact." These intact centers specifically involved the functions of spontaneous breathing and reflexes: eye-opening, yawning, and "certain reflex activities at brainstem and spinal cord levels." As evidence that lower brain activity remained, they report that an electroretinogram (measuring electrical activity of the eye) in patient 1 was normal on day 13. After day 49 there still remained reactivity of the pupils to light in addition to spontaneous respiration.

If this evidence is sound, it strongly suggests that it is empirically as well as theoretically possible to have irreversible loss of cortical function (and therefore loss of consciousness) while lower brain functions remain intact.

This leaves us with the empirical question of the proper criteria for the irreversible loss of consciousness which is thought to have its locus in the neocortex of the cerebrum. Brierley and his colleagues suggest that the EEG alone (excluding the other three criteria of the Harvard report) measures the activity of the neocortex.[19] Presumably this test must also meet the carefully specified conditions of amplifier gain, repeat of the test after a given time period, and exclusion of the exceptional cases, if it is

Table 6.1. LEVELS OF THE DEFINITION OF DEATH

Concept of Death Philosophical or theo- logical judgment of the essentially significant change at death.	Locus of Death Place to look to deter- mine if a person has died.	Criteria of Death Measurements physicians or other officials use to determine whether a person is dead—to be determined by scientific empirical study.
1. The irreversible stopping of the flow of "vital" body fluids, i.e., the blood and breath	Heart and lungs	1. Visual observation of respiration, per- haps with the use of a mirror 2. Feeling of the pulse, possibly supported by electrocardiogram
2. The irreversible loss of the soul from the body	The pineal body? (according to Des- cartes) The respiratory track?	Observation of breath?
3. The irreversible loss of the capac- ity for bodily in- tegration and soc- ial interaction	The brain	1. Unreceptivity and unresponsitivity 2. No movements or breathing 3. No reflexes (except spinal reflexes) 4. Flat electroenceph- alogram (to be used as confirmatory evidence) —All tests to be repeated 24 hours later (excluded con- ditions: hypothermia and central nervous system drug depression)
4. Irreversible loss of consciousness or the capacity for social inter- action	Probably the neocortex	Electroencephalogram

NOTE: *Formal Definition.* Death means a complete change in the status of a living entity characterized by the irreversible loss of those characteristics that are essentially significant to it.

The possible concepts, loci, and criteria of death are much more complex than the ones given here. These are meant to be simplified models of types of positions being taken in the current debate. It is obvious that those who believe that death means the irreversible loss of the capacity for bodily integration (3) or the irreversible loss of consciousness (4) have no reservations about pronouncing death when the heart and lungs have ceased to function. This is because they are willing to use loss of heart and lung activity as shortcut criteria for death, believing that once heart and lungs have stopped, the brain or neocortex will necessarily stop as well.

to be used as the criterion for death according to our fourth concept, irreversible loss of capacity for social interaction. The empirical evidence is not all in, but it would seem that the 2,650 cases of flat EEG without recovery which are cited to support the Harvard criteria would also be persuasive preliminary empirical evidence for the use of the EEG alone as empirical evidence for the irreversible loss of consciousness and social interaction which (presumably) have their locus in the neocortex. What these 2,650 cases would have to include for the data to be definitive would be a significant number of Brierley-type patients where the EEG criteria were met without the other Harvard criteria being met. This is a question for the neurophysiologists to resolve.

There is another problem with the use of electroencephalogram, angiography, or other techniques for measuring cerebral function as a criterion for the irreversible loss of consciousness. Once again we must face the problem of a false positive diagnosis of life. The old heart and lung criteria may provide a false positive diagnosis for a holder of the bodily integrating capacity concept, and the Harvard criteria may give false positive indications for a holder of the consciousness or social interaction concept. Could a person have electroencephalographic activity but still have no capacity for consciousness or social interaction? Whether this is possible empirically is difficult to say, but at least theoretically there are certainly portions of the neocortex which could be functioning and presumably be recorded on an electroencephalogram without the individual having any capacity for consciousness. For instance, what if through an accident or vascular occlusion the motor cortex remained viable but the sensory cortex did not? Even the most narrow criterion of the electroencephalogram alone may still give false positive diagnoses of living for holders of the social interaction concept.

Notes

1. Ad Hoc Committee of the Harvard Medical School to Examine the Definition of Brain Death, "A Definition of Irreversible Coma," *Journal of the American Medical Association* (1968), 205:337–340.

2. Henry K. Beecher, "The New Definition of Death, Some Opposing Views," paper presented at the meeting of the American Association for the Advancement of Science, December 1970, p. 2.

3. Paul Ramsey, "On Updating Procedures for Stating That a Man Has Died," in *The Patient as Person* (New Haven: Yale University Press, 1970), p. 103.

4. J. B. Brierley, J. A. H. Adams, D. I. Graham, and J. A. Simpson, "Neocortical Death after Cardiac Arrest," *Lancet,* September 11, 1971, pp. 560–565.

5. Beecher, "The New Definition of Death," p. 4.

6. René Descartes, "The Passions of the Soul," in *The Philosophical Works of Descartes* (Cambridge: Cambridge University Press, 1911), 1:345.

7. Beecher, "The New Definition of Death," p. 2.

8. Brierly et al., "Neocortical Death."

9. Ad Hoc Committee of the Harvard Medical School, "A Definition of Irreversible Coma," pp. 337–338. See also F. Mellerio, "Clinical and EEG Study of a Case of Acute Poisoning with Cerebral Electrical Silence, Followed by Recovery," *Electroencephalography Clinical Neurophysiology* (1971), 30:270–271.

10. James F. Toole, "The Neurologist and the Concept of Brain Death," *Perspectives in Biology and Medicine* (Summer 1971), p. 602.

11. See, for example, A. A. Hadijidimos, M. Brock, P. Baum, and K. Schurmann, "Cessation of Cerebral Blood Flow in Total Irreversible Loss of Brain Function," in M. Brock, C. Fieschi, D. H. Ingvar, N. A. Lassen, and K. Schurmann, eds., *Cerebral Blood Flow* (Berlin: Springer-Verlag, 1969), pp. 209–212; A. Beis et al., "Hemodynamic and Metabolic Studies in 'Coma Depassé,' " *ibid.*, pp. 213–215.

12. G. E. W. Wolstenholme and Maeve O'Connor, eds., *Ethics in Medical Progress: With Special Reference to Transplantation* (Boston: Little, Brown, 1966), p. 69.

13. *Ibid.*, p. 71.

14. Task Force on Death and Dying of the Institute of Society, Ethics and the Life Sciences, "Refinements in Criteria for the Determination of Death: An Appraisal," *Journal of the American Medical Association* (1972), 221:50–51.

15. Daniel Silverman, Richard L. Masland, Michael G. Saunders, and Robert S. Schwab, "Irreversible Coma Associated with Electrocerebral Silence," *Neurology* (1970), 20:525–533.

16. The inclusion of absence of breathing and reflexes in the criteria suggests this, but does not necessarily lead to this. It might be that, empirically, it is necessary for lower brain reflexes and breathing to be absent for twenty-four hours in order to be sure that the patient not only will never regain these functions but will never regain consciousness.

17. Brierley et al., "Neocortical Death." See also Ricardo Ceballos and Samuel C. Little, "Progressive Electroencephalographic Changes in Laminar Necrosis of the Brain," *Southern Medical Journal* (1971), 64:1370–1376.

18. *Ibid.*, p. 560.

19. Brierley et al., "Neocortical Death."

7

A Proposed Uniform Determination of Death Act

President's Commission for the Study
of Ethical Problems in Medicine
and Biomedical and Behavioral Research

The array of "model laws" and state variations reveals two major problems: first, their diversity, and second, the overly complex or inexact wording that characterizes many of them. Diversity is a problem for several reasons. In the case of enacted statutes, diversity means nonuniformity among jurisdictions. In most areas of the law, provisions that diverge from one state to the next create, at worst, inconvenience and the occasional failure of a finely honed business or personal plan to achieve its intended result. But on the subject of death, nonuniformity has a jarring effect. Of course, the diversity is really only superficial; all the enacted statutes appear to have the same intent. Yet even small differences raise the question: if the statutes all mean the same thing, why are they so varied? And it is possible to think of medical situations—and, even more freely, of legal cases that would be unlikely but not bizarre—in which the differences in statutory language *could* lead to different outcomes.

Reprinted from the Commission's July 1981 final report entitled *Defining Death: A Report on the Medical, Legal and Ethical Issues in the Determination of Death,* pp. 72–79, 80–81. Some footnotes omitted.

More fundamental is the obstacle that diversity presents for the process of statutory enactment. Legislators, presented with a variety of proposals and no clear explanation of the significance of their differences, are (not surprisingly) wary of *all* the choices. Proponents of each of the models (and other critics) compounded this difficulty by objecting to the language of the other statutes. . . .

A uniform proposal that is broadly acceptable would significantly ease the enactment of good law on death throughout the United States. To that end, the Commission's Executive Director met in May 1980 with representatives of the American Bar Association, the American Medical Association, and the National Conference of Commissioners on Uniform State Laws. Through a comparison of the then existing "models" with the objectives that a statute ought to serve, they arrived at a proposed Uniform Determination of Death Act:

1. [*Determination of Death.*] An individual who has sustained either (1) irreversible cessation of circulatory and respiratory functions, or (2) irreversible cessation of all functions of the entire brain, including the brainstem, is dead. A determination of death must be made in accordance with accepted medical standards.

2. [*Uniformity of Construction and Application.*] This act shall be applied and construed to effectuate its general purpose to make uniform the law with respect to the subject of this Act among states enacting it.

This model law has now been approved by the Uniform Law Commissioners, the ABA, and the AMA as a substitute for their previous proposals. It has also been endorsed by the American Academy of Neurology and the American Electroencephalographic Society.

Construction of the Statute

The proposed statute addresses the matter of "defining" death at the level of general physiological standards rather than at the level of more abstract concepts or the level of more precise criteria and tests. The proposed statute articulates alternative standards, since in the vast majority of cases irreversible circulatory and respiratory cessation will be the obvious and sufficient basis for diagnosing death. When a patient is not supported on a respirator, the need to evaluate brain functions does not arise. The basic statute in this area should acknowledge that fact by setting forth the basis on which death *is* determined in such cases (namely, that breathing and blood flow have ceased and cannot be restored or replaced).

It would be possible, as in the statute drafted by the Law Reform Commission of Canada, to propound the irreversible cessation of brain functions as *the* "definition" and then to permit that standard to be met not only by direct measures of brain activity but also "by the prolonged absence of spontaneous cardiac and respiratory functions."[1] Although conceptually acceptable (and vastly superior to the adoption of brain cessation as a primary standard conjoined with a nonspecific reference to other, apparently unrelated "usual and customary procedures"),[2] the Canadian proposal breaks with tradition in a manner that appears to be unnecessary. For most lay people—and in all probability for most physicians as well—the permanent loss of heart and lung function (for example, in an elderly person who has died in his or her sleep) clearly manifests death. Biomedical scientists can explain the brain's particularly important—and vulnerable—role in the organism as a whole and show how temporary loss of blood flow (ischemia) becomes permanent cessation because of the damage it inflicts on the brain. Nonetheless, most of the time people do not, and need not, go through this two-step process. Irreversible loss of circulation is recognized as death because—setting aside any mythical connotations of the heart—a person without blood flow simply cannot live. Thus, the Commission prefers to employ language which would reflect the continuity of the traditional standard and the newer, brain-based standard.

"INDIVIDUAL"

Other aspects of the statutory language, as well as several phrases that were intentionally omitted, deserve special mention. First, the word "individual" is employed here to conform to the standard designation of a human being in the language of the uniform acts. The term "person" was not used here because it is sometimes used by the law to include a corporation. Although that particular confusion would be unlikely to arise here, the narrower term "individual" is more precise and thus avoids the possibility of confusion.

"IRREVERSIBLE CESSATION OF FUNCTIONS"

Second, the statute emphasizes the degree of damage to the brain required for the determination of death by stating "*all* functions of the *entire* brain, *including the brainstem*" (emphasis added). This may be thought doubly redundant, but at least it should make plain the intent to *exclude* from application under the "definition" any patient who has lost only "higher" brain functions or, conversely, who maintains those functions but has suffered solely a direct injury to the brainstem which interferes with the vegetative functions of the body.

The phrase "cessation of *functions*" reflects an important choice. It stands in contrast to two other terms that have been discussed in this field: (a) "loss of activity" and (b) "destruction of the organ."

Bodily parts, and the subparts that make them up, are important for the functions they perform. Thus, detecting a loss of the ability to function is the central aim of diagnosis in this field. After an organ has lost the ability to *function* within the organism, electrical and metabolic *activity* at the level of individual cells or even groups of cells may continue for a period of time. Unless this cellular activity is integrated, however, it cannot contribute to the operation of the organism as a whole. Thus, cellular activity alone is irrelevant in judging whether the organism, as opposed to its components, is "dead."

At the other pole, several commentators have argued that organic *destruction* rather than cessation of functions should be the basis for declaring death.[3] They assert that until an organ has been destroyed there is always the *possibility* that it might resume functioning. The Commission has rejected this position for several reasons. Once brain cells have permanently ceased metabolizing, the body cannot regenerate them. The loss of the brain's functions precedes the destruction of the cells and liquefaction of the tissues.

Theoretically, even *destruction* of an organ does not prevent its functions from being restored. Any decision to recognize "the end" is inevitably restricted by the limits of available medical knowledge and techniques.[4] Since "irreversibility" adjusts to the times, the proposed statute can incorporate new clinical capabilities. Many patients declared dead fifty years ago because of heart failure would not have experienced an *"irreversible* cessation of circulatory and respiratory functions" in the hands of a modern hospital.

Finally, the argument for using "brain destruction" echoes the proposal about "putrefaction" made two centuries ago and overcome by advances in diagnostic techniques. The traditional cardiopulmonary standard relies on the vital signs as a measure of heart-lung function; the declaration of death does not await evidence of destruction. Since the evidence reviewed by the Commission indicates that brain criteria, properly applied, diagnose death as reliably as cardiopulmonary criteria, the Commission sees no reason not to use the same standards of cessation for both. The requirement of "irreversible cessation of functions" should apply to both cardiopulmonary and brain-based determinations.

"IS DEAD"

Most of the model statutes previously proposed state that a person meeting the statutory standards "will [or shall] be considered dead." This formulation, although probably effective in achieving the desired clarification of the place of "brain death" in the law, is somewhat disconcerting since it might be read to indicate that the law will *consider* someone dead who by some other, perhaps wiser, standard *is not* dead. The President's Commission does not endorse this view. If favors stating more directly (as had the Uniform State Law Commissioners in their 1978 proposal) that a person "is dead" when he or she meets one of the standards set forth in the statute.

In declaring that an individual "is dead," physicians imply that at some moment prior to the diagnosis the individual moved from the status of "being alive" to "being dead." The Commission concurs in the view that "death should be viewed not as a process but as the event that separates the process of dying from the process of disintegration."[5] Although it assumes that each dead person became dead at some moment prior to the time of diagnosis, the statute does not specify that moment. Rather, this calculation is left to "accepted medical practices" and the law of each jurisdiction.

Determining the time of passage from living to dead can be troublesome in certain situations; like all aspects of assessing whether a body is dead, it relies heavily on the clinical skills and judgment of the person making the determination. In most cases, it appears to be the custom simply to record the time when a diagnosis of death is made as the time of death. When precision is important for legal purposes, the scientific basis for determining the time of death may be reexamined and resolved through legal proceedings.

A determination of death immediately changes the attitudes and behavior of the living toward the body that has gone from being a person to being a corpse. Discontinuation of medical care, mourning, and burial are examples of customary behavior; people usually provide intimate care for living patients and identify with them, while withdrawing from contact with the dead. In ordinary circumstances, the time at which medical diagnosis causes a change in legal status should be synchronous with the time that social behaviors naturally change.

In some cases of death determined by neurologic criteria, however, it is necessary to allow for repeated testing, observation, or metabolism of drugs. This may interpose hours or even days between the actual time of death and its confirmation. Procedures for certifying time of death, like those for determining the status of being dead, will be a matter for locally "accepted medical standards," hospital rules and custom, community mores and state death certificate law. Present practice in most localities now parallels the determination of death by cardiopulmonary criteria: death by brain criteria is certified at the time that the fact of death is established, that is, after all tests and confirmatory observation periods are complete.

When the time of "brain death" has legal importance, a best medical estimate of the actual time when all brain functions irreversibly ceased will probably be appropriate. When this is a matter of controversy, it becomes a point to be resolved by the law of the jurisdiction. Typically, judges decide this on the basis of expert testimony—as they do with a contested determination of unwitnessed cessation of cardiopulmonary functions.

"ACCEPTED MEDICAL STANDARDS"

The proposed statutes variously describe the basis on which the criteria and tests actually used to diagnose death may be selected. The variations were:

Capron-Kass (1972)   "based on ordinary standards of medical practice"

ABA (1975)   "according to usual and customary standards of medical practice"

NCCUSL (1978)   "in accordance with reasonable medical standards"

AMA (1979)   "in accordance with accepted medical standards"

Despite their linguistic differences, the Capron-Kass, ABA, and AMA models apparently intend the same result: to require the use of diagnostic measures and procedures that have the normal test of scrutiny and adoption by the biomedical community. In contrast, the 1978 Uniform proposal sounded a different note by proposing "reasonableness" as the standard. The problem is: whose reasonableness? Might lay jurors conclude that a medical practice, although generally adopted, was "unreasonable"? It would be unfair to subject a physician (and others acting pursuant to his or her instructions) to liability on the basis of an after-the-fact determination of standards if he or she had been acting in good faith and according to the norms of professional practice and belief. Even the prospect of this liability would unnecessarily disrupt orderly decision-making in this field.

The process by which a norm of medical practice becomes "accepted" varies according to the field and the type of procedure at issue. The statutory language should eliminate wholly idiosyncratic standards or the use of experimental means of diagnosis (except in conjunction with adequate customary procedures). On the other hand, the statute does not require a procedure to be universally adopted; it is enough if, like any medical practice which is later challenged, it has been accepted by a substantial and reputable body of medical men and women as safe and efficacious for the purpose for which it is being employed.[6]

The Commission has also concluded that the statute need not elaborate the legal consequences of following accepted practices. The model statute proposed earlier by the AMA contained separate sections precluding criminal and civil prosecution or liability for determinations of death made in accordance with the statute or actions taken "in good faith in reliance on a determination of death."[7] It is not necessary to address this issue in a statute because the existing common law already eliminates such liability.

PERSONAL BELIEFS

Should a statute include a "conscience clause" permitting an individual (or family members, where the individual is incompetent) to specify the standard to be used for determining his or her death based upon personal or religious beliefs?[8] While sympathetic to the concerns and values that prompt this suggestion, the Commission has concluded that such a provision has no place in a statute on the determination of death. Were a nonuniform standard permitted, unfortunate and mischievous results are easily imaginable.[9]

If the question were what actions (e.g., termination of treatment, autopsy, removal of organs, etc.) could be taken, there might be room for such a conscience clause. Yet, as the question is one of legal *status,* on which turn the rights and interests not only of the one individual but also of other people and of the state itself, the subject is not one for personal (or familial) self-determination.

The statute specifies that death has occurred if *either* cardiopulmonary or brain criteria are met. Although, as a legal matter, there is no personal discretion as to the *fact* of death when either criterion is met, room remains for reasonable accommodation of personal beliefs regarding the actions to be taken once a determination of death has been made. Such actions, whether medical (e.g., maintaining a dead body on a respirator until organs are removed for transplantation) or religious (e.g., withholding religious pronouncement of death until the blood has ceased flowing), can vary with the circumstances. Some subjects in the Commission's hospital survey, for example, were maintained on ventilators for several hours after they were dead, in deference to family wishes or in order for the family to decide whether to donate the deceased's organs.

Notes

1. Law Reform Commission of Canada, *Criteria for the Determination of Death* (Report, No. 15), Minister of Supply and Service, Canada (1981) pp. 7–20.

2. See, e.g., California Health and Safety Code §7180 (West 1975).

3. Paul A. Byrne, Sean O'Reilly, and Paul M. Quay, "Brain Death: An Opposing Viewpoint," *Journal of the American Medical Association* (1979), 242:1985.

4. Already, a hand "destroyed" in an accident can be reconstructed using advanced surgical methods. The functions of the kidney can be artificially restored through extracorporeal devices; an implantable artificial heart has been tested in animals and is now proposed for human trials. It is impossible to predict what other "miracles" biomedical science may some day produce in the restoration of natural functions or their substitution through artificial means.

5. James L. Bernat, Charles M. Culver, and Bernard Gert, "On the Definition and Criterion of Death," *Annals of Internal Medicine* (1981), 94:389: "If we regard death as a process then either the process starts when the person is still living, which confuses the 'process of death' with the process of dying, for we all regard someone who is dying as not yet dead, or the 'process of death' starts when the person is no longer alive, which confuses death with the process of disintegration."

6. *Edwards v. United States,* 519 F.2d 1137 (5th cir. 1975); *Price v. Neyland,* 320 F.2d 674 (D.C. Cir. 1963).

7. Editorial, *Journal of the American Medical Association* (1980), 243:420.

8. Robert M. Veatch, *Death, Dying and the Biological Revolution: Our Last Quest for Responsibility* (New Haven: Yale University Press, 1977), pp. 72–76; Michael T. Sullivan, "The Dying Person—His Plight and His Right," *New England Law Review* (1973), 216:1978.

9. Alexander M. Capron, "Legal Definition of Death," *Annals of the New York Academy of Science* (1978), 315:349, 356–357.

8

Guidelines for the Determination of Death

Report of the Medical Consultants on the Diagnosis
of Death to the President's Commission
for the Study of Ethical Problems in Medicine
and Biomedical and Behavioral Research

The criteria that physicians use in determining that death has
occurred should:

(1) Eliminate errors in classifying a living individual as dead,
(2) Allow as few errors as possible in classifying a dead body as alive,
(3) Allow a determination to be made without unreasonable delay,
(4) Be adaptable to a variety of clinical situations, and
(5) Be explicit and accessible to verification.

Because it would be undesirable for any guidelines to be mandated by legislation or regulation or to be inflexibly established in case law, the proposed Uniform Determination of Death Act appropriately specifies only "accepted medical standards." Local, state, and national institutions and professional organizations are encouraged to examine and publish their practices.

The following guidelines represent a distillation of current

Reprinted from Appendix F of the Commission's July 1981 final report entitled *Defining Death: A Report on the Medical, Legal and Ethical Issues in the Determination of Death*, pp. 161–66. The names of the 56 medical consultants are included in the original report.

practice in regard to the determination of death. Only the most commonly available and verified tests have been included. The time of death recorded on a death certificate is at present a matter of local practice and is not covered in this document.

These guidelines are advisory. Their successful use requires a competent and judicious physician, experienced in clinical examination and the relevant procedures. All periods of observation listed in these guidelines require the patient to be under the care of a physician. Considering the responsibility entailed in the determination of death, consultation is recommended when appropriate.

The outline of the criteria is set forth below in capital and small capital letters. The indented text that follows each outline heading explains its meaning. In addition, the two sets of criteria (cardiopulmonary and neurologic) are followed by a presentation of the major complicating conditions: drug and metabolic intoxication, hypothermia, young age, and shock. It is of paramount importance that anyone referring to these guidelines be thoroughly familiar with the entire documents, including explanatory notes and complicating conditions.

The Criteria for Determination of Death

An individual presenting the findings in *either* section A (cardiopulmonary) *or* section B (neurologic) is dead. In either section, a diagnosis of death requires that *both cessation of functions,* as set forth in subsection 1, *and irreversibility,* as set forth in subsection 2, be demonstrated.

A. AN INDIVIDUAL WITH IRREVERSIBLE CESSATION OF CIRCULATORY AND RESPIRATORY FUNCTIONS IS DEAD.
   1. *CESSATION* IS RECOGNIZED BY AN APPROPRIATE CLINICAL EXAMINATION.
   Clinical examination will disclose at least the absence of responsiveness, heartbeat, and respiratory effort. Medical circumstances may require the use of confirmatory tests, such as an ECG.

2. *IRREVERSIBILITY* IS RECOGNIZED BY PERSISTENT CESSATION OF FUNCTIONS DURING AN APPROPRIATE PERIOD OF OBSERVATION AND/OR TRIAL OF THERAPY. In clinical situations where death is expected, where the course has been gradual, and where irregular agonal respiration or heartbeat finally ceases, the period of observation following the cessation may be only the few minutes required to complete the examination. Similarly, if resuscitation is not undertaken and ventricular fibrillation and standstill develop in a monitored patient, the required period of observation thereafter may be as short as a few minutes. When a possible death is unobserved, unexpected, or sudden, the examination may need to be more detailed or repeated over a longer period, while appropriate resuscitative effort is maintained as a test of cardiovascular responsiveness. Diagnosis in individuals who are first observed with rigor mortis or putrefaction may require only the observation period necessary to establish that fact.

B. AN INDIVIDUAL WITH IRREVERSIBLE CESSATION OF ALL FUNCTIONS OF THE ENTIRE BRAIN, INCLUDING THE BRAINSTEM, IS DEAD.

The "functions of the entire brain" that are relevant to the diagnosis are those that are clinically ascertainable. Where indicated, the clinical diagnosis is subject to confirmation by laboratory tests as described below. Consultation with a physician experienced in this diagnosis is advisable.

1. *CESSATION* IS RECOGNIZED WHEN EVALUATION DISCLOSES FINDINGS OF a *AND* b:

a. CEREBRAL FUNCTIONS ARE ABSENT, AND . . .

There must be deep coma, that is, cerebral unreceptivity and unresponsivity. Medical circumstances may require the use of confirmatory studies such as EEG or blood flow study.

b. BRAINSTEM FUNCTIONS ARE ABSENT.

Reliable testing of brainstem reflexes requires a perceptive and experienced physician using adequate stimuli. Pupillary light, corneal, oculocephalic, oculovestibular, oropharyngeal, and respiratory (apnea) reflexes should be tested. When these reflexes cannot be adequately assessed, confirmatory tests are recommended.

Adequate testing for apnea is very important. An accepted method is ventilation with pure oxygen or an oxygen and carbon dioxide mixture for ten minutes before withdrawal of the ventilator, followed by passive flow of oxygen. (This procedure allows

PaCO2 to rise without hazardous hypoxia.) Hypercarbia adequately stimulates respiratory effort within thirty seconds when PaCO2 is greater than 60 mmHg. A ten minute period of apnea is usually sufficient to attain this level of hypercarbia. Testing of arterial blood gases can be used to confirm this level. Spontaneous breathing efforts indicate that part of the brainstem is functioning.

Peripheral nervous system activity and spinal cord reflexes may persist after death. True decerebrate or decorticate posturing or seizures are inconsistent with the diagnosis of death.

2. *IRREVERSIBILITY* IS RECOGNIZED WHEN EVALUATION DISCLOSES FINDINGS OF a *AND* b *AND* c:

a. THE CAUSE OF COMA IS ESTABLISHED AND IS SUFFICIENT TO ACCOUNT FOR THE LOSS OF BRAIN FUNCTIONS, AND . . .

Most difficulties with the determination of death on the basis of neurologic criteria have resulted from inadequate attention to this basic diagnostic prerequisite. In addition to a careful clinical examination and investigation of history, relevant knowledge of causation may be acquired by computed tomographic scan, measurement of core temperature, drug screening, EEG, angiography, or other procedures.

b. THE POSSIBILITY OF RECOVERY OF ANY BRAIN FUNCTIONS IS EXCLUDED, AND . . .

The most important reversible conditions are sedation, hypothermia, neuromuscular blockade, and shock. In the unusual circumstance where a sufficient cause cannot be established, irreversibility can be reliably inferred only after extensive evaluation for drug intoxication, extended observation, and other testing. A determination that blood flow to the brain is absent can be used to demonstrate a sufficient and irreversible condition.

c. THE CESSATION OF ALL BRAIN FUNCTIONS PERSISTS FOR AN APPROPRIATE PERIOD OF OBSERVATION AND/OR TRIAL OF THERAPY.

Even when coma is known to have started at an earlier time, the absence of all brain functions must be established by an experienced physician at the initiation of the observation period. The duration of observation periods is a matter of clinical judgment, and some physicians recommend shorter or longer periods than those given here.

Except for patients with drug intoxication, hypothermia, young age, or shock, medical centers with substantial experience in diagnosing death neurologically report no cases of brain functions returning following a six hour cessation, documented by clinical examination and confirmatory EEG. In the absence of confirmatory tests, a period of observation of at least twelve hours is recommended when an irreversible condition is well established. For anoxic brain damage where the extent of damage is more difficult to ascertain, observation for twenty-four hours is generally desirable. In anoxic injury, the observation period may be reduced if a test shows cessation of cerebral blood flow or if an EEG shows electrocerebral silence in an adult patient without drug intoxication, hypothermia, or shock.

Confirmation of clinical findings by EEG is desirable when objective documentation is needed to substantiate the clinical findings. Electrocerebral silence verifies irreversible loss of cortical functions, except in patients with drug intoxication or hypothermia. (Important technical details are provided in: American Electroencephalographic Society, *Guidelines in EEG 1980,* Section 4: "Minimum Technical Standards for EEG Recording in Suspected Cerebral Death," pp. 19–24, Atlanta, 1980.) When joined with the clinical findings of absent brainstem functions, electrocerebral silence confirms the diagnosis.

Complete cessation of circulation to the normothermic adult brain for more than ten minutes is incompatible with survival of brain tissue. Documentation of this circulatory failure is therefore evidence of death of the entire brain. Four-vessel intracranial angiography is definitive for diagnosing cessation of circulation to the entire brain (both cerebrum and posterior fossa) but entails substantial practical difficulties and risks. Tests are available that assess circulation only in the cerebral hemispheres, namely radioisotope bolus cerebral angiography and gamma camera imaging with radioisotope cerebral angiography. Without complicating conditions, absent cerebral blood flow as measured by these tests, in conjunction with the clinical determination of cessation of all brain functions for at least six hours, is diagnostic of death.

Complicating Conditions

A. DRUG AND METABOLIC INTOXICATION

Drug intoxication is the most serious problem in the determination of death, especially when multiple drugs are used.

Cessation of brain functions caused by the sedative and anesthetic drugs, such as barbiturates, benzodiazepines, meprobamate, methaqualone, and trichloroethylene, may be completely reversible even though they produce clinical cessation of brain functions and electrocerebral silence. In cases where there is any likelihood of sedative presence, toxicology screening for all likely drugs is required. If exogenous intoxication is found, death may not be declared until the intoxicant is metabolized or intracranial circulation is tested and found to have ceased.

Total paralysis may cause unresponsiveness, areflexia, and apnea that closely simulates death. Exposure to drugs such as neuromuscular blocking agents or aminoglycoside antibiotics, and diseases like myasthenia gravis are usually apparent by careful review of the history. Prolonged paralysis after use of succinylcholine chloride and related drugs requires evaluation of pseudocholinesterase deficiency. If there is any question, low-dose atropine stimulation, electromyogram, peripheral nerve stimulation, EEG, tests of intracranial circulation, or extended observation, as indicated, will make the diagnosis clear.

In drug-induced coma, EEG activity may return or persist while the patient remains unresponsive, and therefore the EEG may be an important evaluation along with extended observation. If the EEG shows electrocerebral silence, short latency auditory or somatosensory evoked potentials may be used to test brainstem function, since these potentials are unlikely to be affected by drugs.

Some severe illnesses (e.g., hepatic encephalopathy, hyperosmolar coma, and preterminal uremia) can cause deep coma. Before irreversible cessation of brain functions can be determined, metabolic abnormalities should be considered and, if possible, corrected. Confirmatory tests of circulation or EEG may be necessary.

B. HYPOTHERMIA

Criteria for reliable recognition of death are not available in the presence of hypothermia (below 32.2°C core temperature). The variables of cerebral circulation in hypothermic patients are not sufficiently well studied to know whether tests of absent or diminished circulation are confirmatory. Hypothermia can mimic brain death by ordinary clinical criteria and can protect against neurologic damage due to hypoxia. Further complications arise since hypothermia also usually precedes and follows death. If these complicating factors make it unclear whether an individual is alive, the only available measure to resolve the issue is to restore normothermia. Hypothermia is not a common cause of difficulty in the determination of death.

C. CHILDREN

The brains of infants and young children have increased resistance to damage and may recover substantial functions even after exhibiting unresponsiveness on neurological examination for longer periods than do adults. Physicians should be particularly cautious in applying neurologic criteria to determine death in children younger than five years.

D. SHOCK

Physicians should also be particularly cautious in applying neurologic criteria to determine death in patients in shock because the reduction in cerebral circulation can render clinical examination and laboratory tests unreliable.

9

Defining Death in Theory and Practice

JAMES L. BERNAT, M.D., CHARLES M. CULVER, M.D., and BERNARD GERT, Ph.D.

In July 1981, the President's Commission for the Study of Ethical Problems in Medicine and Biomedical and Behavioral Research published its first report, *Defining Death: Medical, Legal, and Ethical Issues in the Determination of Death.*[1] The Commission made this subject one of its first studies primarily because of a legal interest: there has been recent disagreement about how best to translate the current physiological understanding of death into acceptable statutory language. But the Commission was also interested in reviewing the dispute between "whole brain" and "higher brain" formulations of death and appraising currently used brain-based tests for death, which have become increasingly varied and sophisticated.

During its meetings, the Commission heard testimony from a variety of experts. Philosophers testified on the conceptual issues involved in defining death; theologians spoke about traditional religious concepts; and neurologists described the

Reprinted from *The Hastings Center Report* (February 1982), 12:5–9, with the permission of the publisher. Copyright © 1982 by the Institute of Society, Ethics and the Life Sciences.

most valid tests for determining cessation of functioning of the brain.

Much of the Commission's report consists of a thorough summary of current knowledge of the physiology of death and how this knowledge has altered understanding of the concept of death itself. Although this presentation is excellent, we believe the model statute that the Commission recommends should not be adopted because there are significant flaws in the Commission's supporting arguments.

There are two distinct, though related, problems in constructing a statutory definition of death. The first is a theoretical concern—providing the correct physiological standard. The second is the practical difficulty of reconciling this standard, which includes a new understanding of death, with the more popular conception of death.

The new understanding of death is largely a consequence of technological advances in life-support systems. Some severely brain-injured patients who have suffered permanent cessation of functioning of the entire brain can be given circulatory and respiratory support such that:

. . . their appearance resembles that of the dead as traditionally perceived: they no longer respond to their environment by sensate and intellectual activity. But their appearance also differs from that traditionally associated with the dead because mechanical support generates breathing, heartbeat, and the associated physical characteristics (e.g., warm, moist skin) of life. (p. 21)

These patients present problems of labeling, for they have some, but not all, of the traditional characteristics that lead one to call a person "dead." Until recently this was rarely, if ever, the case: patients who had some of these characteristics also had all the others. It is not that new technology has changed the concept of death; rather, this technology has made it apparent that previously there had been no clear, precise definition of death.

In his book *Pragmatism,* William James provided a useful example of this kind of definitional problem with regard to the phrase "going around." A squirrel was on the trunk of a tree, and a hunter was on the opposite side. Wishing to see the squirrel, the hunter proceeded to go around the tree; the squirrel, not wishing to be seen, also went around the tree, always facing the hunter but keeping the trunk between them. Had the hunter "gone around" the squirrel or not? James correctly noted that the phrase "going around" was ambiguous; in one sense (going around from north to west, to south, to east, and back to north) the hunter did go around the squirrel, and in the other sense (going around from front, to left, to back, to right, and to front again) he did not. The old sense of "going around" was gone forever. Indeed, there never really was an old, unambiguous sense.

Similarly, one regarded a man as dead if the organism as a whole had permanently ceased to function, if he had permanently stopped breathing, and if his heart had permanently stopped beating. All these usually happened at the same time or within a few minutes of one another, so that people did not consider how they would describe a person if one phenomenon occurred but the other two did not. However, because of modern technology, there are patients whose organism as a whole has permanently ceased to function, but whose respiration and circulation do function through mechanical support systems.

In James' case, there seems no reason for choosing either sense of "going around" as the more important and basic. However, in the case of death clearly the permanent cessation of the organism as a whole is far closer to what has always been meant by death than is permanent absence of breathing and heartbeat. Recognizing this point, the Commission states:

Although absence of breathing and heartbeat may often have been spoken of as "defining" death, review of history and of current medical and popular understanding makes clear that these were merely evidence for the disintegration of the organism as a whole as discussed in Chapter Three. (p. 58)

Thus, the Commission defined the concept of death as the permanent cessation of functioning of the organism as a whole, and developed a statutory definition or standard of death on this basis. We believe that this is the correct approach, and that the report should be judged on how well it has carried out this intention.[2]

The second, practical problem that a new statutory definition must confront results from the rapid increase in the medical understanding of the physiology of death. There is a considerable gap between the understanding of most physicians—who have come to accept the centrality of the functioning of the brain in defining death—and most laypersons who, along with a few practicing physicians, continue to regard the functioning of the heart and lungs as central. Informed medical opinion is now virtually unanimous that a person is dead when and only when the entire brain, including the brainstem, has permanently ceased to function. However, most laypersons continue to believe that the permanent cessation of heartbeat and breathing determines death.

As the Commission acknowledges, the problem lies in incorporating the new medical understanding in a statute without unduly disturbing those who still regard cardiopulmonary function as central.

The Origin of the Problem

After reviewing the anatomy of the brain, and citing clinical examples of individuals with only partial brain damage, the Commission concludes:

The President's Commission, as subsequent chapters explain more fully, regards the cessation of the vital functions of the entire brain—and not merely portions thereof, such as those responsible for cognitive functions—as the only proper neurologic basis for declaring death. This conclusion accords with the overwhelming consensus of medical and legal experts and the public. (p. 18)

A neurologic standard actually lay behind past as well as present tests used by the medical profession for declaring death. Physicians traditionally have determined death by examining patients for total unresponsiveness; lack of any spontaneous movements, including breathing; absence of pupillary light reflexes; and absence of heartbeat. Of these signs, only the last is not directly a sign of cessation of brain functioning. The value of the commonly known tests of death—which detect the permanent absence of spontaneous heartbeat and breathing—depends upon their producing irreversible cessation of functioning of the whole brain.

The Commission traces the history of the use of brain-based tests in death determinations. One landmark was the 1959 description by French neurophysiologists of the characteristics of patients with gross brain damage who have been maintained on respirators, a condition that they aptly termed *coma dépassé* (beyond coma); another was the 1968 report by the Ad Hoc Committee of the Harvard Medical School to Examine the Definition of Brain Death, which listed criteria for diagnosing a permanently nonfunctioning brain. These criteria have since been overwhelmingly validated; no person known to have met them has survived. The Commission also reviews the status of confirmatory tests of permanent cessation of whole brain functioning, including tests of cerebral blood flow and electroencephalography, and points out some of their limitations.

The Commission discusses the role of cessation of ventilation and circulation in the cessation of functioning of the organism as a whole:

For patients who are not artificially maintained, breathing and heartbeat were, and are, reliable signs either of systemic integration and/or of continued brain functioning (depending on which approach one takes to the "whole brain" concept). To regard breathing and respiration as having diagnostic significance when the brain of a respirator-supported patient has ceased functioning, however, is to forget the basic reasoning behind their use in individuals who are not artificially maintained. (p. 37)

The Commission considers and rejects the "higher brain" formulation of death, which depends upon a concept of death defined as "loss of personhood," or in the words of Robert Veatch, its major proponent, "the irreversible loss of that which is essentially significant to the nature of man."[3] By this definition, permanent loss of consciousness and cognition would count as death; thus patients in persistent vegetative states (Karen Ann Quinlan, for example) would be considered dead. These patients have normally functioning brainstems despite severe damage to, or complete loss of, their neocortex. They are permanently comatose but maintain spontaneous respiration and heartbeat, have intact brainstem reflexes such as pupillary constriction to light, and maintain the complex array of neuroendocrine regulatory mechanisms subserved by the brainstem and hypothalamus. While such patients have lost their personhood, they are not dead because they have retained most of the functions of the organism as a whole.

An important weakness of the higher brain formulation of death is the "slippery slope" problem. Just how much neocortical damage is necessary for death? By this definition, would not severely demented patients also be considered dead? Then what about those somewhat less severely brain damaged? Because personhood is an inherently vague concept, strict criteria for its loss are difficult to identify.

The Commission might also have pointed out that the higher brain formulation is unacceptable because it applies only to human beings and not to related species. By the traditional concept of death, we mean the same thing when we say, "Mr. Jones died last night" as when we say, "My dog died last week." Death is a biological concept, so an acceptable definition should be applicable to related species. Such is the case when death is defined as the permanent cessation of functioning of the organism as a whole.

The higher brain formulation is not acceptable as the definition of death. It does have a place in determining possible grounds for nonvoluntary euthanasia, that is, allowing an organism to die when that organism is no longer a person. But the major question—is nonvoluntary euthanasia desirable for patients in persistent vegetative states—should not be answered by blurring the distinction between loss of personhood and death of the organism.

The Commission rightly points out that the problem of formulating a precise statutory definition goes beyond the boundaries of medical authority. They also reject a judicial solution because specifying a standard of death is too fundamental to rely purely on retrospective determination. Furthermore a judicial solution would require too much time, expense, and psychological trauma for those involved. Favoring a legislative solution, they point out that:

A statute on death ought to guide physicians and others in decision making about respirator-maintained patients; it ought also to educate those who must make legal and policy decisions. Legislation will not remove the need for reasoned interpretation—first by physicians and perhaps then by judges—but it can restrict the compass within which they make their choices to one which has been found acceptable by the public. Furthermore, if legislators are guided by a single model bill, the likelihood of statutory law that is uniform in language and intent is greatly increased. (pp. 50–51)

In chapter five of the report, "What 'Definition' Ought to be Adopted?" the Commission confronts the main problem in devising an adequate statutory definition of death. (When the Commission puts the word "definition" in quotation marks, as in this title, it is usually referring to a statutory definition, not an account of the ordinary meaning of the word "death.") The problem is to include in the statute the theoretically correct standard of death—irreversible cessation of all brain functioning—but also allow, for practical purposes, irreversible cessation of cardiopulmonary functions to be used as a test of death in the overwhelming majority of cases. We do not think the Commission's solution to this problem—the Uniform Determination of Death Act (UDDA)—is successful. The UDDA provides:

An individual who has sustained either (1) irreversible cessation of circulatory and respiratory functions, or (2) irreversible cessation of all functions of the entire brain, including the brainstem, is dead. A determination of death must be made in accordance with accepted medical standards. (p. 73)

The Commission rightly notes that "the statute must address the right question" (p. 57). It then states: "The Commission conceives the question to be, 'How, given medical advances in cardiopulmonary support, can the evidence that death has occurred be obtained and recognized?' " We do not think this is the right question at all. Indeed, the UDDA statute does not even attempt to answer this question, which sounds much more like a medical query than one that should be addressed by a statute. The basic question that a statute should address, we believe, is: given medical advances in the understanding of death, what general physiological standards should be used to "define" death?

Another question that might be addressed by a statute is: what practical guide should be given to physicians concerning application of this standard? Note that these are two separate questions: the Commission fails to recognize fully that *two* distinct questions have to be answered, leading to some of the confusion in its report.

When dealing with the conceptual and theoretical bases of the proper standards of death, the report is clear:

In setting forth the standards recommended in this Report, the Commission has used the "whole brain" terms to clarify the understanding of death that enjoys near universal acceptance in our society. The Commission finds the "whole brain" formulations give resonance and depth to the biomedical and epidemiological data presented in Chapter Two . . . the "whole brain" formulations provide a theory that is sufficiently precise, concise and widely acceptable. (p. 36)

The Commission also acknowledges, as noted above, that the heart and lungs play only a subsidiary role:

Although absence of breathing and heartbeat may often have been spoken of as "defining" death, review of history and current medical and popular understanding makes clear that these were merely evidence for the disintegration of the organism as a whole, as discussed in Chapter Three. (p. 58)

However, the Commission does not seem to realize that something that is "merely evidence" should not be presented as a standard of death, for it presents a statute that includes two equal standards of death: (1) "irreversible cessation of circulatory and respiratory functions," and (2) "irreversible cessation of all functions of the entire brain, including the brainstem."

The clearest statement of the Commission's problem in separating conceptual and theoretical considerations from practical ones comes in its discussion of the statute drafted by the Law Reform Commission of Canada:

It would be possible, as in the statute drafted by the Law Reform Commission of Canada, to propound the irreversible cessation of brain functions as *the* "definition" and then to permit that standard to be met not only by direct measures of brain activity but also "by the prolonged absence of spontaneous cardiac and respiratory functions." Although conceptually acceptable (and vastly superior to the adoption of brain cessation as a primary standard conjoined with a nonspecific reference to other apparently unrelated "usual and customary procedures"), the Canadian proposal breaks with tradition in a manner that appears to be unnecessary. (p. 74)[4]

Here the Commission seems to be claiming that the only flaw in the Canadian account is that it "breaks with tradition in a manner that appears to be unnecessary." But this is a very surprising claim. Almost half the state statutes adopted since 1970 use only the brain standard and do not even mention circulation and respiration. Indeed, this is also true of the earlier statutes endorsed by the American Bar Association and the Uniform Brain Death Act put forward by the National Conference of Commissioners on Uniform State Laws.[5]

Since it is hard to take at face value the claim that the Canadian proposal unnecessarily breaks with tradition, it is worth examining how the Commission supports this claim. It correctly points out:

For most lay people—and in all probability for most physicians as well— the permanent loss of heart and lung function (for example, in an elderly person who has died in his or her sleep) clearly manifests death. (p. 74)

But the Canadian statute acknowledges that this is true. The Commission then alludes to the brain's special role:

As previous chapters in this Report recount, biomedical scientists can explain the brain's particularly important—and vulnerable—role in the organism as a whole and show how temporary loss of blood flow (ischemia) becomes a permanent cessation because of the damage that it inflicts on the brain. (p. 74)

This is also compatible with the Canadian statute. Then comes the crucial step in the argument:

Nonetheless, most of the time people do not, and need not, go through this two step process. Irreversible loss of circulation is recognized as death because—setting aside any mythical connotations of the heart—a person without blood flow simply cannot live. Thus, the Commission prefers to employ language which would reflect the continuity of the traditional standard and the newer, brain-based standard. (p. 74)

The Commission's reasoning seems to be as follows: if people do not and need not think about the cessation of brain function in recognizing death from loss of heart and lung function, then cessation of heart and lung function is an independent standard of death. But this reasoning is fallacious. Consider the following parallel argument. If people do not and need not think about cessation of brain function (or of heart and lung function) in recognizing death from someone being smashed flat by a steamroller, then being smashed flat by a steamroller is an independent standard of death. Even if people were commonly smashed flat by steamrollers, it would still not be a standard of death. For a standard of death is not merely that by which we can recognize that someone is dead; it is, based on all of our medical understanding, that which is both a necessary and sufficient condition for death. If the standard is fulfilled, the person is dead; if it is not fulfilled, the person is not dead. Irreversible cessation of all brain functions is such a standard. If it has occurred, the person is dead; if it has not occurred, the person is not dead, no matter what has happened to the heart, lungs, or any other organ.

Let us now see why "irreversible cessation of circulatory and respiratory functions" is not a standard of death. First, this phrase is ambiguous (recall the parallel problem with "going around"). It can mean either irreversible cessation of *spontaneous* circulatory and respiratory functions" or "irreversible cessation of *artificially supported* circulatory and respiratory functions." No such ambiguity exists with regard to cessation of brain functions, for there are no artificially supported brain functions, in the relevant sense. No one would want to call a man in an iron lung and wearing a pacemaker dead, especially if he were still talking to us. Thus, irreversible cessation of spontaneous cardiopulmonary function may be a necessary condition for death, but it is certainly not sufficient. And irreversible cessation of artificially supported circulatory and respiratory functions is also not a standard of death, for though it may be a sufficient condition of death, it is not a necessary condition; it is one of the key points of the Commission's report that when circulation and respiration are being artificially maintained, but all brain functions have irreversibly ceased, the person is dead.

The report does not explain the ambiguous phrase "irreversible cessation of circulatory and respiratory functions"—all the more surprising for the Commission explains almost all the words in the statute, even why it uses "individual" rather than "person" and "is dead" rather than "will be considered dead." Possibly it would have required far more explanation than the Commission was prepared to offer.

There is no acceptable understanding of the phrase "irreversible loss of circulatory and respiratory functions" that provides a genuine standard for death. The Commission failed to realize this difficulty or perhaps it did partly realize it, and for that reason failed even to mention "spontaneous' or "artificially maintained." We think the Commission did not distinguish carefully enough between a *standard,* which must be a necessary and sufficient condition of death if it is to "define" it, and a *test,* which is merely a way of determining death.

No doubt some of the Commission's problems were brought on by its concern with avoiding radical change:

The conservative nature of the reform here proposed will be more apparent if the statute refers explicitly to the existing cardiopulmonary standard for determination of death. The brain-based standard is, after all, merely supplementary to the older standard, which will continue to be adequate in the overwhelming number of cases in the foreseeable future. (p. 59)

However, any standard of death must be adequate in all cases, not merely the overwhelming number. Here is another instance in which the term "spontaneous" becomes important. For the "older standard" was for "irreversible cessation of *spontaneous* circulatory and respiratory functions," and the Commission rightly recognizes that this standard is no longer universally adequate. What it does not seem to realize is that this means it is not really a standard but merely a test. Cardiopulmonary tests may be adequate in the overwhelming number of cases, and brain-based tests may be used in only a small portion of cases, but this belongs in the practical part of the statute, not in the statutory definition of death.

The Commission has thus created a statutory definition of death that is seriously misleading and that contains the most serious flaw that the Commission finds in previous statutes: it provides two independent standards of death, without explaining the relationship between them.

A Modified Solution

The Commission strived to produce a statute that would be adopted by all jurisdictions in the United States, and it presents good arguments for uniform legislation. Since 1970, twenty-seven states have adopted determination-of-death statutes; though the statutes appear to have similar intent, they are confusingly diverse in form and many are ambiguously worded.

The UDDA statute is not desirable, we believe, because it too is ambiguous and it elevates the irreversible cessation of cardiopulmonary functioning to the level of a standard of death, when it is really only a test, although a test that may be used in most circumstances. Permanent cessation of spontaneous cardiopulmonary functioning works as a test of death only in the absence of artificial cardiopulmonary support because only there does it produce the true standard of death—the irreversible cessation of all brain functions. A conceptually satisfactory statute would not need to mention cessation of cardiopulmonary function at all. It would be sufficient to include only irreversible cessation of whole brain functioning and allow physicians to select validated and agreed-upon tests (prolonged absence of spontaneous cardiopulmonary function would be one) to measure irreversible cessation of whole brain function. However, the Commission felt, and we agree, that a statute that included cessation of cardiopulmonary function would be more broadly acceptable and useful.

The solution is to reconcile the claims of conceptual clarity and practical utility. In order to produce a more conceptually acceptable statute of death that would also be useful, we have incorporated into the UDDA statute the distinction between a standard and a test that was recognized by the model statute provided by the Law Reform Commission of Canada, and by the statute we recently proposed. Our proposed statute reads:

An individual who has sustained irreversible cessation of all functions of the entire brain, including the brainstem, is dead

(a) In the absence of artificial means of cardiopulmonary support, death (the irreversible cessation of all brain functions) may be determined by the prolonged absence of spontaneous circulatory and respiratory functions.

(b) In the presence of artificial means of cardiopulmonary support,

death (the irreversible cessation of all brain functions) must be
determined by tests of brain function.
In both situations, the determination of death must be made in accordance with accepted medical standards.

We believe that this statute is conceptually clearer than the
UDDA statute. It identifies the irreversible cessation of all functions of the entire brain, including the brainstem, as the standard
of death, thus making clear that death is a single phenomenon. It
also provides a guide to the practicing physician, pointing out
that he or she may continue to declare death by cardiopulmonary
tests in the majority of deaths uncomplicated by artificial cardiopulmonary support. And in the presence of cardiopulmonary
support, the physician must directly measure the functioning of
the brain. Thus this statute is both practical and conceptually
clear.

Notes

1. President's Commission for the Study of Ethical Problems in Medicine and
Biomedical and Behavioral Research, *Defining Death: Medical, Legal, and Ethical Issues in
the Determination of Death* (Washington, D.C.: GPO, July 1981).
2. James L. Bernat, Charles M. Culver, Bernard Gert, "On the Definition and
Criterion of Death," *Annals of Internal Medicine* (1981), 94:389–394.
3. Robert M. Veatch, *Death, Dying, and the Biological Revolution* (New Haven:
Yale University Press, 1976).
4. Law Reform Commission of Canada, *Criteria for the Determination of Death*
(Ottawa: Law Reform Commission of Canada, March 1981).
5. "House of Delegates Redefines Death, Urges Redefinition of Rape, and Undoes
the Houston Amendments," *American Bar Association Journal* (1975), 61:463–464; and
Uniform Brain Death Act 1, 12 Uniform Laws Annotated, supplement (1980), vol. 15.

10

Commonwealth v. Golston

Supreme Judicial Court of Massachusetts,
373 Mass. 249, 366 N.E.2d 744 (1977)

BRAUCHER, Justice:
The defendant appeals his conviction of murder in the first degree. Among numerous other errors, he claims that the death of the victim was not properly established. We hold that the trial judge correctly accepted the medical concept of "brain death"; alternatively, any error in this respect was harmless beyond a reasonable doubt. . . .

There was evidence of the following facts. About 2 p.m. on Sunday, August 24, 1975, the victim, . . . came out of a store in Dorchester and walked toward his car. The defendant, . . . tiptoed behind him and hit him on the head with a baseball bat. The defendant then went into a building, changed his clothes, and crossed the street to the store, where he worked. When asked why he had hit the man, he said, "For kicks." The victim was taken to a hospital. There a large portion of the front of his skull was removed to relieve pressure on his brain, and he breathed with the aid of an artificial respirator. On August 26, his blood pressure, heartbeat and pulse were not observable, he failed to breathe when taken off the respirator for two minutes, and an electroencephalogram failed to reveal any cerebral electrical activity. On August 28, he again made no attempt to breathe when taken off the respirator, there were no reflex actions or responses to painful stimulation, and a second electroencephalogram showed no evidence of brain wave activity. After consultation with the victim's family, the respirator was removed on August 31, and his heart stopped.

1. *The proof of "brain death."* There was medical testimony that on August 25 only the part of the victim's brain responsible for the most primitive responses, the brain stem, was still to some degree working. On August 26 the remaining brain stem functions, such as responding to painful stimuli and gasping for air, had disappeared; the victim never again exhibited any signs that his brain stem or cortex was functioning. In the opinion of the responsible physician, the victim was then dead, having reached the stage of irreversible "brain death." This opinion was confirmed by an electroencephalogram on August 26 and by another on August 28. The removal of the respirator on August 31 was in accordance with good medical practice. An autopsy the next day revealed a brain without architecture, a decomposed, jelly-like mass, consistent with a brain dead for substantially more than two days. The medical examiner concluded that the victim had been dead since August 28.

According to the testimony, a definition of "brain death" was developed by the Harvard Ad Hoc Committee in 1968. The traditional definition of death as the cessation of the heartbeat is erroneous; death does not occur until the heart has stopped long enough so that there is complete loss of brain function. When the heart is maintained artificially, the brain function must be examined directly. The Harvard Committee developed basic clinical criteria, which are generally accepted by the medical community. Subsequent studies resulted in the establishment by an interagency committee of slightly less rigorous criteria, but the physicians attending the victim applied the original Harvard Committee criteria.

The three basic criteria were (1) unresponsiveness to normally painful stimuli; (2) absence of spontaneous movements or breathing; and (3) absence of reflexes. The diagnosis of "brain death" was to be confirmed by an electroencephalogram, and was to be observed over a twenty-four hour period. No reported individual has ever survived when these criteria were met. In accordance with these criteria, several doctors testified that the victim was dead by August 28.

2. *The judge's instruction on "brain death."* The judge instructed the jury that "as a matter of law, the occurrence of a brain death, if you find it, satisfies the essential element of the crime of murder requiring proof beyond a reasonable doubt of the death of the victim. Brain death occurs when, in the opinion of a licensed physician, based on ordinary and accepted standards of medical practice, there has been a total and irreversible cessation of spontaneous brain functions and further attempts at resuscitation or continued supportive maintenance would not be successful in restoring such functions." The judge also submitted two questions to the jury, to be answered if they found the defendant guilty of murder in either the first or the second degree: (1) whether they found that the element of death in the crime of murder was satisfied by the proof of a brain death; (2) if so, whether the brain death occurred before or after the artificial life support was disconnected. The jury answered the first question, "Yes," and the second, "Before." . . .

So far as we can ascertain, this court has never before decided the question when death occurs for the purposes of the law of homicide. The judge recognized the significant technological advances in the area of artificial life support and applied traditional principles, we think correctly, to the novel case presented. "The rules and principles of the common law . . . are broad and expansive enough to embrace all new cases as they arise." . . . The judge made an "evolutionary restatement" of the rule rather than a substantively new rule. . . . Proof of the same facts would permit conviction under either the old or the new formulation, and there was no lack of fair warning to the defendant. . . .

To avoid misunderstanding, we emphasize that we consider the issue of "brain death" only as it affects conviction. We do not consider the numerous other situations in which the question when death occurs might arise. . . .

THREE
Selective Nontreatment of Handicapped Newborns

The moral problem of selective nontreatment of handicapped newborns has been discussed in hospital nurseries and neonatal intensive care units (NICUs) since the late 1960s. Pediatricians, pediatric surgeons, and neonatologists have written numerous articles on this complex problem, often displaying important differences in their views regarding the extent to which severely premature and seriously handicapped babies should be given life-prolonging treatment.

Advances in medical technology have drastically changed the ability of neonatologists and other pediatricians to treat infants born with congenital abnormalities. Premature and disabled babies who would have died had they been born in the 1950s or early 1960s are now frequently able, with sophisticated technological assistance, to survive. The result is that increasingly smaller infants (sometimes weighing only 600 grams at birth) and disabled infants with serious conditions (for example, infants with spina bifida, or hyaline membrane disease, or congenital heart disease, or intraventricular hemorrhage, or hydrocephalus) are now usually given medical treatment in the first few days and weeks after birth.

The clinical location for this medical treatment is the NICU. Approximately 600 hospitals in the United States now have NICUs. These units admit 200,000 newborns annually, representing 6 percent of all live births in this country. Costs per patient in NICUs range from $2,000 to well over $40,000, with the total annual national cost of neonatal intensive care in the area of $1.5 billion.

As medical technology has advanced to make possible the prolongation of many handicapped infants' lives—but at increasing costs, both financial and otherwise—important ethical questions have been debated by physicians, nurses, parents, ethicists, attorneys, and other concerned individuals. When, if ever, is it morally justifiable not to provide life-prolonging medical treatment for neonates with severe congenital defects? When, if ever, is a baby too young and/or too small to be saved by medical technology? How often—and in which specific kinds of cases—does technological intervention bring about more harm than benefit to the child? If the decision is made that some infants are not to be treated, on which clinical and ethical criteria should that decision be based? If medical treatment is judged not in a particular infant's best interests, how should that infant be managed in the NICU? Who are the appropriate decision makers for these agonizing decisions regarding life, suffering, and death?

There are five ethical options for dealing with several of these questions. The first option, and the most conservative of the five positions, is to argue that all nondying infants should receive life-prolonging medical treatment, no matter how premature or disabled the infants may be. A second option is the most radical of the five positions. Philosophers subscribing to this view are convinced that personhood can be defined according to a limited number of criteria (self-consciousness, a capacity for rationality, and so forth), that newborn infants do not count as persons according to these criteria, and that any seriously disabled newborns may have their lives terminated. A third option is to argue that decisions about treatment or non-treatment are most appropriately made by the parents of handicapped infants, because they are the most involved persons in such cases. A fourth option focuses on the quality of lives disabled infants will likely have, and concludes that only those babies who have a chance for meaningful lives should receive life-prolonging treatment. By contrast, the fifth option concentrates on the projected burden of continued existence to a handicapped infant, rather than on the projected lack of quality, and argues that medical treatment should be withheld from a severely disabled infant only when such treatment is judged not in the child's best interests.

Decisions about selected nontreatment involve the law as well as ethics. Such life and death decisions are obviously not made in a legal vacuum. Rather, decisions about withholding or withdrawing treatment from handicapped newborns are increasingly coming under the scrutiny of the state legislatures, the courts, and the federal government.

State statutes have bearing on selective nontreatment decisions in two ways. First, all states have homicide and neglect laws that can, depending upon the facts in a particular case, be brought against the parents and/or physicians who withhold treatment from a disabled infant. Whenever parents, through either premeditation or negligence, decide to withhold life-prolonging medical treatment from a neonate with a lethal condition, and it can be demonstrated that their failure to provide treatment was the proximate cause of the child's death, they may be liable for a number of legal charges ranging from first-degree murder to involuntary manslaughter to neglect. In addition, physicians who withhold medical treatment from neonates who need and stand to benefit from such treatment are liable for a range of legal charges. It is, however, extremely rare for such charges to be brought against parents or physicians.

Second, several states in the 1980s passed statutes specifically dealing with the protection of handicapped newborns. Louisiana was the first state to have such a law. The Louisiana law states that "no infant born alive shall be denied or deprived of food or nutrients, water, or oxygen by any person whomsoever with the intent to cause or allow the death of the child"

(Act 339 became law in Louisiana in 1982). Because legislators often fail to understand the complexities of cases in NICUs, such laws are generally vague, extremely difficult to interpret, and virtually devoid of specific guidelines for neonatologists who regularly work with children having a wide variety of handicapping conditions.

Cases of selective nontreatment sometimes end up in state or federal courts. In such cases judges may decide that the parents and physicians have acted responsibly, may mandate treatment against the parents' wishes, may appoint a legal guardian to protect a child's best interests, or may charge the parents and/or physicians with criminal conduct. Cases receiving considerable media attention in the 1980s included the Brian West case in Orange County, California; the Elin Daniels case in Miami, Florida; the "Baby Doe" case in Bloomington, Indiana; and the "Baby Jane Doe" case in Stony Brook, New York.

Because of the publicity surrounding the Bloomington case, and the widespread view that the court system failed in that particular case, the federal government has taken on an increasingly active and visible role in cases involving handicapped newborns. That activity can be divided into three overlapping parts. The first part has involved federal regulations. Beginning in 1982, the Department of Health and Human Services attempted to protect the lives of handicapped infants through a series of regulations aimed at the nation's hospitals and pediatricians. The most controversial of these regulations were the multiple revised versions of the "Baby Doe" rules issued in March and July of 1983, January and December of 1984, and April of 1985. The second part of the government's activity has been litigious in nature. As illustrated by the several court battles in the "Baby Jane Doe" case, the Department of Health and Human Services attempted unsuccessfully to enforce some of its selective nontreatment regulations through judicial decisions. The third part of the government's activity has consisted of legislation. In 1984 the Congress revised earlier child abuse laws and stipulated that all handicapped newborns should receive medically indicated treatment unless (a) an infant is dying or is irreversibly comatose, (b) medical treatment in a particular case would be futile, or (c) medical treatment in a specific instance would be inhumane.

The selected readings illustrate some of the medical, legal, and ethical issues involved in decisions to withhold treatment from handicapped newborns. The article by Raymond Duff and A. G. M. Campbell, both of them pediatricians at the Yale-New Haven Hospital at the time of writing, is one of the "classics" on the topic of selective nontreatment. Published in 1973, this article was one of the first medical articles to bring the issue of selective nontreatment out of the NICU into public view. The response to the Duff/Campbell article was intense, as illustrated by the second and third readings in this section. John Robertson, an attorney, and Norman Fost, a pediatrician, responded to the publicized cases of selective nontreatment by pointing out the possible legal liability of the parties involved in such cases. Richard Sherlock, an ethicist, responded by arguing that Duff and Campbell—and other persons making similar decisions—have insufficient criteria for denying life to disabled infants.

The other two selections are more recent and indicate that, in the midst of increased attention to the legal implications of selective nontreatment decisions, debate continues regarding appropriate clinical and ethical criteria for such decisions. The Carson Strong article argues that federal regulations do not adequately consider the impact of handicapped infants upon family units—and that the projected burden of some infants upon some families is a sufficient reason to withhold aggressive treatment. The excerpt from *Selective Nontreatment of Handicapped Newborns,* by contrast, focuses on diagnostic categories as an appropriate way of determining which infants should be allowed to die and which ones should be given treatment to prolong and enhance their lives.

As already indicated, there have been a number of court cases concerned with selective nontreatment decisions. One of these cases, the "Baby Jane Doe" case, involved nine different court hearings in state and federal courts in New York. Some of the hearings focused on the parents' decision to have their daughter's spina bifida lesion given the conservative treatment of an antibiotic dressing (to encourage the skin to grow over the spinal defect), rather than the more aggressive treatment of closing the lesion surgically. The court case selected for inclusion in these readings is the November 17, 1983, decision by the U.S. District Court, which ruled that "the decision of the parents . . . was a reasonable one based on due consideration of the medical options available and on a genuine concern for the best interest of the child."

11

Moral and Ethical Dilemmas in the Special-Care Nursery

RAYMOND S. DUFF, M.D.
AND A. G. M. CAMPBELL, M.D.

Between 1940 and 1970 there was a 58 percent decrease in the infant death rate in the United States.[1] This reduction was related in part to the application of new knowledge to the care of infants. Neonatal mortality rates in hospitals having infant intensive-care units have been above one-half those reported in hospitals without such units.[2] There is now evidence that in many conditions of early infancy the long-term morbidity may also be reduced.[3] Survivors of these units may be healthy, and their parents grateful, but some infants continue to suffer from such conditions as chronic cardiopulmonary disease, short-bowel-syndrome or various manifestations of brain damage; others are severely handicapped by a myriad of congenital malformations that in previous times would have resulted in early death. Recently, both lay and professional persons have expressed increasing concern about the quality of life for these severely impaired survivors and their families. Many pediatricians and others are distressed with the long-term results of

Reprinted from *The New England Journal of Medicine* (October 25, 1973), 289:890-894, with the permission of the publisher. Copyright © 1973 by the Massachusetts Medical Society.

pressing on and on to save life at all costs and in all circumstances. Eliot Slater stated, "If this is one of the consequences of the sanctity-of-life ethic, perhaps our formulation of the principle should be revised."[4]

The experiences described in this communication document some of the grave moral and ethical dilemmas now faced by physicians and families. They indicate some of the problems in a large special-care nursery where medical technology has prolonged life and where "informed" parents influence the management decisions concerning their infants.

Background and Methods

The special-care nursery of the Yale-New Haven Hospital not only serves an obstetric service for over 4,000 live births annually but also acts as the principal referral center in Connecticut for infants with major problems of the newborn period. From January 1, 1970, through June 30, 1972, 1,615 infants born at the hospital were admitted, and 556 others were transferred for specialized care from community hospitals. During this interval, the average daily census was 26, with a range of 14 to 37.

For some years the unit has had a liberal policy for parental visiting, with the staff placing particular emphasis on helping parents adjust to and participate in the care of their infants with special problems. By encouraging visiting, attempting to create a relaxed atmosphere within the unit, exploring carefully the special needs of the infants, and familiarizing parents with various aspects of care, it was hoped to remove much of the apprehension—indeed, fear—with which parents at first view an intensive-care nursery. At any time, parents may see and handle their babies. They commonly observe or participate in most routine aspects of care and are often present when some infant is critically ill or moribund. They may attend, as they choose, the death of their own infant. Since an average of two to three deaths occur each week and many infants are critically ill for long periods, it is obvious that the concentrated, intimate social interactions between personnel, infants, and parents in an emotionally charged atmosphere often make the work of the staff very difficult and demanding. However, such participation and recognition of parents' rights to information about their infant appear to be the chief foundations of "informed consent" for treatment.

Each staff member must know how to cope with any questions and problems brought up by parents, and if he or she cannot help, they must have access to those who can. These requirements can be met only when staff members work closely with each other in all the varied circumstances from simple to complex, from triumph to tragedy. Formal and informal meetings take place regularly to discuss the technical and family aspects of care. As a given problem may require, some or all of several persons (including families, nurses, social workers, physicians, chaplains, and others) may convene to exchange information and reach decisions. Thus, staff and parents function more or less as a small community in which a concerted attempt is made to ensure that each member may participate in and know about the major decisions that concern him or her. However, the physician takes appropriate initiative in final decision making, so that the family will not have to bear that heavy burden alone.

For several years, the responsibilities of attending pediatrician have been assumed chiefly by ourselves, who, as a result, have become acquainted intimately with the problems of the infants, the staff, and the parents. Our almost constant availability to staff, private pediatricians, and parents has resulted in the raising of more and more ethical questions about various aspects of intensive care for critically ill and congenitally deformed infants. The penetrating questions and challenges, particularly of knowledgeable parents (such as physicians, nurses, or lawyers), brought increasing doubts about the wisdom of many of the decisions that seemed to parents to be predicated chiefly on technical considerations. Some thought their child had a right to die since he could not live well or effectively. Others thought that society should pay the costs of care that may be so destructive to the family economy. Often, too, the parents' or siblings' rights to relief from the seemingly pointless, crushing burdens were important considerations. It seemed right to yield to parent wishes in several cases as physicians have done for generations. As a result, some treatments were withheld or stopped with the knowledge that earlier death and relief from suffering would result. Such options were explored with the less knowledgeable parents to ensure that their consent for treatment of their defective children was truly informed. As Eisenberg pointed out regarding the application of technology, "At long last, we are beginning to ask, not *can* it be done, but *should* it be done?"[5] In lengthy, frank discussions, the anguish of the parents was shared, and attempts were made to support fully the reasoned choices, whether for active treatment and rehabilitation or for an early death.

To determine the extent to which death resulted from withdrawing or withholding treatment, we examined the hospital records of all children who died from January 1, 1970, through June 30, 1972.

Results

In total, there were 299 deaths. Each was classified in one of two categories. Deaths in category 1 resulted from pathologic conditions in spite of the treatment given; 256 (86 percent) were in this category. Of these, 66 percent were the result of respiratory problems or complications associated with extreme prematurity (birth weight under 1,000 g). Congenital heart disease and other anomalies accounted for an additional 22 percent (table 11.1).

Deaths in category 2 were associated with severe impairment, usually from congenital disorders: 43 (14 percent) were in this group (table 11.2). These deaths or their timing was associated with discontinuance or withdrawal of treatment. The mean duration of life in category 2 (table 11.3) was greater than

Table 11.1. PROBLEMS CAUSING DEATH IN CATEGORY 1

Problem	No. of Deaths	Percentage
Respiratory	108	42.2
Extreme prematurity	60	23.4
Heart disease	42	16.4
Multiple anomalies	14	5.5
Other	32	12.5
Totals	256	100.0

that in category 1. This was the result of a mean life of 55 days for eight infants who became chronic cardiopulmonary cripples but for whom prolonged and intensive efforts were made in the hope of eventual recovery. They were infants who were dependent on oxygen, digoxin, and diuretics, and most of them had been treated for the idiopathic respiratory-distress syndrome with high oxygen concentrations and positive-pressure ventilation.

Some examples of management choices in category 2 illustrate the problems. An infant with Down's syndrome and intestinal atresia, like the much-publicized one at Johns Hopkins Hospital, was not treated because his parents thought that surgery was wrong for their baby and themselves. He died seven days after birth. Another child had chronic pulmonary disease after positive-pressure ventilation with high oxygen concentrations for treatment of severe idiopathic respiratory-distress syndrome. By five months of age, he still required 40 percent oxygen to survive, and even then, he was chronically dyspneic and cyanotic. He also suffered from cor pulmonale, which was difficult to control with digoxin and diuretics. The nurses, parents, and physicians considered it cruel to continue, and yet difficult to stop. All were attached to this child, whose life they had tried so hard to make worthwhile. The family had endured high expenses (the hospital bill exceeding $15,000), and the strains of the illness were believed to be threatening the marriage bonds and to be causing sibling behavioral disturbances. Oxygen supplementation was stopped, and the child died in about three hours. The family settled down and 18 months later had another baby, who was healthy.

A third child had meningomyelocele, hydrocephalus, and

Table 11.2. PROBLEMS ASSOCIATED WITH DEATH IN CATEGORY 2

Problem	No. of Deaths	Percentage
Multiple anomalies	15	34.9
Trisomy	8	18.6
Cardiopulmonary	8	18.6
Meningomyelocele	7	16.3
Other central nervous system defects	3	7.0
Short-bowel syndrome	2	4.6
Totals	43	100.0

Table 11.3. SELECTED COMPARISONS OF 256 CASES IN CATEGORY 1 AND 43 IN CATEGORY 2

Attribute	Category 1	Category 2
Mean length of life	4.8 days	7.5 days
Standard deviation	8.8 days	34.3
Range	1–69	1–150
Portion living for < 2 days	50.0%	12.0%

major anomalies on every organ in the pelvis. When the parents understood the limits of medical care and rehabilitation, they believed no treatment should be given. She died at five days of age.

We have maintained contact with most families of children in category 2. Thus far, these families appear to have experienced a normal mourning for their losses. Although some exhibited doubts that the choices were correct, all appear to be as effective in their lives as they were before this experience. Some claim that their profoundly moving experience has provided a deeper meaning in life, and from this they believe they have become more effective people.

Members of all religious faiths and atheists were participants as parents and as staff in these experiences. There appeared to be no relation between participation and a person's religion. Repeated participation in these troubling events did not appear to reduce the worry of staff about the awesome nature of the decisions.

Discussion

That decisions are made not to treat severely defective infants may be no surprise to those familiar with special-care facilities. All laymen and professionals familiar with our nursery appeared to set some limits upon their application of treatment to extend life or to investigate a pathologic process. For example, an experienced nurse said about one child, "We lost him several weeks ago. Isn't it time to quit?" In another case, a house officer said to a physician investigating an aspect of a child's disease, "For this child, don't you think it's time to turn off your curiosity so you can turn on your kindness?" Like many others, these children eventually acquired the "right to die."

Arguments among staff members and families for and against such decisions were based on varied notions of the rights and interests of defective infants, their families, professionals, and society. They were also related to varying ideas about prognosis. Regarding the infants, some contended that individuals should have a right to die in some circumstances such as anencephaly, hydranencephaly, and some severely deforming and incapacitating conditions. Such very defective individuals were considered to have little or no hope of achieving meaningful "humanhood."[6] For example, they have little or no capacity to love or be loved. They are often cared for in facilities that have been characterized as "hardly more than dying bins,"[7] an assessment with which, in our experience, knowledgeable parents (those who visited chronic-care facilities for placement of their children) agreed. With institutionalized well children, social participation may be essentially nonexistent, and maternal deprivation severe; this is known to have an adverse, usually disastrous, effect upon the child. The situation for the defective child is probably worse, for he is restricted socially both by his need for care and by his defects. To escape "wrongful life,"[8] a fate rated as worse than death, seemed right. In this regard, Lasagna notes, "We may, as a society, scorn the civilizations that slaughtered their infants, but our present treatment of the retarded is some ways more cruel."[9]

Others considered allowing a child to die wrong for several reasons. The person most involved, the infant, had no choice in the decision. Prognosis was not always exact, and a few children with extensive care might live for months, and occasionally years. Some might survive and function satisfactorily. To a few persons, withholding treatment and accepting death was condemned as criminal.

Families had strong but mixed feelings about management decisions. Living with the handicapped is clearly a family affair, and families of deformed infants thought there were limits to what they could bear or should be expected to bear. Most of them wanted maximal efforts to sustain life and to rehabilitate the handicapped; in such cases, they were supported fully. However, some families, especially those having children with severe defects, feared that they and their other children would become socially enslaved, economically deprived, and permanently stigmatized, all perhaps for a lost cause. Such a state of "chronic sorrow" until death has been described by Olshansky.[10] In some cases, families considered the death of the child right both for the child and for the family. They asked if that choice could be theirs or their doctors.

As Feifel has reported, physicians on the whole are reluctant to deal with the issues.[11] Some, particularly specialists based in the medical center, gave specific reasons for this disinclination. There was a feeling that to "give up" was disloyal to the cause of the profession. Since major research, teaching, and patient–care efforts were being made, professionals expected to discover, transmit, and apply knowledge and skills; patients and families were supposed to cooperate fully even if they were not always grateful. Some physicians recognized that the wishes of families went against their own, but they were resolute. They commonly agreed that if they were the parents of very defective children, withholding treatment would be most desirable for them. However, they argued that aggressive management was indicated for others. Some believed that allowing death as a management option was euthanasia and must be stopped for fear of setting a "poor ethical example" or for fear of personal prosecution or damage to their clinical departments or to the medical center as a whole. Alexander's report on Nazi Germany was cited in some cases as providing justification for pressing the effort to combat disease.[12] Some persons were concerned about the loss through death of "teaching material." They feared the training of professionals for the care of defective children in the future and the advancing of the state of the art would be compromised. Some parents who became aware of this concern thought their children should not become experimental subjects.

Practicing pediatricians, general practitioners, and obstetricians were often familiar with these families and were usually sympathetic with their views. However, since they were more distant from the special-care nursery than the specialists of the medical center, their influence was often minimal. As a result, families received little support from them, and tension in community-medical relations was a recurring problem.

Infants with severe types of meningomyelocele precipitated the most controversial decisions. Several decades ago, those who survived this condition beyond a few weeks usually became hydrocephalic and retarded, in addition to being crippled and deformed. Without modern treatment, they died earlier. Some may have been killed or at least not resuscitated at birth. From the early 1960s, the tendency has been to treat vigorously all infants with meningomyelocele. As advanced by Zachary and Shurtleff, aggressive management of these children became the rule in our unit as in many others.[13] Infants were usually referred quickly. Parents routinely signed permits for operation though rarely had they seen their children's defects or had the nature of various management plans and their respective prognoses clearly explained to them. Some physicians believed that parents were too upset to understand the nature of the problems and the options for care. Since they believed informed consent had no meaning in these circumstances, they either ignored the parents or simply told them that the child needed an operation on the back as the first step in correcting several defects. As a result, parents often felt completely left out while the activities of care proceeded at a brisk pace.

Some physicians experienced in the care of these children and familiar with the impact of such conditions upon families had early reservations about this plan of care.[14] More recently, they were influenced by the pessimistic appraisal of vigorous management schemes in some cases.[15] Meningomyelocele, when treated vigorously, is associated with higher survival rates, but the achievement of satisfactory rehabilitation is at best difficult and usually impossible for almost all who are severely affected. Knowing this, some physicians and some families decide against treatment of the most severely affected. If treatment is not carried out, the child's condition will usually deteriorate from further brain damage, urinary-tract infections, and orthopedic difficulties, and death can be expected much earlier. Two-thirds may be dead by three months, and over 90 percent by one year of age. However, the quality of life during that time is poor, and the strains on families are great, but not necessarily greater than with treatment.[16] Thus, both treatment and nontreatment constitute unsatisfactory dilemmas for everyone, especially for the child and his family. When maximum treatment was viewed as unacceptable by families and physicians in our unit, there was a growing tendency to seek early death as a management option, to avoid that cruel choice of gradual, often slow, but progressive deterioration of the child who was required under these circumstances in effect to kill himself. Parents and staff then asked if his dying needed to be prolonged. If not, what were the most appropriate medical responses?

Is it possible that some physicians and some families may join in a conspiracy to deny the right of a defective child to live or to die? Either could occur. Prolongation of the dying process by resident physicians having a vested interest in their careers has been described by Sudnow.[17] On the other hand, from the fatigue of working long and hard some physicians may give up too soon, assuming that their cause is lost. Families, similarly, may have mixed motives. They may demand death to obtain relief from the high costs and the tensions inherent in suffering, but their sense of guilt in this thought may produce the opposite demand, perhaps in violation of the sick person's rights. Thus, the challenge of deciding what course to take can be most tormenting for the family and the physician. Unquestionably, not facing the issue would appear to be the easier course, at least temporarily; no doubt many patients, families, and physicians decline to join in an effort to solve the problems. They can readily assume that what is being done is right and sufficient and ask no questions. But pretending there is no decision to be made is an arbitrary and potentially devastating decision of default. Since families and patients must live with the problems one way or another in any case, the physician's failure to face the issues may constitute a victimizing abandonment of patients and their families in times of greatest need. As Lasagna pointed out, "There is no place for the physician to hide."

Can families in the shock resulting from the birth of a defective child understand what faces them? Can they give truly "informed consent" for treatment or withholding treatment? Some of our colleagues answer no to both questions. In our opinion, if families regardless of background are heard sympathetically and at length and are given information and answers to their questions in words they understand, the problems of their children as well as the expected benefits and limits of any proposed care can be understood clearly in practically all instances. Parents *are* able to understand the implications of such things as chronic dyspnea, oxygen dependency, incontinence, paralysis, contractures, sexual handicaps, and mental retardation.

Another problem concerns who decides for a child. It may be acceptable for a person to reject treatment and bring about his own death. But it is quite a different situation when others are doing this for him. We do not know how often families and their physicians will make just decisions for severely handicapped children. Clearly, this issue is central in evaluation of the process of decision making that we have described. But we also ask, if these parties cannot make such decisions justly, who can?

We recognize great variability and often much uncertainty in prognoses and in family capacities to deal with defective newborn infants. We also acknowledge that there are limits of support that society can or will give to assist handicapped persons and their families. Severely deforming conditions that are associated with little or no hope of a functional existence pose painful dilemmas for the laymen and professionals who must decide how to cope with severe handicaps. We believe the burdens of decision making must be borne by families and their professional advisers because they are most familiar with the respective situations. Since families primarily must live with and are most affected by the decisions, it therefore appears that society and the health professions should provide only general guidelines for decision making. Moreover, since variations between situations are so great, and the situations themselves so complex, it follows that much latitude in decision making should be expected and tolerated. Otherwise, the rules of society or the policies most convenient for medical technologists may become cruel masters of human beings instead of their servants. Regarding any "allocation of death" policy[18] we readily acknowledge that the extreme excesses of Hegelian "rational utility" under dictatorships must be avoided (Alexander). Perhaps it is less recognized that the uncontrolled application of medical technology may be detrimental to individuals and families. In this regard, our views are similar to those of Waitzkin and Stoeckle.[19]

Physicians may hold excessive power over decision making by limiting or controlling the information made available to patients or families. It seems appropriate that the profession be held accountable for presenting fully all management options and their expected consequences. Also, the public should be aware that professionals often face conflicts of interest that may result in decisions against individual preferences.

What are the legal implications of actions like those described in this paper? Some persons may argue that the law has been broken, and others would contend otherwise. Perhaps more than anything else, the public and professional silence on a major social taboo and some common practices has been broken further. That seems appropriate, for out of the ensuing dialogue perhaps better choices for patients and families can be made. If working out these dilemmas in ways such as those we suggest is in violation of the law, we believe the law should be changed.

Notes

1. Myron E. Wegman, "Annual Summary of Vital Statistics—1970," *Pediatrics* (December 1971), 48:979–983.

2. P. R. Swyer, "The Regional Organization of Special Care for the Neonate," *Pediatric Clinics of North America* (November 1970), 17:761–776.

3. Grace Rawlings, Ann Steward, E. O. R. Reynolds, and L. B. Strang, "Changing Prognosis for Infants of Very Low Birth Weight," *Lancet* (March 1971), 1:516–519.

4. Eliot Slater, "Health Service or Sickness Service?" *British Medical Journal* (December 1971), 4:734–736.

5. Leon Eisenberg, "The Human Nature of Human Nature," *Science* (April 1971), 176:123–128.

6. Joseph Fletcher, "Indicators of Humanhood: A Tentative Profile of Man," *Hastings Center Report* (November 1972), 2:1–4.

7. Howard E. Freeman, Orville G. Brim, Jr., and Greer Williams, "New Dimensions of Dying," in Orville G. Brim, Howard Freeman, Sol Levine, and Norman A. Scotch, eds., *The Dying Patient*, (New York: Russell Sage Foundation, 1970).

8. H. Tristram Engelhardt, "Euthanasia and Children: The Injury of Continued Existence," *Journal of Pediatrics* (July 1973), 83:170–171.

9. Louis Lasagna, *Life, Death and the Doctor* (New York: Knopf, 1968).

10. Simon Olshansky, "Chronic Sorrow: a Response to Having a Mentally Defective Child," *Social Casework* (April 1962), 43:190–193.

11. Herman Feifel, "Perception of Death," *Annals of the New York Academy of Science* (December 1969), 164:669–677.

12. Leo Alexander, "Medical Science under Dictatorship," *New England Journal of Medicine* (July 14, 1949), 241:39–47.

13. R. B. Zachary, "Ethical and Social Aspects of Treatment of Spina Bifida," *Lancet* (August 1968), 2:274–276; and D. B. Shurtleff, "Care of the Myelodysplastic Patient," in Morris Green and Robert Haggerty, eds., *Ambulatory Pediatrics* (Philadelphia: Saunders, 1968).

14. Donald D. Matson, "Surgical Treatment of Myelomeningocele," *Pediatrics* (August 1968), 42: 225–227.

15. J. Lorber, "Results of Treatment of Myelomeningocele," *Developmental Medicine and Child Neurology* (June 1971), 13:279–303.

16. D. W. Hide, H. Perry Williams, and H. L. Ellis, "The Outlook for the Child with a Myelomeningocele for Whom Early Surgery Was Considered Inadvisable," *Developmental Medicine and Child Neurology* (February 1972), 14: 304–307.

17. David Sudnow, *Passing On* (Englewood Cliffs, N.J.: Prentice-Hall, 1967).

18. Bayless Manning, "Legal and Policy Issues in the Allocation of Death," in Orville G. Brim, Jr., Howard Freeman, Sol Levine, and Norman A. Scotch, eds., *The Dying Patient*.

19. H. Waitzkin, and J. D. Stoeckle, "The Communication of Information about Illness," *Advances in Psychosomatic Medicine* (1971), 8:180–215.

12

Passive Euthanasia of Defective Newborn Infants: Legal Considerations

JOHN A. ROBERTSON, J.D., AND NORMAN FOST, M.D.

Parents and physicians now face a dilemma when infants with Down Syndrome, myelomeningocele, and other birth defects require medical or surgical attention merely to stay alive. If parents withhold consent for medical care and the physician acquiesces, the infant may die. To provide the appropriate medical care, however, may maintain the existence of a being with only minimal capacity for personal development and human interaction.

Withholding treatment seems to have become a widespread, if not frequent, event. Widely publicized cases have arisen in Maine, Arizona, New York, Denver, and Los Angeles. Duff and Campbell reported 43 instances over a two-year period in the newborn unit of a university medical center.[1] A number of eminent physicians recently appeared before the Senate Subcommittee on Health and at that time justified the practice. Leading textbooks and journals discuss indications for withholding treatment.[2]

Although the growing visibility of the practice has generated much ethical debate, discussion of the legality of the practice and the appropriateness of current law has been minimal. This absence is unfortunate for several reasons. The first and most important is that parents, physicians, and nurses may be risking criminal liability without awareness of the legal ramifications of their decision. Physicians can hardly assist parents to reach an informed choice concerning treatment if they do not also disclose that their choice may have serious legal consequences. Also, analysis of the law may expose inconsistencies or inadequacies, and thus point the way to changes that will enhance the certitude and security of future decision-making. Finally, the traditional legal concern with procedures for balancing conflicting interests may point the way to a reasonable solution to a perplexing dilemma of modern medicine.

This article briefly reviews the potential criminal liability of parents, physicians, and nurses involved in the decision to withhold ordinary care from defective newborn infants. Finding that any or all of them may be subject to criminal prosecution for murder, manslaughter, neglect, child abuse, or conspiracy, we then discuss some issues relevant to an evaluation of these policies. Finally, we propose a third approach to the problem which avoids the excesses of present law and present practices. *The authors do not contend that the criminal liability here enumerated should necessarily be pursued,* nor is it clear that as a practical matter that this would occur. Rather, we are concerned with elucidating the legal issues so that participants in such decisions can be fully informed, and legal policy, where desirable, altered.

Liability of Parents

Generally, homicide by omission occurs when a person's failure to discharge a *legal* duty to another person causes that person's death. If the required action is intentionally withheld, the crime is either first- or second-degree murder, depending on the extent of premeditation and deliberation. When the omission occurs through gross carelessness or disregard of the consequences of failing to act, the crime is involuntary manslaughter.[3]

In the case of a defective infant the withholding of essential care would appear to present a possible case of homicide by omission on the part of parents, physicians, and nurses, with the degree of homicide depending on the extent of premeditation. Following a live birth, the law generally presumes that personhood exists and that there is entitlement to the usual legal protections, whatever the specific physical and mental characteristics of the infant may be. Every state imposes on parents a legal duty to provide necessary medical assistance to a helpless minor child. If they withhold such care and the child dies, they may be prosecuted for manslaughter or murder, as has frequently occurred when parents have refused or neglected to obtain medical care for nondefective children. Although no parent has yet been prosecuted for withholding care from defective neonates, the well-recognized rule would appear equally applicable to nontreatment of defective infants. Defenses based on religious grounds, or even on poverty, if public assistance is available, have been specifically rejected, and other legal defenses, such as the defense of necessity may not apply. While care may be omitted as "extraordinary" if there is only a minimal chance of survival, when survival is likely, treatment cannot be withheld simply because of cost or the future social disutility of the infant.

In addition to homicide, parents may also be liable under statutes that make it criminal for a parent to neglect to support or to provide necessities, to furnish medical attention, to maltreat, to be cruel to, or to endanger the child's life or health.[4]

Liability of Attending Physician

The attending physician who counsels the parents to withhold treatment, or who merely acquiesces in their decision and takes no steps to save the child's life, may also incur criminal liability. Since withholding needed medical care by the parents would in many states constitute child abuse or neglect, the physician who knows of the situation and fails to report the case to proper authorities would commit a crime in the 20 or so states where failure to report child abuse is a crime. While failure to report is only a misdemeanor, under the common law "misdemeanor-manslaughter rule" a person whose misdemeanor causes the death of another is guilty of manslaughter. Since reporting might have led to appointment of a guardian and thus saved the child's life, the physician who fails to report could be guilty of manslaughter.

The physician may also be guilty of homicide by omission (by the same reasoning discussed under Parental Liability), because he has breached a legal duty to care for the child and thereby caused the child's death. The legal duty of the physician would be to intervene directly by carrying out the procedure, or at least to report the case to public or judicial authorities who may then intervene to save the child. The sources of this duty are several. One is the child abuse-reporting statutes, which impose a legal duty to report instances of parental neglect even in those states where failure to report is not criminal.

The duty may also derive from the physician's initial undertaking of care of the child. Although it may appear that by refusing consent the parents have terminated the physician's legal duty to care for the child, there are at least three possible grounds for arguing that the parents are not able to terminate the physician's obligations to the infant-patient, once the doctor-patient relationship has begun, if the patient will be substantially harmed by his withdrawal.

1. The first argument is based on the law of contract. The attending physician has contracted with the parents to provide care for a third party, the infant. Ordinarily the contract for services will be made with an obstetrician, a general practitioner, and/or a pediatrician before or at birth to provide all necessary medical care. When the child is born, this contractual obligation to provide services begins. Under the law of third party beneficiary contracts, the parties contracting for services to another cannot terminate the obligation to a minor, if the minor would be thereby substantially harmed. Since the parents are powerless to terminate the physician's obligation to care for the child, the physician would have a legal duty to take such steps as are necessary to protect the interests of the child. If emergency treatment were required, the physician would be privileged to proceed without parental consent. In most

cases and where feasible, the physician's duty would be better fulfilled by seeking the appointment of a guardian who could then consent to treatment.

The attending physician's contractual duty to care for the child despite parental denial of consent would not exist if the physician clearly agreed to treat the child only if normal, or, if the parents in engaging the physician made their agreement subject to modification in case of a defective birth. However, neither parents nor physicians are likely in prenatal consultations to be so specific. Prosecution could, of course, change prevailing practices.

2. Even if the contract theory were rejected, physicians would still have a legal duty to care for the child on the traditional tort doctrine that one who assumes the care of another, whether gratuitously or not, cannot terminate such care if the third person would be hurt thereby. This rule is based on the idea that one who undertakes care prevents others who might have come to the infant's aid from doing so. Again, the physician could withdraw or not treat only if he has taken steps to notify public or hospital authorities, which would protect the child by leading to the appointment of a guardian.

3. It could be argued that the physician would have a legal duty to protect the child on the ground that he has placed the child in peril through his role as a source of information for the parents. A person who puts another in peril, even innocently and without malice, incurs a legal duty to act to protect the imperiled person. By giving the parents adverse prognostic information regarding the infant's handicaps, the economic and psychologic burdens to be faced by the parents, and so on, he may be the immediate cause of nontreatment of the infant, by leading the parents to a decision they would not otherwise have made or perhaps even considered. Under this theory even a consultant might be liable if he communicated information which led to a nontreatment decision and death, particularly if the information was incorrect or unfairly presented and then he took no action to save the child.

In addition to liability for homicide by omission or under the misdemeanor-manslaughter rule, the physician may also be subject to homicide liability as an accessory; an accessory is one who "counsels, encourages or aids or abets another to commit a felony."[5] This would be clearest in a case in which the physician counseled or encouraged the parents to withhold treatment. If omission of care by the parent is criminal, then the physician's liability as an accessory follows. If the physician were indifferent to the child's fate, or preferred that it would live but felt obligated to provide the parents with all the facts, it is less likely he would be culpable, since the requisite intent would be lacking.

The attending physician may be guilty of conspiracy to commit homicide or violate the child abuse or neglect laws. Conspiracy is an agreement between two or more parties to achieve an unlawful objective, with (in most jurisdictions) an overt action toward that end. If parents and physician agree that a defective newborn infant should die, and take any action toward that end, conspiracy could exist. Similarly, a staff conference on a particular case could amount to conspiracy, if the attending physician and others agreed that medical or surgical procedures should be withheld from the child.

Liability of Other Physicians and Nurses

Physicians other than the attending physician, such as consultants, house officers, and administrative personnel, might also incur criminal liability under the statutes and common law principles reviewed above.

Nurses who participate or acquiesce in parental decisions to withhold treatment may also be at risk. While a nurse's care is subordinate to the orders of a physician, her legal duty is not fulfilled simply by carrying out physician orders with requisite skill and judgment. In some cases she is required to act independently or directly counter to the physician, if protection of the patient requires it. At the very least, she might be obligated to inform her supervisor. A finding consistent with this view was reached in *Goff vs Doctors Hospital of San Jose*[6] where two nurses, the attending physician, and the hospital were held civilly liable when a patient died from postpartum cervical hemorrhage. The nurses were aware the mother was in peril but did not contact the attending physician, because they thought he would not come. The court found that they had a duty to report the situation to a superior.

The Possibility of Prosecution

The existence of potential criminal liability is no guarantee that parents, physicians, nurses, and hospitals will in fact be prosecuted, nor that any prosecution will be successful. Parents who have actively killed defective children have often been acquitted (though not always), and no parent has been prosecuted for withholding care from, as opposed to actively killing, a defective newborn infant. Similarly, the only physicians prosecuted for homicide in euthanasia situations involved terminally ill patients, and both were acquitted. No doctor has yet been prosecuted for passive euthanasia of a defective newborn infant.

The infrequency of past criminal prosecutions, however, may not be a reliable guide for the future. As the practice becomes more openly acknowledged, pressure may build to prosecute and some prosecution is likely, if only to clarify the law. The manslaughter conviction of a Boston physician for allegedly killing a viable fetus after removal from the uterus during a lawfully performed hysterotomy illustrates the dangers of ignoring the legal issues, and the politics of the process by which a prosecution might be initiated. Physicians, parents, and others may decide that they are willing to risk prosecution, or believe that the law should be broken. Such a position entails risks, and one cannot safely predict from past experience that criminal liability will never in practice be imposed.

Practical Implications for Physicians and Hospitals

Parents and health professionals with experience in the complex and heart-wrenching decisions involving defective newborn infants might justifiably react to this legal synopsis with shock and rage. Such decisions are made by people trying to do what they think is best under extremely difficult circumstances. The suggestion that such sincere and well-intended decisions might be criminal is offensive.

The authors do not intend to suggest, in this review, that such criminal charges should be made, nor do we intend to comment, pro or con, on the ethical issues involved in such decisions. Our primary purpose is to suggest that criminal charges *could* be brought, given a susceptible case and a prosecutor willing to pursue it. Some legal scholars might reasonably disagree with the validity of such charges, and we would not predict that such proceedings would necessarily end in conviction. Many would have moral objections to the initiation of such a trial, whatever the law. But few would dispute that such a case could be brought to court and, conceivably, to conviction. The experiences of Dr. Edelin [in the Boston case] and the participants in the Quinlan case demonstrate dramatically how parents and physicians involved in medical decisions which have occurred countless times without judicial interference can find themselves unexpectedly at the center of a raging controversy.

What are the implications of these possibilities for physicians and hospitals caring for such infants and desirous of avoiding prosecution? First, physicians could consider informing parents that criminal liability might attach to a nontreatment decision, so that parents could be sufficiently informed of the risk to seek legal advice. In addition, such parents might be informed that even if they do not wish to keep the child, they are legally obligated, at least until parental rights are formally terminated, to provide it with needed medical care. If the parents insist on risking prosecution, the physician might then inform them that he is legally obligated to take steps toward saving the infant's life. In some jurisdictions it would be sufficient to report the matter to the child welfare or other authorities prescribed in the child abuse-reporting laws; in others the physician or the hospital might have to initiate neglect proceedings. The parents cannot terminate the physician's legal duties by withholding consent or even by discharging him. The law does not permit a physician to avoid criminal liability by submitting to the wishes of the parents and doing nothing, if this will lead to injury or death of the infant.

To avoid liability, hospitals could adopt rules prohibiting

medical staff from not treating defective newborn infants, or, at least, for following certain procedures when faced with those decisions. The procedure could include reporting such cases to hospital authorities who would then seek a judicial ruling authorizing treatment. Resort to judicial approval, however burdensome and painful in this situation, could perform several useful functions. It would shield parents, physicians, nurses, and hospitals from criminal liability, pass the burden of a difficult decision to a more impartial process, and provide an opportunity to test or challenge the law before rather than after criminal prosecution. If a court ruled for or against treatment, the decision could be appealed to state appellate courts, which could define more precisely the duties involved and, conceivably, permit nontreatment in specific cases. While time would not permit appellate review of most cases, such issues of broad public policy which are sure to recur can be reviewed even though the specific controversy has been resolved by death or treatment.

Evaluation of Legal Policy

Many persons who have experienced the dilemma of caring for defective newborn infants would disagree with current law. Duff and Campbell, for instance, argue that "if working out these dilemmas in ways we suggest is in violation of the law . . . the law should be changed." They would grant parents and their physicians the final discretion to decide whether a defective infant should be treated, and hence live or die:

We believe the burdens of decision making must be borne by families and their profesional advisors because they are most familiar with the respective situations. Since families primarily must live with and are most affected by the decision, it therefore appears that society and the health professions should provide only general guidelines for decision making. Moreover, since variations between situations are so great, and the situations themselves so complex, it follows that much latitude in decision making should be expected and tolerated.[7]

What law, if any, should govern this situation? Ideally, the law should provide clear rules and predictable enforcement while resolving conflicting interests in a way consistent with prevailing moral, personal, professional, and economic values. Satisfactory law in respect to the defective infant dilemma depends on the answers to two questions. First, is there a definable class of human offspring from whom, under prevailing moral standards, ordinary medical care may be withheld without their consent? If withholding care can never be justified, the sole policy question is whether the existing legal structures best implement that goal or whether a new offense and penalty structure should be created. The second question arises after one concludes that withholding care in some instances may be morally justified or socially desirable, and asks who among parents, physicians, and other decision-makers is best equipped to decide when care is to be withheld? Here policy will focus on criteria, procedures, and decision-making processes for implementing a social policy of involuntary passive euthanasia.

It is the first question over which moral and policy issue is most keenly joined and which is therefore most crucial. Supporters of present law argue that there is no reasonable basis for allocating the right to life among human offspring on the basis of physical and mental characteristics, or social contribution—that all are persons and all deserve the legal protections and rights accorded persons. Many defective newborn infants in fact are capable of achieving some meaningful existence; even if they are not, the social and other costs of maintaining them is but a minute portion of health expenditures. State assistance may be available to parents of modest means, and, in any event, parents who do not wish to keep a defective child are free to terminate their legal obligations. Furthermore, a policy of allocating rights according to personal characteristics, capacity, or social utility requires an arbitrary choice among personal and social characteristics reflective of social, cultural, or racial bias which is easily abused and inconsistent with a democratic society. Determining the right to life by the net social utility of a person's future pitches one onto a slippery slope, the bottom of which holds no person or value sacred as against social utility.

Opponents of the law argue that not only may we reasonably and carefully distinguish between human offspring by their capacities, but we can draw narrow boundaries which do not set us onto the slippery slope where all values are subject to social worth assessments. Given high social and personal costs in keeping alive human beings with only marginal ability for personal development or interaction, the delineation of such a class is justified. Proponents of this view need not hold that every child with Down syndrome or myelomeningocele should not be treated. Only that in some cases, such as anencephaly or myelomeningocele with an extremely unfavorable prognosis, the defects are so extensive that nontreatment is morally and socially justified.

Due Process and Decision Making

A choice between these two positions depends ultimately on deeply held philosophical and religious views and is only partially susceptible to rational argument and marshalling of evidence. Rather than attempt to persuade the reader to any one personal view or analyze the ethical issues of specific cases, we suggest that even if after reflection one decides that there is a class of defective newborn infants from whom treatment can be justifiably withheld, it does not follow that parents and physicians should be the sole judge in each case of who shall survive.

The question of specifying the class of defectives and circumstances in which treatment may be justifiably withheld remains. The claim is not that treatment may be withheld from any infant, or even from all infants with some defect, but rather that in some circumstances infants with certain kinds of anomalies should or need not be treated. How then is that class and those circumstances to be identified? What checks or safeguards should exist to be sure than an infant meets those criteria?

The position offered by Duff and Campbell—that parents and physicians should have absolute discretion to decide whether an infant should live or die—appears to go too far. Simply because nontreatment decisions are acceptable in some circumstances of extreme defect, it does not follow that parents and physicians should *always* be free to decide whether all defective infants should live or die. Otherwise they may decide not to treat infants with less extensive defects, whom few persons would agree should die. Indeed, there is no reason to think that parents and physicians would always consider all the factors relevant to a nontreatment decision and reach a socially justified choice. (1) The emotional trauma and conflict of giving birth to a defective newborn infant may make the parents incapable of careful consideration of the issues.[8] (2) Given their own, often conflicting interests, parents and physicians might not scrutinize all factors or balance them out in a fair way. Thus, many parents might decide against treating a baby with Down syndrome, and the physician might agree, even though neither social, financial, or psychic cost in a particular instance would justify nontreatment. (3) Neither parents nor physicians can claim the special expertise in making complex ethical-social judgments which warrant giving them such broad authority.

What is needed, then, is either a set of authoritative criteria describing the limited circumstances in which ordinary care may be withheld from defective newborn infants, or a process of decision-making which minimizes the risk of abuses or mistakes. We do not here attempt to articulate those criteria, other than to point out that if nontreatment is ever justified, it is because the nature of the defect, developmental potential, cost to parent and society, etc. seems overwhelmingly to argue against treatment. Such criteria could be set forth for assessment by the medical and lay community and would have to be revised frequently to incorporate changing medical and social facts. Only in scrutinizing our reasons can we be sure that these decisions are in fact morally defensible. This would reduce the risk of arbitrary decision-making and assure that infants are not being allowed to die for special reasons. One problem concerns the process by which criteria would be formulated. Would a national commission, a legislature, or professional bodies be convened for this purpose? A second major difficulty with specific criteria is the almost limitless and unpredictable complexity of individual cases. Also, defining or articulating criteria in an open public way does lend legitimacy to the practice of taking life on grounds of social utility.

An alternative to the articulation of specific criteria would be a requirement for a better *process* of decision-making. A concern with process demonstrates the solemnity of the commitment to life, and the exceptional nature of any deviation from that commitment. In addition, process can assure that criteria are being accurately applied, that limits exist, and that the possibilities of conflicts of interest are minimized.

The essence of due process is to maximize the probability that decisions will be made impartially after full consideration of all relevant facts and interests, rather than on the uncontested perceptions and self-interest of one party. Such a process can be helpful, even if only advisory to parents and physicians, by exposing or sensitizing them to considerations which they might have ignored on their own. A legal conception of due process would entail turning over decision-making to someone more likely to be disinterested than the parents or their private physician and assuring that the interests of the child are fully represented in that forum. Alternative decision-makers might include one or a group of physicians, a judge, or a mixed lay and medical committee; they could consider the need for decisions and reasons to be stated in writing, and in some cases, judicial review. Although the notion of a "God committee" has been much maligned, experience with institutional "human subjects" committees in recent years suggests that groups can be formed which will improve the ethical acceptability of controversial and complex medical decisions. One last alternative would be a strictly post hoc institutional review process of specific decisions, within the limits of confidentiality, similar to review of other hospital practices as occurs with tissue committees, clinicopathologic conferences, and the like. One objection to this approach is that whatever change it produces is slow, and unjustified deaths might result in the interim.

A crucial theoretical problem in requiring due process would be the setting of limits within which the process must be invoked. If no defective infant can be allowed to die without due process, why should any nonconsenting patient be allowed to die? A requirement for inclusion of all such cases would involve a *reductio ad absurdum,* namely, review of every pediatric patient who dies under the care of a physician, since life can almost always be extended to some degree. The public concern over the defective newborn infant, however, does not seem to extend to patients who are terminally ill and allowed to die.

Judicialization of medical decision-making is often inappropriate, but where long life is at stake, the forms and procecrdure of due process may serve to focus the precise issues and increase impartiality. Such process would limit the cases of passive euthanasia to the clearest ones, and thereby limit the precedent-expanding significance of nontreatment.

Unless those who favor nontreatment are willing to subject their selection criteria to critical scrutiny, the practice could be presumed unjustified, and present legal policy continued. If, as Duff and Campbell say, the law needs to be changed, this should not be done unofficially in newborn nurseries but in the traditional open forums, such as legislatures or courtrooms. By claiming the right to act in ignorance or defiance of existing legal principles and statutes, the physician, parent, nurse, or hospital administrator claims a right which he would not ascribe to others.

We believe that resolution of this controversy by a criminal proceeding would not be desirable. We also believe that public opinion would be supportive of such decisions being made outside the courts, providing the public could be assured that the possibility of abuse is minimal. Such reassurance would at the least depend on a process of institutional or professional review. Alternatively, test cases could be brought anonymously through the legal system. Whatever the mechanism, public scrutiny and involvement is unlikely to disappear and the medical community can probably help patients best by actively participating in the structuring of a resolution, rather than responding to thrusts initiated by others.

Notes

1. R.S. Duff and A.G.M. Campbell, "Moral and Ethical Dilemmas in the Special-Care Nursery," *New England Journal of Medicine* (1973), 289:890.
2. F.D. Ingraham, and D.D. Matson, *Neurosurgery of Infancy and Childhood*

(Springfield, Ill.: Charles C Thomas, 1954); J. Lorber, "Results of Treatment of My-elomeningocele," *Developmental Medicine and Child Neurology* (1971), 13:279.

3. W. LaFave and A. Scott, *Handbook of Criminal Law* (St. Paul: West Publishing, 1972), pp. 182–191.

4. J.A. Robertson, "Involuntary Euthanasia of Defective Newborns: A Legal Analysis," *Stanford Law Review* (1975), 27:213.

5. LaFave and Scott, p. 498.

6. 166 Cal. App. 2d 314, 333 P. 2d 29, 1958.

7. Duff and Campbell, p. 894.

8. John Fletcher, "Attitudes Toward Defective Newborns," *Hastings Center Studies* (1974), 2:21; and A. Mandelbaum and M.E. Wheeler, "The Meaning of a Defective Child to Parents," *Social Casework* (1960), 41:360.

13

Selective Nontreatment of Newborns

RICHARD SHERLOCK, Ph.D.

A mong those who have defended a policy of selective non-treatment of defective newborns, none have been as forceful or direct in stating and defending their views as have Duff and Campbell.[1] It may therefore be presumed that they have worked out a coherent, plausible policy that answers to the most serious objections of their critics. In my estimation, however, their statements on these issues are notable for the lack of a coherent policy, plausibly justified and able to meet objections. The current article ["Deciding the Care of Severely Malformed or Dying Infants"] does nothing to remedy these deficiencies and in this response I propose to show why this is the case.

The fundamental weakness in this article comes from the authors' unwillingness to give us any idea of just when an infant becomes a candidate for nontreatment or merely palliative care. Looking at their section "Options for care" one might guess that this is purely a medical judgment with care being withdrawn only from those infants who are actually dying and only limited

Reprinted from the *Journal of Medical Ethics* (1979), 6:139–40, with the permission of the publisher. Copyright © 1979 by the *Journal of Medical Ethics*.

treatment offered to those who are unlikely to benefit from more aggressive measures. This interpretation, however, does not square with the rest of the paper nor with other published papers by these same authors.[2] Even in this paper we are reminded of lives "severely compromised through handicap" which are a "fate worse than death." Put in other terms the authors seem to claim that there are some lives that are not worth living and that for infants burdened with such handicaps parents should have the right to decide against treatment.

The problem is that we are never told just what these handicaps are or what the criteria are that distinguish those infants whose parents should be allowed to discontinue care from those whose parents should not have any such request honored. Surely the authors do not hold that parents should, for any conceivable reason, be allowed to let their children die, e.g., should a parent be allowed to starve a normal child to death or let a normal infant die on religious grounds? Nowhere have the authors said that they favor such a massive transformation of our moral convictions and legal constraints as to permit these acts to be done without fear of punishment. Yet until they provide some reasonable criteria for distinguishing the above cases from those they will include in a nontreatment regime, the argument they have advanced logically commits them to respecting parental choice in the above cases.

The authors' response to this sort of query is that since such cases vary so much no criteria will be possible. This is an interesting claim but it is hardly sufficient. There are several reasons for this. First, there is simply the logical point that if it is true that no one would wish to support the parental activities noted above, then there are some cases in which parental requests should not be honored. The authors therefore must explain just which cases are so out of line that a parental right to withdraw or not begin therapy should not even be considered.

Secondly, this reliance on parental judgment allows for the worst and most arbitrary factors to be determinative of whether the infant lives or dies. For example, it is a well established fact that parental religiosity correlates highly with a willingness to care for a defective child.[3] Do the authors therefore wish us to adopt a policy that allows the child to live or die simply as a result of the religious convictions of the parents? Such a result is completely at odds with many of our most basic social and legal policies regarding the rights of parents and children as well as the moral convictions that lie behind these policies.

Following directly from the above point we must note that the policy here proposed leads directly to outcomes that will not square with even the most minimal notions of fairness or justice. Suppose, for example, we have two infants with the same medical status and prognosis. If we believe that these infants have a life not worth living then to allow one set of parents to choose nontreatment while another chooses life-saving therapy is hardly even minimally fair to the second infant. If death is really better than life for these infants why should we entertain a parental request to "inflict" continued life on one infant?

The final consideration that should lead our authors to develop the criteria that they have not yet provided is more practical. As the study of Professor Robertson has shown, the activities outlined in the article with respect to non-dying but defective infants are currently illegal in American law.[4] Given this state of affairs the authors certainly would want to see the law changed. However, one cannot change the law without providing some criteria for distinguishing the cases where nontreatment is possible from those where it is not, unless one wishes to repeal all legal prohibitions against child neglect and abuse.

The above reflections suggest that authors cannot avoid the central question of what it is that makes a life one that is not worth living. Until they do provide an answer to this question their policy remains unworkable, vague, and very implausible.

There is, however, a second crucial issue that the authors have not dealt with, one that may be as serious as the first: why should we adopt this policy just with regard to infants? Surely neonates are not the only human beings with severe developmental abnormalities. In institutions all over the Western world there are hundreds of thousands of persons with the very same conditions that the authors suggest justify a decision not to treat. Furthermore, an assessment at birth of the prognosis and life prospects of the child is notoriously uncertain. So too is any judgment about the impact of this child on the family. While these problems are not eliminated they are certainly diminished if we are considering 5–10 year old children, especially those in institutions where the environmental factors can be closely controlled. We surely would have a better view of their lives and potential and the impact on the family. In short, if there is any justification at all for what Duff and Campbell propose for newborns then there is better justification for a similar policy with respect to children at any age.

Yet do these authors wish to propose that if children at an institution contract a potentially fatal illness such as pneumonia they should not be treated in the hope that they will die? Or, if, as is often the case, those with the severest problems begin to choke on their food should the physicians and nurses stand by and watch them die? Frankly, I seriously doubt that they wish to endorse such a serious transformation of our moral attitudes and social policies. But the objection remains. Until the authors can distinguish what they do propose from these cases, the policy that they have suggested logically commits them to support a policy of death, not better care for severely retarded children.

The authors, of course, suggest that many safeguards exist that will protect us from bad decisions, but the only effective safeguard will be a clear, consistent statement of just when and why parents should be allowed to choose death for their children. Vague appeals to "suffering" or "burden" or "hardship" will not do, for parents also suffer with a 10 year old severely retarded child and an adolescent burned out on heroin. As we know, some parents will choose death for any number of questionable reasons. (Jehovah's Witnesses' cases are only the cream of a much more bizarre crop from the religious underworld). Until we know, for example, just why parents should not be allowed to choose death over transfusion for a normal child, the statement that there are safeguards will be meaningless.[5]

In sum, the authors must show us what the precise range of cases is, in terms of age and disability, in which they would honor a parental request for nontreatment. Furthermore, they must offer a plausible rationale for such a set of criteria, one that goes beyond vague appeals to "suffering" or family burdens. Without such a development in their argument the policy they wish us to adopt commits us to courses of action in relevantly similar cases that are at odds with the moral convictions of a great many well informed and sensitive physicians and policy makers and much current law and social policy as well.

Frankly, I seriously doubt that an effective answer is to be found to the objections I raise. At least no answer has yet been forthcoming from the many writers who seem to agree with these authors. Some have simply resigned themselves to identifying who should make the decision; others have proposed vague guidelines and criteria, arbitrarily drawn, and logically applicable to a far greater range of cases than those that a given writer wishes to consider for nontreatment. Unless those who favor selective nontreatment for defective infants can develop more precise guidelines and rationales the fundamental weakness of this position will remain: it will commit us to courses of action and to social policies that are at odds with one of the oldest and most basic moral principles in the medical profession—to provide life saving therapy to all of those who need it.

Notes

1. A. G. M. Campbell and R. S. Duff, "Deciding the Care of Severely Malformed or Dying Infants," *Journal of Medical Ethics* (1979), 5:65–67.

2. R. S. Duff and A. G. M. Campbell, "Moral and Ethical Dilemmas in the Special Care Nursery." *New England Journal of Medicine* (1973), 289:890–894; and R. S. Duff and A. G. M. Campbell, "On Deciding the Care of Severely Handicapped or Dying Persons," *Pediatrics* (1976), 57:487–493.

3. G. H. Zuk, "The Religious Factor and the Role of Guilt in Parental Acceptance of the Retarded Child," *American Journal of Mental Deficiency* (1959), 64:139–147.

4. J. Robertson, "Involuntary Euthanasia of Defective Newborns: A Legal Analysis," *Stanford Law Review* (1975), 27:213–267.

5. R. Veatch, *Death, Dying and the Biological Revolution* (New Haven: Yale University Press, 1976), pp. 125–128.

6. My overall assessment of these policies is somewhat similar to that outlined by P. Ramsey, *Ethics at the Edges of Life* (New Haven: Yale University Press, 1978), pp. 189–267.

14

Defective Infants and Their Impact on Families: Ethical and Legal Considerations

CARSON STRONG, Ph.D.

On July 5, 1983, the United States Department of Health & Human Services (HHS) proposed a revision of its earlier-issued "Baby Doe rules" on treatment decisions for defective infants.[1] Although the initial rules issued by HHS on this topic had been struck down by Judge Gerhard Gesell of the United States District Court in April 1983, HHS continued the 24-hour hotline, and a spokesman declared: "We're not going to give up." As promised, HHS issued its revised rules less than three months later; the new rules propose a continuation of the hotline and the requirement that medically indicated treatment not be withheld from any handicapped child.

These proposed regulations reflect the widespread reproach which has been directed toward physicians and parents who decide to withhold treatment from defective newborns. The Baby Doe case in Bloomington, Indiana, which precipitated the HHS rules, is the most recent example. This case involved an infant with Down syndrome and an esophageal atresia, which required treatment if the infant were to survive. Media coverage

Reprinted from *Law, Medicine and Health Care* (September, 1983), 11:168–171, 181, with the permission of the publisher. Copyright © 1983 by the American Society of Law and Medicine. Some footnotes omitted.

resulted in nationwide condemnation of the parents' decision to withhold corrective surgery. An Indiana state representative was quoted: "Certainly the child has a right to life. I can't imagine any court denying the child a chance to live."[2] The HHS Office for Civil Rights reacted immediately to the case by putting all hospitals and health care providers on notice that withholding life-saving treatment from defective infants would result in withdrawal of federal financial assistance.[3]

Another, earlier, example of withholding treatment from a defective infant is the well-known case at Johns Hopkins Hospital in Baltimore, concerning the withholding of surgery to correct a duodenal atresia in a neonate with Down syndrome. A distinguished theologian argued that the participants in that incident were wrong in withholding surgery, emphasizing that "a mongoloid infant is human, and thus has the intrinsic value of humanity and the rights of a human being."[4] A widely distributed film about the case expressed, on balance, disapproval of the decision not to treat.[5]

These disapproving attitudes give little consideration to the harms which can occur to families as a result of raising a child with serious impairments. Health professionals who work with such families are aware of such harms, and numerous studies have documented their nature and frequency. The issue I address is this: should our social policies concerning aggressive treatment of defective newborns take into account the hardships which may occur to families? I argue that they should, that the policy proposed by HHS as well as the policy currently embodied in our common law are inadequate in this regard, and that any of several alternatives would be preferable to those policies. Specifically, we should either provide sufficient financial and professional support to these families or permit the participants in these tragic dilemmas to take into account family burdens in making their decisions.

Harms to Families

The results of a few selected studies serve to indicate some of the typical harms which can occur to families raising defective infants. One example is a study by Gath in which thirty families with newborns having Down syndrome were periodically interviewed during the first two years following the birth. The purpose of the investigation was to determine the impact of the child upon family relationships when the child is brought up within the family. It was found that marital breakdown or severe marital disharmony occurred in nine (30 percent) of the families. In a matched control group of thirty families with a normal infant, there were no instances of such marital disturbance.[6]

A number of reports on familial hardships have focused on families of spina bifida children. In a study of 59 such families, Tew, Payne and Laurence found that the proportion of families having severe discord or a broken marriage increased from 3.5 percent at the time of birth to 31.5 percent nine years later. In a matched control group of families with normal children, the figures were 6.9 percent at the child's birth and 7 percent nine years later. Despite the increased proportion of marital discord, the authors found that there was no correlation between changes in the quality of the marital relationship and the severity of the child's handicap. In fact, among families of a slightly handicapped child there was a slightly higher percentage of severe discord or broken marriage than among families with a severely handicapped child.[7]

In studying 37 families with adolescents having spina bifida, Dorner found that the need for frequent trips to the hospital caused a major disorganization of family routine in 30 percent of the families, using measures such as total time taken, financial loss, and problems with transport.[8] A major disruption of the parents' social lives occurred in 41 percent of the families. Ten of 36 mothers had been to their family doctors with psychiatric problems during the year prior to the study. Fourteen of the mothers were on tranquilizers or anti-depressants at the time of the study and had been for an extended period. Fifty-three percent of the mothers complained of sleep disturbance, loss of appetite, anxiety, lack of energy, or depression.

In a report on families of non-retarded children with cerebral palsy, Wortis and Margolies stated that a major problem was the physical strain and exhaustion caused by the frequent need to lift or carry the child—a problem which gained magnitude as the child grew older. Another finding was that the parents expressed considerable anxiety concerning the child's future, particularly in regard to who would care for the child after the parents died. As those authors put it, "In analyzing the home situations we found that every family had problems of a more or less serious nature relating to the presence of the handicapped child."[9]

Other harms which may occur include loss of career opportunities, maladjustment and poor school performance on the part of siblings, and restrictions on the ability to travel or relocate.

There is evidence that physicians often allow parents to consider the impact of a handicapped child on the family when making decisions concerning withholding treatment. In a national survey in 1975, physicians who were involved in these decisions were asked whether they would acquiesce in a parental decision to withhold surgery in a newborn with intestinal atresia if the infant also had Down syndrome. A "yes" response was given by 76.8 percent of the pediatric surgeons and 49.5 percent of the pediatricians surveyed. The respondents were asked to rank in order of importance the following factors in deciding whether to withhold treatment from severely damaged infants: (a) infant's probable I.Q.; (b) potential quality of life; (c) cost to society; (d) possible adverse effects on the family; and (e) parents' willingness to raise the child at home.[10] Factor (d) was ranked first or second by 49.8 percent of the pediatric surgeons, being surpassed only by factor (b). Forty percent of the pediatricians ranked factor (d) first or second.

As these studies indicate, the potential harm to a family is clearly a relevant consideration in decisions to provide aggressive treatment to a defective newborn.

. . . .

Limiting Enforced Sacrifice

The above discussion suggests that our current social policies do not sufficiently consider the potential harms to families. This shortcoming could be corrected in various ways. One approach would be to provide treatment in all cases in which continued life is reasonably believed to be in the interests of the infant *and* to provide financial and professional support to the families. This approach, advocated by the President's Commission for the Study of Ethical Problems in Medicine and Biomedical and Behavioral Research,[11] would be preferable to our current policies in that it would better promote the various conflicting values. It would promote the respect for life and the avoiding of harm to families. Such an approach might involve a comprehensive federal commitment to victims of congenital disease similar to the support now being provided in the area of catastrophic renal disease. Perhaps it would involve investing more resources in the institutional care of impaired children.

It is not at all clear, however, that we will pursue such avenues in the near future. Our society is faced with limited revenues and many competing needs. Since this envisioned social policy would involve large financial expenditures, many individuals may ask whether there are better ways to spend our tax dollars. Although the approach in question would be a worthy one, the problem involves showing that it should have priority in relation to other worthy social ends.

Alternatively, there could be a greater effort to identify potential adoptive parents. This approach is suggested by the fact that in the Baby Doe case, several concerned individuals offered to adopt the child. It is doubtful, however, that this approach would, by itself, adequately resolve the problem. It is not clear that, if this were a routine policy, there would be enough people willing to become adoptive parents. In addition, questions can be raised concerning the long-term consequences for such adoptive families and for the children. Would there be a significant incidence of family disruption as described in the studies discussed above? This approach, to be effective, might have to be supplemented by substantial support for the families, whether natural or adoptive, which raise impaired children.

If we choose not to make a commitment to provide support to families, then we should take into account harms to families in our social policies concerning the providing of aggressive treatment to defective infants and in our moral evaluation of such cases. In that event, it should be considered acceptable, both morally and legally, to withhold aggressive treatment when the pursuit of such treatment is likely to place an overwhelming burden on the family. Specifically, when parents are at risk for such harms, they should be given the opportunity to provide considerable input in life-or-death decisions which may arise concerning aggressive treatment. If it is the decision of the parents to withhold treatment in such a situation, that decision should be respected. In the absence of a commitment to support families, there should be no federal regulation which restricts parental decisionmaking in such cases, and our principles of common law should give due weight to the potential harms to families.

Perhaps it will be thought that this recommendation is in opposition to the widely recognized principle that there is a limit to parental autonomy. When parental action is likely to cause serious (and avoidable) harm to the child, we consider it justifiable to interfere with parental liberty in order to prevent that harm. Examples include cases in which parents refuse consent on religious grounds for life-saving treatment for their child. The recommendation of this article, however, does not oppose that principle, but rather calls for a qualification to it. Just as we recognize limits to parental autonomy, so we should recognize limits to what we require of parents for the sake of their children. When interference with parental liberty would cause a grave burden to the family, we should consider such interference to be unwarranted.

Guidelines for Decisionmaking

Given these considerations, a difficult question arises. How does one identify those cases in which a significant burden to the family appears likely? Pertinent to this problem in any given case are various empirical factors, including the infant's prognosis for handicap and survival, as well as the availability of institutional placement, foster care, or adoption. In addition to these empirical factors, an evaluative judgment is involved. That is, one must determine how much burden is sufficient to justify parental decisionmaking in life-or-death situations, given the concomitant possibility of the withholding of treatment. We would need guidelines, at the professional level as well as the institutional or local level, which attempt to address this question, assuming that we do not provide substantial financial assistance to families.

Those who are familiar with the clinical dimensions of this issue know that in individual cases there is often a great deal of uncertainty concerning the empirical factors mentioned above. Thus, the guidelines would have to allow some degree of discretionary judgment by physicians and parents in particular cases. One purpose of the guidelines is to identify types of situations in which, based on past experience, it is reasonable to believe that the infant's condition will be such that the family would need assistance in order to avoid being substantially burdened. Such professional guidelines would perhaps best be formulated by an interdisciplinary body. The guidelines should take into account the available research data dealing with correlations between the infant's clinical condition and long-term neurological outcome. Since new avenues of research are opening in this area, the guidelines would have to be updated periodically in light of new data. We would need supplementary guidelines at the institutional, or perhaps regional, level because the availability of community resources for families varies with locality. These local guidelines would help to identify types of cases in which the lack of available public support might have a serious adverse impact on the family.

The primary purpose of such professional and local guidelines would be to protect families from harm by providing parents with the opportunity of decisionmaking about aggressive treatment in those cases in which it is reasonable to believe that the infant's survival would be deleterious to the family. Such guidelines would also promote the ethical goal of treating similar cases in similar ways.

Yet, such guidelines may not provide sufficient protection to families, since the physicians involved in these cases would typically have the power to act according to their own interpretations of the guidelines. Therefore, parents should have recourse to the courts in cases of disagreement with physicians, just as physicians today seek court orders for the continuation of treatment. Furthermore, the proposed guidelines should be considered a legally acceptable resource for judges to draw upon in resolving such disputes. This would help remedy two shortcomings of the court decisions discussed above: the failure to recognize harms to families as a relevant consideration, and the failure to take into account the available empirical data which are pertinent to that consideration.

Of course, the suggestion that we need guidelines for decisionmaking concerning defective newborns is not a new one. My recommendation differs from previous proposals, however, because it gives explicit attention to the potential hardships to families.

Respect for Family Integrity

Support for the idea that such guidelines would be an improvement over our current policies can be found in our society's well-established concern to promote and protect the well-being of families. This concern about families is expressed as follows by the President's Commission:

> Families are very important units in society. Not only do they provide the setting in which children are raised, but the interdependence of family members is an important support and means of expression for adults as well. Americans have traditionally been reluctant to intrude upon the functioning of families, both because doing so would be difficult and because it would destroy some of the value of the family, which seems to need privacy and discretion to maintain its significance.[12]

Because we value family autonomy, parents are accorded a wide range of discretion in making decisions about children. In the law, there is a strong presumption in favor of family privacy and autonomy against coercive state intervention.[13]

Thus, a defense of parents' ability to withhold treatment because of the onerous financial and emotional burdens of a severely impaired child has its basis in principles already recognized in law. The presumption in favor of family autonomy is illustrated in the common law involving cases in which parents

refuse medical treatment for their children. The court will interfere with parental authority only when it is outweighed by considerations of great magnitude, such as death or other serious
harm to the child. Generally, the courts arrive at their decisions
by balancing family autonomy against the other relevant considerations. In this balancing of competing interests, it is inconsistent to overlook the harms to the family which can arise from
state interference. Protecting the values of family life seems to
require not only respect for family autonomy but also the
avoidance of causing serious harm to families. To the extent
that interference would harm the family, the argument for interfering is less compelling. When the harm is likely to be significant, the considerations other than family autonomy (which
include nonmaleficence toward families) may not be weighty
enough to override that autonomy. Judicial restraint appears to
be indicated in such situations.

It may be objected that the retarded have the same rights
as anyone else, and that such guidelines would unjustifiably discriminate against the retarded. Yet, in this analysis, the morally
relevant factor is not retardation, but rather is the burden to the
family. It should be emphasized that retardation does not necessarily result in serious harms to the family. For example, when
adequate institutional resources are available, serious harm to the
family can be avoided. In such cases, the withholding of aggressive life-saving treatment for the retarded child is not warranted,
at least not on the basis of protecting the interests of the family.
Also, severe burdens can occur without retardation. An example
is a child with neuromuscular disease without cortical damage, as
in some spina bifida cases. In such instances, the burden to the
family is just as much a relevant factor as in instances involving
retardation. The issue can be regarded as a conflict between the
rights of the individual and the interests in protecting the integrity of families. The rights of the impaired infant are important,
of course, but they are not absolute.

In conclusion, our current policies can be faulted for failing
to take into account the disruption of family life which can be
caused by aggressive life-saving treatment of impaired children
without parental consent. In particular, the courts can be criticized
for not recognizing the burdens that these forced decisions place

on families when no relief is provided by governmental programs. We should either provide support to families to substantially reduce the hardships they undergo or take into account those hardships in deciding whether to withhold aggressive treatment.

Notes

1. "Nondiscrimination on the Basis of Handicap Relating to Health Care for Handicapped Infants," *Federal Register* (July 5, 1983), 48:30846.

2. "Evansville Couple Races Clock, Law to Save 'Condemned' Baby," *Evansville Courier,* April 15, 1982, p. 1.

3. "Discriminating Against the Handicapped by Withholding Treatment or Nourishment: Notice to Health Care Providers," *Federal Register* (June 16, 1982), 47:26027.

4. J. M. Gustafson, "Mongolism, Parental Desires, and the Right to Life," *Perspectives in Biology and Medicine* (Summer 1973), 16(4):529, 530.

5. *Who Should Survive?* produced by the Joseph P. Kennedy, Jr., Foundation, distributed by Lowengard & Brotherhood, Hartford, Conn.

6. A. Gath, "The Impact of an Abnormal Child Upon the Parents," *British Journal of Psychiatry* (1977), 130:405.

7. B. J. Tew, H. Payne, K. M. Laurence, "Must a Family with a Handicapped Child Be a Handicapped Family?" *Developmental Medicine and Child Neurology* (1974), 16(Supp. 32):95.

8. S. Dorner, "Psychological and Social Problems of Families of Adolescent Spina Bifida Patients: A Preliminary Report," *Developmental Medicine and Child Neurology* (1973), 15(Supp. 29):24.

9. H. Z. Wortis, J. A. Margolies, "Parents of Children with Cerebral Palsy," *Medical Social Work* (January 1955), 4:110.

10. A. Shaw, J. C. Randolph, and B. Manard, "Ethical Issues in Pediatric Surgery: A National Survey of Pediatricians and Pediatric Surgeons," *Pediatrics* (October 1977), 60(4):588. Similar results were reported in I. D. Todres, et al., "Pediatricians' Attitudes Affecting Decision-Making in Defective Newborns," *Pediatrics* (1977), 60(2):197.

11. President's Commission for the Study of Ethical Problems in Medicine and Biomedical and Behavioral Research, *Deciding to Forego Life-Sustaining Treatment* (Washington, D.C.: GPO, March, 1983), pp. 218, 228–29.

12. *Ibid.,* p. 215.

13. D. A. Shatten and R. S. Chabon, "Decisionmaking and the Right to Refuse Life-Saving Treatment for Defective Newborns," *Journal of Legal Medicine* (1982), 3(1):59, 72, citing "Medical Care for the Child at Risk: On State Supervention of Parental Autonomy," *Yale Law Journal* (1977), 86:645, 651.

15

Clinical Applications

ROBERT F. WEIR, Ph.D.

The argument was previously advanced that selective nontreatment decisions should be governed primarily by diagnostic
categories. If a newborn has an anomalous condition that can be
effectively treated, the child should generally be given the recommended treatment. In contrast, if a newborn has a diagnostic
condition that cannot be effectively treated, the child should generally be spared from efforts at life prolongation, because such
efforts will be futile and/or harmful to the child.

In addition, it was argued that selecting by diagnostic categories is consistent with the principles of nonmaleficence and justice. According to the principle of nonmaleficence, it is justifiable
to withhold life-prolonging treatment from all infants who have
conditions that "overmaster" them (to use the Hippocratic terminology) and that seem impervious to even the most advanced
medical procedures. To persist in trying to treat such infants is to
go counter to their best interests and thereby to inflict unwarranted harm on them. According to an egalitarian interpretation of

Reprinted from *Selective Nontreatment of Handicapped Newborns*, pp. 234–41, with
the permission of Oxford University Press. Copyright © 1984 Oxford University Press.
Footnotes renumbered.

justice, it is morally correct to withhold treatment from all infants born with the same kind of severe anomalous condition—as long as all available means of treating the condition are judged to be counter to those infants' best interests. To take another approach by comparing infants across major diagnostic lines is to engage in unfair quality-of-life assessments, because any less-than-normal infant will lose out in such a comparison.

It is now time to be more specific about which diagnostic conditions call for selective nontreatment. Any serious effort to do this kind of ethical line-drawing must meet three interrelated requirements: indicate as clearly as possible *where* the line is to be drawn between conditions to treat and those not to treat, provide reasons as to *why* the treatment/nontreatment line is drawn where it is, and apply the proposed line-drawing to actual cases.

It is improbable that all persons reading these words will agree with my placement of all the diagnostic conditions to be discussed below, especially since there are differences of opinion in the pediatric medical community regarding some of the conditions. Nevertheless, it seems reasonable that selection by diagnostic categories should be done by placing any of the congenital anomalies in one of three groups: anomalous conditions that should not be treated because efforts to save newborns with these conditions will not succeed; anomalous conditions that should not be treated because of the consensus judgment that life-prolonging treatment is not in the best interests of these infants; and anomalous conditions that should be treated because life-prolonging treatment is in the best interests of these infants. This threefold grouping of congential anomalies results in the placement of diagnostic conditions as follows:

1. *Withhold efforts at treatment* (desist unsuccessful rescue): anencephaly; other untreatable neurological conditions (e.g., craniorachischisis totalis, myeloschisis, massive subarachnoid hemorrhage, Chiari II malformation); infantile polycystic kidney disease; untreatable types of congenital heart disease (e.g., hypoplastic left ventricle); and multiple severe anomalies requiring repetitious efforts at resuscitation.
2. *Withhold or withdraw treatment* (allow to die): hydran-

encephaly; trisomy 18; trisomy 13; Lesch-Nyhan syndrome; Tay-Sachs disease; lissencephaly; cri-du-chat syndrome; and metachromatic leukodystrophy.

3. *Treat to prolong and enhance life*: hydrocephalus; most cases of prematurity; esophageal atresia with tracheo-esophageal fistula; duodenal atresia; most cases of congenital heart disease; most cases of intraventricular hemorrhage; trisomy 21 (Down's syndrome); hyaline membrane disease; most cases of spina bifida cystica; Apert's syndrome; diaphragmatic hernia; most cases of congenital kidney disease; abnormalities of the abdominal wall; exstrophy of the cloaca; neurofibromatosis; phenylketonuria; maple syrup urine disease; homocystinuria; cystic fibrosis; congenital hypothyroidism; and others too numerous to mention.

The reasons for drawing the treatment/nontreatment line in this manner are fairly straightforward. The congenital anomalies placed in the first nontreatment group seem, on the basis of current medical evidence, to be untreatable. Most of the conditions are rapidly fatal within the first few days of life.[1] At most, aggressive efforts at treatment may salvage these neonates for a short period of time, but for questionable moral reasons. Vigorous attempts at treatment with these generally acknowledged lethal cases appear to be done for the interests (and egos) of the medical personnel involved, not for the interests of the newborns subjected to futile rescue efforts.

When combined with the anomalous conditions in the first nontreatment group, the diagnostic conditions placed in the second nontreatment group represent less than 1 percent of all neonates. Nevertheless, good reasons are required to deny treatment to the nondying newborns whose conditions place them in this nontreatment group because, in contrast to the newborns in group 1, the nontreatment of infants in group 2 is done by choice. The reasons for nontreatment, in general terms, are that when infants are accurately diagnosed as having one of the anomalous conditions in the second group, a careful prognosis indicates that the lives that can be prolonged for an indeterminate period of time will not be in the best interests of the infants and children who have to endure them. Rather than proving beneficial to these children, life-prolonging treatment will subject them to a fate worse than death.

More specifically, there are several reasons for thinking that death, not severely handicapped life, is in the best interests of infants having any of the anomalous conditions in the second nontreatment group. First, a correct diagnosis of most of these conditions leads to a prognosis of *extremely short life expectancy.* Although some infants with some of these conditions (e.g., Lesch-Nyhan, Tay-Sachs, cri-du-chat) live for a few years after birth, the odds are very high that most newborns in the second nontreatment group will die in their first year of life even if given some forms of treatment. No matter how much sustaining treatment is given, continued life is simply not likely for most of these neonates.

Second, there is *no curative or corrective* treatment for these conditions. Little can be done for these children other than marginal life prolongation, palliative care, and institutionalization in a custodial ward. For the conditions with late onset dates (Lesch-Nyhan, Tay-Sachs, and the late infantile form of metachromatic leukodystrophy), the lack of effective treatment means that infants who appear normal during their first few months of life will experience progressive neurological and physical deterioration that is simply impossible to prevent or minimize.

Third, virtually all of the infants in the second nontreatment group who manage to survive beyond their first year end up with *serious neurological deficiencies.* In most cases the neurological deficiencies are very serious. With rare exceptions, infants with these conditions develop into children with severe (below 50 I.Q.) to profound (below 25 I.Q.) mental retardation.

Fourth, there are a *multiplicity of other serious medical problems* that accompany the neurological deficiences in these conditions. Most of the infants have some form of congenital heart disease. Most of them also have hypotonia, apnea, seizures, and numerous other clinical features of their particular anomalous conditions.

It may be helpful to focus on some of the conditions in the second group. Newborns who inherit the autosomal recessive condition of Tay-Sachs disease (one form of G_{M2}-gangliosidosis) appear normal for approximately six months, then have an inexorable decline toward a totally vegetative existence followed by death when they are three or four years of age. The progressive loss of contact with parents and the environment is characterized by profound mental retardation, convulsions, paralysis, blindness, inability to feed orally, and severe weight loss.[2]

Male neonates who inherit the X-linked recessive condition of Lesch-Nyhan syndrome also appear normal at birth, then at approximately six months begin a process of neurological and physiological deterioration first evidenced by athetosis (ceaseless, involuntary writhing movements). Along with severe mental deficiency, the most striking neurological feature of this condition is compulsive self-mutilation that requires placing the elbows in splints, wrapping the hands in gauze, and sometimes extracting the teeth. Even then, children with this condition often bang their heads against inanimate objects or take out their aggression on other persons.[3]

Infants (usually girls) with trisomy 18 generally do not survive the first two months of life. The 10 percent who live past the 12-month point do so with serious abnormalities of the brain, congenital heart disease, problems with apnea and cyanosis, hypertonia, severe gastrointestinal and renal deformities, dislocated hips, and virtually no chance to live to a second birthday.[4]

Metachromatic leukodystrophy is a rare autosomal recessive disease, with the late infantile form being the most common type of the condition. Neonates with the disease appear normal but have a serious disturbance of the white matter in the cerebral hemispheres that results in a diffuse loss of myelin in the central nervous system. Symptoms of the condition appear late in the first year of life, then progress through four clinical stages until, at the age of three or four, children with the condition are decerebrate, bedridden, quadriplegic, blind, without verbal sounds, and in need of tube feeding.[5]

Cri-du-chat syndrome (or 5p— syndrome) is a chromosomal disorder involving a deletion of the short arm of the fifth chromosome. The commonly used name for the condition is a reference to the catlike cry of infants having the disorder. In addition to this unusual cry, the most important aspect of this syndrome is the profound retardation that affects intellectual and motor development. Other symptoms of the condition include severely slowed growth, hypertonia, microcephaly, congenital heart disease, scoliosis, and inability to speak.[6]

The severity of these conditions—and the absence of effective treatment—forces one to conclude that death is preferable to severely handicapped existence for these children. Most reasonable persons—whether parents, physicians, other proxies, or other thoughtful individuals—will agree that the combination of harmful conditions accompanying these birth defects represents a fate worse than death for these afflicted newborns.

By contrast, infants with any of the anomalous conditions listed in the third group should be given treatment to prolong and to enhance their lives. The reasons for drawing the line at this point are several. First, the majority of the conditions *do not involve mental deficiency* at all, thus indicating that these neonates are potential persons in a way that newborns in the first two groups are not. Most of the anomalies in these conditions are physiological ones of one sort or another. Furthermore, for the disorders that do involve the possibility of neurological damage (e.g., hydrocephalus, phenylketonuria, intraventricular hemorrhage) or actual mental deficiency (e.g., trisomy 21), there is either a good chance of effectively treating the condition or at least a reasonable chance that the mental handicap will be rather mild.

Second, there is *curative or corrective treatment* available for most of the mental and physical handicaps associated with these conditions. In some instances (e.g., esophageal or duodenal atresia) the treatment is curative. In other instances (e.g., hydrocephalus, diaphragmatic hernia) the treatment is usually corrective. In other instances (e.g., phenylketonuria, maple syrup urine disease, homocystinuria) the treatment involves nothing more sophisticated than a special diet to adjust an underlying error of metabolism. Even for most cases of spina bifida cystica, in which surgery can neither cure nor correct the paralysis below the lesion, there is reasonably effective treatment for most of the physical and mental problems associated with the condition.

Third, most of these conditions *do not require institutional-*

ization if the affected infants are given appropriate treatment sufficiently early. Of course some parents may choose to institutionalize children with more severe forms of Down's syndrome or spina bifida or some of the other conditions that present ongoing problems, but these disorders do not usually have the degree of severity (as those in the second nontreatment group do) that necessitates placement in a handicapped children's facility. In fact, most children in this third group tend to do better if given care, emotional support, and friendship outside of an institutional setting.

Fourth, as already implied, infants with conditions listed in the third group have significantly *longer life expectancy* than newborns in the second group. A number of the conditions (e.g., congenital heart disease, hyaline membrane disease) cause neonatal fatalities if not effectively treated, but on the whole the availability of effective treatment means that neonates with these conditions will live many years beyond infancy.

Fifth, *very few adolescents or adults* with any of these conditions indicate that they *wish they had never survived infancy.* Even individuals with serious, ongoing handicaps (such as those associated with the more severe cases of spina bifida) rarely indicate to researchers that they would prefer no life to the life they have had. They may covet the normalcy they see in other persons, but they do not want to give up the abnormal lives they have for the alternative of death.

Of the various diagnostic conditions in the treatment group, Down's syndrome and spina bifida stand out because of the frequency of their occurrence and the conflicting points of view regarding the merits of life-prolonging treatment. Down's syndrome is unquestionably a serious congenital anomaly that no one would choose to have, and that no prospective parents would choose as the genetic composition of any of their children. As previously mentioned, the most serious feature of this disorder is moderately severe to severe mental retardation (typically in the 25–60 I.Q. range). However, the mental deficiency is occasionally milder, with some Down's syndrome children having I.Q. scores in the 60–80 range. In addition, these children have physical abnormalities ranging from relatively minor ones (e.g., shortened fingers, slanting eyes with inner canthal folds) to much more serious ones in some cases such as congenital heart disease (in 40 percent of the cases), esophageal or duodenal atresia (in 4 percent of the cases), and increased susceptibility to infections.[7]

Likewise, spina bifida cystica is a serious congenital anomaly that adults would never choose for themselves or their as yet unconceived children. During pregnancy it is possible to screen for spina bifida cases using the combination of ultrasonography, amniocentesis, and alpha-fetoprotein assays. Once born, infants with spina bifida have a number of physical abnormalities that have been previously discussed. In addition, these children often have hydrocephalus. Whether mental deficiency becomes an acquired feature of spina bifida cases with hydrocephalus depends on the effectiveness of shunting and the medical team's ability to prevent central nervous system infections (ventriculitis and/or meningitis). As a consequence, I.Q. scores in one study of children with spina bifida range from 102 in cases without hydrocephalus, to 95 for shunted hydrocephalus, to 72 for shunted cases with a history of ventriculitis.[8]

The day may come when spina bifida cases will be prevented or drastically reduced in number by having women take multivitamin supplements before and during pregnancy, or by having mandatory screening for spina bifida cases during pregnancy by running laboratory tests on the blood serum of pregnant women. Until that time, the question remains the same for cases of Down's syndrome and cases of spina bifida: is life-prolonging treatment in the best interests of these birth-defective infants? My answer is affirmative in cases of Down's syndrome and in the great majority of spina bifida cases. Children born with either of these anomalous conditions obviously do not have normal lives ahead of them. In this respect, they lack the chance for the quality of life that most normal children enjoy. Children born with either of these conditions also do not have desirable lives—except when these lives are compared with the alternative of death. The argument that these handicapped lives (or others in the treatment group) represent a fate worse than death is neither persuasive nor supported by studies of these children when they reach adolescence and adulthood.[9]

Notes

1. See Donald C. Fyler and Peter Lang, "Neonatal Heart Disease," in Gordon B. Avery, ed., *Neonatology: Pathophysiology and Management of the Newborn,* 2d ed. (Philadelphia: Lippincott, 1981), pp. 438–72; and Joseph J. Volpe and Richard Koenigsberger, "Neurologic Disorders," in Avery, *Neonatology,* pp. 910–963.

2. See Edwin H. Kolodny, "Tay Sachs Disease," in R. M. Goodman and Arno Motulsky, eds., *Genetic Disease among Ashkenazi Jews* (New York: Raven Press, 1979), pp. 217–229; Michael M. Kaback, D. L. Rimoin, and J. S. O'Brien, eds., *Tay-Sachs Disease: Screening and Prevention* (New York: Alan R. Liss, 1977); and Hans Galjaard, *Genetic Metabolic Diseases* (Amsterdam, New York, and Oxford: Elsevier/North Holland Biomedical Press, 1980), pp. 266–281.

3. See William L. Nyhan, "The Lesch-Nyhan Syndrome," *Annual Review of Medicine* (1973), 24:41–60; and John B. Stanbury et al., eds., *The Metabolic Basis of Inherited Disease,* 5th ed. (New York: McGraw-Hill, 1983), pp. 1115–1138.

4. See M. E. Hodes et al., "Clinical Experience with Trisomies 18 and 13," *Journal of Medical Genetics* (1978), 15:48–60.

5. See Galjaard, *Genetic Metabolic Diseases,* pp.215–25; and Stanbury el al., *Metabolic Basis of Inherited Disease,* pp. 881–901.

6. See William L. Nyhan and Nadia O. Sakati, *Genetic and Malformation Syndromes in Clinical Medicine* (Chicago: Year Book Medical Publishers, 1976), pp. 128–131; David W. Smith, *Recognizable Patterns of Human Malformation* (Philadelphia: Saunders, 1970), pp. 48–49; and E. Neibuhr, "The Cri-du-Chat Syndrome: Epidemiology, Cytogenetics, and Clinical Features," *Human Genetics* (1978), pp. 227–234.

7. David W. Smith and Ann Asper Wilson, *The Child with Down's Syndrome* (Philadelphia: Saunders, 1973), pp. 21–44.

8. David G. McLone et al., "Central Nervous System Infections as a Limiting Factor in the Intelligence of Children with Myelomeningocele," *Pediatrics* (September 1982), 70:338–342.

9. See Smith and Wilson, *The Child with Down's Syndrome,* pp. 91–105; Kathleen Evans, Veronica Hickman, and C. O. Carter, "Handicap and Social Status of Adults with Spina Bifida Cystica," *British Journal of Preventive and Social Medicine* (1974), 28:85–92; S. Dorner, "Adolescents with Spina Bifida: How They See Their Situation," *Archives of Disease in Childhood* (June 1976), 51:439–44; K. M. Laurence and Ann Beresford, "Degree of Physical Handicap, Education and Occupation of 51 Adults with Spina Bifida," *British Journal of Preventive and Social Medicine* (September 1976), 30:197–202.

16

United States v. University Hospital of the State University of New York at Stony Brook

U.S. District Court, E.D. New York,
575 F.Supp. 607 (1983)

WEXLER, District Judge:

In this action, plaintiff, the United States of America, seeks an order directing that one of the defendants, University Hospital of the State University of New York at Stony Brook, allow the Department of Health and Human Services access to the medical records of a handicapped infant, hereinafter referred to as "Baby Jane Doe." Plaintiff contends that plaintiff is entitled to such an order pursuant to Section 504 of the Rehabilitation Act of 1973, . . . which provides, in pertinent part:

> No otherwise qualified handicapped individual in the United States . . . shall, solely by reason of his handicap, be excluded from participation in, be denied the benefits of, or be subjected to discrimination under any program or activity receiving Federal financial assistance. . . .

Facts

1. On October 11, 1983, Baby Jane Doe was born, suffering from spina bifida, hydrocephalus, microcephaly, bilateral

upper extremity spasticity, a prolapsed rectum, and a malformed brain stem.

2. The parents of Baby Jane Doe have refused to give consent to the University Hospital . . . for the performance of surgical procedures upon Baby Jane Doe to treat the spinal defect and to drain the water from the infant's skull caused by the hydrocephalic condition, but have instead opted for a conservative treatment involving good nutrition and the administration of antibiotics and dressing of the exposed spinal sac to encourage the skin to grow over and protect it. . . .

5. On October 21, 1983, the Appellate Division of the Supreme Court of the State of New York determined that Baby Jane Doe was not in imminent danger of death, and that the parents of Baby Jane Doe, in refusing permission for the operations, made a reasonable choice among possible medical treatments, acting with the best interests of the child in mind. . . .

7. During the period in which the state court proceedings were taking place, the Department of Health and Human Services received a complaint that Baby Jane Doe was being discriminatorily denied medically indicated treatment on the basis of her physical and mental handicaps. . . .

9. Since October 22, 1983, the Department of Health and Human Services . . . has repeatedly requested that the University Hospital . . . provide the Department with access to all of Baby Jane Doe's medical records. The University Hospital, acting in part on the refusal of Baby Jane Doe's parents to consent to the release of the records, has refused to release the records. . . .

It is undisputed that the defendant University Hospital has at all times been willing to perform the surgical procedures in question, if only the parents of Baby Jane Doe would consent to such procedures. Further, the defendant University Hospital lacks the legal right to perform such procedures, unless there is consent by either the child's natural guardians (i.e., her parents), or by some other legally appointed guardian. It would appear, therefore, that the defendant University Hospital has failed to perform the surgical procedures in question, not because Baby Jane Doe is handicapped, but because her parents have refused to consent to such procedures. The defendant University Hospital has therefore not violated the Rehabilitation Act by subjecting a handicapped individual to discrimination solely by reason of her handicap. . . .

In any case, the papers submitted to the Court demonstrate conclusively that the decision of the parents to refuse consent to the surgical procedures was a reasonable one based on due consideration of the medical options available and on a genuine concern for the best interests of the child. . . .

The reasonableness of the parents' choice is apparent from the Appellate Division's summary of the medical testimony offered at the [state] Supreme Court hearing:

> The record confirms that the failure to perform the surgery will not place the infant in imminent danger of death, although surgery might significantly reduce the risk of infection. On the other hand, successful results could also be achieved with antibiotic therapy. Further, while the mortality rate is higher where conservative medical treatment is used, in this particular case the surgical procedures also involved a greater risk of depriving the infant of what little function remains in her legs, and would also result in recurring urinary tract and possibly kidney infections, skin infections and edemas of the limbs.

Right To Privacy

Defendants have contended that release of Baby Jane Doe's medical records to the Department of Health and Human Services without the consent of the child's parents would violate the constitutional right to privacy and New York state legislation concerning the confidentiality of the doctor-patient relationship. . . .

The defendants' reliance upon the constitutional right of privacy is extremely weak. In the instant action, plaintiff is, at least implicitly, alleging the possibility that the parents of Baby Jane Doe, in refusing their consent to surgical procedures, were not acting in the best interests of the child. . . . In the instant action, the Court has found that the parents in question are in fact acting upon a reasonable interpretation of the child's best interests. Under different facts, however, it is quite possible that an assertion by a parent on behalf of a handicapped child of the child's right to privacy made to preclude the release of the child's medical records to officials would not be sustained as a valid invocation of the constitutional right to privacy. This would be particularly so in those situations in which the officials in question provide a guarantee that such medical records will be kept confidential, and in which the officials possess a firm basis for believing that the child is in grave danger. . . .

FOUR

Treatment Abatement with Critically Ill Patients

Advances in medical technology have drastically changed the clinical setting, the medical personnel, and the treatment options available to most critically ill patients. The clinical setting has changed with the creation of Intensive Care Units (ICUs), established specifically to provide continuous, specialized treatment and monitoring of critically ill patients in a special care area. Now many hospitals have gone beyond a single ICU to multiple ICUs offering specialized care for cardiac patients, surgical patients, trauma patients, neonatal patients, and so forth.

The medical personnel who care for critically ill patients have changed with the establishment of critical care medicine as a subspecialty of internal medicine, anesthesia, pediatrics, and surgery. In addition to having medical specialists trained in particular organ systems, many critically ill patients who have multiple vital organ failures now have access to an interdisciplinary critical care team. By moving beyond a traditional, compartmentalized approach to medicine, the personnel in critical care medicine offer patients care for life-threatening problems which arise when several organ systems begin to fail.

The options for diagnosing and treating critically ill patients have gone through remarkable changes in recent years. Depending upon the condition(s) bringing about critical illness, patients may be offered a multitude of diagnostic and therapeutic alternatives: ultrasound, computerized tomography (CT) scanning, nuclear magnetic resonance (NMR), mechanical ventilation, chemotherapy and radiation therapy, intravenous feeding, antibiotics, inotropic and antiarrhythmic drugs, cardiopulmonary resuscitation (CPR), hemodialysis, organ transplants, coronary bypass surgery, an artificial heart, and so on.

Such changes in medicine have brought about numerous issues in the fields of biomedical ethics and health care law. The year 1976 may be taken as an illustrative example. Among the notable events in medicine, law, and ethics that year, three stand out as having unusual importance for the issue of treatment abatement. First, Karen Ann Quinlan, a 21-year-old woman, collapsed at a party in April 1975, was rushed to a hospital and placed on a respirator, and remained on the respirator as she became the focal point of a legal battle in New Jersey that continued until March 1976. The point at issue in the legal controversy was the right of treatment termination: did Karen's parents, who had decided that their now incompetent, brain-damaged, comatose daughter was no longer being helped by the respirator, have the right to have the respirator removed? In March 1976 the Supreme Court of New Jersey ruled that the "right of privacy" permits "termination of treatment in the circumstances of this case," thereby allowing the respirator to be removed from Karen. Second, the Massachusetts General Hospital took the lead among hospitals by publishing guidelines for dividing critically ill patients into four treatment groups. The groups ranged from Class A patients, who are to be given "maximal therapeutic effort without reservation," to Class D patients, for whom "all therapy can be discontinued . . . though maximum comfort to the patient may be continued" (*New England Journal of Medicine,* August 12, 1976). Third, California became the first state to pass a Natural Death Act. Californians, who like all American citizens have the legal right to refuse life-prolonging treatment, were given a specific legal mechanism in September 1976 to facilitate the carrying out of that right. Thus events in three states demonstrated that life-prolonging technology is sometimes limited by the medical conditions of critically ill patients and by the right of those patients (or their guardians) to refuse treatment.

Succeeding years have seen continued attention given to the issue of treatment abatement. Three national groups have played important roles in emphasizing the importance of the issue. Concern for Dying, an educational organization headquartered in New York, increased its efforts in the late 1970s to publicize and distribute the document known as the "Living Will." Millions of Americans have now signed copies of this document, asking that they "be allowed to die and not be kept alive by medications, artificial means or 'heroic measures.' " The Society for the Right to Die, also based in New York, has focused its efforts on the passage of natural death acts in state legislatures. The results of these efforts are reflected in the readings in this section, with the number of states having natural death acts increasing from 11 (Battin article) to 12 (CFD Legal Advisers' article) to 15 (Wanzer et al. article) to 36 at the time of this writing. The President's Commission for the Study of Ethical Problems in Medicine, whose views on the issue of the determination of death are included in part 2, also addressed the issue of treatment abatement. The Commission's lengthy report, entitled *Deciding to Forego Life-Sustaining Treatment,* was issued in 1983.

Of course, treatment abatement would not be a controversial "issue" if there were not individuals and organizations opposing the recent events mentioned above. Some right-to-life groups (for example, the National Right-to-Life Committee, the Christian Action Council, and the American Life Lobby) have opposed efforts to facilitate the legal right to refuse life-prolonging treatment, because they believe that treatment abatement decisions are the "first step" toward societal acceptance of suicide and euthanasia. Some conservative religious organizations (most notably, some officials and groups within the Catholic Church) have joined in the opposition to natural death acts, occasionally going so far as to claim that treatment abatement decisions are "contrary to the Judeo-Christian tradition." Some physicians and physicians' organizations have opposed natural-death-act legislation, for a number of reasons: they believe such legislation is unnecessary, it can lead to abuse, it will mean additional paper-work for physicians, and it will oversimplify and romanticize the complex medical factors that often characterize cases involving critically ill patients. And some individual physicians and hospital administrators have opposed efforts by competent patients and by the legal guardians of incompetent patients to refuse life-sustaining treatment, thereby necessitating a number of "right-to-die" court decisions.

In the midst of this ongoing debate, a number of ethical and legal factors need to be kept in mind. First, it is important to distinguish among categories of critically ill patients. The ethical and legal questions involved in treatment termination decisions differ significantly depending upon whether the patient is (a) competent to make such decisions, (b) is not and never has been competent to make such decisions (for example, infants and severely retarded adults), or (c) is not now competent, but previously was competent (with the present incompetency due to a permanent loss of consciousness, or advanced senility).

Second, cases involving treatment abatement decisions need to be kept separate from other types of death-related cases. Treatment abatement cases are different from determination-of-death cases for the obvious reason that the critically ill patient in the former type of case is unquestionably alive, even if possibly incompetent for some reason. Treatment abatement cases are different from suicide cases because a critically ill patient in the former type of case does not necessarily regard life as intolerable or want to die, but simply wants to live for whatever length of time is possible apart from the life-support procedures currently being used. And treatment abatement cases are different from voluntary euthanasia cases in that the patient does not request to be killed, but to be allowed to live and die apart from selected medical treatments that are regarded as futile or undesirable.

Third, some of the debate about the appropriateness of treatment abatement in particular cases hangs on distinctions commonly used in ethics and law. Whether the distinctions are unquestionably accepted, rejected as untenable, or interpreted in yet another way, at least three such distinctions have wide usage in written opinions about treatment abatement decisions. The killing/letting die distinction often surfaces when questions are raised about the morality and legality of removing critically ill patients from respirators, especially when the questions concern whether the removal of a respirator is or is not morally equivalent to intentionally killing the patient. The ordinary/extraordinary distinction, although interpreted in many ways, is present when persons discuss whether a particular kind of treatment (for example, artificial feeding) is obligatory or possibly optional as a means of prolonging the life of a given patient. The distinction between withholding/withdrawing treatment appears when physicians question whether it is better not to start a particular treatment than to make the difficult decision (morally and psychologically) to stop the treatment once it has proven to be ineffective.

The selected readings address many of the issues involved in treatment abatement decisions. The first article, written by Sidney Wanzer and nine other physicians, argues that hopelessly ill patients should be given no treatment other than "general nursing care and efforts to make the patient comfortable." The second article, written by the legal advisers committee of Concern for Dying, proposes a model Act for the right to refuse treatment, in the belief that such an Act will promote patient autonomy and respect for persons. Pabst Battin's article, by contrast, points out that respect for patient autonomy can sometimes have cruel results, especially when the termination of treatment leads to a more painful experience of dying than a patient had anticipated when declining life-sustaining treatment.

The last two articles address an issue that has come into prominence in the 1980s. Joanne Lynn and James Childress, the former a physician and the latter an ethicist, are convinced that there are times when it is morally permissible to withhold food and fluids from critically ill patients. Daniel Callahan, also an ethicist and the Director of the Hastings Center, disagrees because he experiences "a deep-seated revulsion at the stopping of feeding" and believes that "feeding of the hungry . . . is the most fundamental of all human relationships."

Because of the differences between cases involving competent patients and those involving proxy decisions for incompetent patients, this section contains excerpts from two court cases. The first case concerns the right of Abe Perlmutter, a 73-year-old competent patient with ALS (amyotrophic lateral sclerosis), to have a respirator removed from his trachea. The court decision, later affirmed (in 1980) by the Supreme Court of Florida, was that the patient "should be allowed to make his choice to die with dignity." The second case is the widely publicized case of Claire Conroy, an 84-year-old nursing home patient with serious, irreversible physical and mental impairments and a limited life expectancy. The decision by the Supreme Court of New Jersey, on the basis of an appeal from Conroy's nephew and guardian, was to allow the removal of Conroy's nasogastric tube because the continued use of the tube to provide her with medicines and food was judged contrary to her best interests.

17

The Physician's Responsibility Toward Hopelessly Ill Patients

SIDNEY H. WANZER, M.D., S. JAMES ADELSTEIN, M.D.,
RONALD E. CRANFORD, M.D.,
DANIEL D. FEDERMAN, M.D., EDWARD D. HOOK, M.D.,
CHARLES G. MOERTEL, M.D., PETER SAFAR, M.D.,
ALAN STONE, M.D., HELEN D. TAUSSIG, M.D.,
AND JAN VAN EYS, M.D., Ph.D.

Efforts to define policies on withholding or withdrawing life-sustaining procedures from hopelessly ill patients are a relatively recent development. In 1976, when two major hospitals publicly announced their protocols in treating the hopelessly ill, the *Journal* marked the event with an editorial titled "Terminating Life Support: Out of the Closet!"[1]

Since then, the subject of permitting patients to die has emerged into the open. The courts have issued several well-publicized decisions since the 1976 Quinlan case,[2] and legislatures in 15 states and the District of Columbia have enacted "natural death" acts (California, 1976; Idaho, 1977; Arkansas, 1977; New Mexico, 1977; Nevada, 1977; Oregon, 1977; North Carolina, 1977; Texas, 1977; Washington, 1979; Kansas, 1979; Alabama, 1981; District of Columbia, 1982; Vermont, 1982; Delaware, 1982; Virginia, 1983; and Illinois, 1983). Moreover, medical institutions have made public statements of "no code" policies.[3] As medical technology has advanced, numerous articles in profes-

Reprinted from *The New England Journal of Medicine* (April 12, 1984), 310:955–959, with the permission of the publisher. Copyright © 1984 by the Massachusetts Medical Society.

sional journals have dealt with various aspects of the subject, along with much discussion and debate of crucial ethical questions. However, the formulation of universally accepted guidelines for physicians treating the hopelessly ill has remained difficult. As Hilfiker states, "it is time we publicly examined our role in these situations, offered each other some guidelines, and came to some consensus about our responsibility."[4]

The present [essay], written by a group of experienced physicians from various disciplines and institutions, is an attempt to meet this need. We have not addressed the special questions surrounding treatment decisions for neonates and minors (a subject in itself) but have limited the scope of the paper to the irreversibly ill adult. Basic to our considerations are two important precepts: the patient's role in decision making is paramount, and a decrease in aggressive treatment of the hopelessly ill patient is advisable when such treatment would only prolong a difficult and uncomfortable process of dying.

The Patient's Role in Decision Making

The patient's right to make decisions about his or her medical treatment is clear. That right, grounded in both common law and the constitutional right of privacy, includes the right to refuse life-sustaining treatment—a fact affirmed in the courts and recently supported by a presidential commission.[5] Ideally, the right is exercised when the diagnosis and treatment are clear, the physician is skilled and sensitive, and the patient is competent and informed. Circumstances, however, are often less than ideal. In writing about "specific clinical and psychologic problems that may complicate the concept of patient autonomy and the right to die with dignity," Jackson and Youngner have illustrated a number of factors that can interfere with appropriate decision making even if the patient's competency is not in question.[6] Disease, pain, drugs, and a variety of conditions altering mental states may severely reduce the patient's capacity for judgment. Since these circumstances can fluctuate, competency can be lost and regained, requiring reevaluation at intervals.

The principal obstacle to a patient's effective participation in decision making is lack of competence, and only when competence is lacking can others substitute their judgment for that of the patient. Therefore, the assessment of competence is a critical issue. Although legal determination of incompetence may at times be a matter for court review, this step can be safely bypassed when there is unanimity on the part of the physician and others consulted—family and close friends, and psychiatrists, if indicated. In arriving at the determination of incompetence, the physician must coordinate the various evaluations and opinions and document them clearly in the medical records. We believe that a hopelessly ill patient's refusal of life-sustaining treatment is not in itself a reason to question the patient's competency, no matter what the personal values of the physician or family may be.

If the terminally ill patient's ability to make decisions becomes progessively reduced, the physician must rely increasingly on the presumed or prestated wishes of the patient. It helps if there is a longstanding relationship between patient and physician, but in fact many adults have no personal physician. Terminally ill patients are often cared for by specialists or members of house staff who do not know what the patient would have wished or may not have the time or experience to handle difficult problems of this kind. Under these circumstances, it becomes important to have other means of determining the patient's desires. A written statement, prepared in advance of the patient's illness and diminished decision-making capacity, can be helpful in indicating to the physician the patient's preference with respect to terminal treatment.[7] Such advance directions, or "living wills," are recognized by law in 15 states and the District of Columbia, and even in states where they have not been legally authorized, they provide important though not binding evidence of a patient's wishes.

Another aid to decision making in which the patient cannot participate effectively is a proxy, designated in advance by the patient to speak on his or her behalf.[8] This option has only recently been provided by law in a few states—either as part of the state's "living will" legislation (Delaware's Death with Dignity Act of 1982 and Virginia's Natural Death Act of 1983) or (in California) as an amendment to the durable-power-of-attorney statute, extending the authorization to health-care decisions.[9] Since the clinical circumstances of a future illness and available treatment options are unpredictable, a proxy chosen by the patient offers the advantage of decision making based on both an intimate knowledge of the patient's wishes and the physician's recommendations.

Neither the living will nor the proxy appointment is a perfect mechanism for projecting a patient's wishes into a period of future incompetency. The living will cannot predict all the various alternatives that become possible as acute illnesses arise, and in many cases, the document is not updated with any regularity. A proxy may not be available at the time of need, or he or she may have a conflict of interest, either emotionally or legally. Nevertheless, in spite of imperfections, the living will and the proxy can be of real assistance to the physician trying to decide the best course of treatment for the dying patient. In their absence, the physician must ascertain from family and friends the attitudes and wishes the patient would have expressed had competence been maintained.

The Physician's Role in Decision Making

The patient's right to accept or refuse treatment notwithstanding, the physician has a major role in the decision-making process. He or she has the knowledge, skills, and judgment to provide diagnosis and prognosis, to offer treatment choices and explain their implications, and to assume responsibility for recommending a decision with respect to treatment.

The physician's schooling, residency training, and professional oath emphasize positive actions to sustain and prolong life; the educational system has only recently given attention to ethical questions surrounding the intentional reduction of medical intervention. Physicians do not easily accept the concept that it may be best to do less, not more, for a patient. The decision to pull back is much more difficult to make than the decision to push ahead with aggressive support, and today's sophisticated and complex medical technology invites physicians to make use of all the means at their disposal—a temptation that must be recognized when evaluating how much or how little to do for the patient.

Coupled with the traditional pressures for aggressive treatment is the uncertainty of diagnosis and prognosis, making it difficult to predict the length and quality of the patient's life with or without treatment. If the attending physician is not expert in the particular area of the patient's illness, he or she should consult with those who are. If there is disagreement concerning the diagnosis or prognosis or both, the life-sustaining approach should be continued until reasonable agreement is reached. However, insistence on certainty beyond a reasonable point can handicap the physician dealing with treatment options in apparently hopeless cases. The rare report of a patient with a similar condition who survived is not an overriding reason to continue aggressive treatment. Such negligible statistical possibilities do not outweigh the reasonable expectations of outcome that will guide treatment decisions.

Physicians are strongly influenced by their personal values and unconscious motivations. Although they should not be forced to act against their moral codes, they should guard against being excessively influenced by unexamined inner conflicts, a tendency to equate a patient's death with professional failure, or unrealistic expectations.

Fear of legal liability often interferes with the physician's ability to make the best choice for the patient. Assessment of legal risks is sometimes made by lawyers whose primary objective is to minimize liability, whether real or imagined. Unfortunately, this may be done at the expense of humane treatment and may go against the expressed wishes of the patient or family. A recent case in California involving murder charges against two physicians who withdrew all life support from a comatose patient created a climate of heightened apprehension in the medical community.[10] The action taken against the physicians was the first and only such criminal case in U.S. legal history.[11] Fortunately, the charges were dismissed by the California Court of Appeal. Treatment of a dying patient always takes place in the context of changing law and changing social policy, but in spite of legal uncertainties, appropriate and compassionate care should have priority over undue fears of criminal or civil liability.

Another possible influence on the physician's thinking is consideration of monetary costs to society and the use of scarce treatment resources in the care of the hopelessly ill. In the past, cost was rarely an important factor in decision making, but today, as society tries to contain the soaring cost of health care, the physician is subject to insistent demands for restraint, which cannot be ignored. Financial ruin of the patient's family, as well as the drain on resources for treatment of other patients who are not hopelessly ill, should be weighed in the decision-making process, although the patient's welfare obviously remains paramount.

Communication with the Patient

When a physician discusses life-threatening illness with a patient, a number of questions arise. Is the patient capable of accepting the information? How much information should the patient be given? When should the physician inform the patient of a fatal illness? Can information be imparted without destroying all hope? There are no absolute answers to these questions, but the following principles seem reasonable.

Although some physicians and families avoid frank discussions with patients, in our view, practically all patients, even disturbed ones, are better off knowing the truth. A decision not to tell the patient the truth because of fear of his or her emotional or psychological inability to handle such information is rarely if ever justified, and in such a case the burden of proof rests on the person who believes that the patient cannot cope with frank discussion. The anxiety of dealing with the unknown can be far more upsetting that the grief of dealing with a known, albeit tragic, truth. A failure to transmit to the patient knowledge of terminal illness can create barriers in communication, and the patient is effectively placed in isolation at a time when emotional sharing is most needed.

The dying patient should be given only as much information as he or she wishes to handle. Some patients want to know every detail, whereas others, who have a limited ability to understand or a limited desire to know, want only the most general information.

The discussion of critical illness and the patient's right to accept or refuse life-prolonging treatment should occur as early as possible in the course of disease; ideally, it will already have taken place at a time when the patient was healthy. However, regardless of any discussions that may or may not have taken place, when fatal illness occurs, the physician—if possible, one with whom the patient has already developed rapport, not a stranger—should tell the patient of an unfavorable diagnosis or prognosis as soon as the information is firm. Such discussions may have to be repeated, since patients often find it difficult to assimilate all they need to know at any one time, and as illness progresses, continued communication will be required to meet changing needs.

When the prognosis is bad, the physician must help the terminally ill patient understand and deal with the prognosis and alternatives for treatment without destroying all hope. This can be done by reassuring the patient that he or she will not be abandoned and by emphasizing the positive measures that can be used for support. The emotional distress that accompanies such discussions is usually more than offset by the security of a consensus about terminal care.

Another important consideration with respect to doctor-patient communication is the matter of informed consent. There are three basic prerequisites for informed consent: the patient must have the capacity to reason and make judgments, the decision must be made voluntarily and without coercion, and the patient must have a clear understanding of the risks and benefits of the proposed treatment alternatives or nontreatment, along with a full understanding of the nature of the disease and the prognosis. Fulfillment of the third condition requires that the physician take the time to discuss the issues fully with the patient and outline the differences among alternatives, which are sometimes very difficult to estimate. Nevertheless, it is the physician's responsibility to ensure, as much as possible, that all the conditions for informed consent are met. In addition to being thoroughly informed, the patient must also understand clearly his or her right to make choices about the type of care to be received—a right many patients are not aware of. This is the cornerstone of all decision making and is the basis on which informed consent rests.

The preeminence of the patient's choice does not preclude the physician's responsibility to make and to share with the patient a personal judgment about what the patient should do. Patients often ask a trusted physician, "What would you do?" A direct answer is in order. Some patients want every possible day of life, regardless of how limited the quality, whereas others apparently prefer early death to prolongation of a very limited life on a day-to-day basis. Given what the physician knows about the individual patient, some order of preference for available treatment choices can be offered. In any case, it is unfair simply to provide a mass of medical facts and options and leave the patient adrift without any further guidance on the alternative courses of action and inaction.

The physician's traditional role as a source of comfort to patients and their families becomes especially important when the decision has been made to withhold treatment that prolongs dying. Competent patients who have chosen to be allowed to die may experience a resultant feeling of abandonment. The family may share this feeling on behalf of the dying patient and have difficulty grappling with the consequences of a decision in which they may or may not have played a part. Assiduous attention to the patient's physical and emotional comfort at this point is essential. The physician's availability at such times can be a source of great psychological comfort to both patient and family.

The physician has a special obligation to listen to the doubts and fears expressed by patients who are hopelessly or terminally ill. Although a rare patient may contemplate suicide, the physician cannot participate by assisting in the act, for this is contrary to law. On the other hand, the physician is not obligated to assume that every such wish is irrational and requires coercive intervention.

The Provision of Appropriate Care

Patients who require only the fourth level of care (comfort) are usually those clearly in the terminal phase of an irreversible illness. For such patients, routine monitoring procedures, including daily temperature, pulse, and blood-pressure readings, may be discontinued. Diagnostic measures, such as blood tests and x-ray films, may be omitted except when required to relieve an uncomfortable or painful condition. Antibiotics need not be administered for pneumonia or other infections. Certain mechanical interventions, such as urethral catheterization, may increase overall comfort and thus be justified, but any mechanical or surgical intervention should be discouraged if it does not accomplish the aim of making the patient comfortable.

Naturally or artificially administered hydration and nutrition may be given or withheld, depending on the patient's comfort. If these supports are to be withheld or withdrawn, however, the physician must be sensitive to the symbolic meaning of this step. The provision of food and water is so important symbolically that family, friends, and staff need to understand that many patients in a terminal situation are not aware of thirst or hunger. Everything done for the patient at the fourth level of care should meet only the test of whether it will make the patient more comfortable and whether it will honor his or her wishes. Any actions that withhold a form of treatment should be clearly discussed with interested parties and documented in the record.

INDIVIDUALIZING TREATMENT

The Competent Patient
Although relief of pain and suffering is the primary consideration in the care of all hopelessly ill patients, differences in patients' disabilities dictate differences in the appropriate form and intensity of their care.

Levels of Care
It can be useful for the physician and other medical personnel to designate the level of care for the hopelessly ill patient that is appropriate at a given stage of the disease process. In this way the treatment goal can be addressed logically and openly. The physician should bring nurses and other health-care personnel into discussions concerning the level of therapy for an individual patient, since they are in close and frequent communication with the patient and his or her family. Decisions about care

should be carefully documented in the record, and all appropriate personnel should be aware of them.

General levels of care can be described as follows: (1) emergency resuscitation; (2) intensive care and advanced life support; (3) general medical care, including antibiotics, drugs, surgery, cancer chemotherapy, and artificial hydration and nutrition; and (4) general nursing care and efforts to make the patient comfortable, including pain relief and hydration and nutrition as dictated by the patient's thirst and hunger. Although the program of care must be individualized, since every patient is unique, these four levels of treatment should be considered and discussed with the patient, the family, and other health-care personnel. Certainly, the competent patient has a right to know that such variations in approach exist.

In treating patients who are generally alert but are dying of a progressive illness, such as cancer, the physician must be especially sensitive to their need for relief from pain and suffering. Aggressive treatment in response to this need is often justified even if under other circumstances the risk of such treatment would be medically undesirable (e.g., it would result in respiratory depression). The level of care to be provided should reflect an understanding between patient and physician and should be reassessed from time to time. In many cases neither intensive care nor emergency resuscitation is desired by the patient and his or her family; there may be a wish only for comfort, with general medical treatment given solely to provide relief from distress.

When the facilities provided by an acute-care hospital are not essential to the comfort and dignity of the dying patient, he or she should be moved to a more appropriate setting, if possible. Care at home or in a less regimented environment, such as a hospice, should be encouraged and facilitated.

The Incompetent Patient

Patients with brain death.[12] Patients with irreversible cessation of all functions of the brain, determined in accordance with accepted medical standards, are considered medically and legally dead, and no further treatment is required.

Patients in a persistent vegetative state.[13] In this state the neocortex is largely and irreversibly detroyed, although some brainstem functions persist. When this neurologic condition has been established with a high degree of medical certainty and has been carefully documented, it is morally justifiable to withhold antibiotics and artificial nutrition and hydration, as well as other forms of life-sustaining treatment, allowing the patient to die. This obviously requires careful efforts to obtain knowledge of the patient's prior wishes and the understanding and agreement of the family. Family attitudes will clearly influence the type of care given in these cases.

Severely and irreversibly demented patients. Patients in this category, most of them elderly, are at one end of the spectrum of decreasing mental capacity. They do not initiate purposeful activity but passively accept nourishment and bodily care.

When the severely demented patient has previously made his or her wishes known and when there is intercurrent illness, it is ethically permissible for the physician to withhold treatment that would serve mainly to prolong the dying process. When there is no prior expression or living will and when no family or advocate is available, the physician should be guided by the need to provide the most humane kind of treatment and the need to carry out the patient's wishes insofar as they are ascertainable.

Severely and irreversibly demented patients need only care given to make them comfortable. If such a patient rejects food and water by mouth, it is ethically permissible to withhold nutrition and hydration artificially administered by vein or gastric tube. Spoon feeding should be continued if needed for comfort. It is ethically appropriate not to treat intercurrent illness except with measures required for comfort (e.g., antibiotics for pneumonia can be withheld). For this category of patients, it is best if decisions about the handling of intercurrent illness are made prospectively, before the onset of an acute illness or threat to life. The physician must always bear in mind that senseless perpetuation of the status quo is decision by default.

Elderly patients with permanent mild impairment of competence. Many elderly patients are described as "pleasantly senile." Although somewhat limited in their ability to initiate activities and communicate, they often appear to be enjoying their moderately restricted lives. Freedom from discomfort should be an overriding objective in the care of such a patient. If emergency resuscitation and intensive care are required, the physician should provide these measures sparingly, guided by the patient's prior wishes, if known, by the wishes of the patient's family, and by an assessment of the patient's prospects for improvement.

Conclusions

Few topics in medicine are more complicated, more controversial, and more emotionally charged than treatment of the hopelessly ill. Technology competes with compassion, legal precedent lags, and controversy is inevitable. The problem is least troublesome when an informed patient and an empathetic physician together confront a clearly defined outlook. We have tried to outline a reasonable approach that is useful even when these ideal circumstances do not obtain. Our recommendations cannot resolve all conflicts, provide simple formulas, or comprehensively address the wide range of issues involved in caring for the hopelessly ill patient, but they are intended to offer some clarification and support for those who bear the social responsibility of deciding whether to forego life-sustaining treatment for the hopelessly ill.

Notes

1. C. Fried, "Terminating Life Support: Out of the Closet!" *New England Journal of Medicine* (1976), 295:390–391.

2. *In re Quinlan,* 70 N.J. 10, 355 A. 2d 647 (1976); *Superintendent of Belchertown State School v. Saikewicz,* 373 Mass. 728, 370 N.E. 2d 417 (Mass. 1977); *In re Dinnerstein,* 380 N.E. 2d 134 (Mass. App. 1978);*Satz v. Perlmutter,* Florida 362 So. 2d 160 (Fla. App. 1978), affirmed by Florida Supreme Court, 379 So. 2d 379 (1980); *Severns v. Wilmington Medical Center, Inc. et al.,* Del. Supr. 421A.2d 1334 (1980); *In re Spring,* 405 N.E. 2d 115 (1980); *In re Eichner* (Fox), Ct. of App., 52 N.Y.S. 2d 266 (1981); and *In re Storar,* Ct. of App., 52 N.Y. 2d 363, 420 N.E. 2d 64, 438 N.Y.S. 2d 255 (1981).

3. President's Commission for the Study of Ethical Problems in Medicine and Biomedical and Behavioral Research, *Deciding to Forego Life-Sustaining Treatment* (Washington, D.C.: GPO, 1983), pp. 236–239.

4. D. Hilfiker, "Allowing the Debilitated to Die: Facing Our Ethical Choices," *New England Journal of Medicine* (1983), 308:716–719.

5. President's Commission, *Deciding to Forego Life-Sustaining Treatment.*

6. D.L. Jackson and S. Youngner, "Patient Autonomy and Death with Dignity: Some Clinical Caveats," *New England Journal of Medicine* (1979), 301:404–408.

7. S. Bok, "Personal Directions for Care at the End of Life," *New England Journal of Medicine* (1976), 295:367–369.

8. A.S. Relman, "Michigan's Sensible Living Will." *New England Journal of Medicine* (1979), 300:1270–72.

9. "Durable Power of Attorney for Health Care," SB 762 (Keene) Ch. 1204 Stats 1983.

10. H. Nelson, "Life-Support Court Edict Leaves Physicians Cautious," *Los Angeles Times,* October 31, 1983.

11. J. Kirsch, "A Death at Kaiser Hospital," *California* (November 1982), pp.79ff.

12. Report of the Ad Hoc Committee of the Harvard Medical School to Examine the Definition of Brain Death, "A Definition of Irreversible Coma," *Journal of the American Medical Association* (1968), 205:377–340; A. Grenvik, D.J. Powner, J.V. Snyder, M.S. Jastremski, R. A. Babcock, and M.G. Loughhead, "Cessation of Therapy in Terminal Illness and Brain Death." *Critical Care Medicine* (1978), 6:284–291; and Report of the Medical Consultants on the Diagnosis of Death to the President's Commission for the Study of Ethical Problems in Medicine and Biomedical and Behavioral Research, "Guidelines for the Determination of Death," *Journal of the American Medical Association* (1981), 246:2184–2186.

13. A. Grenvik et al., "Cessation of Therapy in Terminal Illness and Brain Death," *Critical Care Medicine* (1978), 6:284–291; and a Report of the Clinical Care Committee of the Massachusetts General Hospital, "Optimum Care for Hopelessly Ill Patients," *New England Journal of Medicine* (1976), 295:362–364.

18

The Right To Refuse Treatment: A Model Act

Legal Advisers Committee of Concern for Dying

The most important right that patients possess is the right of self-determination, the right to make the ultimate decision concerning what will or will not be done to their bodies.[1] This right, embodied in the informed consent doctrine, has a critical and essential corollary: the right to refuse treatment.[2] Unless the right to refuse treatment is honored, the right of self-determination degenerates into a "right" to agree with one's physician.

Courts have recently declared that both the common law[3] and the United States Constitution[4] protect an individual's right to refuse medical treatment. These decisions might be seen as arguments against legislation that would reaffirm and enhance this right since such legislation might be viewed as either unnecessary or undesirable and confusing. On the other hand, cases continue to recur in which individuals are treated despite their competent objections or withdrawal of consent.[5] And although courts universally recognize the patient's right to refuse treat-

Reprinted from the American Journal of Public Health (August 1983), 73:918–21, with the permission of the publisher. Copyright © 1983 by the American Journal of Public Health. Footnotes renumbered.

ment, they have differed in their enunciation of the proper standards to be followed in implementing this right.[6] We believe the
centrality of the right to refuse treatment makes its periodic
reaffirmation appropriate, and a clear articulation of its applica-
bility in particular contexts is a proper subject for legislation.

Living Will and Natural Death Statutes

To help promote the right of self-determination by preventing
unwanted heroic medical interventions, many commentators
have proposed, and 12 states and the District of Columbia have
adopted, so-called "living will" or "natural death" statutes.[7] The
primary purpose of these statutes is to provide competent individuals with a mechanism to set forth in a document, called a
"living will," what they do and do not want done to them in
case they become mentally incompetent and require medical intervention to keep them alive.

   The rationale is that, with the advent of more effective
medical technology, patients may have their lives prolonged
painfully, expensively, fruitlessly, and against their wills. By
signing a prior statement, the patient hopes to avoid a technological imperative which commands that that which can be done,
must be done, and instead keep some control over his or her
medical treatment.

   Although specific provisions of these statutes vary, a typical statute allows patients to direct the withholding or withdrawal of medical treatment in the event the patient becomes
terminally ill. Most current "living will" statutes basically permit
physicians to honor a terminally ill patient's directive not to be
treated if the physician agrees that treatment is not indicated.
This, of course, can be done in the absence of any statute;[8] and
the current statutes do not so much enhance patients' rights as
they enhance provider privileges (i.e., physicians typically are
granted immunity if they follow a patient's directive, but are not
required to follow it if they do not want to).[9]

Previous Model Acts

Model statutes suggested by other commentators have been of three basic kinds: 1) syntheses of the best features of existing legislation and proposals;[10] 2) proposals to extend the right to refuse treatment to nonterminally ill patients;[11] and 3) proposals to permit the individual to designate another person to make the treatment decisions when the individual is unable to make them.[12] We believe all of these efforts are laudatory, and have attempted to incorporate in our own model the best of each current proposal. However, we also believe it is time to move beyond the limitations of "living will" and "natural death" legislation, and propose a model that incorporates all the features necessary in what might be considered "second generation" legislation. Such legislation:

should not be restricted to the terminally ill, but should apply to all competent adults and mature minors;

should not limit the types of treatment an individual can refuse   (e.g., to "extraordinary" treatment), but should apply to all medical interventions;

should permit individuals to designate another person to act on their behalf and set forth the criteria under which the designated person is to make decisions;

should require health care providers to follow the patient's wishes and provide sanctions for those who do not do so;

should require health care providers to continue to provide palliative care to patients who refuse other interventions.

The Model Legislation

The specific provisions of our proposal are set forth in the appendix to this article. Many of the sections are self-explanatory, but some merit additional comment. No specific form or document is included because we believe the individual's wishes will be more likely to be set forth if their own words are used.

It should be stressed initially that the right being reaffirmed is the right to refuse treatment implicit in any meaningful concept of individual liberty. Living will statutes, on the other hand, usually rely on a vaguely articulated "right to die" which has no legal pedigree. We include both adults and mature minors in the purview of the Act because we believe minors who understand the nature and consequences of their actions should not be forced to undergo medical treatment against their will.

COMPETENCE

The definitions seek to clarify the scope of the right by including all "competent" individuals who can understand the nature and consequences of their decisions. Thus while mature minors and previously competent individuals are included, individuals who have never been competent or who did not express their wishes while competent are not within the scope of the proposal. The competent person's understanding must be attested to by two adult witnesses at the time of an oral refusal. While the Act's definition of competence is consistent with the law of most states on this subject, hospitals may wish to develop objective criteria, procedures, and documentation requirements to assess competency accurately.

The competence standard used is a functional one, based on the individual's ability to give informed consent. It rejects any notion that a patient's decision must be consistent with the "medically rational choice" as defined by the physician. Competence is *the* crucial issue, since a lack of competence, or even the questioning of an individual's competence, deprives the individual of the power to make treatment decisions.

For example, in *Lane v. Candura*, a 77-year-old woman refused to permit amputation of her gangrenous leg. Her physician believed that this decision, which would lead to her death, was medically irrational, and that Mrs. Candura was incompetent.[13] As is often the case, Mrs. Candura's competence was not questioned at any time when she agreed to undergo recommended surgical procedures. The court noted that Candura's occasional fluctuations in mental lucidity did not affect her basic ability to understand what the doctor wanted to do and what would happen if he didn't: she knew that the doctor wanted to amputate her leg, and that he believed she would otherwise die. The court also clarified that the competent patient's decision must be respected even when, as in this case, physicians or others considered it unfortunate, medically irrational, or misguided. Using these principles, the court refused to appoint a guardian for Mrs. Candura since she had exhibited a reasonable appreciation of the issues surrounding the treatment refusal. Other courts have validated a competence definition substantially identical to the one used in this Act.[14]

The proposed Act aims at protecting the autonomy of not only terminally ill patients, but those who are not terminally ill as well. If we do not raise our sensitivity regarding respect for the nonterminal patient's right to autonomy, it is extremely unlikely that the rights of terminal patients will be respected. The Act also applies to patients like Karen Ann Quinlan who, while in a hopeless, persistent vegetative state, do not suffer from an underlying, terminal illness.

DESIGNATING A PROXY

The President's Commission for the Study of Ethical Problems in Medicine has recently noted that "by combining a proxy directive with specific instructions, an individual could control both the content and the process of decision-making about care in case of incapacity."[15] Concern for Dying's Act incorporates this suggestion by permitting the declarant to both define what interventions are refused, and to name an authorized individual to make decisions consistent with the declarant's desires as expressed in the declaration. Thirty-seven states currently have durable power of attorney laws that arguably permit such a designation, provided that the individual gives specific authorization regarding medical treatment. However, these statutes were passed long before living wills became an issue, and although we believe courts should honor medical decisions made by a proxy named under a durable power of attorney statute, there have been no reported cases on this issue to date.[16]

There is no time limit to the validity of declarations, just as there is no time limit on ordinary wills or on donations made under Uniform Anatomical Gift Acts. The primary protection regarding the authenticity of the wishes of a person is the requirement for two witnesses to certify that they believe the person understood what he was signing and did it voluntarily. We have not restricted the individuals who can be either witnesses or

Don Meloche

DEMANDE DE CONSULTATION

Patient référé par   Hôpital ☐   Bureau privé ☐

Nom du patient:

No assurance sociale:

Adresse:

Téléphone:

DIAGNOSTIC:

RECOMMANDATIONS:

authorized persons (e.g., the attending physician or relatives who might benefit under a will are not excluded because we think this unnecessarily implies bad faith on the part of categories of individuals and unnecessarily restricts the autonomy of a person to choose his own proxy and witnesses). Further, criminal penalties exist for falsification and forgery, and, if a physician or relative wants to harm the declarant, there are much easier ways to do it than by utilizing this mechanism. A second protection for the declarant is that revocation of a declaration is made easy. But the intent to revoke must be specific. Merely signing a blanket hospital admissions form that "consents" to whatever treatment physicians at the hospital wish to render is insufficient indication of revocation of a declaration.

RESPONSIBILITY OF PROVIDERS

The Model Act further clarifies that refusal of treatment does not terminate the physician–patient relationship, and that a physician who declines to follow the patient's wishes must transfer the patient to a physician who will. The Act recognizes that some providers may have different belief or value systems from the people they care for as patients, and attempts to establish a realistic procedure which allows the ethical views of both parties to be respected. However, the Act also recognizes that the patient is most immediately affected by failure to carry out a treatment-refusal decision, since the patient's own future and quality of life are at stake. Consequently, when a patient's directive and provider's view differ, the patient's directive must prevail over the physician's views on the rare occasions where transfer is impossible.

Providers who follow the procedures outlined in this Act are relieved of liability pursuant to any civil, criminal, or administrative action. However, providers who abandon their patients or refuse to comply with valid declarations are subject to sanctions. They may face civil actions including charges of negligence and battery. Administrative sanctions may include license revocation, suspension, or other disciplinary action by the state board of professional registration.

Other sections of the Act make it clear that this method of refusing treatment is not exclusive, but in addition to any other methods recogized by law; that the refusal of treatment is not suicide; that a treatment refusal does not affect any insurance policy; and that regardless of refusals, palliative care must be given unless specifically refused by the patient himself.

Summary

In summary, this model Right to Refuse Treatment Act clearly enunciates the competent person's right to refuse treatment, does not limit the exercise of this right to terminally ill patients or to extraordinary or heroic measures, and provides a mechanism by which a competent person can declare his or her intentions concerning treatment in the event of future incompetence, and can name another person to enforce this declaration.

The Act is designed to promote autonomy and respect for persons, by enhancing the individual's right to accept or reject medical treatments recommended by health care providers. It protects all competent persons, and incompetent persons who executed a declaration while they were competent. It provides that individuals may execute a written, signed declaration setting forth their intentions on treatment and refusal decisions and permits them to designate authorized individuals to make treatment decisions on their behalf, should they become incompetent in the future. The Act expresses, upholds, and clarifies recognized patient rights to autonomy and inviolability, recognition of which accords with the ethics of the medical profession; shields complying physicians, witnesses, and authorized persons acting in good faith, from liability; and provides sanctions for those who violate its provisions.

It has been almost three-quarters of a century since Judge Benjamin Cardozo wrote, regarding medical care that, "Every human being of adult years has a right to determine what shall be done with his own body."[17] Today's medical care would be incomprehensible to a physician practicing when these words were written. Nonetheless, medicine's success in radically improving its ability to prolong life has made the right of self-determination an even more vital principle. By proposing this Act, the Legal Advisers of Concern for Dying reaffirm the right to self-determination in the hope that the discussion fostered will enhance the liberty of all citizens.

Appendix

RIGHT TO REFUSE TREATMENT ACT

Section 1. Definitions

"Competent person" shall mean an individual who is able to understand and appreciate the nature and consequences of a decision to accept or refuse treatment.

"Declaration" shall mean a written statement executed according to the provisions of this Act which sets forth the declarant's intentions with respect to medical procedures, treatment or nontreatment, and may include the declarant's intentions concerning palliative care.

"Declarant" shall mean an individual who executes a declaration under the provisions of this Act.

"Health care provider" shall mean a person, facility or institution licensed or authorized to provide health care.

"Incompetent person" shall mean a person who is unable to understand and appreciate the nature and consequences of a decision to accept or refuse treatment.

"Medical procedure or treatment" shall mean any action taken by a physician or health care provider designed to diagnose, assess, or treat a disease, illness, or injury. These include, but are not limited to, surgery, drugs, transfusions, mechanical ventilation, dialysis, resuscitation, artificial feeding, and any other medical act designed for diagnosis, assessment or treatment.

"Palliative care" shall mean any measure taken by a physician or health care provider designed primarily to maintain the patient's comfort. These include, but are not limited to, sedatives and pain-killing drugs; nonartificial, oral feeding; suction; hydration; and hygienic care.

"Physician" shall mean any physician responsible for the declarant's care.

Section 2.

A competent person has the right to refuse any medical procedure or treatment, and any palliative care measure.

Section 3.

A competent person may execute a declaration directing the withholding or withdrawal of any medical procedure or treatment or any palliative care measure, which is in use or may be used in the future in the person's medical care or treatment, even if continuance of the medical procedure or treatment could prevent or postpone the person's death from being caused by the person's disease, illness or injury. The declaration shall be in writing, dated and signed by the declarant in the presence of two adult witnesses. The two witnesses must sign the declaration, and by their signatures indicate they believe the declarant's execution of the declaration was understanding and voluntary.

Section 4.

If a person is unable to sign a declaration due to a physical impairment, the person may execute a declaration by communicating agreement after the declaration has been read to the person in the presence of the two adult witnesses. The two witnesses must sign the declaration, and by their signatures indicate the person is physically impaired so as to be unable to sign the declaration, that the person understands the declaration's terms, and that the person voluntarily agrees to the terms of the declaration.

Section 5.

A declarant shall have the right to appoint in the declaration a person authorized to order the administration, withholding, or withdrawal of medical procedures and treatment in the event that the declarant becomes incompetent. A person so authorized shall have the power to enforce the provisions of the declaration and shall be bound to exercise this authority consistent with the declaration and the authorized person's best judgment as to the actual desires and preferences of the declarant. No palliative care measure may be withheld by an authorized person unless explicitly provided for in the declaration. Physicians and health care providers caring for incompetent declarants shall provide such authorized persons all medical information which would be available to the declarant if the declarant were competent.

Section 6.

Any declarant may revoke a declaration by destroying or defacing it, executing a written revocation, making an oral revocation, or by any other act evidencing the declarant's specific intent to revoke the declaration.

Section 7.

A competent person who orders the withholding or withdrawal of treatment shall receive appropriate palliative care unless it is expressly stated by the person orally or through a declaration that the person refuses palliative care.

Section 8.

This act shall not impair or supersede a person's legal right to direct the withholding or withdrawal of medical treatment or procedures in any other manner recognized by law.

Section 9.

No person shall require anyone to execute a declaration as a condition of enrollment, continuation, or receipt of benefits for disability, life, health or any other type of insurance. The withdrawal or withholding of medical procedures or treatment pursuant to the provisions of this Act shall not affect the validity of any insurance policy, and shall not constitute suicide.

Section 10.

This Act shall create no presumption concerning the intention of a person who has failed to execute a declaration. The fact that a person has failed to execute a declaration shall not constitute evidence of that person's intent concerning treatment or nontreatment.

Section 11.

A declaration made pursuant to this Act, an oral refusal by a person, or a refusal of medical procedures or treatment through an authorized person, shall be binding on all physicians and health care providers caring for the declarant.

Section 12.

A physician who fails to comply with a written or oral declaration and to make necessary arrangements to transfer the declarant to another physician

who will effectuate the delaration shall be subject to civil liability and professional disciplinary action, including license revocation or suspension. When acting in good faith to effectuate the terms of a declaration or when following the direction of an authorized person appointed in a declaration under Section 5, no physician or health care provider shall be liable in any civil, criminal, or administrative action for withholding or withdrawing any medical procedure, treatment, or palliative care measure. When acting in good faith, no witness to a declaration, or person authorized to make treatment decisions under Section 5, shall be liable in any civil, criminal, or administrative action.
Section 13.

A person found guilty of willfully concealing a declaration, or falsifying or forging a revocation of a declaration, shall be subject to criminal prosecution for a misdemeanor [the class or type of misdemeanor is left to the determination of individual state legislatures].
Section 14.

Any person who falsifies or forges a declaration or who willfully conceals or withholds information concerning the revocation of a declaration, with the intent to cause a withholding or withdrawal of life-sustaining procedures from a person, and who thereby causes life-sustaining procedures to be withheld or withdrawn and death to be hastened, shall be subject to criminal prosecution for a felony [the class or type of felony is left to the determination of individual state legislatures.]
Section 15.

If any provision or application of this Act is held invalid, this invalidity shall not affect other provisions or applications of the Act which can be given effect without the invalid provision or application, and to this end the provisions of this Act are severable.

Notes

1. G.J. Annas, L.H. Glantz, and B.F. Katz, *Informed Consent to Human Experimentation: The Subject's Dilemma* (Cambridge, Mass.: Ballinger, 1977).

2. N.L. Cantor, "A Patient's Decision to Decline Life-Saving Medical Treatment: Bodily Integrity Versus the Preservation of Life," *Rutgers Law Review* (1973), 26:228–264.

3. *In re Eichner*, 52 N.Y. 2d 363 (1981).

4. *Belchertown v. Saikewicz*, 370 N.E. 2d 417 (Ma. 1977).

5. *Satz v. Perlmutter*, 362 So. 2d 160 (Fla. Dist. Ct. App. 1978), affirmed, 379 So. 2d 359 (Fla. 1980); and *William James Foster v. Wallace W. Tourtellotte*, Dist. Ct. Order CV 81-5046-RMT (Mx), U.S. Dist. Ct. Central Dist. California (Nov. 16, 1981) (Takasugi, J).

6. *In re Quinlan*, 70 N.J. 10, 355 A.2d 647 (1976). See also *In re Eichner, Belcher-town v. Saikewicz.*

7. Alabama Code secs. 22-8A-1 to 22-8A-10 (Supp. 1981); Arkansas Stat. Ann. secs. 81-3801-3804 (Supp. 1981); California Health and Safety Code secs. 7185-7195 (Deering Supp. 1982); District of Columbia Code secs. 6-2421 to 2430 (Supp. 1982); Delaware Code Ann. tit. 16, secs. 2501-2509 (1982); Idaho Code secs. 39-4501 to 4508 (Supp. 1982); Kansas Stat. Ann. secs. 65-28.101 to 65-28.109 (Supp. 1981); Nevada Rev. Stat. secs. 449.540-.690 (1979); New Mexico Stat. Ann. secs. 24-7-1 to 24-7-11 (1981); North Carolina Gen. Stat. secs. 90-320 to 90-322 (1981); Oregon Rev. Stat. secs. 97.050-.090 (1981); Texas Rev. Civ. Stat. Ann. art. 4590h secs. 1-11 (Vernon 1982); 18 Vermont Stat. Ann. secs. 5251-5262 (1982); Washington Rev. Code. Ann. 70.122.010-70.122.905 (West 1982).

8. B. Dickens, "The Right to Natural Death," *McGill Law Journal* (1981), 26:847-879; E.W. Keyserling, *Sanctity of Life or Quality of Life* (Ottawa: Law Reform Commission of Canada, 1981); and Law Reform Commission of Canada, *Euthanasia, Aiding Suicide, and Cessation of Treatment*, Working Paper 28 (Ottawa: Law Reform Commission of Canada, 1982). See also Cantor, "A Patient's Decision", 228-264.

9. L. Kutner, "Due Process of Euthanasia: The Living Will, A Proposal," *Indiana Law Journal* (1969), 44:539–554; G.J. Annas, L.H. Glantz, and B.F. Katz, *The Rights of Doctors, Nurses, and Allied Health Professionals* (Cambridge, Mass.: Ballinger, 1981); S. Stephenson, "The Right To Die: A Proposal for Natural Death Legislation," *University of Cincinnati Law Review* (1980), 49:228-243; Beraldo, "Give Me Liberty and Give Me Death: The Right To Die and the California Natural Death Act," *Santa Clara Law Review* (1980), 20:971–991; Walters, "The Kansas Natural Death Act," *Washburn Law Journal* (1980), 19:519–535; Kutner, "The Living Will: Coping with the Historical Event of Death," *Baylor Law Review* (1975), 27:39–63; C. Hand, "Death with Dignity and the Terminally Ill: The Need for Legislative Action," *Nova Law Review* (1980), 4:257-269; Kite, "The Right to Die a Natural Death and the Living Will," *Texas Tech Law Review* (1982), 13:99–128; and Havens, "In re Living Will," *Nova Law Review* (1981), 5:446–470.

10. *Yale Law School Model Bill* (New York: Society for the Right to Die, Legislative Handbook 1981), pp. 23–26; R.P. Kaplan, "Euthanasia Legislation: A Survey and a Model Act," *American Journal of Law and Medicine* (1976), 2:41–99; and S. Stephenson, "The Right To Die: A Proposal for Natural Death Legislation." pp. 228-243.

11. G. Grisez and J.M. Boyle, *Life and Death with Liberty and Justice* (Notre Dame: University of Notre Dame Press, 1979), pp. 109–120.

12. R. Veatch, *Death, Dying and the Biological Revolution* (New Haven: Yale University Press, 1976), pp. 199–201; and A.S. Relman, "Michigan's Sensible Living Will," *New England Journal of Medicine* (1979), 300:270–271.

13. *Lane v. Candura*, 6 Mass. App. 377, 376 N.E. 2d 1232 (1978).

14. *In re Osborne*, 294 A. 2d 372 (D.C. 1972); *In re Melido*, 88 Misc. 2d 974, 390 N.Y.S. 2d 523 (1976), *In re Yetter*, 62 Pa. D. & C. 2d 619 (1973), and A.E. Doudera and J.D. Peters, eds., *Legal and Ethical Aspects of Treating*

15. President's Commission for the Study of Ethical Problems in Medicine and Biomedical and Behavioral Research, *Making Health Care Decisions* (Washington, DC: GPO, 1982), 1:155–160.

16. *Ibid.* Also "Legal Problems of the Aged and Infirm—The Durable Power of Attorney—Planned Protective Services and the Living Will," *Real Property, Probate and Trust Journal* (1978), 13:1-42.

17. *Scholendorf v. Society of New York Hospitals*, 211 N.Y. 125, 129 (1914).

19

The Least Worst Death

M. PABST BATTIN, Ph.D.

In recent years "right-to-die" movements have brought into the public consciousness something most physicians have long known: that in some hopeless medical conditions, heroic efforts to extend life may no longer be humane, and the physician must be prepared to allow the patient to die. Physician responses to patients' requests for "natural death" or "death with dignity" have been, in general, sensitive and compassionate. But the successes of the right-to-die movement have had a bitterly ironic result: institutional and legal protections for "natural death" have, in some cases, actually made it more painful to die.

There is just one legally protected mechanism for achieving natural death: refusal of medical treatment. It is available to both competent and incompetent patients. In the United States, the competent patient is legally entitled to refuse medical treatment of any sort on any personal or religious grounds, except perhaps where the interests of minor children are involved. A number of court cases, including *Quinlan, Saikewicz, Spring,* and

Reprinted from the *Hastings Center Report* (April 1983), 13:13–16, with the permission of the publishers. Copyright © 1983 by the Institute of Society, Ethics and the Life Sciences.

Eichner,[1] have established precedent in the treatment of an incompetent patient for a proxy refusal by a family member or guardian. In addition, eleven states now have specific legislation protecting the physician from legal action for failure to render treatment when a competent patient has executed a directive to be followed after he is no longer competent. A durable power of attorney, executed by the competent patient in favor of a trusted relative or friend, is also used to determine treatment choices after incompetence occurs.

An Earlier but Not Easier Death

In the face of irreversible, terminal illness, a patient may wish to die sooner but "naturally," without artificial prolongation of any kind. By doing so, the patient may believe he is choosing a death that is, as a contributor to the *New England Journal of Medicine* has put it, "comfortable, decent, and peaceful";[2] "natural death," the patient may assume, means a death that is easier than a medically prolonged one.[3] That is why he is willing to undergo death earlier and that is why, he assumes, natural death is legally protected. But the patient may conceive of "natural death" as more than pain-free; he may assume that it will allow time for reviewing life and saying farewell to family and loved ones, for last rites or final words, for passing on hopes, wisdom, confessions, and blessings to the next generation. These ideas are of course heavily stereotyped; they are the product of literary and cultural traditions associated with conventional death-bed scenes, reinforced by movies, books, and news stories, religious models, and just plain wishful thinking. Even the very term "natural" may have stereotyped connotations for the patient: something close to nature, uncontrived, and appropriate. As a result of these notions, the patient often takes "natural death" to be a painless, conscious, dignified, culminative slipping-away.

Now consider what sorts of death actually occur under the rubric of "natural death." A patient suffers a cardiac arrest and is not resuscitated. Result: sudden unconsciousness, without pain, and death within a number of seconds. Or a patient has an infection that is not treated. Result: the unrestrained multiplication of microorganisms, the production of toxins, interference with organ function, hypotension, and death. On the way there may be fever, delirium, rigor or shaking, and light-headedness; death usually takes one or two days, depending on the organism involved. If the kidneys fail and dialysis or transplant is not undertaken, the patient is generally more conscious, but experiences nausea, vomiting, gastrointestinal hemorrhage (evident in vomiting blood), inability to concentrate, neuromuscular irritability or twitching, and eventually convulsions. Dying may take from days to weeks, unless such circumstances as high potassium levels intervene. Refusal of amputation, although painless, is characterized by fever, chills, and foul-smelling tissues. Hypotension, characteristic of dehydration and many other states, is not painful but also not pleasant: the patient cannot sit up or get out of bed, has a dry mouth and thick tongue, and may find it difficult to talk. An untreated respiratory death involves conscious air hunger. This means gasping, an increased breathing rate, a panicked feeling of inability to get air in or out. Respiratory deaths may take only minutes; on the other hand, they may last for hours. If the patient refuses intravenous fluids, he may become dehydrated. If he refuses surgery for cancer, an organ may rupture. Refusal of treatment does not simply bring about death in a vacuum, so to speak; death always occurs from some specific cause.

Many patients who are dying in these ways are either comatose or heavily sedated. Such deaths do not allow for a period of conscious reflection at the end of life, nor do they permit farewell-saying, last rites, final words, or other features of the stereotypically "dignified" death.

Even less likely to match the patient's conception of natural death are those cases in which the patient is still conscious and competent, but meets a death that is quite different than he had bargained for. Consider the bowel cancer patient with widespread metastases and a very poor prognosis who—perhaps partly out of consideration for the emotional and financial resources of his family—refuses surgery to reduce or bypass the tumor. How, exactly, will he die? This patient is clearly within his legal rights in refusing surgery, but the physician knows what the outcome is very likely to be: obstruction of the intestinal tract will occur, the bowel wall will perforate, the abdomen will become distended, there will be intractable vomiting (perhaps with a fecal character to the emesis), and the tumor will erode into adjacent areas, causing increased pain, hemorrhage, and sepsis. Narcotic sedation and companion drugs may be partially effective in controlling pain, nausea, and vomiting, but this patient will *not* get the kind of death he thought he had bargained for. Yet, he was willing to shorten his life, to use the single legally protected mechanism—refusal of treatment—to achieve that "natural" death. Small wonder that many physicians are skeptical of the "gains" made by the popular movements supporting the right to die.

When the Right to Die Goes Wrong

Several distinct factors contribute to the backfiring of the right-to-die cause. First, and perhaps the most obvious, the patient may misjudge his own situation in refusing treatment or in executing a natural-death directive: his refusal may be precipitous and ill informed, based more on fear than on a settled desire to die. Second, the physician's response to the patient's request for "death with dignity" may be insensitive, rigid, or even punitive (though in my experience most physicians respond with compassion and wisdom). Legal constraints may also make natural death more difficult than might be hoped: safeguards often render natural-death requests and directives cumbersome to execute, and in any case, in a litigation-conscious society, the physician will often take the most cautious route.

But most important in the apparent backfiring of the right-to-die movement is the underlying ambiguity in the very concept of "natural death." Patients tend to think of the character of the experience they expect to undergo—a death that is "comfortable, decent, peaceful"—but all the law protects is the refusal of medical procedures. Even lawmakers sometimes confuse the two. The California and Kansas natural-death laws claim to protect what they romantically describe as "the natural process of dying." North Carolina's statute says it protects the right to a "peaceful and natural" death. But since these laws actually protect only refusal of treatment, they can hardly guarantee a peaceful, easy death. Thus, we see a widening gulf between the intent of the law to protect the patient's final desires, and the outcomes if the law is actually followed. The physician is caught in between: he recognizes his patient's right to die peacefully, naturally, and with whatever dignity is possible, but foresees the unfortunate results that may come about when the patient exercises this right as the law permits.

Of course, if the symptoms or pain become unbearable the patient may change his mind. The patient who earlier wished not to be "hooked up on tubes" now begins to experience difficulty in breathing or swallowing, and finds that a tracheotomy will relieve his distress. The bowel cancer patient experiences severe discomfort from obstruction, and gives permission for decompression or reductive surgery after all. In some cases, the family may engineer the change of heart because they find dying too hard to watch. Health care personnel may view these reversals with satisfaction: "See," they may say, "he really wants to live after all." But such reversals cannot always be interpreted as a triumph of the will to live; they may also be an indication that refusing treatment makes dying too hard.

Options for an Easier Death

How can the physician honor the dying patient's wish for a peaceful, conscious, and culminative death? There is more than one option.

Such a death can come about whenever the patient is conscious and painfree; he can reflect and, if family, clergy, or friends are summoned at the time, he will be able to communicate his wishes. Given these conditions, death can be brought on in various direct ways. For instance, the physician can administer a lethal quantity of an appropriate drug. Or the patient on severe dietary restrictions can violate his diet: the kidney-failure patient, for instance, for whom high potassium levels are fatal, can simply overeat on avocados. These ways of producing death are, of course, active euthanasia, or assisted or unassisted suicide. For many patients, such a death would count as "natural" and would satisfy the expectations under which they had chosen to die rather than to continue an intolerable existence. But for many patients (and for many physicians as well) a death that involves deliberate killing is morally wrong. Such a patient could never assent to an actively caused death, and even though it might be physically calm, it could hardly be emotionally or psychologically peaceful. This is not to say that active euthanasia or assisted suicide are morally wrong, but rather that the force of some patients' moral views about them precludes using such practices to achieve the kind of death they want. Furthermore, many physicians are unwilling to shoulder the legal risk such practices may seem to involve.

But active killing aside, the physician can do much to grant the dying patient the humane death he has chosen by using the sole legally protected mechanism that safeguards the right to die: refusal of treatment. This mechanism need not always backfire. For in almost any terminal condition, death can occur in various ways, and there are many possible outcomes of the patient's present condition. The patient who is dying of emphysema could die of respiratory failure, but could also die of cardiac arrest or untreated pulmonary infection. The patient who is suffering from bowel cancer could die of peritonitis following rupture of the bowel, but could also die of dehydration, of pulmonary infection, of acid–base imbalance, of electrolyte deficiency, or of an arrhythmia.

As the poet Rilke observes, we have a tendency to associate a certain sort of end with a specific disease: it is the "official death" for that sort of illness. But there are many other ways of dying than the official death, and the physician can take advantage of these. Infection and cancer, for instance, are old friends; there is increased frequency of infection in the immuno-compromised host. Other secondary conditions, like dehydration or metabolic derangement, may set in. Of course certain conditions typically occur a little earlier, others a little later, in the ordinary course of a terminal disease, and some are a matter of chance. The crucial point is that certain conditions will produce a death that is more comfortable, more decent, more predictable, and more permitting of conscious and peaceful experience than others. Some are better, if the patient has to die at all, and some are worse. Which mode of death claims the patient depends in part on circumstances and in part on the physician's response to conditions that occur. What the patient who rejects active euthanasia or assisted suicide may realistically hope for is this: the least worst death among those that could naturally occur. Not all unavoidable surrenders need involve rout; in the face of inevitable death, the physician becomes strategist, the deviser of plans for how to meet death most favorably.

He does so, of course, at the request of the patient, or, if the patient is not competent, the patient's guardian or kin. Patient autonomy is crucial in the notion of natural death. The physician could of course produce death by simply failing to offer a particular treatment to the patient. But to fail to *offer* treatment that might prolong life, at least when this does not compromise limited or very expensive resources to which other patients have claims, would violate the most fundamental principles of medical practice; some patients do not want "natural death," regardless of the physical suffering or dependency that prolongation of life may entail.

A scenario in which natural death is accomplished by the patient's selective refusal of treatment has one major advantage over active euthanasia and assisted suicide: refusal of treatment is clearly permitted and protected by law. Unfortunately, however, most patients do not have the specialized medical knowledge to use this self-protective mechanism intelligently. Few are aware that some kinds of refusal of treatment will better serve their desires for a "natural death" than others. And few patients realize that refusal of treatment can be selective. Although many patients with life-threatening illness are receiving multiple kinds of therapy, from surgery to nutritional support, most assume that it is only the major procedures (like surgery) that can be refused. (This misconception is perhaps perpetuated by the standard practice of obtaining specific consent for major procedures, like surgery, but not for minor, ongoing ones.) Then, too, patients may be unable to distinguish therapeutic from palliative procedures. And they may not understand the interaction between one therapy and another. In short, most patients do not have enough medical knowledge to foresee the consequences of refusing treatment on a selective basis; it is this that the physician must supply.

It is already morally and legally recognized that informed consent to a procedure involves explicit disclosure, both about the risks and outcomes of the proposed procedure and about the risks and outcomes of alternative possible procedures. Some courts, as in *Quackenbush*,[4] have also recognized the patient's right to explicit disclosure about the outcomes of refusing the proposed treatment. But though it is crucial in making a genuinely informed decision, the patient's right to information about the risks and outcomes of alternative kinds of refusal has not yet been recognized. So, for instance, in order to make a genuinely informed choice, the bowel cancer patient with concomitant infection will need to know about the outcomes of each of the principal options: accepting both bowel surgery and antibiotics; accepting antibiotics but not surgery; accepting surgery but not antibiotics; or accepting neither. The case may of course be more complex, but the principle remains: To recognize the patient's right to autonomous choice in matters concerning the treatment of his own body, the physician must provide information about all the legal options open to him, not just information sufficient to choose between accepting or rejecting a single proposed procedure.

One caveat: It sometimes occurs that physicians disclose the dismal probable consequences of refusing treatment in order to coerce patients into accepting the treatment they propose. This may be particularly common in surgery that will result in ostomy of the bowel. The patient is given a graphic description of the impending abdominal catastrophe—impaction, rupture, distention, hemorrhage, sepsis, and death. He thus consents readily to the surgery proposed. The paternalistic physician may find this maneuver appropriate, particularly since ostomy surgery is often refused out of vanity, depression, or on fatalistic grounds. But the physician who frightens a patient into accepting a procedure by describing the awful consequences of refusal is not honoring the patient's right to informed, autonomous choice: he has not described the various choices the patient could make, but only the worst.

Supplying the knowledge a patient needs in order to choose the least worst death need not require enormous amounts of additional energy or time on the part of the physician; it can be incorporated into the usual informed consent disclosures. If the patient is unable to accommodate the medical details, or instructs the physician to do what he thinks is best, the physician may use his own judgment in ordering and refraining from ordering treatment. If the patient clearly prefers to accept less life in hopes of an easy death, the physician should act in a way that will allow the least worst death to occur. In principle, however, the competent patient, and the proxy deciders for an incompetent patient, are entitled to explicit disclosure about all the alternatives for medical care. Physicians in burn units are already experienced in telling patients with very severe burns, where survival is unprecedented, what the outcome is likely to be if aggressive treatment is undertaken or if it is not—death in both cases, but under quite different conditions. Their expertise in these delicate matters might be most useful here. Informed refusal is just as much the patient's right as informed consent.

The role of the physician as strategist of natural death may be even more crucial in longer-term degenerative illnesses, where both physician and patient have far more advance warning that the patient's condition will deteriorate, and far more opportunity to work together in determining the conditions of the ultimate death. Of course, the first interest of both physician and patient will be strategies for maximizing the good life left. Nevertheless, many patients with long-term, eventually terminal illnesses, like multiple sclerosis, Huntington's chorea, diabetes, or chronic renal failure, may educate themselves considerably about the expected courses of their illnesses, and may display a good deal of anxiety about the end stages. This is particularly true in hereditary conditions where the patient may have watched a parent or relative die of the disease. But it is precisely in these conditions that the physician's opportunity may be greatest for humane guidance in the unavoidable matter of dying. He can help the patient to understand what the long-term options are in refusing treatment while he is competent, or help him to execute a natural-death directive or durable power of attorney that spells out the particulars of treatment refusal after he becomes incompetent.

Of course, some diseases are complex, and not easy to explain. Patients are not always capable of listening very well, especially to unattractive possibilities concerning their own ends. And physicians are sometimes reluctant to acknowledge that their efforts to sustain life will eventually fail. Providing such information may also seem to undermine whatever hope the physician can nourish in the patient. But the very fact that the patient's demise is still far in the future makes it possible for the physician to describe various scenarios of how that death could occur, and at the same time give the *patient* control over which of them will actually happen. Not all patients will choose the same strategies of ending, nor is there any reason that they should. What may count as the "least worst" death to one person may be the most feared form of death to another. The physician may be able to increase the patient's psychological comfort immensely by giving him a way of meeting an unavoidable death on his own terms.

In both acute and long-term terminal illnesses, the key to good strategy is flexibility in considering *all* the possibilities at hand. These alternatives need not include active euthanasia or suicide measures of any kind, direct or indirect. To take advantage of the best of the naturally occurring alternatives is not to cause the patient's death, which will happen anyway, but to guide him away from the usual, frequently worst, end.

In the current enthusiasm for "natural death" it is not patient autonomy that dismays physicians. What does dismay them is the way in which respect for patient autonomy can lead to cruel results. The cure for that dismay lies in the realization that the physician can contribute to the *genuine* honoring of the patient's autonomy and rights, assuring him of "natural death" in the way in which the patient understands it, and still remain within the confines of good medical practice and law.

Notes

1. *In re Quinlan*, 355 A. 2d 647 (N.J. 1976); *Superintendent of Belchertown v. Saikewicz*, 370 N.E. 2d 417 (Mass. 1977); *In re Spring*, Mass. App., 399 N.E. 2d 493; *In re Eichner*, 73 A.D. 2d 431 (2nd Dept. 1980).

2. S. S. Spencer, " 'Code' or 'No Code': A Nonlegal Opinion," *New England Journal of Medicine* (1979), 300:138–140.

3. See Dallas M. High's analysis of the various senses of the term "natural death" in ordinary language, in "Is 'Natural Death' an Illusion?" *Hastings Center Report* (August 1978), pp. 37–42.

4. *In re Quackenbush*, 156 N.J. Super. 282, 353 A. 2d 785 (1978).

20

Must Patients Always Be Given Food and Water?

JOANNE LYNN, M.D. AND JAMES F. CHILDRESS, Ph.D.

M any people die from the lack of food or water. For some, this lack is the result of poverty or famine, but for others it is the result of disease or deliberate decision. In the past, malnutrition and dehydration must have accompanied nearly every death that followed an illness of more than a few days. Most dying patients do not eat much on their own, and nothing could be done for them until the first flexible tubing for instilling food or other liquid into the stomach was developed about a hundred years ago. Even then, the procedure was so scarce, so costly in physician and nursing time, and so poorly tolerated that it was used only for patients who clearly could benefit. With the advent of more reliable and efficient procedures in the past few decades, these conditions can be corrected or ameliorated in nearly every patient who would otherwise be malnourished or dehydrated. In fact, intravenous lines and nasogastric tubes have become common images of hospital care.

Providing adequate nutrition and fluids is a high priority

Reprinted from the *Hastings Center Report* (October 1983), 13:17–21, with the permission of the publishers. Copyright © 1983 by the Institute of Society, Ethics and the Life Sciences. Some footnotes omitted.

for most patients, both because they suffer directly from inadequacies and because these deficiencies hinder their ability to overcome other diseases. But are there some patients who need not receive these treatments? This question has become a prominent public policy issue in a number of recent cases. In May 1981, in Danville, Illinois, the parents and the physician of newborn conjoined twins with shared abdominal organs decided not to feed these children. Feeding and other treatments were given after court intervention, though a grand jury refused to indict the parents. Later that year, two physicians in Los Angeles discontinued intravenous nutrition to a patient who had severe brain damage after an episode involving loss of oxygen following routine surgery. Murder charges were brought, but the hearing judge dismissed the charges at a preliminary hearing. On appeal, the charges were reinstated and remanded for trial.

In April 1982, a Bloomington, Indiana, infant who had tracheoesophageal fistula and Down syndrome was not treated or fed, and he died after two courts ruled that the decision was proper but before all appeals could be heard. When the federal government then moved to ensure that such infants would be fed in the future, the Surgeon General, Dr. C. Everett Koop, initially stated that there is never adequate reason to deny nutrition and fluids to a newborn infant.

While these cases were before the public, the nephew of Clare Conroy, an elderly incompetent woman with several serious medical problems, petitioned a New Jersey court for authority to discontinue her nasogastric tube feedings. Although the intermediate appeals court has reversed the ruling, the trial court held that he had this authority since the evidence indicated that the patient would not have wanted such treatment and that its value to her was doubtful.

In all these dramatic cases and in many more that go unnoticed, the decision is made to deliberately withhold food or fluid known to be necessary for the life of the patient. Such decisions are unsettling. There is now widespread consensus that sometimes a patient is best served by not undertaking or continuing certain treatments that would sustain life, especially if these entail substantial suffering.[1] But food and water are so central to an array of human emotions that it is almost impossible to consider them with the same emotional detachment that one might feel toward a respirator or a dialysis machine.

Nevertheless, the question remains: should it ever be permissible to withhold or withdraw food and nutrition? The answer in any real case should acknowledge the psychological contiguity between feeding and loving and between nutritional satisfaction and emotional satisfaction. Yet this acknowledgment does not resolve the core question.

Some have held that it is intrinsically wrong not to feed another. The philosopher G. E. M. Anscombe contends: "For wilful starvation there can be no excuse. The same can't be said quite without qualification about failing to operate or to adopt some courses of treatment."[2] But the moral issues are more complex than Anscombe's comment suggests. Does correcting nutritional deficiencies always improve patients' well-being? What should be our reflective moral response to withholding or withdrawing nutrition? What moral principles are relevant to our reflections? What medical facts about ways of providing nutrition are relevant? And what policies should be adopted by the society, hospitals, and medical and other health care professionals?

In our effort to find answers to these questions, we will concentrate upon the care of patients who are incompetent to make choices for themselves. Patients who are competent to determine the course of their therapy may refuse any and all interventions proposed by others, as long as their refusals do not seriously harm or impose unfair burdens upon others. A competent patient's decision regarding whether or not to accept the provision of food and water by medical means such as tube feeding or intravenous alimentation is unlikely to raise questions of harm or burden to others.

What then should guide those who must decide about nutrition for a patient who cannot decide? As a start, consider the standard by which other medical decisions are made: one should decide as the incompetent person would have if he or she were competent, when that is possible to determine, and advance that person's interests in a more generalized sense when individual preferences cannot be known.

The Medical Procedures

There is no reason to apply a different standard to feeding and hydration. Surely, when one inserts a feeding tube, or creates a gastrostomy opening, or inserts a needle into a vein, one intends to benefit the patient. Ideally, one should provide what the patient believes to be of benefit, but at least the effect should be beneficial in the opinions of surrogates and caregivers.

Thus, the question becomes: is it ever in the patient's interest to become malnourished and dehydrated, rather than to receive treatment? Posing the question so starkly points to our need to know what is entailed in treating these conditions and what benefits the treatments offer.

The medical interventions that provide food and fluids are of two basic types. First, liquids can be delivered by a tube that is inserted into a functioning gastrointestinal tract, most commonly through the nose and esophagus into the stomach or through a surgical incision in the abdominal wall and directly into the stomach. The liquids used can be specially prepared solutions of nutrients or a blenderized version of an ordinary diet. The nasogastric tube is cheap; it may lead to pneumonia and often annoys the patient and family, sometimes even requiring that the patient be restrained to prevent its removal.

Creating a gastrostomy is usually a simple surgical procedure, and, once the wound is healed, care is very simple. Since it is out of sight, it is aesthetically more acceptable and restraints are needed less often. Also, the gastrostomy creates no additional risk of pneumonia. However, while elimination of a nasogastric tube requires only removing the tube, a gastrostomy is fairly permanent, and can be closed only by surgery.

The second type of medical intervention is intravenous feeding and hydration, which also has two major forms. The ordinary hospital or peripheral IV, in which fluid is delivered directly to the bloodstream through a small needle, is useful only for temporary efforts to improve hydration and electrolyte concentrations. One cannot provide a balanced diet through the veins in the limbs: to do that requires a central line, or a special catheter placed into one of the major veins in the chest. The latter procedure is much more risky and vulnerable to infections and technical errors, and it is much more costly than any of the other procedures. Both forms of intravenous nutrition and hydration commonly require restraining the patient, cause minor infections and other ill effects, and are costly, especially since they ordinarily require the patient to be in a hospital.

None of these procedures, then, is ideal; each entails some distress, some medical limitations, and some costs. When may a procedure be foregone that might improve nutrition and hydration for a given patient? Only when the procedure and the resulting improvement in nutrition and hydration do not offer the patient a net benefit over what he or she would otherwise have faced.

Are there such circumstances? We believe that there are; but they are few and limited to the following three kinds of situations: 1. The procedures that would be required are so unlikely to achieve improved nutritional and fluid levels that they could be correctly considered futile; 2. The improvement in nutritional and fluid balance, though achievable, could be of no benefit to the patient; 3. The burdens of receiving the treatment may outweigh the benefit.

When Food and Water May Be Withheld

FUTILE TREATMENT

Sometimes even providing "food and water" to a patient becomes a monumental task. Consider a patient with a severe clotting deficiency and a nearly total body burn. Gaining access to the central veins is likely to cause hemorrhage or infection, nasogastric tube placement may be quite painful, and there may be no skin to which to suture the stomach for a gastrostomy tube. Or consider a patient with severe congestive heart failure who develops cancer of the stomach with a fistula that delivers food from the stomach to the colon without passing through the intestine and being absorbed. Feeding the patient may be possible, but little is absorbed. Intravenous feeding cannot be tolerated because the fluid would be too much for the weakened heart. Or consider the infant with infarction of all but a short segment of bowel. Again, the infant can be fed, but little if anything is absorbed. Intravenous methods can be used, but only for a short time (weeks or months) until their complications, including thrombosis, hemorrhage, infections, and malnutrition, cause death.

In these circumstances, the patient is going to die soon, no matter what is done. The ineffective efforts to provide nutrition and hydration may well directly cause suffering that offers no counterbalancing benefit for the patient. Although the procedures might be tried, especially if the competent patient wanted them or the incompetent patient's surrogate had reason to believe that this incompetent patient would have wanted them, they cannot be considered obligatory. To hold that a patient must be subjected to this predictably futile sort of intervention just because protein balance is negative or the blood serum is concentrated is to lose sight of the moral warrant for medical care and to reduce the patient to an array of measurable variables.

NO POSSIBILITY OF BENEFIT

Some patients can be reliably diagnosed to have permanently lost consciousness. This unusual group of patients includes those with anencephaly, persistent vegetative state, and some preterminal comas. In these cases, it is very difficult to discern how any medical intervention can benefit or harm the patient. These patients cannot and never will be able to experience any of the events occurring in the world or in their bodies. When the diagnosis is exceedingly clear, we sustain their lives vigorously mainly for their loved ones and the community at large.

While these considerations probably indicate that continued artificial feeding is best in most cases, there may be some cases in which the family and the caregivers are convinced that artificial feeding is offensive and unreasonable. In such cases, there seems to be no adequate reason to claim that withholding food and water violates any obligations that these parties or the general society have with regard to permanently unconscious patients. Thus, if the parents of an anencephalic infant or of a patient like Karen Quinlan in a persistent vegetative state feel strongly that no medical procedures should be applied to provide nutrition and hydration, and the caregivers are willing to comply, there should be no barrier in law or public policy to thwart the plan.[3]

DISPROPORTIONATE BURDEN

The most difficult cases are those in which normal nutritional status or fluid balance could be restored, but only with a severe burden for the patient. In these cases, the treatment is futile in a broader sense—the patient will not actually benefit from the improved nutrition and hydration. A patient who is competent can decide the relative merits of the treatment being provided, knowing the probable consequences, and weighing the merits of life under various sets of constrained circumstances. But a surrogate decision maker for a patient who is incompetent to decide will have a difficult task. When the situation is irremediably ambiguous, erring on the side of continued life and improved nutrition and hydration seems the less grievous error. But are there situations that would warrant a determination that this patient, whose nutrition and hydration could surely be improved, is not thereby well served?

Though they are rare, we believe there are such cases. The treatments entailed are not benign. Their efforts are far short of ideal. Furthermore, many of the patients most likely to have inadequate food and fluid intake are also likely to suffer the most serious side effects of these therapies.

Patients who are allowed to die without artificial hydration and nutrition may well die more comfortably than patients who receive conventional amounts of intravenous hydration.[4] Terminal pulmonary edema, nausea, and mental confusion are more likely when patients have been treated to maintain fluid and nutrition until close to the time of death.

Thus, those patients whose "need" for artificial nutrition and hydration arises only near the time of death may be harmed by its provision. It is not at all clear that they receive any benefit in having a slightly prolonged life, and it does seem reasonable to allow a surrogate to decide that, for this patient at this time, slight prolongation of life is not warranted if it involves measures that will probably increase the patient's suffering as he or she dies.

Even patients who might live much longer might not be

well served by artificial means to provide fluid and food. Such patients might include those with fairly severe dementia for whom the restraints required could be a constant source of fear, discomfort, and struggle. For such a patient, sedation to tolerate the feeding mechanisms might preclude any of the pleasant experiences that might otherwise have been available. Thus, a decision not to intervene, except perhaps briefly to ascertain that there are no treatable causes, might allow such a patient to live out a shorter life with fair freedom of movement and freedom from fear, while a decision to maintain artificial nutrition and hydration might consign the patient to end his or her life in unremitting anguish. If this were the case a surrogate decision maker would seem to be well justified in refusing the treatment.

Inappropriate Moral Constraints

Four considerations are frequently proposed as moral constraints on foregoing medical feeding and hydration. We find none of these to dictate that artificial nutrition and hydration must always be provided.

THE OBLIGATION TO PROVIDE "ORDINARY" CARE

Debates about appropriate medical treatment are often couched in terms of "ordinary" and "extraordinary" means of treatment. Historically, this distinction emerged in the Roman Catholic tradition to differentiate optional treatment from treatment that was obligatory for medical professionals to offer and for patients to accept.[5] These terms also appear in many secular contexts, such as court decisions and medical codes. The recent debates about ordinary and extraordinary means of treatment have been interminable and often unfruitful, in part because of a lack of clarity about what the terms mean. Do they represent the premises of an argument or the conclusion, and what features of a situation are relevant to the categorization as "ordinary" or "extraordinary"?[6]

Several criteria have been implicit in debates about ordinary and extraordinary means of treatment; some of them may be relevant to determining whether and which treatments are obligatory and which are optional. Treatments have been distinguished according to their simplicity (simple/complex), their naturalness (natural/artificial), their customariness (usual/unusual), their invasiveness (noninvasive/invasive), their chance of success (reasonable chance/futile), their balance of benefits and burdens (proportionate/disproportionate), and their expense (inexpensive/costly). Each set of paired terms or phrases in the parentheses suggests a continuum: as the treatment moves from the first of the paired terms to the second, it is said to become less obligatory and more optional.

However, when these various criteria, widely used in discussions about medical treatment, are carefully examined, most of them are not morally relevant in distinguishing optional from obligatory medical treatments. For example, if a rare, complex, artificial, and invasive treatment offers a patient a reasonable chance of nearly painless cure, then one would have to offer a substantial justification not to provide that treatment to an incompetent patient.

What matters, then, in determining whether to provide a treatment to an incompetent patient is not a prior determination that this treatment is "ordinary" per se, but rather a determination that this treatment is likely to provide this patient benefits that are sufficient to make it worthwhile to endure the burdens that accompany the treatment. To this end, some of the considerations listed above are relevant: whether a treatment is likely to succeed is an obvious example. But such considerations taken in isolation are not conclusive. Rather, the surrogate decision maker is obliged to assess the desirability to this patient of each of the options presented, including nontreatment. For most people at most times, this assessment would lead to a clear obligation to provide food and fluids.

But sometimes, as we have indicated, providing food and fluids through medical interventions may fail to benefit and may even harm some patients. Then the treatment cannot be said to be obligatory, no matter how usual and simple its provision may be. If "ordinary" and "extraordinary" are used to convey the conclusion about the obligation to treat, providing nutrition and fluids would have become, in these cases, "extraordinary." Since this phrasing is misleading, it is probably better to use "proportionate" and "disproportionate," as the Vatican now suggests,[7] or "obligatory" and "optional."

Obviously, providing nutrition and hydration may sometimes be necessary to keep patients comfortable while they are dying even though it may temporarily prolong their dying. In such cases, food and fluids constitute warranted palliative care. But in other cases, such as a patient in a deep and irreversible coma, nutrition and hydration do not appear to be needed or helpful, except perhaps to comfort the staff and family. And sometimes the interventions needed for nutrition and hydration are so burdensome that they are harmful and best not utilized.

THE OBLIGATION TO CONTINUE TREATMENTS ONCE STARTED

Once having started a mode of treatment, many caregivers find it very difficult to discontinue it. While this strongly felt difference between the ease of withholding a treatment and the difficulty of withdrawing it provides a psychological explanation of certain actions, it does not justify them. It sometimes even leads to a thoroughly irrational decision process. For example, in caring for a dying, comatose patient, many physicians apparently find it harder to stop a functioning peripheral IV than not to restart one that has infiltrated (that is, has broken through the blood vessel and is leaking fluid into surrounding tissue), especially if the only way to reestablish an IV would be to insert a central line into the heart or to do a cutdown (make an incision to gain access to the deep large blood vessels).[8]

What factors might make withdrawing medical treatment morally worse than withholding it? Withdrawing a treatment seems to be an action, which, when it is likely to end in death, initially seems more serious than an omission that ends in death. However, this view is fraught with errors. Withdrawing is not always an act: failing to put the next infusion into a tube could be correctly described as an omission, for example. Even when withdrawing is an act, it may well be morally correct and even morally obligatory. Discontinuing intravenous lines in a patient now permanently unconscious in accord with that patient's well-informed advance directive would certainly be such a case. Furthermore, the caregiver's obligation to serve the patient's interests through both acts and omissions rules out the exculpation that accompanies omissions in the usual course of social life. An omission that is not warranted by the patient's interests is culpable.

Sometimes initiating a treatment creates expectations in the minds of caregivers, patients, and family that the treatment will be continued indefinitely or until the patient is cured. Such expectations may provide a reason to continue the treatment as a way to keep a promise. However, as with all promises, caregivers could be very careful when initiating a treatment to explain the indications for its discontinuation, and they could modify preconceptions with continuing reevaluation and education during treatment. Though all patients are entitled to expect the continuation of care in the patient's best interests, they are not and should not be entitled to the continuation of a particular mode of care.

Accepting the distinction between withholding and withdrawing medical treatment as morally significant also has a very unfortunate implication: caregivers may become unduly reluctant to begin some treatments precisely because they fear that they will be locked into continuing treatments that are no longer a value to the patient. For example, the physician who had been unwilling to stop the respirator while the infant, Andrew Stinson, died over several months is reportedly "less eager to attach babies to respirators now."[9] But if it were easier to ignore malnutrition and dehydration and to withhold treatments for these problems than to discontinue the same treatments when they have become especially burdensome and insufficiently beneficial for this patient, then the incentives would be perverse. Once a treatment has been tried, it is often much clearer whether it is of value to this patient, and the decision to stop it can be made more reliably.

The same considerations should apply to starting as to stopping a treatment, and whatever assessment warrants withholding should also warrant withdrawing.

THE OBLIGATION TO AVOID BEING THE UNAMBIGUOUS CAUSE OF DEATH

Many physicians will agree with all that we have said and still refuse to allow a choice to forego food and fluid because such a course seems to be a "death sentence." In this view death seems to be more certain from malnutrition and dehydration than from foregoing other forms of medical therapy. This implies that it is acceptable to act in ways that are likely to cause death, as in not operating on a gangrenous leg, only if there remains a chance that the patient will survive. This is a comforting formulation for caregivers, to be sure, since they can thereby avoid feeling the full weight of the responsibility for the time and manner of a patient's death. However, it is not a persuasive moral argument.

First, in appropriate cases discontinuing certain medical treatments is generally accepted despite the fact that death is as certain as with nonfeeding. Dialysis in a patient without kidney function or transfusions in a patient with severe aplastic anemia are obvious examples. The dying that awaits such patients often is not greatly different from dying of dehydration and malnutrition.

Second, the certainty of a generally undesirable outcome such as death is always relevant to a decision, but it does not foreclose the possibility that this course is better than others available to this patient. Ambiguity and uncertainty are so common in medical decision making that caregivers are tempted to use them in distancing themselves from direct responsibility. However, caregivers are in fact responsible for the time and manner of death for many patients. Their distaste for this fact should not constrain otherwise morally justified decisions.

THE OBLIGATION TO PROVIDE SYMBOLICALLY SIGNIFICANT TREATMENT

One of the most common arguments for always providing nutrition and hydration is that it symbolizes, expresses, or conveys the essence of care and compassion. Some actions not only aim at goals, they also express values. Such expressive actions should not simply be viewed as means to ends; they should also be viewed in light of what they communicate. From this perspective food and water are not only goods that preserve life and provide comfort; they are also symbols of care and compassion. To withhold or withdraw them—to "starve" a patient—can never express or convey care.

Why is providing food and water a central symbol of care and compassion? Feeding is the first response of the community to the needs of newborns and remains a central mode of nurture and comfort. Eating is associated with social interchange and community, and providing food for someone else is a way to create and maintain bonds of sharing and expressing concern. Furthermore, even the relatively low levels of hunger and thirst that most people have experienced are decidedly uncomfortable, and the common image of severe malnutrition or dehydration is one of unremitting agony. Thus, people are rightly eager to provide food and water. Such provision is essential to minimally tolerable existence and a powerful symbol of our concern for each other.

However, *medical* nutrition and hydration, we have argued, may not always provide net benefits to patients. Medical procedures to provide nutrition and hydration are more similar to other medical procedures than to typical human ways of providing nutrition and hydration, for example, a sip of water. It should be possible to evaluate their benefits and burdens, as we evaluate any other medical procedure. Of course, if family, friends, and caregivers feel that such procedures affirm important values even when they do not benefit the patient, their feelings should not be ignored. We do not contend that there is an obligation to withhold or to withdraw such procedures (unless consideration of the patient's advance directives or current best interest unambiguously dictates that conclusion); we only contend that nutrition and hydration may be foregone in some cases.

The symbolic connection between care and nutrition or hydration adds useful caution to decision making. If decision makers worry over withholding or withdrawing medical nutrition and hydration, they may inquire more seriously into the circumstances that putatively justify their decisions. This is generally salutary for health care decision making. The critical inquiry may well yield the sad but justified conclusion that the patient will be served best by not using medical procedures to provide food and fluids.

A Limited Conclusion

Our conclusion—that patients or their surrogates, in close collaboration with their physicians and other caregivers and with careful assessment of the relevant information, can correctly decide to forego the provision of medical treatments intended to correct malnutrition and dehydration in some circumstances—is quite limited. Concentrating on incompetent patients, we have argued that in most cases such patients will be best served by providing nutrition and fluids. Thus, there should be a presumption in favor of providing nutrition and fluids as part of the broader presumption to provide means that prolong life. But this presumption may be rebutted in particular cases.

We do not have enough information to be able to determine with clarity and conviction whether withholding or withdrawing nutrition and hydration was justified in the cases that have occasioned public concern, though it seems likely that the Danville and Bloomington babies should have been fed and that Claire Conroy should not.

It is never sufficient to rule out "starvation" categorically. The question is whether the obligation to act in the patient's best interests was discharged by withholding or withdrawing particular medical treatments. All we have claimed is that nutrition and hydration by medical means need not always be provided. Sometimes they may not be in accord with the patient's wishes or interests. Medical nutrition and hydration do not appear to be distinguishable in any morally relevant way from other life-sustaining medical treatments that may on occasion be withheld or withdrawn.

Notes

1. The President's Commission for the Study of Ethical Problems in Medicine and Biomedical and Behavioral Research, *Deciding to Forego Life-Sustaining Treatment* (Washington, D. C.: GPO, 1982).

2. G. E. M. Anscombe, "Ethical Problems in the Management of Some Severely Handicapped Children: Commentary 2," *Journal of Medical Ethics* (1981), 7:122.

3. President's Commission, *Deciding to Forego Life-Sustaining Treatment,* pp. 171–196.

4. Joyce V. Zerwekh, "The Dehydration Question," *Nursing83* (January 1983), 47–51, with comments by Judith R. Brown and Marion B. Dolan.

5. James J. McCartney, "The Development of the Doctrine of Ordinary and Extraordinary Means of Preserving Life in Catholic Moral Theology before the Karen Quinlan Case," *Linacre Quarterly* (1980), 47:215ff.

6. President's Commission, *Deciding to Forego Life-Sustaining Treatment,* pp. 82–90. For an argument that fluids and electrolytes can be "extraordinary," see Carson Strong, "Can Fluids and Electrolytes be 'Extraordinary' Treatment?" *Journal of Medical Ethics* (1981), 7:83–85.

7. The Sacred Congregation for the Doctrine of the Faith, *Declaration on Euthanasia,* Vatican City, May 5, 1980.

8. See Kenneth C. Micetich, Patricia H. Steinecker, and David C. Thomasma, "Are Intravenous Fluids Morally Required for a Dying Patient?" *Archives of Internal Medicine* (May 1983), 143:975–978.

9. Robert and Peggy Stinson, *The Long Dying of Baby Andrew* (Boston: Little, Brown, 1983), p. 355.

21

On Feeding the Dying

DANIEL CALLAHAN, Ph.D.

Feeling and sentiment are rarely absent from a well-ordered moral life. They serve to reinforce our convictions, warn us clamorously when some cherished values are in danger, and alert us that the consequences of some action may carry untoward ethical insults. If they are not always reliable guides, their absence is even more hazardous, as anyone who has dealt with a sociopath is painfully aware.

What, then, are we to make of those circumstances in which our traditional or characteristic moral sentiments no longer seem appropriate? The recent and vigorous appearance of a debate on the provision of nutrition to dying, or comatose, or vegetative patients seems to signal such a circumstance. The issue is not entirely new, and references to it can be found in some older manuals of moral theology. But it was never a widely discussed topic.

Why has it reemerged now? First, I suspect not simply because of a few well-publicized cases, but because a denial of

Reprinted from the *Hastings Center Report* (October 1983), 13:22, with the permission of the publishers. Copyright © 1983 by the Institute of Society, Ethics and the Life Sciences.

nutrition may in the long run become the only effective way to make certain that a large number of biologically tenacious patients actually die. Given the increasingly large pool of superannuated, chronically ill, physically marginal elderly, it could well become the nontreatment of choice. Second, because we have now become sufficiently habituated to the idea of turning off a respirator, we are psychologically prepared to go one step further. Indeed, a consistent line of opinion, from the older manuals through to the present, is that there is no logical or moral difference between the two actions.

My problem is less with the rigor of those arguments than it is in knowing what to do with a stubborn emotional repugnance against a discontinuance of nutrition. By the logic of the argument that nutrition can be burdensome "treatment," the family of Karen Ann Quinlan would long ago have been justified in asking that her feeding be discontinued. Even Paul Ramsey, never casual or lax about such matters, wrote in the *Hastings Center Report* in February 1976 that "the IV is as aimless as the respirator. It, too, is only prolonging Karen's dying" (p. 16). But he also reported that her father, Joseph Quinlan, was amazed when asked if he wanted the intravenous feeding stopped: "Oh no, that is her nourishment."

No one, so far as I can recall, criticized Mr. Quinlan for that decision. But that was almost ten years ago, when it was still uncommon to turn off respirators and the arguments for doing so were less secured in public and professional opinion. It has taken almost that long for the old distinction between killing and allowing to die, omission and commission, to have some public bite. Yet if we have now come to accept and institutionalize that distinction, and if artificial feeding and artificial respirators are taken to be morally identical, then it is possible to ask a disturbing question: If the feeding of Karen Anne Quinlan is (a) no more than a prolongation of her dying, and (b) morally no different an act than the long since discontinued artificial respiration, and (c) costly to society (paid for by Medicaid)—well, then, what possible rational case could be made to allow her father to indulge that sentiment, particularly at public expense?

Do I perhaps go too far in my question? No one, to be sure, has argued that feeding *must* be discontinued when it will do no more good than artificial respiration, only that it *may* be discontinued under such conditions. But we would do well here to recall the customary history of allowable but nonmandatory medical interventions. In the case of the definition of death, for example, it is no longer customary to allow a person who has suffered from death of the whole brain to be maintained on a respirator simply because the family wants that done. Hard rationality prevails: the respirator does the (dead) patient no good; therefore it must be discontinued. Is it an extravagant exercise of the imagination to envision a time in the future when a similar logic will prevail: feeding does an (irreversibly comatose) patient no good; therefore it must be stopped?

The only impediment to the enactment of that kind of policy is a cluster of sentiments and emotions that is repelled by the idea of starving someone to death, even in those cases where it might be for the patient's own good. Unless we begin now to reeducate public emotions, we can be certain that the offending sentiments will be perpetuated into another generation. Many will live on who, but for greater rationality and logical consistency, would mercifully have been—what can we euphemistically call it?—deintubated.

I would like to cast a vote against that kind of educational program. The feeding of the hungry, whether because they are poor or because they are physically unable to feed themselves, is the most fundamental of all human relationships. It is the perfect symbol of the fact that human life is inescapably social and communal. We cannot live at all unless others are prepared to give us food and water when we need them. If the duty of parents toward infants provides a perfect example of inescapable moral obligation, the giving of nourishment is its first and most basic manifestation.

It is a most dangerous business to tamper with, or adulterate, so enduring and central a moral emotion, one in which the repugnance against starving people to death could be, on occasion, greater than that which a more straitened rationality would call for.

Yet, that said, I cannot deny the moral licitness of the discontinuation of feeding under some circumstances (for example, those specified by Lynn and Childress). Can this struggle between head and heart be resolved? Yes. I see no social disaster in the offing if there remains a deep-seated revulsion at the stopping of feeding even under legitimate circumstances. No doubt some people will live on in ways beneficial neither to them nor to others. No doubt a good bit of money will be wasted indulging rationally hard-to-defend anti-starvation policies. That strikes me as a tolerable price to pay to preserve—with ample margin to spare—one of the few moral emotions that could just as easily be called a necessary social instinct.

22

Satz v. Perlmutter

District Court of Appeal of Florida,
363 So.2d 160 (1978)

LETTS, Judge:

The state here appeals a trial court order permitting the removal of an artificial life sustaining device from a competent, but terminally ill adult. We affirm.

Seventy-three year old Abe Perlmutter lies mortally sick in a hospital, suffering from amyotrophic lateral sclerosis (Lou Gehrig's disease) diagnosed in January 1977. There is no cure and normal life expectancy, from time of diagnosis, is but two years. In Mr. Perlmutter, the affliction has progressed to the point of virtual incapability of movement, inability to breathe without a mechanical respirator and his very speech is an extreme effort. Even with the respirator, the prognosis is death within a short time. Notwithstanding, he remains in command of his mental faculties and legally competent. He seeks, with full approval of his adult family, to have the respirator removed from his trachea, which act, according to his physician, based upon medical probability, would result in "a reasonable life expectancy of less than one hour." Mr. Perlmutter is fully aware of the inevitable result of such removal, yet has attempted to remove it for himself (hospital personnel, activated by an alarm, reconnected it). He has repeatedly stated to his family, "I'm miserable, take it out," and at a bedside hearing, told the obviously concerned trial judge that whatever would be in store for him if the respirator were removed, "it can't be worse than what I'm going through now."

Pursuant to all of the foregoing, and upon the petition of Mr. Perlmutter himself, the trial judge entered a detailed and thoughtful final judgment which included the following language:

ORDERED AND ADJUDGED that Abe Perlmutter, in the exercise of his right of privacy, may remain in defendant hospital or leave said hospital, free of the mechanical respirator now attached to his body and all defendants and their staffs are restrained from interfering with Plaintiff's decision.

We agree with the trial judge.

The State's position is that it (1) has an overriding duty to preserve life, and (2) that termination of supportive care, whether it be by the patient, his family or medical personnel, is an unlawful killing of a human being . . . The hospital, and its doctors, while not insensitive to this tragedy, fear not only criminal prosecution if they aid in removal of the mechanical device, but also civil liability. In the absence of prior Florida law on the subject, their fears cannot be discounted.

The pros and cons involved in such tragedies which bedevil contemporary society, mainly because of incredible advancement in scientific medicine, are all exhaustively discussed in *Superintendent of Belchertown v. Saikewicz.* . . . As *Saikewicz* points out, the right of an individual to refuse medical treatment is tempered by the State's:

1. Interest in the preservation of life.
2. Need to protect innocent third parties.
3. Duty to prevent suicide.
4. Requirement that it help maintain the ethical integrity of medical practice.

In the case at bar, none of these four considerations surmount the individual wishes of Abe Perlmutter. Thus we adopt the view of the line of cases discussed in *Saikewicz* which would allow Abe Perlmutter the right to refuse or discontinue treatment based upon "the constitutional right to privacy . . . an expression

of the sanctity of individual free choice and self-determination."
We would stress that this adoption is limited to the specific facts
now before us, involving a competent adult patient. The problem
is less easy of solution when the patient is incapable of understanding and we, therefore, postpone a crossing of that more complex
bridge until such time as we are required to do so. . . .

It is our conclusion . . . that when these several public policy interests are weighed against the rights of Mr. Perlmutter, the
latter must and should prevail. Abe Perlmutter should be allowed
to make his choice to die with dignity, notwithstanding over a
dozen legislative failures in this state to adopt suitable legislation in
this field. It is all very convenient to insist on continuing Mr.
Perlmutter's life so that there can be no question of foul play, no
resulting civil liability and no possible trespass on medical ethics.
However, it is quite another matter to do so at the patient's sole
expense and against his competent will, thus inflicting never ending physical torture on his body until the inevitable, but artificially
suspended, moment of death. Such a course of conduct invades
the patient's constitutional right of privacy, removes his freedom
of choice, and invades his right to self-determination.

23

In the Matter of Claire C. Conroy

Supreme Court of New Jersey,
98 N.J. 321, 486 A.2d 1209 (1985)

SCHREIBER, Justice:

At issue here are the circumstances under which life-sustaining treatment may be withheld or withdrawn from incompetent, institutionalized, elderly patients with severe and permanent mental and physical impairments and a limited life expectancy.

Plaintiff, Thomas C. Whittemore, nephew and guardian of Claire Conroy, an incompetent, sought permission to remove a nasogastric feeding tube, the primary conduit for nutrients, from his ward, an eighty-four-year-old bedridden woman with serious and irreversible physical and mental impairments who resided in a nursing home. . . .

In 1979 Claire Conroy, who was suffering from an organic brain syndrome that manifested itself in her exhibiting periodic confusion, was adjudicated an incompetent, and plaintiff, her nephew, was appointed her guardian. The guardian had Ms. Conroy placed in the Parkview Nursing Home. . . .

Ms. Conroy was hospitalized on two occasions at Clara Maas Hospital. . . . During the latter hospitalization the diagnostic evaluation showed that Ms. Conroy had necrotic gangrenous ulcers on her left foot. Two orthopedic surgeons recommended that to save her life, her leg should be amputated. However, her nephew refused to consent to the surgery because he was confident that she would not have wanted it. Contrary to the doctors' prognosis, Ms. Conroy did not die from the gangrene.

During this second hospitalization, Dr. Kazemi observed that Ms. Conroy was not eating adequately, and therefore, on July 23, 1982, he inserted a nasogastric tube that extended from her nose through her esophagus to her stomach. Medicines and food were then given to her through this tube. On October 18, the tube was removed, and Ms. Conroy was fed by hand through her mouth for two weeks. However, she was unable to eat a sufficient amount in this manner, and the tube was reinserted on November 3.

When Ms. Conroy was transferred from the hospital to the nursing home on November 17, 1982, the tube was left in place. It continued to be used for the same purposes thereafter. . . .

At the time of trial [February 1983], Ms. Conroy was no longer ambulatory and was confined to bed, unable to move from a semi-fetal position. She suffered from arteriosclerotic heart disease, hypertension, and diabetes mellitus; her left leg was gangrenous to her knee; she had several necrotic decubitus ulcers on her left foot, leg, and hip; an eye problem required irrigation; she had a urinary catheter in place and could not control her bowels; she could not speak; and her ability to swallow was very limited. On the other hand, she interacted with her environment in some limited ways: she could move her head, neck, hands, and arms to a minor extent; she was able to scratch herself, and had pulled at her bandages, tube, and catheter; she moaned occasionally when moved or fed through the tube . . . and she smiled on occasion when her hair was combed, or when she received a comforting rub.

Dr. Kazemi and Dr. Davidoff . . . testified that Ms. Conroy was not brain dead, comatose, or in a chronic vegetative state. . . .

The medical testimony was inconclusive as to whether, or to what extent, Ms. Conroy was capable of experiencing pain. . . .

Both doctors testified that if the nasogastric tube were removed, Ms. Conroy would die of dehydration in about a week. Dr. Davidoff believed that the resulting thirst could be painful but that Ms. Conroy would become unconscious long before she died. . . . Dr. Kazemi stated that he did not think it would be acceptable medical practice to remove the tube and that he was in favor of keeping it in place. As he put it, "she's a human being and I guess she has a right to live if it's possible." Ms. Rittel, the nurse, also thought the tube should not be removed since in her view it was not an extraordinary treatment. The nursing home had taken no position on the subject. . . .

Mr. Whittemore testified . . . that he now sought removal of the nasogastric tube because, in his opinion, she would have refused the amputation and "would not have allowed [the nasogastric tube] to be inserted in the first place."

Ms. Conroy was a Roman Catholic. The Rev. Joseph Kukura, a Roman Catholic priest and an associate professor of Christian Ethics . . . testified that acceptable church teaching could be found in a document entitled "Declaration on Euthanasia" . . . Father Kukura said that life-sustaining procedures could be withdrawn if they were extraordinary. . . . Here, he said, the hope of recovery and of returning to cognitive life, even with the nasogastric feeding, was not a reasonable possibility. . . . It was his judgment that removal of the tube would be ethical, even though the ensuing period until her death would be painful.

The trial court decided to permit removal of the tube. . . . The guardian *ad litem* appealed. While the appeal was pending, Ms. Conroy died with the nasogastric tube intact. Nevertheless, the Appellate Division decided to resolve the meritorious issues. . . .

The Appellate Division . . . held that a guardian's decision may never be used to withhold nourishment, as opposed to the treatment or attempted curing of a disease, from an incompetent patient who is not comatose, brain dead, or vegetative, and whose death is not irreversibly imminent. . . . The court concluded that withdrawal of Ms. Conroy's nasogastric tube would be tantamount to killing her—not simply letting her die—and that such active euthanasia was ethically impermissible. . . . The Appellate Division therefore reversed the trial court's judgment. . . .

The starting point in analyzing whether life-sustaining treatment may be withheld or withdrawn from an incompetent patient is to determine what rights a competent patient has to accept or reject medical care. It is therefore necessary at the outset of this discussion to identify the nature and extent of a patient's rights that are implicated by such decisions. . . .

Whether based on common-law doctrines or on constitutional theory, the right to decline life-sustaining medical treatment is not absolute. In some cases, it may yield to countervailing societal interests in sustaining the person's life. Courts and commentators have commonly identified four state interests that may limit a person's right to refuse medical treatment: preserving life, preventing suicide, safeguarding the integrity of the medical profession, and protecting innocent third parties. . . .

In view of the case law, we have no doubt that Ms. Conroy, if competent to make the decision and if resolute in her determination, could have chosen to have her nasogastric tube withdrawn. Her interest in freedom from nonconsensual invasion of her bodily integrity would outweigh any state interest in preserving life or in safeguarding the integrity of the medical profession. In addition, rejecting her artificial means of feeding would not constitute attempted suicide, as the decision would probably be based on a wish to be free of medical intervention rather than a specific intent to die. . . . Finally, removal of her feeding tube would not create a public health or safety hazard, nor would her death leave any minor dependents without care or support. . . .

More difficult questions arise in the context of patients who, like Claire Conroy, are incompetent to make particular treatment decisions for themselves. Such patients are unable to exercise directly their own right to accept or refuse medical treatment. In attempting to exercise that right on their behalf, substitute decision-makers must seek to respect simultaneously both aspects of the patient's right to self-determination—the right to live, and the right, in some cases, to die of natural causes without medical intervention. . . .

In light of these rights and concerns, we hold that life-sustaining treatment may be withheld or withdrawn from an incompetent patient when it is clear that the particular patient would have refused the treatment under the circumstances involved. . . . The question is not what a reasonable or average person would have chosen to do under the circumstances but what the particular patient would have done if able to choose for himself. . . .

We hesitate, however, to foreclose the possibility of humane actions, which may involve termination of life-sustaining treatment, for persons who never clearly expressed their desires about life-sustaining treatment but who are now suffering a prolonged and painful death. . . . We therefore hold that life-sustaining treatment may also be withheld or withdrawn from a patient in Claire Conroy's situation if either of two "best interests" tests—a limited-objective or a pure-objective test—is satisfied. . . .

We emphasize that in making decisions whether to administer life-sustaining treatment to patients such as Claire Conroy, the primary focus should be the patient's desires and experience of pain and enjoyment—not the type of treatment involved. Thus, we reject the distinction that some have made between actively hastening death by terminating treatment and passively allowing a person to die of a disease as one of limited use in a legal analysis. . . .

For a similar reason, we also reject any distinction between withholding and withdrawing life-sustaining treatment. . . . This distinction is more psychologically compelling than logically sound. . . .

We also find unpersuasive the distinction relied upon by some courts, commentators, and theologians between "ordinary" treatment, which they would always require, and "extraordinary" treatment, which they deem optional. . . .

Some commentators, as indeed did the Appellate Division here, have made yet a fourth distinction, between the termination of artifical feedings and the termination of other forms of life-sustaining medical treatment. . . . Certainly, feeding has an emotional significance. . . . However, artificial feedings such as nasogastric tubes, gastrostomies, and intravenous infusions are significantly different from bottle-feeding or spoon-feeding—they are medical procedures with inherent risks and possible side effects, instituted by skilled health-care providers to compensate for impaired physical functioning. Analytically, artificial feeding by means of a nasogastric tube or intravenous infusion can be seen as equivalent to artificial breathing by means of a respirator. Both prolong life through mechanical means when the body is no longer able to perform a vital bodily function on its own. . . .

Furthermore, while nasogastric feeding and other medical procedures to ensure nutrition and hydration are usually well tolerated, they are not free from risks or burdens. . . . Nasogastric tubes may lead to pneumonia, cause irritation and discomfort, and require arm restraints for an incompetent patient. . . . Finally, dehydration may well not be distressing or painful to a dying patient. . . . Thus, it cannot be assumed that it will always be beneficial for an incompetent patient to receive artificial feeding or harmful for him not to receive it. . . .

Under the analysis articulated above, withdrawal or withholding of artificial feeding, like any other medical treatment, would be permissible if there is sufficient proof to satisfy the subjective, limited-objective, or pure-objective test. A competent patient has the right to decline any medical treatment, including artificial feeding, and should retain that right when and if he becomes incompetent. . . .

We have not attempted to set forth guidelines for decision-making with respect to life-sustaining treatment in a variety of other situations that are not currently before us. Innumerable variations are possible. . . .

The judgment of the Appellate Division is reversed. In light of Ms. Conroy's death, we do not remand the matter for further proceedings.

FIVE
Euthanasia

Euthanasia, or intentional killing, is one of the perennial ethical issues in death and dying. Discussions of euthanasia, however, are often confusing for a number of reasons. First, there are terminological problems brought about by two very different usages of "euthanasia." Some persons use the term in an etymological manner to signify a "good death" (the term is derived from two Greek roots with this meaning). By contrast, other persons use the term in its more modern sense of "an act of killing someone who is hopelessly ill for reasons of mercy."

Second, some people who write about the morality of euthanasia distinguish between "passive" (or "negative") euthanasia and "active" (or "positive") euthanasia. The exact meaning of this distinction is not always clear. Depending upon the writer or speaker, the distinction may be meant to suggest a significant difference between omissions and acts, or between letting a patient die and killing a patient, or between a disease being the causative factor in a patient's death and a human agent being the cause of the patient's death, or between a nonintentional termination of a patient's life and the intentional termination of a patient's life. Because of these variable meanings, the distinction between passive and active euthanasia is not particularly helpful. Greater clarity can be gained by discussing the differences and similarities between (a) cases of treatment abatement and (b) cases of euthanasia, with the term "euthanasia" being used only in reference to cases involving intentional killing.

Third, some discussions of euthanasia move back and forth indiscriminately between considerations of the morality of euthanasia and considerations of the legalization of euthanasia. Of course, questions about the moral permissibility of intentionally killing patients cannot responsibly take place in a legal vacuum, especially since such acts are clearly against the law. Nevertheless, for analytical purposes it is helpful to distinguish as much as possible between the rightness or wrongness of individual *acts* of euthanasia, as opposed to the related but separate question of whether such acts should be given legal status as acceptable *practices*.

In addition to dealing with these problems, a serious consideration of the morality—and, separately, the possible legalization—of euthanasia needs to address several questions. Is euthanasia a theoretical issue only (as discussions of euthanasia often seem to suggest), or have there been actual cases of patients being killed for reasons of mercy? Euthanasia often seems to be a somewhat "unreal" issue, no doubt due to the illegality of intentionally killing patients. Because of this illegal status, actual cases of euthanasia seldom occur and even less seldom receive publicity. But they do occur, and a few cases involving physicians, nurses, relatives, and friends who have killed patients for reasons of mercy have resulted in court decisions. In most of the cases, the defendants were acquitted. Some examples in the United States:

    the 1950s Hermann Sander, M.D. (New Hampshire, 1950)
                    Herman Nagel (Arizona, 1953)
                    Otto Werner (Illinois, 1958)
    the 1960s William Reinecke (Illinois, 1967)
                    Robert Washkin (Illinois, 1969)
    the 1970s Lester Zygmaniak (New Jersey, 1973)
                    Vincent Montemarano, M.D. (New York, 1974)

the 1980s   Hans Florian (Florida, 1983)
            Dorothy Healy, R.N. (California, 1984)
            Roswell Gilbert (Florida, 1985)

If the passive/active distinction is not helpful, are there distinctions between types of euthanasia that are helpful to make? The passive/active distinction, however it is interpreted, tends to focus on differences in the moral agent's intention or action. Another way of distinguishing between types of euthanasia is to emphasize the patient's perspective in terms of preferences and choices. When competent, dying patients decide that death is preferable to a continually painful existence and request that they be killed, the subsequent intentional killing of the patient for reasons of mercy by the physician (or someone else) is *voluntary euthanasia.* When comatose or other incompetent patients are intentionally killed for reasons of mercy, the causation of their deaths is correctly described as *nonvoluntary euthanasia,* because they were unable to express a desire or preference regarding the continuation or termination of their lives. When competent patients express a desire to continue living, any subsequent killing of the patient by someone else is *involuntary euthanasia* (in moral terms) or murder (in legal terms).

What are the standard features of various euthanasia cases? To emphasize the important differences between voluntary euthanasia cases and nonvoluntary euthanasia cases, it is helpful to isolate the characteristic features of such cases. The result is as follows:

Voluntary Euthanasia	*Nonvoluntary Euthanasia*
1. patient's medical condition appears irreversible	1. same
2. patient has intractable pain or other intolerable condition	2. patient is incompetent (permanent comatosis, advanced senility)
3. patient is unable to commit suicide	3. same
4. patient prefers death to continuation of intolerable life	4. patient preferences unknown and unknowable

5. patient requests to
   be killed

5. patient unable to make
   such a request

6. physician (or someone)
   intentionally kills
   patient

6. same

7. moral agent's motive
   is compassion or mercy

7. same

What are the recurring philosophical arguments regarding the morality of voluntary euthanasia, and the possibility of the legalization of voluntary euthanasia? Such arguments fall into three categories. The first group of arguments concentrates on the traditional distinction between killing and letting die, with some writers claiming that the distinction has no significant moral meaning and other writers attempting to show that there are important moral differences between killing patients and allowing patients to die by terminating futile or unwanted medical treatment. Other arguments address the question of the justifiability of acts of voluntary euthanasia. Some writers are convinced that voluntary euthanasia can never be justified as a moral act because they claim such acts are unnecessary, violate the sanctity of human life, go counter to God's commandments, preclude the possibility of discovering a wrong prognosis or a medical cure, and/or brutalize the persons doing the killing; others maintain that voluntary euthanasia is occasionally justifiable on the grounds of mercy, patient autonomy, utility, and/or universalizability. The third group of arguments extends the debate about voluntary euthanasia into the area of public policy, with some writers putting forth proposals for the legalization of voluntary euthanasia—but most writers (often using variations of the wedge argument) being convinced that voluntary euthanasia should never be given legal sanction because of the inevitable problem of abuse.

Have there been serious attempts to legalize voluntary euthanasia? The answer is affirmative, with most such attempts having occurred fairly recently. For example, the Netherlands appears ready to legalize "aid-in-dying," which includes voluntary euthanasia and assisting rational suicide efforts. The

Criminal Court in Rotterdam set forth guidelines in 1981 for "non-criminal aid-in-dying," the Netherlands Medical Association followed suit in 1984, and the matter is before the Netherlands Supreme Court as this is being written.

A major effort was made in 1969 to legalize voluntary euthanasia in Great Britain. A "Voluntary Euthanasia Bill," actively supported by the Voluntary Euthanasia Society in England, was defeated on its second reading before the House of Lords. Had this effort succeeded, a critically ill patient suffering from an "irremediable condition" (certified by two physicians) would have had the legal option of requesting "the painless inducement of death." A revised bill, again supported by the Voluntary Euthanasia Society, is before Parliament at the present time.

In the United States the movement to legalize voluntary euthanasia is now led by the Hemlock Society, an organization based in Los Angeles. Established in 1980, this society has over 10,000 members and actively promotes the legalization of voluntary euthanasia for the terminally ill.

The selected readings contain some of the most important arguments about the morality and the possible legalization of euthanasia. The first two selections disagree about the killing/letting die distinction. James Rachels, a philosopher at the University of Alabama, argues that "the bare difference" between killing patients and allowing them to die is morally insignificant, and supports his claim with two hypothetical cases that have been widely discussed in recent years. Tom Beauchamp, a philosopher at Georgetown University, and James Childress, a religious ethicist at the University of Virginia, are two of the persons who have seriously considered Rachels' cases and arguments—and they remain convinced that the killing/letting die distinction is morally important.

The other selections disagree about the morality of voluntary euthanasia. Peter Singer, a philosopher at Monash University (Australia), thinks that voluntary euthanasia is morally justifiable *and* that it should be a legal option for terminally ill patients. Arthur Dyck, a religious ethicist at Harvard, is convinced that voluntary euthanasia is *neither* morally justifiable nor legally desirable. And Daniel Maguire, a religious ethicist at Marquette University, concludes that "death by choice" is a morally and legally sound option for contemporary society.

In terms of the law, cases of euthanasia present unusual difficulties for an editor of a book of readings. As noted above, such cases are rare in American jurisprudence. In addition, since such cases involve criminal prosecutions, there is no opinion or decision from the bench. Still another problem is that euthanasia cases are handled at the level of trial courts, and the decisions of trial courts (except those in the federal system) are not usually reported in legal publications.

Nevertheless, such cases do occur. The last "mercy killing" case involving a physician as the defendant was the case of Vincent Montemarano that took place in New York (Nassau County) in 1974. Accused of murder, Montemarano was found not guilty after trial, as indicated by the disposition of the case at the end of this section. The most recent euthanasia case took place in Florida (Broward County) in 1985. Roswell Gilbert, aged 76, was found guilty of having murdered his wife after 51 years of marriage, and was sentenced to life in prison. Already turned down by the Florida cabinet in a bid for clemency, the case is now under appeal in Florida. The judgment and sentence in the case conclude this section.

24

Active and Passive Euthanasia

JAMES RACHELS, Ph.D.

The distinction between active and passive euthanasia is thought to be crucial for medical ethics. The idea is that it is permissible, at least in some cases, to withhold treatment and allow a patient to die, but it is never permissible to take any direct action to kill the patient. This doctrine seems to be accepted by most doctors, and it was endorsed in a statement adopted by the House of Delegates of the American Medical Association on December 4, 1973:

The intentional termination of the life of one human being by another—mercy killing—is contrary to that for which the medical profession stands and is contrary to the policy of the American Medical Association.

The cessation of the employment of extraordinary means to prolong the life of the body when there is irrefutable evidence that biological death is imminent is the decision of the patient and/or his immediate family. The advice and judgment of the physician should be freely available to the patient and/or his immediate family.

Reprinted from *The New England Journal of Medicine* (January 9, 1975) 292:78–80, with the permission of the publisher. Copyright © 1975 by the Massachusetts Medical Society.

However, a strong case can be made against this doctrine. In what follows I will set out some of the relevant arguments, and urge doctors to reconsider their views on this matter.

To begin with a familiar type of situation, a patient who is dying of incurable cancer of the throat is in terrible pain, which can no longer be satisfactorily alleviated. He is certain to die within a few days, even if present treatment is continued, but he does not want to go on living for those days since the pain is unbearable. So he asks the doctor for an end to it, and his family joins in the request.

Suppose the doctor agrees to withhold treatment, as the conventional doctrine says he may. The justification for his doing so is that the patient is in terrible agony, and since he is going to die anyway, it would be wrong to prolong his suffering needlessly. But now notice this. If one simply withholds treatment it may take the patient longer to die, and so he may suffer more than he would if more direct action were taken and a lethal injection given. This fact provides strong reason for thinking that, once the initial decision not to prolong his agony has been made, active euthanasia is actually preferable to passive euthanasia, rather than the reverse. To say otherwise is to endorse the option that leads to more suffering rather than less, and is contrary to the humanitarian impulse that prompts the decision not to prolong his life in the first place.

Part of my point is that the process of being "allowed to die" can be relatively slow and painful, whereas being given a lethal injection is relatively quick and painless. Let me give a different sort of example. In the United States about one in 600 babies is born with Down's syndrome. Most of these babies are otherwise healthy—that is, with only the usual pediatric care, they will proceed to an otherwise normal infancy. Some, however, are born with congenital defects such as intestinal obstructions that require operations if they are to live. Sometimes, the parents and the doctor will decide not to operate, and let the infant die. Anthony Shaw describes what happens then.

When surgery is denied [the doctor] must try to keep the infant from suffering while natural forces sap the baby's life away. As a surgeon whose natural inclination is to use the scalpel to fight off death, standing by and watching a salvageable baby die is the most emotionally exhausting experience I know. It is easy at a conference, in a theoretical discussion, to decide that such infants should be allowed to die. It is altogether different to stand by in the nursery and watch as dehydration and infection wither a tiny being over hours and days. This is a terrible ordeal for me and the hospital staff—much more so than for the parents who never set foot in the nursery.[1]

I can understand why some people are opposed to all euthanasia, and insist that such infants must be allowed to live. I think I can also understand why other people favor destroying these babies quickly and painlessly. But why should anyone favor letting "dehydration and infection wither a tiny being over hours and days?" The doctrine that says that a baby may be allowed to dehydrate and wither, but may not be given an injection that would end its life without suffering, seems so patently cruel as to require no further refutation. The strong language is not intended to offend, but only to put the point in the clearest possible way.

My second argument is that the conventional doctrine leads to decisions concerning life and death made on irrelevant grounds.

Consider again the case of the infants with Down's syndrome who need operations for congenital defects unrelated to the syndrome to live. Sometimes there is no operation, and the baby dies, but when there is no such defect, the baby lives on. Now, an operation such as that to remove an intestinal obstruction is not prohibitively difficult. The reason why such operations are not performed in these cases is, clearly, that the child has Down's syndrome and the parents and doctor judge that because of that fact it is better for the child to die.

But notice that this situation is absurd, no matter what view one takes of the lives and potentials of such babies. If the life of such an infant is worth preserving, what does it matter if it needs a simple operation? Or, if one thinks it better that such a baby should not live on, what difference does it make that it happens to have an unobstructed intestinal tract? In either case, the matter of life and death is being decided on irrelevant grounds. It is the Down's syndrome, and not the intestines, that is the issue. The matter should be decided, if at all, on that basis, and not be allowed to depend on the essentially irrelevant question of whether the intestinal tract is blocked.

What makes this situation possible, of course, is the idea that when there is an intestinal blockage, one can "let the baby die," but when there is no such defect there is nothing that can be done, for one must not "kill" it. The fact that this idea leads to such results as deciding life or death on irrelevant grounds is another good reason why the doctrine should be rejected.

One reason why so many people think that there is an important moral difference between active and passive euthanasia is that they think killing someone is morally worse than letting someone die. But is it? Is killing, in itself, worse than letting die? To investigate this issue, two cases may be considered that are exactly alike except that one involves killing whereas the other involves letting someone die. Then, it can be asked whether this difference makes any difference to the moral assessments. It is important that the cases be exactly alike, except for this one difference, since otherwise one cannot be confident that it is this difference and not some other that accounts for any variation in the assessments of the two cases. So, let us consider this pair of cases:

In the first, Smith stands to gain a large inheritance if anything should happen to his six-year-old cousin. One evening while the child is taking his bath, Smith sneaks into the bathroom and drowns the child, and then arranges things so that it will look like an accident.

In the second, Jones also stands to gain if anything should happen to his six-year-old cousin. Like Smith, Jones sneaks in planning to drown the child in his bath. However, just as he enters the bathroom Jones sees the child slip and hit his head, and fall face down in the water. Jones is delighted; he stands by, ready to push the child's head back under if it is necessary, but it is not necessary. With only a little thrashing about, the child drowns all by himself, "accidentally," as Jones watches and does nothing.

Now Smith killed the child, whereas Jones "merely" let the child die. That is the only difference between them. Did either man behave better, from a moral point of view? If the difference between killing and letting die were in itself a morally important matter, one should say that Jones' behavior was less reprehensible than Smith's. But does one really want to say that? I think not. In the first place, both men acted from the same motive, personal gain, and both had exactly the same end in view when they acted. It may be inferred from Smith's conduct that he is a bad man, although that judgment may be withdrawn or modified if certain further facts are learned about him—for example, that he is mentally deranged. But would not the very same thing be inferred about Jones from his conduct? And would not the same further considerations also be relevant to any modification of this judgment? Moreover, suppose Jones pleaded, in his own defense, "After all, I didn't do anything except just stand there and watch the child drown. I didn't kill him; I only let him die." Again, if letting die were in itself less bad than killing, this defense should have at least some weight. But it does not. Such a "defense" can only be regarded as a grotesque perversion of moral reasoning. Morally speaking, it is no defense at all.

Now it may be pointed out, quite properly, that the cases of euthanasia with which doctors are concerned are not like this at all. They do not involve personal gain or the destruction of normal healthy children. Doctors are concerned only with cases in which the patient's life is of no further use to him, or in which the patient's life has become or will soon become a terrible burden. However, the point is the same in these cases: the bare difference between killing and letting die does not, in itself, make a moral difference. If a doctor lets a patient die, for humane reasons, he is in the same moral position as if he had given the patient a lethal injection for humane reasons. If his decision was wrong—if, for example, the patient's illness was in fact curable—the decision would be equally regrettable no matter which method was used to carry it out. And if the doctor's decision was the right one, the method used is not in itself important.

The AMA policy statement isolates the crucial issue very well; the crucial issue is "the intentional termination of the life of one human being by another." But after identifying this issue, and forbidding "mercy killing," the statement goes on to deny that the cessation of treatment is the intentional termination of a life. This is where the mistake comes in, for what is the cessation of treatment, in these circumstances, if it is not "the intentional termination of the life of one human being by another?" Of course it is exactly that, and if it were not, there would be no point to it.

Many people will find this judgment hard to accept. One reason, I think, is that it is very easy to conflate the question of whether killing is, in itself, worse than letting die, with the very different question of whether most actual cases of killing are more reprehensible than most cases of letting die. Most actual cases of killing are clearly terrible (think, for example, of all the murders reported in the newspapers), and one hears of such cases every day. On the other hand, one hardly ever hears of a case of letting die, except for the actions of doctors who are motivated by humanitarian reasons. So one learns to think of killing in a much worse light than of letting die. But this does not mean that there is something about killing that makes it in itself worse than letting die, for it is not the bare difference between killing and letting die that makes the difference in these cases. Rather, the other factors—the murderer's motive of personal gain, for example, contrasted with the doctor's humanitarian motivation—account for different reactions to the different cases.

I have argued that killing is not in itself any worse than letting die; if my contention is right, it follows that active euthanasia is not any worse than passive euthanasia. What arguments can be given on the other side? The most common, I believe, is the following:

"The important difference between active and passive euthanasia is that in passive euthanasia, the doctor does not do anything to bring about the patient's death. The doctor does nothing, and the patient dies of whatever ills already afflict him. In active euthanasia, however, the doctor does something to bring about the patient's death: he kills him. The doctor who gives the patient with cancer a lethal injection has himself caused his patient's death; whereas if he merely ceases treatment, the cancer is the cause of the death."

A number of points need to be made here. The first is that it is not exactly correct to say that in passive euthanasia the doctor does nothing, for he does do one thing that is very important: he lets the patient die. "Letting someone die" is certainly different, in some respects, from other types of action—mainly in that it is a kind of action that one may perform by way of not performing certain other actions. For example, one may let a patient die by way of not giving medication, just as one may insult someone by way of not shaking his hand. But for any purpose of moral assessment, it is a type of action nonetheless. The decision to let a patient die is subject to moral appraisal in the same way that a decision to kill him would be subject to moral appraisal: it may be assessed as wise or unwise, compassionate or sadistic, right or wrong. If a doctor deliberately let a patient die who was suffering from a routinely curable illness, the doctor would certainly be to blame for what he had done, just as he would certainly be to blame if he had needlessly killed the patient. Charges against him would then be appropriate. If so, it would be no defense at all for him to insist that he didn't "do anything." He would have done something very serious indeed, for he let his patient die.

Fixing the cause of death may be very important from a legal point of view, for it may determine whether criminal charges are brought against the doctor. But I do not think that this notion can be used to show a moral difference between active and passive euthanasia. The reason why it is considered bad to be the cause of someone's death is that death is regarded as a great evil—and so it is. However, if it has been decided that euthanasia—even passive euthanasia—is desirable in a given case, it has also been decided that in this instance death is no greater an evil than the patient's continued existence. And if this is true, the usual reason for not wanting to be the cause of someone's death simply does not apply.

Finally, doctors may think that all of this is only of academic interest—the sort of thing that philosophers may worry about but that has no practical bearing on their own work. After all, doctors must be concerned about the legal consequences of what they do, and active euthanasia is clearly forbidden by the law. But even so, doctors should also be concerned with the fact that the law is forcing upon them a moral doctrine that may well be indefensible, and has a considerable effect on their practices. Of course, most doctors are not now in the position of being coerced in this matter, for they do not regard themselves as merely going along with what the law requires. Rather, in statements such as the AMA policy statement that I have quoted, they are endorsing this doctrine as a central point of medical ethics. In that statement, active euthanasia is condemned not merely as illegal but as "contrary to that for which the medical profession stands," whereas passive euthanasia is approved. However, the preceding considerations suggest that there is really no moral difference between the two, considered in themselves (there may be important moral differences in some cases in their *consequences*, but, as I pointed out, these differences may make active euthanasia, and not passive euthanasia, the morally preferable option). So, whereas doctors may have to discriminate between active and passive euthanasia to satisfy the law, they should not do any more than that. In particular, they should not give the distinction any added authority and weight by writing it into official statements of medical ethics.

Notes

1. A. Shaw, "Doctor, Do We Have a Choice?" *New York Times Magazine*, January 30, 1972, p. 54.

25

Killing and Letting Die

TOM L. BEAUCHAMP, Ph.D.
AND JAMES F. CHILDRESS, Ph.D.

A sixty-eight-year-old doctor, who suffered severely from terminal carcinoma of the stomach, collapsed with a massive
pulmonary embolism. He survived because one of his young
colleagues performed a pulmonary embolectomy. Upon recovery the doctor-patient requested that no steps should be taken to
prolong his life if he suffered another cardiovascular collapse. He
even wrote an authorization to this effect for the hospital records.
He reasoned that his pain was too much to bear given his dismal
prospects. He thus asked to be *allowed to die* under certain conditions, but he did not ask to be *killed*. In [another] case . . . a
defective infant needed an operation to correct a tracheoesophageal fistula. The parents and physicians determined that survival
was not in this infant's best interests and decided to allow the
infant to die rather than to perform an operation. In both cases,
we need to ask whether certain actions, such as intentionally not
trying to overcome a cardiovascular collapse and not performing

Reprinted from *Principles of Biomedical Ethics,* 2nd ed., pp. 115–120, 122–126, with
the permission of Oxford University Press. Copyright © 1979, 1983, by Oxford University Press.

an operation, can legitimately be described as "allowing to die" rather than "killing," and whether such actions are justifiable.

For many people, it is important to distinguish killing and letting die, and to prohibit the former while authorizing the latter in some range of cases. For example, after prohibiting "mercy killing" or the "intentional termination of the life of one human being by another,"[1] the AMA House of Delegates held that cessation of treatment is morally justified when the patient and/or the patient's immediate family, with the advice and judgment of the physician, decide to withhold or stop the use of "extraordinary means to prolong life when there is irrefutable evidence that biological death is imminent." Although several terms in this statement—such as "extraordinary," "irrefutable," and "imminent"—need careful examination, it is clear that the statement authorizes some instances of allowing to die by withholding or stopping treatment, while it excludes killing. Whether letting particular patients die—such as the sixty-eight-year-old man suffering from terminal carcinoma of the stomach and the defective infant needing an operation—is morally acceptable would depend on several conditions. But if their deaths involve killing rather than being merely "allowed deaths," they are not justifiable according to the AMA House of Delegates' statement.

In recent years, the distinction between killing and letting die has come under frequent attack. Some critics focus on developments in biomedical technology that appear to make it difficult to classify acts as instances either of killing or of letting die. Unplugging the respirator is now a standard example of this problem. Other critics dismiss the distinction itself, holding that it is a "moral quibble"without any "moral bite." As we explore the arguments for and against this distinction, it is important to emphasize that acceptance or rejection of the *distinction* does not necessarily determine *moral conclusions* about particular cases. For instance, it is possible to reject the distinction and to hold that some cases of what have been called "killing" and "letting die" are morally permissible, or that all cases are morally prohibited; and it is also possible to affirm the distinction and yet to hold that most cases of letting die and all cases of killing are morally wrong. Even if the distinction is morally significant, the label "killing" or the label "letting die" should not dictate a conclusion about a particular case. For example, it would be absurd to affirm the moral significance of the distinction and then to accept *all* cases of letting die as morally fitting. Even instances of letting die must meet other criteria such as the detriment-benefit calculation, and some cases of allowed death involve egregious negligence.

In a widely discussed argument for rejecting both the distinction between active and passive euthanasia and the AMA's policy statement, James Rachels contends that killing is not, in itself, worse than letting die.[2] That is, the "bare difference" between acts of killing and acts of letting die is not in itself a morally relevant difference. Part of his strategy is to sketch two cases that differ only in that one involves killing, while the other involves allowing to die. He contends that if there is no morally relevant difference between these cases, the "bare difference" between killing and allowing to die is demonstrated to be morally irrelevant. In his two cases, two young men want their six-year-old cousins dead so that they can gain large inheritances. Smith drowns his cousin while the boy is taking a bath. Jones plans to drown his cousin, but as he enters the bathroom he sees the boy slip and hit his head; Jones stands by, doing nothing, while the boy drowns. Smith killed his cousin; Jones merely allowed his cousin to die.

While we agree with Rachels that both acts are equally reprehensible because of the motives, ends, and actions, we do not accept his conclusion that these examples show that the distinction between killing and letting die is morally irrelevant. Several rejoinders to Rachels are in order. First, Rachels' cases and the cessations of treatment envisioned by the AMA are so markedly disanalogous that it is not clear what Rachels' argument shows. In some cases of unjustified acts, including both of Rachels' examples, we are not interested in moral distinctions per se. As Richard Trammell points out, some examples have a "masking" or "sledgehammer" effect; the fact that "one cannot distinguish the taste of two wines when both are mixed with green persimmon juice, does not imply that there is no distinction between the wines."[3] Since Rachels' examples involve two morally unjustified acts by agents whose motives and intentions are despicable, it is not surprising that some *other* features of their situations, such as killing and letting die, do not strike us as morally compelling considerations.

Second, while Rachels' cases involve two *unjustified* actions, one of killing and the other of letting die, the AMA statement distinguished cases of *unjustified killing* from cases of *justified letting die*. The AMA statement does not, however, claim that the moral difference is identical to the distinction between killing and letting die. It does not even imply that the "bare difference" between (passive) letting die and (active) killing is the only difference or even a morally sufficient difference between the justified and unjustified cases. Its point is rather that the justified actions in medicine are confined to (passive) letting die. While the AMA statement holds that "mercy killing" in medicine is unjustified in all circumstances, it does not hold that letting die is right in all circumstances or that killing outside medicine is always wrong. For an act that results in an earlier death for the patient to be justified, it is necessary that it be describable as an act of "letting die," but this description is not sufficient to justify the act; nor is the bare description of killing sufficient to make *all* acts of killing wrong. This AMA pronouncement is meant to hold only in the context of the physician–patient relationship.

Third, in Rachels' cases Smith and Jones are *morally* responsible and *morally* blameworthy for the deaths of their respective cousins, even if Jones, who allowed his cousin to drown, is not *causally* responsible. The law might find only Smith, who killed his cousin, guilty of homicide (because of the law's theory of proximate cause), but morality condemns both actions because of the agents' motives and their commissions and omissions. While we would not condemn a nonswimmer for failing to jump into deep water to try to rescue a drowning child, we find Jones' actions reprehensible because he (morally) should have rescued the child. Even if he had no other special duties to the child, the duty of beneficence . . . requires affirmative action. The point of the cases envisioned by the AMA is that the physician is always morally prohibited from killing patients but is not morally bound to preserve life in *all* cases. According to the AMA, the physician has a right—and perhaps a duty—to stop treatment if and only if three conditions are met: (1) the life of the body is being preserved by extraordinary means, (2) there is irrefutable evidence that biological death is imminent, and (3) the patient and/or the family consents.

Fourth, even if the distinction between killing and letting die is morally irrelevant in some contexts, it does not follow that it is always morally irrelevant. The fact that the distinction does not show up in every sort of case does not mean that it is morally unimportant under all circumstances. Rachels does effectively undermine any attempt to rest judgments about ending life on the "bare difference" between killing and letting die, but his target may be a straw man. Many philosophers and theologians have argued that there are *independent* moral, religious, and other reasons for defending the distinction and for prohibiting killing while authorizing allowing to die in some circumstances.

One theologian has argued, for example, that we can discern the moral significance of the distinction between killing and letting die only by "placing it in the religious context out of which it grew."[4] That context is the biblical story of God's actions toward his creatures. In that context it makes *sense* to talk about "placing patients in God's hands," just as it is important not to usurp God's prerogatives by desperately struggling to prolong life when the patient is irreversibly dying. But even if the distinction between killing and letting die originated within a religious context, and even if it makes more sense in that context than in some others, it can be defended on nontheological grounds without being reduced to a claim about a "bare difference." However important the religious context was for the origin of the distinction, religious doctrines are not presupposed by the distinction and independent moral grounds are sufficient to support it.

Some nontheological arguments in favor of the distinction between killing and allowing to die invoke both moral and practical considerations. They hold that the distinction enables us to express and maintain certain principles such as nonmaleficence and to avoid certain harmful consequences. Probably no single reason by itself is sufficient to support the moral relevance of the distinction and thus to prohibit killing while permitting some intentionally allowed deaths. But several reasons together indicate that the distinction is worth retaining or, in effect, that our current practices should be maintained with some clarifications and modifications. We now turn to this set of reasons.

The most important arguments for the distinction between killing and letting die depend on a distinction between *acts* and *practices*.[5] It is one thing to justify an act, i.e., to hold that it is right; it is another to justify a general practice. Many beliefs about principles and consequences are applied to practices or rules rather than directly to acts. For example, we might justify a rule of confidentiality because it encourages people to seek therapy and because it promotes respect for persons and their privacy. Such a rule might, however, lead to undesirable results in *particular* cases. Likewise, a rule that prohibits "active killing," while permitting some "allowed deaths," may be justifiable, even though it excludes some acts of killing that in and of themselves might appear to be justifiable. Such a rule would not permit us to kill a patient who suffers from terrible pain, who rationally asks for "mercy," i.e., to be killed, and who will probably die within three weeks. According to the rule of double effect, we should, of course, use measures to alleviate the patient's pain even though these would hasten death; we should allow the patient to die, but not kill the patient. It may be necessary to prohibit by rule and policy some acts that do not appear to be wrong in some circumstances in order to maintain a viable practice that, for the most part, expresses our principles and avoids seriously undesirable consequences. Thus, although particular acts of killing may not violate the duty of nonmaleficence and may even be humane and compassionate, a policy of authorizing killing would probably violate the duty of nonmaleficence by creating a grave risk of harm in many cases.

According to one line of argument, the prohibition of killing even for "mercy" expresses principles and values that provide a basis of trust between patients and health care professionals. Trust involves the expectation that others will respect moral limits. When we trust medical practitioners, we expect them to promote our welfare and, at least, to do us no harm without a corresponding prospect of benefit. The prohibition of killing in medical contexts is a basic expression of the ethos of care for the patient's life and health as well as the duty of maleficence. Some claim that it is instrumentally as well as symbolically important, for its removal would weaken a "climate, both moral and legal, which we are not able to do without."[6] David Louisell, for example, contends that "euthanasia would threaten the patient–physician relationship: confidence might give way to suspicion. . . . Can the physician, historic battler for life, become an affirmative agent of death without jeopardizing the trust of his dependents?"[7]

If rules permitting active killing were introduced into a society, it is not implausible to suppose that the society over time would move increasingly in the direction of involuntary euthanasia—e.g., in the form of killing defective newborns for such reasons as the avoidance of social burdens. There could be a general reduction of respect for human life as a result of the official removal of some barriers to killing. Rules against killing in a moral code are not isolated; they are threads in a fabric of rules, based in part on nonmaleficence, that support respect for human life. The more threads we remove, the weaker the fabric becomes. If we focus on attitudes and not merely rules, the general attitude of respect for life may be eroded by shifts in particular areas. Determination of the probability of such an erosion depends not only on the connectedness of rules and attitudes, but also on various forces in the society. . . .

In addition to fears of abuse, including abuse of the mentally disturbed and others who cannot consent, there are other legitimate fears. First, easy resort to killing to relieve pain and suffering may divert attention and resources from other strategies that may be effective, such as the hospice movement. Second, consider the following two types of wrongly diagnosed patients.[8] 1. Patients wrongly diagnosed as hopeless, and who will survive even if a treatment *is* ceased (in order to allow a natural death). 2. Patients wrongly diagnosed as hopeless, and who will survive only if the treatment is *not ceased* (in order to allow a natural death). If a social rule of allowing some patients to die were in effect, doctors and families who followed it would only lose patients in the second category. But if killing were permitted, at least some of the patients in the first category would be needlessly lost. Thus, a rule prohibiting killing would save some lives that would be lost if *both* killing and allowing to die were permitted. Of course, such a consequence is not a decisive reason for a policy of (only) allowing to die, for the numbers in categories (1) and (2) are likely to be small and other reasons for killing, such as extreme pain and autonomous choice, might be weighty. But it is certainly a morally relevant reason.

Proponents of the practice of killing some patients appeal to a range of exceptional cases to show the utility of the practice. Among the strongest reasons for killing some patients is to relieve unbearable and uncontrollable pain and suffering. No one would deny that pain and suffering can so ravage and dehumanize patients that death appears to be in their best interests. Prolonging life and refusing to kill in such circumstances may appear to be cruel and even to violate the duty of nonmaleficence. Often proponents of "mercy killing" appeal to nonmedical situations to show that killing may be more humane and compassionate than letting die—as, for example, in the case of a truck driver inextricably trapped in a burning wreck who cries out for "mercy" and asks to be killed. In such tragic situations we are reluctant to say that those who kill at the behest of the victim act wrongly. Furthermore, juries often find persons who have killed a suffering relative not guilty by reason of temporary insanity.

There are, nevertheless, serious objections to building into *medical practice* an explicit exception licensing physicians to kill their patients in order to relieve uncontrollable pain and suffering. One objection is that it is not clear that many, if any, cases in medical practice are really parallel to the person trapped in a burning wreck. The physician may be able to relieve pain and suffering short of killing—even if death is hastened—by means that are not available to a bystander at the scene of an accident. A second objection holds that we should not construct a social or professional ethic on borderline situations and emergency cases, even if medical practitioners confront some cases of unmanageable pain and suffering. It is dangerous to generalize from emergencies, for hard cases may make bad social and professional ethics as well as bad law. As Charles Fried writes,

The concept of emergency is only a tolerable moral concept if somehow we can truly think of it as exceptional, if we can truly think of it as a circumstance that, far from defying our usual moral universe, suspends it for a limited time and thus suspends usual moral principles. It is when emergencies become usual that we are threatened with moral disintegration, dehumanization.[9]

Third, there are ways to "accept" acts of killing in exceptional circumstances without altering the rules of practice in order to accommodate them. As mentioned earlier, juries often find those who kill their suffering relatives not guilty by reason of temporary insanity, as occurred in the Zygmaniak case in New Jersey.[10] In June 1973, George Zygmaniak was in a motor-cycle accident that left him paralyzed from the neck down. This paralysis was considered to be irreversible, and Zygmaniak begged his brother, Lester, to kill him. Three days later, Lester brought a sawed-off shotgun into the hospital and shot his brother in the head, after having told him, "Close your eyes now, I'm going to shoot you." Verdicts like "not guilty by reason of temporary insanity" do not *justify* the act of killing a suffering relative. They differ from a verdict of not guilty on grounds of self-defense, for self-defense does justify killing, at least in some circumstances. Verdicts like not guilty by reason of temporary insanity thus function to *excuse* the agent by finding that he or she lacked the conditions of responsibility necessary to be legally guilty.

Others have proposed that we maintain the legal rule against killing even if physicians and others sometime have to engage in justified conscientious or civil disobedience. Concurring with Robert Veatch, Paul Ramsey holds that "civil disobedience— the courage to go against the rules when morally warranted—may be better than to allow for exceptions in a rule of general practice."[11] But what conditions might justify conscientious refus-als in medical practice to follow the rule against killing patients? According to Ramsey, when dying patients are totally inaccessible to our care, when our care is a matter of indifference to them because of intractable pain or a deep coma, "there is no longer any morally significant distinction between omission and commission, between standing aside and directly dispatching them."[12] "Total inaccessibility" is a limit of care itself; for care can become totally useless. It is not clear, however, that Ramsey's distinction between dying and nondying patients can carry his argument. Nor is it clear whether he considers someone in a deep and prolonged state of unconsciousness as dying, and if so, whether such a view is justifiable. In addition, it is necessary to ask whether Ramsey's exception can be limited to the cases that he endorses; it too may be the thin edge of the wedge. Nevertheless, even if pain and suffering of a certain magnitude can in principle justify active killing, as long as other conditions are met, they may only justify acts of conscientious refusal to follow the rule of practice, not basic changes in the rule itself.

Finally, which side in the debate has the burden of proof—the proponents or the opponents of a practice of selective killing? Anthony Flew has argued that supporters of the current practice of prohibiting killing must bear the burden of proof because the prohibition of *voluntary* euthanasia violates the principle of liberty by refusing to respect individual autonomy.[13] However, a policy of voluntary euthanasia, based on either a negative right to die (a right to noninterference) or a positive right to die (a right to be killed), would involve such a change in society's vision of the medical profession and medical attitudes that a shift in the burden of proof to the proponents of change is inevitable. The prohibition of killing is not arbitrary even when cases of voluntary request are factored in. It expresses some important moral principles, values, and attitudes whose loss, or serious alteration, could have major negative consequences. Because the current practice of prohibiting killing while accepting some "allowed deaths" has served us well, if not perfectly, it should be altered only with the utmost caution. Lines are not easy to draw and maintain, but in general we have been able to follow the line between killing and letting die in medical practice. Before we undertake any major changes, we need strong evidence that these changes are really needed in order to avoid important harms or secure important benefits, and that the good effects will outweigh the bad effects.

Notes

1. It is a mistake to view these expressions as synonymous, though the present statement appears to.

2. James Rachels, "Active and Passive Euthanasia," *New England Journal of Medicine* (January 9, 1975), 292:78–80. For valuable discussions of the distinction between

killing and letting die, see Bonnie Steinbock, ed., *Killing and Letting Die* (Englewood Cliffs, N.J.: Prentice-Hall, 1980); and John Ladd, ed., *Ethical Issues Relating to Life and Death* (New York: Oxford University Press, 1979).

3. Richard L. Trammell, "Saving and Taking Life," *Journal of Philosophy* (1975), 72: 131–137.

4. Gilbert Meilaender, "The Distinction Between Killing and Allowing to Die," *Theological Studies* (1976), 37: 467–470.

5. See John Rawls, "Two Concepts of Rules," *Philosophical Review* (1955), 64: 3–32.

6. G. J. Hughes, S. J., "Killing and Letting Die," *The Month* (1975), 236:42–45.

7. David Louisell, "Euthanasia and Biothanasia: On Dying and Killing," *Linacre Quarterly* (1973), 40: 234–258.

8. We owe most of this argument to James Rachels.

9. Charles Fried, "Rights and Health Care—Beyond Equity and Efficiency," *New England Journal of Medicine* (July 31, 1975), 293:245.

10. For a discussion of this case, see Paige Mitchell, *Act of Love: The Killing of George Zygmaniak* (New York: Knopf, 1976).

11. See Paul Ramsey, *Ethics at the Edges of Life* (New Haven: Yale University Press, 1978), p. 217; Robert Veatch, *Death, Dying, and the Biological Revolution* (New Haven, Conn.: Yale University Press, 1976) p. 97.

12. Ramsey, *Ethics at the Edges of Life,* pp. 195, 214, 216; cf. Ramsey, *The Patient as Person* (New Haven: Yale University Press, 1970), pp. 161–164.

13. Anthony Flew, "The Principle of Euthanasia," in A. B. Downing, ed., *Euthanasia and the Right to Death: The Case of Voluntary Euthanasia* (London: Peter Owen, 1969), pp. 30–48.

26

Justifying Voluntary Euthanasia

PETER SINGER, D. Phil.

Under existing laws people suffering unrelievable pain or distress from an incurable illness who ask their doctors to end their lives are asking their doctors to become murderers. Although juries are extremely reluctant to convict in cases of this kind the law is clear that neither the request, nor the degree of suffering, nor the incurable condition of the person killed, is a defense to a charge of murder. Advocates of voluntary euthanasia propose that this law be changed so that a doctor could legally act on a patient's desire to die without further suffering.

The case for voluntary euthanasia has some common ground with the case for nonvoluntary euthanasia, in that the reason for killing is to end suffering. The two kinds of euthanasia differ, however, in that voluntary euthanasia involves the killing of a person, a rational and self-conscious being and not merely a conscious being. (To be strictly accurate it must be said that this is not always so, because although only rational and self-conscious beings can consent to their own deaths, they may not be rational

Reprinted from *Practical Ethics*, pp. 140–46, with permisson of the publisher. Copyright © 1979 by Cambridge University Press.

and self-conscious at the time euthanasia is contemplated—the doctor may, for instance, be acting on a prior written request for euthanasia if, through accident or illness, one's rational faculties should be irretrievably lost. For simplicity we shall, henceforth, disregard this complication.) . . .

Let us return to the general principles about killing proposed [earlier]. I argued that the wrongness of killing a conscious being which is not self-conscious, rational or autonomous, depends on utilitarian considerations. It is on this basis that I have defended nonvoluntary euthanasia. On the other hand it is, as we saw, plausible to hold that killing a self-conscious being is a more serious matter than killing a merely conscious being. We found four distinct grounds on which this could be argued:

1. The classical utilitarian claim that since self-conscious beings are capable of fearing their own death, killing them has worse effects on others.
2. The preference utilitarian calculation which counts the thwarting of the victim's desire to go on living as an important reason against killing.
3. A theory of rights according to which to have a right one must have the ability to desire that to which one has a right, so that to have a right to life one must be able to desire one's own continued existence.
4. Respect for autonomous decisions of rational agents.

Now suppose we have a situation in which a person suffering from a painful and incurable disease wishes to die. If the individual were not a person—not rational or self-conscious—euthanasia would, as I have said, be justifiable. Do any of the four grounds for holding that it is normally worse to kill a person provide reasons against killing when the individual is a person?

The classical utilitarian objection does not apply to killing that takes place only with the genuine consent of the person killed. That people are killed under these conditions would have no tendency to spread fear or insecurity, since we have no cause to be fearful of being killed with our own genuine consent. If we do not wish to be killed, we simply do not consent. In fact, the argument from fear points in favor of voluntary euthanasia, for if voluntary euthanasia is not permitted we may, with good cause, be fearful that our deaths will be unnecessarily drawn out and distressing.

Preference utilitarianism also points in favor of, not against, voluntary euthanasia. Just as preference utilitarianism must count a desire to go on living as a reason against killing, so it must count a desire to die as a reason for killing.

Next, according to the theory of rights we have considered, it is an essential feature of a right that one can waive one's rights if one so chooses. I may have a right to privacy; but I can, if I wish, film every detail of my daily life and invite the neighbors to my home movies. Neighbors sufficiently intrigued to accept my invitation could do so without violating my right to privacy, since the right has on this occasion been waived. Similarly, to say that I have a right to life is not to say that it would be wrong for my doctor to end my life, if she does so at my request. In making this request I waive my right to life.

Lastly, the principle of respect for autonomy tells us to allow rational agents to live their own lives according to their own autonomous decisions, free from coercion or interference; but if rational agents should autonomously choose to die, then respect for autonomy will lead us to assist them to do as they choose.

So, although there are reasons for thinking that killing a self-conscious being is normally worse than killing any other kind of being, in the special case of voluntary euthanasia most of these reasons count for euthanasia rather than against. Surprising as this result might at first seem, it really does no more than reflect the fact that what is special about self-conscious beings is that they can know that they exist over time and will, unless they die, continue to exist. Normally this continued existence is fervently desired; when the foreseeable continued existence is dreaded rather than desired however, the desire to die may take the place of the normal desire to live. Thus the case for voluntary euthanasia is arguably much stronger than the case for nonvoluntary euthanasia.

Some opponents of the legalization of voluntary euthanasia might concede that all this follows, if we have a genuinely free and rational decision to die: but, they add, we can never be sure that a request to be killed is the result of a free and rational decision. Will not the sick and elderly be pressured by their relatives to end their lives quickly? Will it not be possible to commit outright murder by pretending that a person has requested euthanasia? And even if there is no pressure of falsification, can anyone who is ill, suffering pain, and very probably in a drugged and confused state of mind, make a rational decision about whether to live or die?

These questions raise technical difficulties for the legalization of voluntary euthanasia, rather than objections to the underlying ethical principles; but they are serious difficulties nonetheless. Voluntary euthanasia societies in Britain and elsewhere have sought to meet them by proposing that euthanasia should be legal only for a person who:

1. is diagnosed by two doctors as suffering from an incurable illness expected to cause severe distress or the loss of rational faculties; and
2. has, at least 30 days before the proposed act of euthanasia, and in the presence of two independent witnesses, made a written request for euthanasia in the event of the situation described in (1) occurring.

Only a doctor could administer euthanasia, and if the patient was at the time still capable of consenting, the doctor would have to make sure that the patient still wished the declaration to be acted upon. A declaration could be revoked at any time.

These provisions, though in some respects cumbersome, appear to meet most of the technical objections to legalization. Murder in the guise of euthanasia would be far-fetched. Two independent witnesses to the declaration, the 30 day waiting period, and—in the case of a mentally competent person—the doctor's final investigation of the patient's wishes would together do a great deal to reduce the danger of doctors acting on requests which did not reflect the free and rational decisions of their patients.

It is often said, in debates about euthanasia, that doctors can be mistaken. Certainly some patients diagnosed by competent doctors as suffering from an incurable condition have survived. Possibly the legalization of voluntary euthanasia would, over the years, mean the deaths of one or two people who would otherwise have recovered. This is not, however, the knock-down argument against euthanasia that some imagine it to be. Against a very small number of unnecessary deaths that might occur if euthanasia is legalized we must place the very large amount of pain and distress that will be suffered by patients who really are terminally ill if euthanasia is not legalized. Longer life is not such a supreme good that it outweighs all other considerations. (If it were, there would be many more effective ways of saving life— such as a ban on smoking, or on cars that can drive faster than 10 m.p.h.—than prohibiting voluntary euthanasia.) The possibility that two doctors may make a mistake means that the person who opts for euthanasia is deciding on the balance of probabilities, and giving up a very slight chance of survival in order to avoid suffering that will almost certainly end in death. This may be a perfectly rational choice. Probability is, as Bishop Butler said, the guide of life, and we must follow its guidance right to the end. Against this, some will reply that improved care for the terminally ill has eliminated pain and made voluntary euthanasia unnecessary. Elisabeth Kübler-Ross, whose *On Death and Dying* is perhaps the best-known book on care for the dying, has claimed that none of her patients request euthanasia. Given personal attention and the right medication, she says, people come to accept their deaths and die peacefully without pain.

Kübler-Ross may be right. It may be possible, now, to eliminate pain. It may even be possible to do it in a way which leaves patients in possession of their rational faculties and free from vomiting, nausea, or other distressing side-effects. Unfortunately only a minority of dying patients now receive this kind of care. Nor is physical pain the only problem. There can also be other distressing conditions, like bones so fragile they fracture at sudden movements, slow starvation due to a cancerous growth, inability to control one's bowels or bladder, difficulty in breathing and so on.

Take the case of Jean Humphry, as described in *Jean's Way*. This is not a case from the period before effective painkillers: Jean Humphry died in 1975. Nor is it the case of someone unable to get good medical care: she was treated at an Oxford hospital and if there were anything else that could have been done for her, her husband, a well-connected Fleet St. journalist, would have been better placed than most to obtain it. Yet Derek Humphry writes:

when the request for help in dying meant relief from relentless suffering and pain and I had seen the extent of this agony, the option simply could not be denied . . . And certainly Jean deserved the dignity of selecting her own ending. She must die soon—as we both now realized—but together we would decide when this would be.

Perhaps one day it will be possible to treat all terminally ill patients in such a way that no one requests euthanasia and the subject becomes a non-issue; but this still distant prospect is no reason to deny euthanasia to those who die in less comfortable conditions. It is, in any case, highly paternalistic to tell dying patients that they are now so well looked after they need not be offered the option of euthanasia. It would be more in keeping with respect for individual freedom and autonomy to legalize euthanasia and let patients decide whether their situation is bearable—let them, as Derek Humphry puts it, have the dignity of selecting their own endings. Better that voluntary euthanasia be an unexercised legal right than a prohibited act which, for all we know, some might desperately desire.

Finally, do these arguments for voluntary euthanasia perhaps give too much weight to individual freedom and autonomy? After all, we do not allow people free choices on matters like, for instance, the taking of heroin. This is a restriction of freedom but, in the view of many, one that can be justified on paternalistic grounds. If preventing people becoming heroin addicts is justifiable paternalism, why isn't preventing people having themselves killed?

The question is a reasonable one, because respect for individual freedom can be carried too far. John Stuart Mill thought that the state should never interfere with the individual except to prevent harm to others. The individual's own good, Mill thought, is not a proper reason for state intervention. But Mill may have had too high an opinion of the rationality of a human being. It may occasionally be right to prevent people making choices which are obviously not rationally based and which we can be sure they will later regret. The prohibition of voluntary euthanasia cannot be justified on paternalistic grounds, however, for voluntary euthanasia is, by definition, an act for which good reasons exist. Voluntary euthanasia occurs only when, to the best of medical knowledge, a person is suffering from an incurable and painful or distressing condition. In these circumstances one cannot say that to choose to die quickly is obviously irrational. The strength of the case for voluntary euthanasia lies in this combination of respect for the preferences, or autonomy, of those who decide for euthanasia; and the clear rational basis of the decision itself.

27

Beneficent Euthanasia and Benemortasia: Alternative Views of Mercy

ARTHUR DYCK, Ph.D.

Debates about the rightness or wrongness of mercy killing generate heated displays of emotion. There are those who consider it so cruel deliberately to end the lives of relatively powerless individuals who are dying that they tend to imagine that only people who are merciless, like the prototypical Nazi agent, could sanction such acts. At the same time, there are others who find it so cruel to wait for death if a dying person is suffering that they tend to regard opponents of mercy killing as insensitive moral legalists, willing to be inhuman for the sake of obedience to absolute rules. Both the proponents and opponents of mercy killing think of themselves as merciful, but each finds it virtually impossible to think of the other as merciful. Perhaps the reader holds the view that moral debates generally engage our deepest emotions. Regardless of our views on that topic, I would like to examine some of the reasons for the strong disagreements that exist between proponents and opponents of mercy killing.

The debate over mercy killing involves different under-

Reprinted from Marvin Kohl, ed., *Beneficent Euthanasia*, pp. 117–18, 124–29, with the permission of the publisher. Copyright © 1975 by Prometheus Books. Some footnotes renumbered.

standings of what it means to show mercy. Indeed, *Webster's New World Dictionary* attaches at least two quite different meanings to the word *mercy*.[1] On the one hand, mercy refers to a constraint against acting in certain ways. Mercy defined in this way is "a refraining from harming or punishing offenders, enemies, persons in one's power, etc." To kill someone is a commonly recognized form of harm, so that refraining from killing someone, particularly someone in one's power, can be seen as being merciful. The association of "mercy" and "failing to kill or be killed" is rendered explicit when the dictionary further defines mercy as "a fortunate thing; thing to be grateful for; blessing (a *mercy* he wasn't killed)."

On the other hand, the dictionary defines mercy as "a disposition to forgive, pity, or be kind" and as "kind or compassionate treatment; relief of suffering." Those who advocate mercy killing under certain circumstances emphasize this meaning of mercy. For them, killing can be justified when it is done out of kindness for the relief of suffering. Because proponents of mercy killing wish to observe and uphold the general prohibition against killing, they limit relief of suffering to instances where suffering can no longer be seen as serving any useful purpose. They speak, therefore, of needless or unnecessary suffering.

So far I have used the term *mercy killing* where many now use the word *euthanasia*. Originally the Greek word *euthanasia* meant painless, happy death. This meaning still appears as one definition of the term. However, a second meaning is now usually added that specifies euthanasia as an "act or method of causing death painlessly, so as to end suffering: advocated by some as a way to deal with persons dying of incurable, painful diseases."[2] Increasingly, euthanasia has come to be equated with mercy killing. For the purposes of this essay, therefore, I will use *mercy killing* and *euthanasia* as synonyms referring to the deliberate inducement of a quick, painless death.

The problem I wish to pose in this essay is whether or not the desire and obligation to be merciful or kind commits us to a policy of euthanasia. Some have claimed that there is a moral obligation to be kind or beneficent and that beneficent euthanasia is, therefore, not only morally justified but morally obligatory. This is a claim that deserves the careful scrutiny of any morally conscientious person. Having examined the arguments for beneficent euthanasia, I will then consider the possibility of an alternative notion of what mercy or kindness requires in those situations where mercy killing would appear to be morally justified or even obligatory.

.   .   .   .

An Ethic of Benemortasia

It is not possible here to do more than sketch some of the main contours of a policy that accepts mercy as a moral obligation but rejects beneficent euthanasia or mercy killing. Such a sketch will, however, clarify the different conceptions of mercy and human dignity that distinguish an ethic of benemortasia from an ethic of beneficent euthanasia.

Because euthanasia no longer functions as a merely descriptive term for a happy or good death, it is necessary to invent another term for this purpose. I have chosen the word "benemortasia," which is derived from two familiar Latin words, *bene* (good) and *mors* (death). What *bene* in benemortasia means depends upon the ethical framework that one adopts in order to interpret what it is to experience a good death, or at least what would be the most morally responsible way to behave in the face of death, either one's own or that of others. The ethic of benemortasia suggested in this essay is concerned with how we ought to behave toward those who are dying or whose death would appear to be a merciful event. It is not necessarily the only ethic one might or should adopt, nor is it complete in scope as presented here.

The ethic of benemortasia that I wish to argue for recognizes mercy or kindness as a moral obligation. Mercy is understood in at least two ways: first, it is merciful not to kill; second, it is merciful to provide care for the dying and the irremediably handicapped where consent is obtained without coercion. (Instances where voluntary consent to care being offered cannot be obtained from its intended recipients, as in cases of comatose or

severely retarded patients, raise special issues that will be discussed later.)

The injunction not to kill is part of a total effort to prevent the destruction of human beings and of the human community. It is an absolute prohibition in the sense that no society can
be indifferent about the taking of human life. Any act, insofar as
it is an act of taking a human life, is wrong; that is to say, taking
a human life is a wrong-making characteristic of actions.

To say, however, that killing is prima facie wrong does
not mean that an act of killing may never be justified.[3] For example, a person's effort to prevent someone's death may lead to
the death of the attacker. However, we can morally justify that
act of intervention because it is an act of saving a life, but not
because it is an act of taking a life. If it were simply an act of
taking a life, it would be wrong.

Advocates of beneficent euthanasia would generally agree
that one should not kill innocent people, particularly those who
are as powerless to defend themselves as the dying and the handicapped. However, restraint against harming people is not enough.
What about positive actions to relieve pain and suffering?

For our ethic of benemortasia, at least the following kinds
of care can be given to patients who are considered to be immi-
nently dying: (1) relief of pain, (2) relief of suffering, (3) respect
for a patient's right to refuse treatment, and (4) universal provision of health care.

1. *Relief of pain.* There is widespread agreement among
those who oppose beneficent euthanasia but who believe in
mercy that pain relief can be offered to patients even when it
means shortening the dying process. This is not considered
killing or assisting in a killing because the cause of death is the
terminal illness of the patient, and the shortening of the dying
process has to do with a choice on the part of a patient to live
with less pain during his last days. All of us make choices about
whether we will seek pain relief. When we are not terminally ill
we also make choices about the kind of care we do or do not
seek. There is no reason to deny such freedom to someone who
is dying. Indeed, there is every reason to be especially solicitous
of a person who is terminally ill. There is no legal or moral
objection to the administration of pain relief provided it is for

that purpose and not for the purpose of killing someone. This means that one does not knowingly give an overdose of a pain reliever, but rather concentrates on dosages that are sufficient for relief of pain, knowing that at some point the dose administered will be final. Indeed, the official regulations of Roman Catholic hospitals in this country explicitly permit hastening the dying process through the adminstration of pain relief.

2. *Relief of suffering.* Suffering is not the same as pain, although in instances where pain is extremely excruciating, it is virtually impossible to avoid suffering. We know, for example, that physicians can relieve suffering in a variety of ways. There is some evidence that patients who know they are dying generally suffer less and are less inclined to ask for pain relief than those who do not know that they are dying. We know also that one of the major sources of suffering for dying people is loneliness and lack of companionship. Our ethic of benemortasia would consider it not only merciful but part of good care in the strictest medical sense to make provision for companionship, whether with medical, paramedical, or other kinds of persons brought to the hospital expressly for this purpose. Churches and other voluntary organizations often assist in this way. Note also the splendid care provided by someone like Elisabeth Kübler-Ross, who is an opponent of beneficent euthanasia but a staunch proponent and practitioner of mercy in the form of relief of suffering.[4]

3. *A patient's right to refuse treatment.* Dying patients are also living patients. They retain the same right as everyone else voluntarily to leave the hospital or to refuse specific kinds of care. Indeed, the right to refuse care is legally recognized. No new law is required to allow patients to exercise their rights. One of the important good effects of the whole discussion of euthanasia is that all of us, including health professionals, are becoming more sensitive to this right to refuse care. Given the concern not to kill, one would continue to expect that physicians who hold out some hope of saving a life would usually presuppose consent to try to save patients who in a desperate state may be expressing a wish to die.

Those who are irreversibly comatose or those who . . . have no functioning of the cerebral cortex, no use of muscles, and so forth, pose special difficulties, both for an ethic of beneficent euthanasia and an ethic of benemortasia. In such instances we are dealing with very tragic circumstances. No decision we make is totally satisfactory from a moral point of view. From the standpoint of our ethic of benemortasia, there is a strong presumption to continue supporting the irreversibly comatose and the severely brain-damaged until there is virtually no reasonable hope of sustaining life, apart from measures that go far beyond ordinary care. There comes a point when the decision to let die can be made out of mercy and also out of the recognition that for the irreversibly comatose death is inevitable and that for the severely brain-damaged child it would be merciful to withhold more than ordinary care in the face of the next serious bout of illness, recognizing also that such episodes of illness will be frequent and devastating. The difference between beneficent euthanasia and our ethic of benemortasia is that, whereas the former would deliberately induce death, the latter, as a last resort after making every effort to save and repair life, mercifully retreats in the face of death's inevitability.

4. *Universal health care.* In order to be merciful as well as just in the provision of care for dying and severely handicapped people, no single person or family should have to bear alone the burden of extensive medical costs. It is notorious that poor people are more often and much sooner let go as dying persons than those who have ample financial resources. Those concerned with mercy should also bear in mind that the much higher rates of maternal and infant death suffered by blacks is one of the more subtle, systemic ways in which a society can permit euthanasia. It is difficult to imagine that anyone could call such subtle forms of euthanasia in any sense merciful or beneficent. Discussions of beneficent euthanasia should not overlook these subtle forms of injustice to people in need of care.

So far, in discussing an ethic of benemortasia, I have stressed the ways in which mercy can be extended to patients without inducing death. However, the proponents of beneficent euthanasia would not be completely satisfied in all cases with the form that mercy takes in our ethic of benemortasia. [They] emphasize a quick, painless death. Our ethic of benemortasia emphasizes erring on the side of the protection of life, while still minimizing suffering. In order to understand this remaining difference between beneficent euthanasia and our ethic of benemortasia, it is necessary to see that they differ with respect to their notions of what constitutes human dignity.

Proponents of beneficent euthanasia tend to rest their case on the following kinds of presuppositions: (1) that the dignity that attaches to personhood by reason of the freedom to make moral choices demands also the freedom to take one's own life or to have it taken when this freedom is absent or lost; (2) that there is such a thing as a life not worth living, a life that lacks dignity, whether by reason of distress, illness, physical or mental handicaps, or even sheer despair for whatever reason; (3) that what is sacred or supreme in value is the "human dignity" that resides in the rational capacity to choose and control life and death.

Our ethic of benemortasia as outlined here rests on the following kinds of presuppositions about human dignity: (1) that the dignity that attaches to personhood by reason of the freedom to make moral choices includes the freedom to refuse noncurative, life-prolonging interventions when one is dying, but does not extend to taking one's life or causing the death of someone who is dying, because that would be unjustified killing; (2) that every life has some worth; (3) that notions of dignity are judged on the basis of what is right, merciful, and just, obligations that the dying and those who care for them share. Being less than perfect, humans require constraints on their decisions regarding the dying. No human being or human community can presume to know who deserves to live or die. From a religious perspective, some would leave that kind of decision to God.[5]

There are two critical differences between these two sets of presuppositions. Whereas in the ethic of beneficent euthanasia, life of a certain kind, or life having dignity, is what has value, in our ethic of benemortasia, life as such retains some value whatever form it takes. This does not mean that an opponent of beneficent euthanasia cannot let die or administer pain relief that may hasten death. What it means is that life as a value is always a consideration; that is one reason why the onus is on those who believe a person should be allowed to die to give stringent and compelling reasons for their belief.

Another critical difference between these two ethical views is that the notion of mercy in our ethic of benemortasia is controlled by what is considered right, particularly the injunction not to kill, on which a wide moral and social consensus exists. The notion of mercy in an ethic of beneficent euthanasia as depicted, for example, by [Marvin] Kohl and Joseph Fletcher[6] is controlled by the conception of human dignity. One of the reasons that Kohl and Fletcher insist upon including quick death is their belief that certain lives are quite undignified and only become dignified in death. It is for this reason that Fletcher can speak of a right to die.

It is precisely this appeal to some notion of dignity to justify killing that evokes "wedge" arguments. As I indicated previously, there are serious and widespread differences among people about what constitutes human dignity. If who shall live and who shall die is made contingent upon these widely divergent views of human dignity, moral and legal policies that justify mercy killing can in principle justify a very narrow and/or a very wide range of instances in which it will be claimed that we as a society are obligated to kill someone. No one using "wedge" arguments against beneficent euthanasia need predict whether at a given moment in history a country like the United States will or will not, if euthanasia becomes lawful, use such laws to indulge in widespread killing of helpless people. The point of the wedge argument is that logically and actually there is no provision made by proponents of beneficent euthanasia for limiting in principle the notion of human dignity and for guaranteeing some kind of concensus about what constitutes human dignity. In the absence of such a consensus, it is understandable that some people having certain notions of human dignity will welcome a policy of beneficent euthanasia, whereas others will be fearful of their lives should euthanasia be legalized.

The debate concerning what constitutes human dignity cannot be easily resolved. There are deep philosophical and religious differences that divide people on that issue. However, the injunction not to kill is not divisive in this way. Much of the emotion generated by the debate over euthanasia finds its source precisely in the understandable and deep uneasiness that many individuals feel when they are asked to move away from a stringent notion of refraining from acts of killing, regarding which there is widespread agreement, and to make judgments about who shall live and who shall die on the basis of conceptions of human dignity, regarding which there are deep religious, ethnic, philosophical, and other differences. Anyone who would argue for beneficent euthanasia needs to confront this difficult and divisive aspect of his proposal. [Proponents of euthanasia] will either have to present a notion of human dignity on which widespread agreement can be obtained or make a case for beneficent euthanasia that does not depend on such a complex set of assumptions about human dignity. Until one or the other of these cases is rendered plausible by proponents of beneficent euthanasia, many of us will continue to work out and try to refine an ethic of benemortasia.

Notes

1. *Webster's New World Dictionary,* 2d college ed., David B. Guralnik, ed., (Englewood Cliffs, N.J.: Prentice-Hall, and New York: World, 1970), p. 889.

2. *Ibid.,* p. 484.

3. W. D. Ross, *The Right and the Good* (London: Oxford University Press, 1930).

4. Elisabeth Kübler-Ross, *On Death and Dying* (New York: Macmillan, 1970).

5. See Arthur J. Dyck, "An Alternative to the Ethic of Euthanasia," in R. H. Williams, ed., *To Live and To Die: When, Why and How?* (New York: Springer-Verlag, 1973), pp. 98–112, for a fuller discussion of the way in which these presuppositions emerge.

6. See Marvin Kohl, "Understanding the Case for Beneficent Euthanasia," *Science, Medicine and Man* (1973), 1:111–121; and Kohl, "Beneficent Euthanasia," *The Humanist* (July/August 1974), pp. 9–11. Also see Joseph Fletcher, "The Patient's Right to Die," in A. B. Downing, ed., *Euthanasia and the Right to Death* (New York: Humanities Press, 1971).

28

Deciding for Yourself: The Objections

DANIEL MAGUIRE, S.T.D.

I t is fair to say that if you do not know the objections to your position, you do not know your position. This was a firm conviction in the great medieval universities, where the position of the adversaries was given unique prominence. The *Summa* of Thomas Aquinas, for example, leads off each article with the objections to his position, and quite regularly he makes the principal points of his case not in exposition but rather in response to the objections. There is a wisdom in this medieval tactic (I refuse to accept the term *medieval* as pejorative) that we could well reappraise and reappropriate. In modern terms, it recognized the dialectical nature of our approach to truth, or, more simply, it recognized that the delicate reality of truth is grasped by our minds only in the tension of point and counterpoint, position and counterposition. "We know in part," said Paul the Apostle with masterful epistemological insight. And only by staying in contact with the parts that others are on to can we move our knowledge from more imperfect to less imperfect. That said, let us look at the main objections to the idea of choosing to end your own life by positive means.

The Domino Theory

Writing in the *Indiana Law Journal,* Luis Kutner observes matter-of-factly that efforts to legalize "voluntary euthanasia" have been persistently rejected because they "appear to be an entering wedge which opens the door to possible mass euthanasia and genocide."[1] What Kutner says is a commonplace in the literature that treats of death by choice. He is evoking, of course, the ghost of Nazi Germany, where some 275,000 people are thought to have perished in "euthanasia centers." There is no precedent that is more regularly brought forward than this one, and well it should be, for what happened in Germany did not happen in an ancient tribe centuries ago, but in a modern state with which we have not a few bonds of cultural kinship.

Analogies, of course, are our way of knowing. We meet something new and immediately a number of similar or analogous realities come to mind. We come to know the unknown by relating it to the related known. That is all well and good. But analogies are also tricky, and the mind can indulge in false analogues. By this I mean that we can compare a present situation to a past one and be so impressed by the possible similarities that we miss the differences.

It is argued that German euthanasia in the Nazi period began at a more moderate level. It was to involve only the severely and hopelessly sick. Originally, it was not to be allowed for Jews since it was seen as a privilege for "true" Germans. But once begun it grew and spread preposterously, until thousands of socially unproductive, defective, and, eventually, racially "tainted" persons were liquidated. "Useless eaters," Hitler called them. And it all started, as Leo Alexander writes, "from small beginnings."[2] The conclusion drawn from this is that if we allow any exceptions, any "small beginnings," we too shall fall into the excesses of the

Nazis. For this reason positive acts to end the lives of consenting persons, or life-ending actions taken by those persons themselves, are to be seen as absolutely unconscionable.

Let me begin to confront this Nazi analogy by the technique which past logicians called *retorqueo argumentum* . . . turning the example back on the one who uses it. This technique does not disprove the argument offered, but it does conduct exploratory surgery on its presuppositions.

Therefore, let it be similarly argued that the Nazi war machine began from "small beginnings." It began when the first humans began to kill one another to settle differences. Through the process of military evolution, this grew to the preposterous point of *Blitzkrieg* and the Nazi military atrocities of World War II. Therefore, relying on the Nazi experience and relying on many other ghastly historical examples of the abuse of military kill-power (which can make this case stronger than that against euthanasia) we can conclude that all forms of killing, even in self-defense, should be morally banned. We should, in a word, become absolute pacifists, and not allow the "small beginnings," which have throughout history generated bloodbath after bloodbath. If the Nazi analogy forbids euthanasia, then it should also, and indeed *a fortiori,* given the history of military carnage, forbid war.

We could make a similar *retorqueo* argument regarding sterilization. The Nazi practice of eugenic sterilization might be argued as the basis for an absolutist stance against all sterilization. Add to the Nazi experience here the excesses revealed in the United States, where children were sterilized apparently without consent (*Time,* July 23, 1973). Given these facts of abuse, should not the possibility of abuse be precluded by an absolute moral ban on sterilization?

Similarly, and finally, could not a case be constructed against the morality of developing and retaining nuclear weapons by citing the Hiroshima and Nagasaki atrocities? Such attacks could happen again. Development and deployment are not even "small beginnings." Therefore, if the thrust of the Nazi analogy used against death by choice is valid, all these should be considered, again *a fortiori,* as beyond the moral pale.

The answer that would be given to my *retorqueo* arguments here would be that I am overworking analogies and not noting the differences between past and present situations. I would make the same response to the analogy regarding death by choice.

There are many differences between our setting and that of Nazi Germany, however many alarming similarities can be found. I shall note four of them. First, the euthanasia program of the Nazis was an explicit repudiation of the individualistic philosophy that animates this country. Mercy killing for the benefit of the patient was not the point in Germany, and was rejected. People were killed because their life was deemed to be of no value to German society. The uselessness of the patient to the community was decisive. Though this idea was resisted heroically by many Germans, and though the mass destruction of mental patients even had to be revoked by the Nazis due to public outcry, still the German context was all too susceptible to this collectivist form of ethic. The motif of individual rights simply was not as ingrained in the society of Nazi Germany as it is today in our society. Indeed, in our society, it tends to be exaggerated. This makes for a major difference to which the Nazi analogists should advert.

A second weakness in the Nazi analogy is that our society is not nearly so homogeneous as German society. American society, we are discovering as we emerge from illusions of oneness, is made up of "unmeltable ethnics" and conflicting cultures. This does not mean that the whole country cannot get jelled into oneness when civil religion gets activated by some national crisis, though even that is getting more difficult to do. But it does suggest that on matters of individual morality, our pluralism is incorrigible. This would seem to augur well for the possibilities of critical debate on any issue such as death by choice. Again, it is a difference worth noting before we concede that the Nazi "parade of horrors" will be our portion if we admit the possibility of some exceptions in the area of voluntary imposition of death.

A third reason to limit the Nazi analogy is the Nazi experience itself. We now have that grotesque episode emblazoned on our cultural memory. The stark experiences of Nazism have become important symbols in our collective consciousness. This does not mean that knowledge is virtue, but it does suggest that deeply ingrained knowledge of human wickedness can help to deter. The wickedness has a harder time now slipping in unbeknownst. Our *when* is different from their *when,* and that is a difference. Their experience gives us a vantage point that makes our situation to that degree advantageously dissimilar.

Fourth and finally, the opening of the question of voluntary dying is now arising in an atmosphere where death is being reevaluated as a potential good, not in an atmosphere where the utilitarian value of certain lives is the issue. How a question arises is important for the conclusions that may follow. The question currently is not whether life is worth living, but whether death, in its own good time, is worth dying. This cultural reevaluation of death is another major and influential difference.

In conclusion then, on the Nazi analogy, it is illuminating. It gives us an example of the iniquity of men that in our earlier naïveté we might have thought implausible. It must never be allowed to leak out of our memories, for of such chastening memories is moral progress made. We must face the painful fact that the Nazis were, like us, members of the species that calls itself *sapiens,* but is nevertheless capable of staggering malice. One can grant all of this and still be able to say that the decision to end life voluntarily in certain cases may be moral if there is proportionate reason to do so.

The domino or wedge theory, however, may be presented in more subtle dress. It is inferred that if we allow exceptions even in the case of a mature adult who wishes his death in the face of unbearable alternatives, the logic of the dominoes will still obtain and send us cascading all the way to compulsory imposition of death. As G. K. Chesterton put it: "Some are proposing what is called euthanasia; at present only a proposal for killing those who are a nuisance to themselves; but soon to be applied to those who are a nuisance to other people."[3] At the very least, it is argued, there will be as a result of this a general erosion of the respect for the sanctity of life. Those who object in this fashion do not see exceptions as the harbingers of a new Hitlerian *Reich* but as slackenings in our already precarious grasp of the sacredness of life. . . .

This possibility of abuse might suggest two remedies: keep the taboo (on the grounds that where there are *no* exceptions there can be no *abusive* exceptions) or make the necessary distinctions where there are differences and strive to contain the possible abuses. There is an old Latin axiom that pertains to this problem: *abusus non tollit usum,* the fact that something can be abused does not mean that it should not be used. Rather, the use should be promoted if it is good, and the abuse curtailed by every means available.

To say that there is no possible way of curtailing abuse if we grant the morality of some voluntary, self-imposed (or assisted) acts of death by choice, and then to conclude that because of that impossibility, no such act can be moral, is an immense and unwarranted leap. Such an argument would not be accepted in other contexts. Suppose one were to argue that all investigatory or experimental medicine, even when performed on consenting subjects, is immoral on the grounds of the extreme danger of abuse. If one were to impose the logic of the domino, a similar case could be made. One could say that, theoretically, the domino or wedge theory does not hold, but given the nature of man, abuse will follow upon use, involuntary experimentation upon voluntary. To support such a case one could turn to Dr. Henry K. Beecher, who reports on the kinds of experiments that go on. He is not selecting rare and extraordinary cases, but assures us that "examples can be found wherever experimentation in man occurs to any significant extent."[4]

To cite a few of his randomly selected examples: 31 subjects, 29 of them black, were used in a study of cyclopropane. Toxic levels of carbon dioxide were achieved and maintained for considerable lengths of time, creating a condition that often leads to fatal fibrillation of the heart.

Whether or not the subjects gave consent, this type of experimentation is a sort of medical roulette. Without the consent of the subjects, the experiment would be gross in its immorality. With the consent, the case becomes open to discussion, but one wonders whether 31 subjects could be found to accept experiments at these stakes if they were really informed as to the nature of the stakes.

In another case, 22 human subjects were injected with live cancer cells. They were "merely told they would be receiving 'some cells.' " One of the investigators admitted that he would not have submitted to such a risky experiment himself.

A final example concerns the treatment of patients suffering from acute streptococcic pharyngitis. For experimental reasons, penicillin was withheld from 525 men despite the investigator's avowed knowledge that "penicillin and other antibiotics will prevent the subsequent development of rheumatic fever." Dr. Beecher reports the result: "Thus, 25 men were crippled, perhaps for life." He adds the significant data that the subjects were not informed, did not consent, and were not aware that any kind of experiment was being performed.

Note well, Dr. Beecher is not detailing experiments conducted in Nazi Germany, but "practices found in industry, in the universities, and university hospitals and private hospitals, in the government, the army, the air force, the navy, the Public Health Service, the National Institutes of Health, and the Veterans Administration." He cites a salient and portentous motive for research experimentation by observing that, in recent years, few if any doctors achieved professorships until they proved themselves productive in investigatory research. From the patient's viewpoint, that introduces a conflict of interest. In spite of these gory examples, which Beecher says "are by no means rare" and which indicate not what might happen but what has happened, I would not see the domino theory as proving that all human experimentation is immoral. Neither do I find my colleagues in ethics rushing to that conclusion. A harsh judgment must be levied against abuses of investigatory medicine, and defenses against them must be mounted, but experimental medicine, under proper conditions, justified by proportionate reasons, may be morally good. The abuse does not make all use wrong.

The matter of experimentation is, I judge, especially useful because it shows the fallacy in the use of the domino or wedge theory used against death by choice. Whereas actual and very impressive abuses in experimentation (including death, mutilation, and deception) do not lead to the conclusion that all experimentation is immoral, the *potential* abuses of death by choice are offered to support the judgment that all death by choice is immoral. If it can be shown that the dangers inherent in death by choice are worse and unavoidable, the case against death by choice will stand. Short of that, this argument fails.

Also, those who argue this way leave themselves open to

the charge of the British philosopher Anthony Flew. Flew argues for voluntary euthanasia only. He does not argue the case for ending the lives of those who are not in a position to consent because they are permanently unconscious. Flew is impatient with those who respond to this argument by saying that they cannot countenance the involuntary euthanasia which presumably would follow from the voluntary kind. His retort: "Anyone, therefore, who dismisses what is in fact being contended on the gratuitously irrelevant grounds that he could not tolerate compulsory euthanasia, may very reasonably be construed as thereby tacitly admitting inability to meet and to overcome the case actually presented."[5]

The domino or wedge theory warns us against the possible diminishment of respect for life that may flow from the acknowledgment of another exception to the principle that forbids killing. To this extent it is to be taken seriously. It focuses our attention on foreseeable effects, and good ethics requires this because effects *partially* constitute the moral object. The domino theory does not, however, prove that every single act of voluntary death by choice is immoral. To attempt to achieve so much so simplistically is to fall under the indictment of the ancient adage: *qui nimis probat, nihil probat.* He who proves too much, proves nothing. . . .

Playing God

In one form or other the objection is often heard that to take steps to end life is playing God, for it is God's prerogative to determine the end of life, not man's. To terminate a life is to violate the property rights of God. As the objection is often phrased, it sounds like a program of pure pacifism. Interrogation, however, usually reveals that the objector does not object to killing in war. There, apparently, we have a permit from God to go at it, using appropriate ethical calculations.

The objection is, at root, a kind of religious, biologistic determinism. Now that, admittedly, is a mouthful. In more kindly language, what the objection implies is that God's will is identified with the processes of man's physical and biological nature. When God wants you to die, your organs will fail or disease will overcome you. Organic collapse is the medium through which God's will is manifested. Positive action to accelerate death, however, would amount to wrestling the matter out of God's hands and taking it into your own. It is a sin of arrogant presumption.

If this objection were taken literally, it would paralyze technological man. And this, of course, would mean that it would paralyze medicine. For if it is wrong to accelerate death, by what right do we delay it by ingenious cures and techniques? Is not medicine tampering with God's property rights by putting off the moment of death and thus frustrating God in his effort to reclaim his property?

Men who believe that God's will is manifested through the physical facts and events of life would have to sit back and await the good pleasure of Nature. All efforts to step in and take over by reshaping the earth in accord with our own designs would be blasphemous. We are here at the level of discourse expressible in the statement: if God wanted to you to fly, he would have given you wings.

The mentality of this objection is utterly at odds with genuine Christian theology. According to the Christian view, man is created in the image of the creator God. He is thus himself commissioned to creativity, a co-creator with God destined to exercise fruitful and ingenious stewardship over the earth. He is not a pawn of the earth's forces, but a participator in God's providence, invited by his nature and his God to provide for himself and for others. This, of course, is not to say that Christian theology is committed to death by choice. It is, however, to say that the presuppositions of the "playing God" objection are not Christian even though Christians are among those who offer it.

Philosophically, there is in the "playing God" objection a problem with the idea of authority. Many people have difficulty believing that they have moral authority over their dying. One of the principal reasons why this question is opening up for reconsideration today is that the idea of authority is being rethought. This is due in no small part to technological man's new awareness of his abilities. Professor Diana Crane alludes to this when she says that there has been a change in social attitudes toward human intervention at both the beginning and the end of life. Birth and Death are now viewed as events which need not be blindly accepted by human beings. . . . Suicide and euthanasia are being tolerated to a greater extent, or at least viewed differently. Consequently, we are in the midst of developing new ethics.[6]

The natural course of events is less and less seen as normative. Unlike his ancestors, technological man is inclined to rise up, not lie down before fate. Obviously, he can overdo this, as our ecocatastrophe bears witness. But it is an apparently irreversible fact of our lives that we envision ourselves less as *Homo actus* (man acted upon) and more as *Homo agens* (man achieving). . . .

Notice, however, that we are not entirely parting company with the ancients on the issue of whether direct termination of life could be moral, but only on how we know that it can be moral. Moral authority is now seen as discoverable. Applied to the question of death by choice, we need not await a miraculous divine revelation of the sort that Abraham is said to have had, to assume this freedom. Rather we must probe and see whether there are proportionate and good reasons to recognize this moral dominion over our dying. To do this is not to play God but, if you will, to play man. It is to do what is proper to man as man, a being with power to deliberate and to act on his deliberations when that action appears to achieve what is good.

Christians and other religious persons who would oppose mercy killing must not pretend there is a divine edict against it. Father Bernard Häring, who opposes euthanasia, puts it this way: "In earlier times, the general argument, 'You may not choose when to fall into the arms of God who alone is Lord over life and death' seemed sufficient. Today however, it is not as simple as that because Christian Scientists and the Witnesses of Jehovah invoke this argument equally in proscribing blood transfusions."[7] Häring might also have added that the same argument was used by Catholics and others against the control of birth as is now used against the control of death. When Häring goes on to argue against euthanasia, he does what he has to do. He tries to find reasons against it. The reasons that he offers (e.g., "the wedge reaction") I do not find compelling, but his manner of argumentation is correct. He is seeking reasons to support a position that is not self-evident one way or the other.

Consent or Despair?

We are considering the objections against death by choice when the patient makes the decision for himself. These cases are easier to judge morally than cases where the decision is made for someone else now unconscious. How can we judge that a person has made a free decision for death? Is the patient just undergoing a temporary period of depression? Or could it be something worse than depression—his relatives? Could those who care for him be tiring of the burden and communicating to him subtly that he avail himself of his moral freedom for death by choice? Could there be, as in the mystery stories, an eager band of relatives chafing at the bit in anticipation of a rich legacy? Though this is more of a danger when we speak of deciding for someone who has lapsed into coma, the desire for death could be prompted by the selfish needs of others.

It is, of course, a fact that a person suffering does have his moments of despair when he feels that his resources of patience are spent and he can endure no more. Then he says with Job (7:15): "Strangling I would welcome rather, and death itself, than these my sufferings!" However, Job did have better days. "After his trials, Job lived on until he was a hundred and forty years old, and saw his children and his children's children up to the fourth generation" (Job 42:16). Job's story of despair, then, had a happy ending. A terminal patient cannot perhaps expect as much, although there are remarkable cases of remission of the worst of illnesses. Still, the possibility for a premature wish for death is a real problem.

Dr. G. E. Schreiner of Georgetown University Hospital reports on a kidney patient who asked to be taken off dialysis. The result of this, of course, would be his death. Dr. Schreiner gave the patient a very thorough dialysis treatment to put him in excellent chemical shape and then asked him if he still wanted to discontinue. "Don't listen to me," he replied. "That's my uremia talking, not me. I want to stay in the program." Another patient, however, said the same thing and was given the same special treatment. He persisted in his desire to stop treatment, and so he withdrew and died. (Interestingly, Dr. Schreiner says, "We allowed him to withdraw," as though the decision were the doctors' and not the patient's, even though the patient was in full and reflective possession of his senses.)

In other illnesses, it is not possible to give a treatment that will provide such favorable physical conditions for a decision. The problem of temporary depression is more difficult in these cases. Some proposed euthanasia bills have tried to meet this problem. The Voluntary Euthanasia bill offered in 1969 in England proposed a 30-day waiting period after a person made a declaration for death by euthanasia. The declaration could be revoked at any time in that period. In some cases, this could leave a person in unrelievable pain for a longer period than he might wish, but it does represent an effort to guarantee real consent.

The ways in which relatives and/or medical personnel could suction the desire to live out of a patient are not easily warded off by legislation. At the level of morality, however, the sin of such persons is heinous. We spoke of the danger of making a sick person feel useless and therefore worthless as though our ability to be of use was the base of our human dignity. Likewise, uncomfortable as we tend to be with suffering and the approach of death, it is possible to insinuate some of our inability to cope with the fact of dying. This, too, could create a premature desire for the release of death.

Most important in this regard is an awareness that it may be the patient's uremia or something else that is requesting death. If the patient is open to it, good counseling can help him evaluate his situation. Sometimes, the closer you are to the patient, the less help you would be in this kind of a decision; other kinds of closeness can give a friend or relative better qualifications than a professional counselor. Overall, the problem of consent is not insuperable, but it is also not to be minimized.

Suppose a Cure is Found

In 1921, George R. Minot was found to have diabetes at the age of 36. For the next two years he fought a losing battle to control his disease by diet, the only means then available. In 1923, insulin became available and Dr. Minot's life was saved. After this, Minot went to work on a series of experiments that culminated in his 1927 report that large quantities of liver could bring about the regeneration of red cells in the bone marrow. This was an effective treatment of pernicious anemia and won for Minot the Nobel prize in 1934.

This story called dramatic attention to the possibility of a new cure being found to bring sudden and unexpected help for a disease that had been fatal. Many people use this argument against death by choice, the idea being that a cure might be just around the corner. Medical science has surprised us before.

The problem of what medicine might do is compounded by what medicine might not be able to do. I refer to the not very fine art of prognosis. Dr. Lasagna calls this art "an elusive one" and notes that "many an embarrassed doctor has failed to outlive the patient whose immediate doom he prophesied." There are also numerous cases of regression of a disease, including cancer, for no apparent reason. Dr. Lasagna writes: "Even where questionable cases are ruled out because of inadequate information, there are still a sizable number of patients considered by cancer experts to show spontaneous disappearance of what appears to be typical malignant disease."[8]

Therefore, prognosis is fallible, diseases go into unaccountable remission, the power of life is unpredictable. How could we ever impose death—an irreversible condition—since, where there is life, there is hope?

In response, I would say that for all its fallibility, prognosis can enjoy a high degree of certainty. The percentage of correct diagnosis is exceptionally high in cancer cases, and these are the patients most likely to opt for death by choice. Other terminal conditons, especially in their later stages, are open to very precise prognosis. These are cases where there is life but no hope.

With regard to the possibility of a cure, there are advanced cases where death would remain a certainty even if a cure were to be found today, due to the extent of deterioration. Also, as Anthony Flew says: "the advance of medicine has not reached a stage where all diseases are curable. And no one seriously thinks that it has. At most this continuing advance has suggested that we need never despair of finding cures *some day*."

This objection sins by abstraction. It tenders a vague hope for medical miracles as an argument against death by choice. In particular cases this vague hope can be dismissed by the concrete facts.

They Shoot Horses, Don't They?

Euthanasia is a bad word. It is bad for two reasons: first, it means too many different things to too many people. Second, it is bad because it connotes an attitude on suffering that is false.

As to its indefiniteness, Paul Ramsey says that in current usage it means direct killing and that efforts to use the term in some other way do not succeed.[9] Yet, for example, lawyer Arval Morris uses it in another way when he says that Pius XII did not uniformly condemn euthanasia. As direct killing Pius certainly did condemn it. The Euthanasia Educational Fund uses the term in two senses and therefore must employ the modifiers active and passive. A *New York Times* editorial (July 3, 1973) speaks of the frequent practice of euthanasia in this country and abroad, and then explains that normally this takes the form of a cessation of extraordinary measures. Moralist Gerald Kelly has to point out that he is not using the term euthanasia to denote the mere giving of drugs to a dying patient to ease his pain, as some theologians do.[10] Some use the qualifier "pure" euthanasia to describe the use of pain-killers which do not shorten life.[11] Also, in some cases the term has been used to describe dangerous medical experiments performed on human beings. As a result of this confusion, many people sense the need to move away from that term and develop terms that do justice to the various and different ways of meeting death. And so we meet the terms orthothanasia, agathanasia, benemortasia, dysthanasia, antidysthanasia, and mercy killing.

Most often, however, the term euthanasia has reference to direct killing with an accent on relief of suffering. Thus a dictionary definition calls it "an act or method of causing death painlessly, so as to end suffering; advocated by some as a way to deal with the victims of incurable disease." The Voluntary

Euthanasia bill of 1969 in England defined euthanasia as "the painless inducement of death." It is to this accent on painlessness that a false philosophy of suffering easily attaches. One of the bad arguments that persistently surfaces in the literature defending euthanasia is in reference to what we do for animals. As the argument goes, we see it as cruel and inhumane to leave an animal in hopeless pain and so we "put him to sleep." Could we do less for one of our own?

Because of this kind of argument, one of the arguments that is brought against any liberalization of the moral right to death by choice is that those who press such a right are infected by a crassly materialistic philosophy of suffering. Since a mistaken philosophy of suffering is reductively a mistaken philosophy of man, this objection is serious. In responding to it, I find myself responding to those who support death by choice with bad arguments (They shoot horses . . .) and to those who rely on those bad arguments to object to death by choice.

The philosophical error involved here is one that should be refutable by observation. Horses and men are different in some rather impressive ways. A horse can be relieved of his suffering but he does not have the human power to transcend that suffering by giving it meaning.

Man is a meaning seeker. Where he finds meaning he is fulfilled, and, by a remarkable alchemy, he can find meaning in the most unlikely experiences. Put in another way, man's consciousness, unlike that of the horse, is open to and geared to the pursuit of the possible that is latent in the actual. The human spirit has a divining power that can detect redemptive possibilities in a situation that would otherwise be crushing and destructive. Were Helen Keller a horse, born blind and deaf, it might have been best to shoot her. Being a person amid other persons, her exquisite possibilities could be and were realized.

Our suffering is human suffering and that means that it is suffering with possibilities. These possibilities may not always be realized, for though we be godly we are not gods. We experience limit. But still, the human capacity to transcend gives human suffering a qualitative distinctiveness.

There is no suggestion here that we return to the views of the past which gave suffering a per se value. Such a value suffering does not have, but rather assumes its meaning, value or disvalue, from the special circumstances of the sufferer. Christians see the crucifixion sufferings of Jesus as meaningful not because they have a sadistic love of crucifixions, but because the circumstances of this particular one lent it a special meaning. Only a sadomasochistic philosophy could see suffering as a value in itself. Of itself it is a disvalue to be alleviated if at all possible. Where no relief is possible, suffering at times can be made meaningfully redemptive through the creative spirit of the sufferer.

First of all, the suffering can be of benefit to the sufferer. As the British lawyer Norman St. John-Stevas put it: "The final stage of an incurable illness can be a wasteland, but it need not be. It can be a vital period in a person's life, reconciling him to life and to death and giving him an interior peace. This is the experience of people who have looked after the dying" (quoted in *America,* May 2, 1970). It should be noted, of course, that what is suggested here is something that *might* be achieved. It is also possible that it could not be and that a final agony will destroy peace rather than enhance it. In spite of all best efforts, the final stage of life may be a wasteland. It is then that the question of terminating that life takes on potential meaning, since death may be the only peace achievable.

There are possible ways also in which final suffering could be helpful to others. For one thing, the dying, while they still have sufficient consciousness, could help the living to come to a more realistic consciousness of death. Many of the dying have been doing this and Dr. Elisabeth Kübler-Ross has, in her writings, brought their teaching to a wide audience.[12]

Persons with a terminal illness who are still very alert of mind and imagination, or persons who have a serious illness such as kidney failure with a consequent need for dialysis, could see their illness as a platform from which to address the needs of their society. The sick could look for opportunities to help the well. With their unique credentials, and while their strength lasts, they could do more than they might realize. By working creatively with politicians and legislators, national health organizations, medical and legal societies, news media, writers, etc.—and in ways as yet unthought of which their healthy imaginations will bring forth—the lobby of the dying and the gravely ill could become a healing force in society. They could seek ways to address the sick priorities of our nation. They could call attention to the needs of the neglected poor of our land and of the third world. They could bear witness to the medical problems of the poor and to the need for better health insurance programs. They could educate legislators and others on the need for legislation to protect their right to die.

The words and feelings of those who stand at the brink of death have a special power. There is in literature a genre of "farewell addresses," real or imagined, but carefully preserved and attended to. The words of those who will soon leave us merit a natural and spontaneous esteem. We would have a healthier society if the dying found ways to speak to those who will survive them for a while.

While urging the positive possibilities of the suffering-dying, we cannot foreclose the sad possibility that a person's condition may be such that the value of terminating life might supersede all other values. There is such a thing as unbearable and undefeatable suffering of the sort that only death can end. In that event, it would be another mark of the distinctively human approach to death to procure the only relief imaginable. For the human person, unlike the horse, knows that he is going to die, knows that death can be a friend, and knows how to bring on death at a time when he can suffer no more. He has the capacity for death by choice; the horse does not.

Killing for the Sake of Life

Arthur J. Dyck of Harvard Divinity School opposes death by choice of the kind of which we have been speaking. He writes that "any act, insofar as it is an act of taking a human life, is wrong, that is to say, taking a human life is a wrong-making characteristic of actions." This, however, does not make Dyck an absolute pacifist. Some killing is good killing. Here is how he justifies that:

To say, however, that killing is prima facie wrong does not mean that an act of killing may never be justified. For example, a person's effort to prevent someone's death may lead to the death of the attacker. However, we can morally justify that act of intervention only because it is an act of saving a life, not because it is an act of taking a life. If it were simply an act of taking a life, it would be wrong.[13]

This particular argument of Dyck's has some basic weaknesses. First of all, most of the killing that is done in the self-defense situation of war, for example, is not done to save life in the physical sense of keeping someone alive. Most wars are fought to protect the quality of human life. They are fought because it is decided that a change in the quality of life is more important than submissive behavior that would probably let more people live but in conditions that are intolerable. Some wars, like the India–Pakistan war, can have the purported or even real purpose of ending an ongoing slaughter and therefore of "saving life." Other wars, such as wars of national independence, are waged for the same reason that tyrants are assassinated, to change the quality of life which had become intolerable under the reigning powers.

Obviously, war, tyrannicide, and killing in self-defense are different from death by choice in a medical context. In the latter case, however, the motive for imposing death is that the quality of this person's life, wracked as he may be by an undefeatable and overwhelming pain, is intolerable. Obviously, in a narrow physical sense he is not "saving" his life by choosing to end it. He does, however, decide that he is saving himself by so choosing since the minimal requirements for personal existence have been obliterated by his condition. It would be sheer materialism to identify the patient's person and personal good with physical perdurance of life in any state.

Furthermore, as Dyck says, the mandate against killing derives from the perception that "no society can be indifferent about the taking of human life." Ending the life of a person who wants it ended because of unsupportable agony is the very opposite of indifference to life. The respect for human life in this case leads to a respect for human death. Ultimately it is the experience of the value of the person that leads to the recognition of the value of death as well as the value of life.

It can also be said in response to Dyck's position that,

although he is working out of a Christian perspective, he seems to ignore the Christian belief in an afterlife. It is Christian belief that death does not end life; it merely changes its condition. The ancient preface for the Mass of the Dead says that "life is changed, not taken away" in death. For a Christian and for anyone who believes in an afterlife, to "terminate life" is not to terminate life, but to move on to a new life. With such a faith, death is not nearly so drastic. It has lost its sting of finality. This would seem to make it easier for a Christian to see death as a friend, especially when he has, through his illness, lost all ability to respond and react to the invitation of his God to join him in the building up of this earth. . . .

The Sense of Profanation

It might further be objected that there is something sacrosanct about a person's life, even his physical life. The proper attitude toward this life is awe, reverence, and support. Tampering with it, experimenting with it, or certainly ending it, is a profanation of the sacred. There is something jarring about the very idea. This, perhaps, is the reason why people have been so slow to accept the idea of mercy killing and why such killing is illegal in almost every land. This is a serious objection, based upon something (the sense of profanation) which I have presented as fundamental to good ethics.

In response, it can be said that the sense of profanation is a two-edged sword. It can, as I have mentioned, also be evoked by the sight of a person whose life is being agonizingly prolonged when truly personal living has become impossible because of unrelenting pain. In such a case, not to allow such a person the right to abbreviate his suffering could seem to subject this person to the dictates of his disease. Not being able to choose death when death is experienced as an essential benefit could easily seem degrading and profaning of personhood. Why should the disease have all the say, and the patient none? By succumbing to such moral determinism, is not the sacred power of deliberation and choice profaned?

It must be remembered, too, that the sense of profanation does not of itself constitute an independent argument. Ethics is holistic. All the questions must be asked and all the evaluational capacities of the human spirit tapped before moral judgment is pronounced. Moral discourse must operate with a system of checks and balances. No one activity or faculty, whether it be *Gemüt,* the sense of profanation, the use of principle, etc., must be allowed an unquestioned hegemony.

In the second part of this objection, it was suggested that maybe the negative stance of most law regarding mercy killing constitutes an argument (based on group experience) against mercy killing. To this, it must be said that law is rarely a pioneer which stakes out new vistas for moral freedom. Law normally has deep historical roots which can either be an illuminating asset or a recalcitrant drag on moral progress. Law has the weaknesses as well as the strengths of the past. On the positive side we must trust it as the fruit of much experience. On the negative side we must reject its myopia when we come to see an issue better. That is why law must be open to reform, or it becomes demonic.

Thomas Jefferson is an eloquent witness to the stranglehold of inadequate law. In 1816 he wrote:

I know also that laws and institutions must be hand in hand with the progress of the human mind. . . . As new discoveries are made, new truths disclosed, and manners and opinions change with the change of circumstances, institutions must advance also, and keep pace with the times. We might as well require a man to wear still the coat which fitted him when a boy, as civilized society to remain ever under the regimen of their barbarous ancestors.[14]

Before concluding that the voice of the law is the voice of God, it is well to look at the values and disvalues that the law has embodied in the past. Look how long law resisted the right of conscientious objection to war. With the greatest struggle and patience, the Quakers managed to win from government exemption to military service on conscientious grounds. And this was in 1802. For centuries this right, now generally seen as sacred, was denied by law. Long denied too was the right of women to vote and of black persons to be free. For the reasons offered in this [essay] and for reasons that others offer, I judge that current laws are denying a human right when they inhibit the individual's right to death by choice. In this case, law is a tabernacle of taboo, and not a beacon of light.

The Hippocratic Oath

Hippocrates lived in the fifth century B.C. In his time, medicine was terribly intertwined with superstition and decadent religiosity. Hippocrates is generally credited with instituting a revolution that desacralized medicine. Morris H. Saffron, the Archivist and Historian of the State Medical Society of New Jersey, says of Hippocrates: "To his majestic figure, subsequent generations of physicians turned as to a demigod, attributing to him many tracts written centuries after his death, so that the Hippocratic Corpus as it now stands, includes more than 70 works."[15] Of all the works attributed to Hippocrates, there is no part more influential than his famous oath, which has guided physicians for centuries. The key passage relevant to death by choice is this: "I will neither give a deadly drug to anybody, if asked for, nor will I make a suggestion to this effect."

This passage is thought to show the influence of Pythagorean philosophy on Hippocratic thought. Pythagoras denied the right of an individual to take his own life. It is to these words of the oath that many people repair when contradicting the right to death by choice.

The prestige of this oath is enormous. Dr. H. Pitney van Dusen, former president of Union Theological Seminary, says that he does not think "there is any other profession that is wedded to such an ancient document, not even the clerical profession with its Ten Commandments."[16] Many physicians argue from this oath against death by choice as though they have an unwavering reliance on the self-sufficiency of this text that can only be compared to the attitude of a fundamentalist sectarian to his Bible. Undoubtedly, this attitude has been productive of much good, but it is again a one-rubric approach to the ethical issues involved and it has all the deficiencies that accrue to simplism in ethics.

In an effort to open the euthanasia issue to discussion, Joseph Fletcher has taken the tack of finding contradictions in the oath (a tactic also used against fundamentalist interpreters of the Bible). Fletcher notes that the oath promises two things: first, to relieve suffering, and second, to prolong and protect life. Then he argues: "When the patient is in the grip of an agonizing and fatal disease, these two promises are incompatible. Two duties come into conflict. To prolong life is to violate the promise to relieve pain. To relieve the pain is to violate the promise to prolong and protect life."[17]

More directly to the point, however, the oath has proved itself an invaluable encapsulation of some of the highest ideals in medical history. It is, however, not inspired by God, or by Apollo or Aesculapius, who are mentioned in the historical form of the oath. It is not a divine substitute for doing ethics. It is not oracular. Though it is good, it is perfectible. In fact, a modified form of the Hippocratic oath was adopted by the General Assembly of the World Medical Association meeting in Geneva in 1948. This form of the oath was also included in the International Code of Medical Ethics, which was adopted in 1949 and is used by physicians and medical schools. This version does not include the passage that swears against giving or counseling the use of something that would cause death. This omission did not constitute an endorsement of mercy killing in any form, but it does present a declaration that would admit of either a pro or con position on death by choice.

Declaration of Geneva: I solemnly pledge myself to consecrate my life to the service of humanity. I will give to my teachers the respect and gratitude which is their due; I will practice my profession with conscience and dignity; the health of my patient will be my first consideration; I will respect the secrets which are confided in me; I will maintain by all means in my power the honor and noble traditions of the medical profession. My colleagues will be my brothers; I will not permit considerations of religion, nationality, race, party politics, or social standing to intervene between my duty and my patient. I will maintain the utmost respect for human life from the time of conception; even under threat, I will not use my medical knowledge contrary to the laws of humanity. I make these promises solemnly, freely, and upon my honor.[18]

One could maintain "the utmost respect for human life" and observe the "laws of humanity" by recognizing that the inducement of death when death is good and befitting is a reasonable and good service to human persons. The decision to do this, of course, would not be the doctor's, since he does not have the moral authority to make these decisions for anyone. His expertise does not in any way equip him to make moral decisions for his patients. He may be asked to administer the injection that causes death. In that case his conscience must guide his own response. The decision to initiate is not his; the decision to cooperate is.

Of Laws and Insurance Companies

Objection: if morality is based on reality, one of the realities of life is the law. In the United States, for example, it is illegal to induce one's own death or to help someone to end his life. Therefore, if all the arguments of ethics point to the fact that a particular act of termination might be moral, the arguments fail by reason of the illegality. It is not moral to act in a way that puts you and others at odds with the law. On top of that, insurance companies take a dim view of this sort of thing and will probably claim exemption from liability for the death. Thus your insurance is wiped out, and how could that be rational or moral?

There are practical objections. To spin out a theory that detaches from such concrete realities as law and insurance is hardly acceptable. And, indeed, it would not only make bad sense but bad ethics. First of all, then, the objection is heavy with overtones of that pernicious confusion that identifies legality and morality. In reply let it be said (again) that what is illegal may be moral, even heroically so. Of this, we have said enough previously.

Second, it is not illegal to kill yourself in all states. And modern law does not punish you by stripping you of your estate. However, in some jurisdictions, self-killing is a crime and those who aid or abet a person normally incur responsibility before the law in any jurisdiction. We have alluded to the Texas case *Sanders v. State,* where it was judged that aiding a person to kill himself is not a crime since self-killing is not a crime. This case, however, was later overruled in Texas in *Aven v. State,* which held that one who furnishes poison to another, knowing that the purpose of the latter is to commit suicide, and who assists in administering the poison which is the cause of death, is guilty of murder. Therefore, there can be no doubt about it. Death by choice does not enjoy the formal protection of the law. The tendency, as we have seen, is to treat these cases leniently, but this offers precarious promise at best. Anyone who attempts death by choice and succeeds obviously has little to fear from the law. Also, if he attempts and fails, he has little to fear even though in some states the attempt is an indictable offense. The hopes for leniency here are well founded. Assisting someone to die is, however, still legally perilous.

There are three options available in the face of this legal situation. Abstain from assisting in death by choice; assist and admit and hope for the best as Dr. Postma and Dr. Sander did; or assist clandestinely. The first course presents no legal problems. It could present moral problems if the patient's request for assistance is well considered and apparently justifiable. Then, it could be judged wrong not to give assistance such as making pills available. On the other hand, even if you felt that this person had a clear moral right to death by choice, it would be morally proper to weigh your consequent legal problems against his extended agony. Notice here again that omission is not an escape from moral choice. In such a case it is a moral choice and not necessarily a good one.

The second solution is the Postma-Sander solution. This requires considerable moral courage. Even though Dr. Postma escaped punishment in the form of a jail sentence, she must have been seriously punished by the trial and by the intense publicity visited upon her private sorrow.

Dr. Sander also had his ordeal even though he was found not guilty in the crowded, cheering courtroom. His right to practice medicine in New Hampshire was temporarily revoked and he was ousted by state and local medical societies. Reportedly, he was at one point reduced to plowing neighbors' fields for four dollars an hour. No one could be morally bound to endure what might have to be endured for assisting someone to die by positive means . . . no matter how deserving the case. Normally, we are not morally bound to heroic acts. We are here in the realm of what some moralists call ultraobligation. It could also, of course, be called the realm of moral opportunity.

Persons who do move ahead of the law here may, by their heroism, succeed in updating the law. Even within the conceptual inadequacies of the relevant American law, ingenious lawyers might be able to explore the possibility of defending this kind of action as being within the legitimate perimeters of religious freedom. Other defenses might also present themselves to the creative lawyers. The time might now be ripe for the development of precedents here.

The third course is the clandestine one. It has been suggested that there has been many an unrecorded use made of drugs such as bichloride of mercury, potassium, and some of the barbituates. This may be, but how would one judge morally? All of the reality-revealing questions would have to be asked, especially the question of who was making the decision. Only then could this course of action be judged. This clandestine course is not a priori wrong. Conscientious objection in the form of both overt and clandestine action is a necessary corrective for those situations where reality demands what the law forbids. Thus assisting a consenting person to achieve death by choice would not be wrong on the sole count of illegality.

But what of insurance? Insurance companies may protect themselves from liability by a suicide clause, at least at the beginning of a policy. The term suicide would include all forms of self-killing, whether the person was well or dying, sane or mentally ill. So someone planning to abbreviate the process of dying in which he finds himself, has to weigh the possibility of loss of coverage. In proportional calculus this might outweigh the gains of an earlier death . . . or it might not. But what of the morality of a person surreptitiously hastening his death in a way that allows him to keep his insurance coverage intact? Insurance companies presume that death occurs without human intervention, even though they often pay in cases of self-killing if the person has been a policyholder for a reasonably long period.

As a moralist, I would suggest that insurance companies should make distinctions where there are differences in the area of self-killing. Motive and other circumstances are, after all, reality-constituting factors. If a man who is repentant over being a poor provider takes out a policy to make his family beneficiaries, and then does himself in, in a way that makes his death look accidental, he is guilty of fraud. His generosity is at the expense of the company and other policyholders.

This is not the same as the case of a person who in extreme neurotic depression kills himself. In such a case, the darkness and terror of overwhelming emotions might plunge him into this act. This, it would seem, should be recognized as death from fatal illness. Uncontrollable depression can be fatal. It would seem wrong to punish this person posthumously by withholding payment on his policy. It can be said quite accurately that in such cases, death occurs because of illness. Normally, psychiatry will be able to attest to the active presence of serious illness preceding death in such a case. Obviously, if someone is emotionally ill when he takes out a policy, this should be revealed, since he has, by this reasoning, a potentially fatal illness. But if this kind of illness struck after the policy was taken out and while the policy is yet young, insurance coverage should not be lost any more than if the person had succumbed to rapidly developing cancer. To do otherwise reveals an archaic and cruel conception of mental illness.

There is also a difference between a person who, in ending his life, interrupts a healthy process and one who interrupts a dying process. A person dying of bone cancer who takes an overdose of barbituates is not the same as the spurned lover who throws himself off a bridge. In the latter case, there might be good reasons to withhold payment on the policy. It may seem unromantic to suggest it, but this venal fact of life might be something of a deterrent to at least some frustrated lovers. Still, even here, such a desperate act is not calculated to be too frequent in our culture and insurance empires would not be likely to crumble if they covered such pathetic cases.

In the former case, involving the person dying of bone cancer, acceleration of his death should not in any way affect coverage. If it does, then the insurer is, in effect, punishing the insured for not holding the insurer's moral position on death by choice. There would seem to be something immoral and possibly unconstitutional about this. At any rate, the patient is, in this case, already in the dying process. The reasonable acceleration of that process should not be subject to financial punishment.

Notes

1. Luis Kutner. "Due Process of Euthanasia: The Living Will, A Proposal," *Indiana Law Journal* (Summer 1969), 44: 539–554.

2. Leo Alexander. "Medical Science under Dictatorship," *New England Journal of Medicine* (July 14, 1949), 241:39–47.

3. Quoted by Yale Kamisar. "Euthanasia Legislation: Some Non-Religious Objections," in A. B. Downing, ed., *Euthanasia and the Right to Death* (Los Angeles: Nash Publishing, 1969), p. 115.

4. Henry K. Beecher. "Medical Research and the Individual," in Daniel Labby, ed., *Life or Death: Ethics and Options* (Seattle: University of Washington Press, 1968), p. 139.

5. Anthony Flew. "The Principle of Euthanasia," in A. B. Downing, ed., *Euthanasia and the Right to Death*.

6. Quoted by Arval Morris. "Voluntary Euthanasia," *Washington Law Review* (April 1970), 45:241.

7. Bernard Häring. *Medical Ethics* (Notre Dame, Ind.: Fides Publishers, 1973), p. 149.

8. Louis Lasagna. *Life, Death, and the Doctor* (New York: Knopf, 1968), p. 229.

9. Paul Ramsey. *The Patient as Person* (New Haven: Yale University Press, 1970), p. 149.

10. Gerald Kelly. "The Duty of Using Artificial Means of Preserving Life," *Theological Studies* (June 1950), 11:203.

11. Helen Silving. "Euthanasia: A Study of Comparative Criminal Law," *University of Pennsylvania Law Review* (December 1954), 103:351.

12. Elisabeth Kübler-Ross. *On Death and Dying* (New York: Macmillan, 1969).

13. Arthur J. Dyck. "An Alternative to the Ethic of Euthanasia," in Robert H. Williams, ed., *To Live and to Die: When, How, and Why?* (New York: Springer-Verlag, 1973), p. 103.

14. Saul K. Padover, ed., *Thomas Jefferson on Democracy* (New York: Mentor, 1939), p. 67.

15. Morris H. Saffron. "Euthanasia in the Greek Tradition," in *Attitudes Toward Euthanasia* (New York: Euthanasia Educational Fund, 1970), p. 5.

16. Henry P. van Dusen. *The Right to Die with Dignity* (New York: Euthanasia Educational Fund, 1971), p. 9.

17. Joseph Fletcher. *Morals and Medicine* (Princeton, N.J.: Princeton University Press, 1954), p. 172.

18. From G. E. W. Wolstenholme and Maeve O'Connor, eds., *Ethics in Medical Progress* (Boston: Little, Brown, 1966), p. 222.

29

People v. Montemarano

Nassau County Court,
Mineola, New York (February 5, 1974)

COUNTY COURT   NASSAU COUNTY

Indictment # 37707

THE PEOPLE OF THE STATE OF NEW YORK

-against-

Vincent A. Montemarano

I certify that:

On June 25, 1973 the Grand Jury of Nassau County filed Indictment # 37707 accusing Vincent A. Montemarano of the crimes of Murder.

On June 27, 1973 the defendant was arraigned before the Court and Plead Not Guilty to the Indictment.

On   Feb.   5,   1974   the defendant appeared before the
Hon.   Raymond L. Wilkes   and was found not guilty after
trial.

SIGNED: Mineola, New York————————————————————————
                                    County Clerk
                          HAROLD W. McCONNELL

30

People v. Gilbert

Broward County Court,
Fort Lauderdale, Florida (May 9, 1985)

JUDGMENT

The Defendant, <u>ROSWELL WARD GILBERT</u>,
being personally before this

Court represented by <u>Joseph A. Varon and Harry Gulkin</u>,
his attorney of record, and having

(*Check Applicable Provision*)

☒ Been tried and found guilty of the following crime(s)

☐ Entered a plea of guilty to the following crime(s)

☐ Entered a plea of nolo contendere to the following crime(s)

COUNT	CRIME	OFFENSE STATUTE NUMBER(S)	DEGREE OF CRIME	CASE NUMBER
I	MURDER IN THE FIRST DEGREE	782.04	CF	

and no cause having been shown why the Defendant should not be adjudicated guilty, IT IS ORDERED THAT the Defendant is hereby ADJUDICATED GUILTY of the above crime(s)

****

The Defendant is hereby ordered to pay the sum of fifteen dollars ($15.00) pursuant to F.S. 960.20 (Crimes Compensation Trust Fund). The Defendant is further ordered to pay the sum of two dollars ($2.00) as a court cost pursuant to F.S.943.25(4).

☐ The Defendant is ordered to pay an additional sum of two dollars ($2.00) pursuant to F.S.943.25(8).
(This provision is optional; not applicable unless checked).

(Check if Applicable) ☐ The Defendant is further ordered to pay a fine in the sum of $_____
pursuant to F.S.775.0835.
(This provision refers to the optional fine for the Crimes Compensation Trust Fund, and is not applicable unless checked and completed. Fines imposed as part of a sentence pursuant to F.S. 775.083 are to be recorded on the Sentence page(s)).

☐ The Court hereby imposes additional court costs in the sum of $_____

Imposition of Sentence ☐ The Court hereby stays and withholds
Stayed and Withheld   the imposition of sentence as to count(s).
(Check if Applicable)

_____

and places the Defendant on probation for a period of _____
under the supervision of the Department of Corrections (conditions of probation set forth in separate order.)

Sentence Deferred   ☐ The Court hereby defers imposition of
Until Later Date   sentence until _____.
(Check if Applicable)   (date)

The Defendant in Open Court was advised of his right to appeal from this Judgment by filing notice of appeal with the Clerk of Court within thirty days following the date sentence is imposed or probation is ordered pursuant to this adjudication. The Defendant was also ad-

vised of his right to the assistance of counsel in taking said appeal at the
expense of the State upon showing of indigence.

JUDGE

Defendant ROSWELL WARD GILBERT

Case Number 85-2596CF

SENTENCE

(as to Count _____ I _____) The Defendant, being personally
before this Court, accompanied by his attorney,
___Joseph A. Varon___, and having been adjudicated guilty
herein, and the Court having given the Defendant an opportunity to
be heard and to offer matters in mitigation of sentence, and to show
cause why he should not be sentenced as provided by law, and no
cause being shown.

(Check either provision)
if applicable)

☐ and the Court having on _____ deferred imposition of sentence until this
date.

☐ and the Court having placed the Defendant on probation and having subsequently revoked the Defendant's probation by separate order entered herein.

IT IS THE SENTENCE OF THE LAW that:

☐ The Defendant pay a fine of $ _____, plus $ _____ as
the 5% surcharge required by F.S.960.25.

☒ The Defendant is hereby committed to the custody of the Department of Corrections

☐ The Defendant is hereby committed to the custody of the Sheriff of
Broward County, Florida.
(Name of local corrections authority to be inserted at printing, if
other than Sheriff)

To be imprisoned (check one; unmarked sections are inapplicable)

XX For a term of Natural Life, mandatory 25 years before eligible for Parole.

☐ For a term of _____

☐ For an indeterminate period of 6 months to _____ years.

***

In the event the above sentence is to the Department of Corrections, the Sheriff of Broward County, Florida is hereby ordered and directed to deliver the Defendant to the Department of Corrections together with a copy of the Judgment and Sentence.

The Defendant in Open Court was advised of his right to appeal from this Sentence by filing notice of appeal within thirty days from this date with the Clerk of this Court, and the Defendant's right to the assistance of counsel in taking said appeal at the expense of the State upon showing of indigency.

In imposing the above sentence, the Court further recommends

_____

_____

_____

DONE AND ORDERED in Open Court at Broward County, Florida, this ____9____ day of ____May____ A.D., 19__85__ .
BROWARD COUNTY, FLORIDA

_____

JUDGE

SIX
Suicide

Albert Camus, in *The Myth of Sisyphus*, declares that suicide is the only truly serious philosophical problem. He means that, in a world which often seems absurd, even the most complex problems can eventually be thought through, worked out, or coped with. But the question of life's meaning remains—as does suicide as a possible option for persons who conclude that life has lost its meaning for them. The philosophical problem is justifying that act of self-destruction.

Camus concludes that suicide is not a justifiable option—even if one believes that God does not exist and the world is absurd. An increasing number of persons, however, disagree. According to the National Center for Health Statistics, more than 27,500 Americans each year kill themselves (a rate of 12 per 100,000), and the number of these reported suicides has increased by 25 percent over the past decade. The number of actual suicides is probably several times higher than those reported, since many acts of self-destruction are interpreted as natural deaths by physicians and surviving relatives. Most of these suicides are by males (approximately 20,500), even though women attempt suicide more often but with less success.

Many of these suicides occur in two age categories. Men and women over the age of 65 sometimes decide to kill themselves because of poor health, economic problems, the loss of meaningful work, the deaths of spouses and close friends, and the persistent feelings of rejection and uselessness. Persons in their late teens and early twenties sometimes decide to destroy themselves because they cannot cope with the pressures placed upon them, cannot compete successfully with others, cannot endure a broken romance, and/or cannot handle feelings of rejection and loneliness. Reported suicides in this 15–24 age category are now twice as high as ten years ago, with suicide ranking as the third leading cause of death among teenagers aged 15–19 and the second leading cause of death for persons aged 20–24.

Traditionally, and particularly in the West, the morality of such acts of self-destruction has been a subject of considerable debate, with the dominant moral position viewing suicide as unjustifiable. Under the influence of the Western religions (Judaism, Christianity, and Islam), suicide has been interpreted in most European and American societies as an egregious act—to the point of having legal punishments established to deter persons who might consider self-destruction. For example, several European societies for centuries had laws permitting shameful acts of disrespect toward the corpse (stoning, stabbing, burying in a shallow grave at a community crossroads) of a person who committed suicide, prohibiting the burial of such a body in a consecrated cemetery, and preventing survivors of a death by suicide from inheriting money or property as a consequence of the death.

Philosophical support for these societal practices came from a number of writers, but principally from Augustine and Aquinas. Augustine (354–430) regarded suicide as wrong because it violates the biblical injunction against killing. For him, the sixth commandment (Exodus 20:13) prohibits any act of murder, including "self-murder." Thomas Aquinas (1225–1274) examined the issue of suicide at some length, especially in his *Summa Theologica.* For Thomas, the question "Whether It Is Lawful to Kill Oneself?" must receive a resounding negative answer, for three reasons. First, suicide is a transgression against oneself and a mortal sin because it goes contrary to the natural inclination of self-preservation. Second, suicide is a transgression against God because (citing Deuteronomy 32:39) God alone has the right to pronounce the sentence of life or death. Third, suicide is a transgression against the human community (as Aristotle had observed) because it harms the relatives and friends who survive.

By sharp contrast, a few philosophers argued that suicide was justifiable in a variety of circumstances. Seneca (4 B.C.–A.D. 65), a Roman philosopher who accepted Plato's theory of the soul's immortality, believed that this life is only preparation for another form of existence. Consequently, whenever there are problems in life, suicide (or "taking off") becomes a rational moral choice. David Hume (1711–1776) agreed, and argued that Aquinas' position on suicide is wrong. First, suicide cannot be a transgression against ourselves because no one throws away a life worth living, but only a life which is made worse than death by advanced age, infirmity, or misfortune. Second, suicide cannot be a transgression against God because the physical laws of matter and motion, not being disrupted by suicidal deaths, suggest that God (if God exists) has not strictly reserved the disposal of human lives for himself. Third, suicide cannot be a transgression against community, at least not always, because suicides do not inevitably inflict harm upon society.

Today, many of the traditional practices regarding suicide seem strange, if not questionable. In the United States, for instance, virtually all of the 50 states updated their wrongful death statutes in the mid-1970s by decriminalizing suicide. The same can be said about attempted suicide, with the great majority of states abrogating this common law crime during the 1970s. These changes reflect the general recognition that persons who kill themselves can hardly be punished by law, and that persons who unsuccessfully attempt to kill themselves are more likely to benefit from medical treatment than from social stigmatization. However, most states retain laws making "aiding and abetting" suicide attempts a criminal offense.

Some of the contemporary philosophical arguments about suicide also differ from the ones that influenced European societies in earlier centuries. Serious debate continues, of course, regarding the morality of individual acts of suicide. Some writers maintain that suicide is justifiable on the grounds of autonomy, respect for persons, and (occasionally) utility; others are convinced that suicide can rarely, if ever, be justified as a moral act because they claim such acts are irrevocable, fail to exercise stewardship over God's gift of life, do not (on balance) serve useful purposes, violate God's commandment against killing, and are almost always more harmful than beneficial for survivors.

In addition to this debate, current discussions of suicide often explore questions not usually found in the traditional philosophical literature on suicide. What features distinguish suicide from other forms of dying and/or killing? Is suicide ever the rational thing to do in a particular set of circumstances? Even if one thinks that suicide is wrong, is the person who commits suicide always blameworthy? When, if ever, are we morally obligated to try to prevent suicide? Are there moral limits beyond which we may not go in restricting another person's liberty, even in trying to prevent that person from self-destruction?

The selected readings address several of these contemporary questions about the morality of suicide and suicide prevention. Tom Beauchamp analyzes the concept of suicide, and proposes that suicide be defined as "an act [in which] a person intentionally brings about his own death in circumstances where others do not coerce him to the action." Richard Brandt, a retired philosopher at the University of Michigan, discusses the morality and rationality of suicide, concluding that in certain circumstances the decision to kill oneself can be a rational choice. Karen Lebacqz, a religious ethicist, and Tristram Engelhardt, a philosopher, argue that suicide can be justifiable in at least three situations, and that there are moral limits beyond which we may not go in suicide prevention.

The last two articles disagree about the morality of suicide prevention. Edwin Shneidman, a professor of thanatology at UCLA, is convinced that suicide is self-evidently wrong and that all members of society are morally obligated to take whatever steps may be necessary to prevent others from self-destruction. Thomas Szasz, a psychiatrist at the Upstate Medical Center (New York), counters by claiming that suicide falls within the right of self-determination and that suicide prevention centers frequently infringe upon a rational expression of human freedom.

The legal case that concludes this section is the unusual suicide attempt of Elizabeth Bouvia. Competent, articulate, yet physically unable to commit suicide because of cerebral palsy, Bouvia argued that she should be assisted in committing suicide by starving to death in Riverside (California) General Hospital. Attorneys for the hospital disagreed, claiming that participation in bringing about such a death might incriminate the medical staff and that such a death would have devastating effects on the medical staff and patients in the hospital. In 1986, an appellate court ruled unanimously that Bouvia, at the time a patient in another hospital, was entitled to have a nasogastric tube removed according to her wishes.

31

What Is Suicide?

TOM L. BEAUCHAMP, Ph.D.

Although debate about the legality, rationality, and morality of suicide has increased in recent years, only fragmentary attention has been devoted to the development of an adequate definition of suicide. Because significantly different moral, social, and legal sanctions will be implied by the classification of an act as suicide, euthanasia, murder, or accidental death, the development of an adequate definition will have important practical consequences. The way we classify actions is indicative of the way we think about them, and in the present case such classifications have immediate relevance for medicine, ethics, and law.

A start in the direction of a definition of "suicide" is the following: The death of a person is a suicide only if: (1) the person's own death is intentionally self-caused, and (2) the person's action is noncoerced. However, two special problems prevent this simple definition from being fully adequate.

Reprinted from Tom L. Beauchamp and Seymour Perlin, eds., *Ethical Issues in Death and Dying* (Englewood Cliffs, N.J.: Prentice-Hall, 1978), pp. 97–102, with the permission of the author and publisher. Copyright © 1977 by Tom. L. Beauchamp.

The Problem of Treatment Refusal

The first class of difficult cases for the above definition involves persons who suffer from a terminal illness or mortal injury, and who refuse some medical therapy without which they will die, but with which they could live for some period beyond the point they would die without the therapy. For example, refusal to allow a blood transfusion, or an amputation, or refusal of further kidney dialysis are now familiar facts of hospital life. But are they suicides? Two facts about such cases are noteworthy. First, these acts certainly *can* be suicides, because *any* means productive of death potentially can be used to the end of suicide. Pulling the plug on one's respirator is not relevantly different from plunging a knife into one's heart, if the reason for putting an end to life is identical in the two cases. Second, suicidal acts can also be sacrificial. For example, if a person were suffering from a costly terminal disease, then it would be an altruistic (even if perhaps misguided) action to take his own life in order to spare his family the inordinate cost of providing the care; but it would nonetheless be suicide.

Still, the seriously suffering person with end-stage renal disease who refuses to continue dialysis and dies a "natural" death does not strike most as a suicide. Why not? Three features of such situations need to be distinguished in order to answer this question:

1. whether the death is *intended* by the agent,
2. whether an *active* means to death is selected,
3. whether a *nonfatal condition* is present (no terminal disease or mortal injury exists).

The more we have unmistakable cases of actions by an agent that involve an *intentionally caused death* using an *active* means where there is a *nonfatal* condition, the more inclined we are to classify such acts as suicides, whereas the more such conditions are absent the less inclined we are to call the acts suicides. For example, if a seriously but not mortally wounded soldier turns his rifle on himself and intentionally brings about his death, it is a suicide. But what about the seriously ill patient of ambiguous intentions, suffering from a terminal illness, and refusing yet another blood transfusion?

Although considerations of terminal illness and of intention are important, the main source of our present definitional problem is the active/passive distinction. A passively allowed, "natural" death seems foreign to the notion of suicide, both because the death is at least in part not caused by the agent and because the "cide" part of "suicide" entails "killing," which is commonly contrasted with allowing to die. In the face of this complex mixture of elements the following generalization may be offered about such cases: An act is *not* a suicide if the person who dies suffers from a terminal disease or from a mortal injury which, by refusal of treatment, he passively allows to cause his death—even if the person intends his death. However, this analysis does not seem adequate for all cases; for example, think of a patient with a terminal condition who could easily avoid dying for a long time but who chooses to end his life immediately by not taking cheap and painless medication. This counterexample might incline us toward the view that a time restriction is also needed. But this restriction probably could not be reasonably formulated, and I am inclined to think that we have reached the conceptual boundaries of our notion of suicide. We have come as close to an understanding as the concept permits. If in the end the analysis offered has become slightly reforming (one that requires that we change the ordinary meaning of "suicide" somewhat), the vagaries of the concept itself are perhaps responsible.

The Problem of Sacrificial Deaths

There remains the problem of so-called "altruistically motivated (or other-regarding) suicide." Here the key notion responsible for our not classifying some intentional self-killings as suicides seems to be that of *sacrifice*. Perhaps those who sacrifice their lives are not conceived as "suicides" for an interesting reason: because we see such actions as from the suicide's point of view having plausible claim to being justified for *other-regarding*—not *self-regarding*—reasons, and hence we logically exclude them from the realm of the suicidal.

Sadly, exclusions based on self-sacrificial acts will not help much in structuring a definition of suicide unless further qualifications are introduced. The monk in Vietnam who pours gasoline over his body and burns himself to death as a protest against his government does not do so for his own sake but for the sake of his beloved countrymen, just as the father who kills himself in the midst of a famine so that his wife and children may have enough to eat acts from self-sacrificial motives. Many cases of this general description provide paradigms of suicidal actions but would have to be declared nonsuicides if the approach were taken that other-regarding, sacrificial acts fail to qualify as suicides.

In the face of this new complexity, a course paralleling the one for refusal-of-treatment cases may be taken: An act is *not* a suicide if the person is caused to die by a life-threatening condition he does not intend to bring about through his own actions. Interestingly, this approach does not turn on the notion of sacrifice, the original problem compelling consideration of these cases. It makes no difference whether the action is sacrificial or nonsacrificial, so long as the condition causing death is not brought about *by the agent* for the purpose of ending his life. This conclusion is somewhat troublesome, because the agent does intend his death in those cases of sacrifice where a person has the option either to save his life or to act in protection of others' lives, and then specifically chooses a course of action that brings about his own death. Nonetheless, in such cases *it cannot be said that he brings about the life-threatening condition causing his death in order to cause his death,* and that fact is the crucial matter.

There are further parallels between this kind of case and the refusal of treatment cases previously discussed. Three relevant ingredients can again be distinguished:

1. whether the death is *intended* by the agent,
2. whether the death is *caused* by the agent (or is caused to the agent),
3. whether the action is *self-regarding* (or is other-regarding).

Here the main source of confusion is not the "active/passive" distinction, but rather is the parallel "caused by/caused to" distinction. To cause one's own death in order to die is to kill oneself, but to have death caused by some alien condition in the course of an action with multiple objectives may not be. Here we might say that the killing/being killed distinction is involved, and that it functions rather like the killing/letting die distinction previously discussed. At any rate, we have again reached the boundaries of our concept of suicide, which is here being contrasted with the concept of an externally caused death. A person might be using an externally caused means as a socially acceptable and convenient way of ending his life, and hence it might be a suicide. But we have seen that this is true of any means to death whatsoever.

A good test case for the above analysis is the now classic case of Captain Oates, who walked into the Antarctic snow to die, because he was suffering from an illness that hindered the progress of a party attempting to make its way out of a severe blizzard.[1] According to R. F. Holland, Oates was not a suicide because: "in Oates's case I can say, 'No [he didn't kill himself]; the blizzard killed him.' Had Oates taken out a revolver and shot himself I should have agreed he was a suicide."[2] I cannot agree with Holland's estimate. On the analysis offered above, Oates' heroic sacrifice is a suicide because of the active steps that he took to bring about his death. Although the climatic conditions proximately caused his death, he *brought about* the relevant life-threatening condition causing his death (exposure to the weather) in order that he die. There is no relevant difference between death by revolver and death by exposure to freezing weather when both equally are life-threatening conditions used to cause one's own death. However, the Oates case is not an easy one to declare a suicide. It is a close call precisely because there is both multiple causation and multiple intent: the action is a heroic way of being *causally responsible* for placing oneself in *conditions which cause* death, and death was intended as a merciful release from an intolerable burden, not only because of Oates' suffering but also because of his knowledge that he was imperilling the lives of his colleagues. Moreover, his release from these burdens is apparently his major objective. No wonder the Oates case has become a classic in literature on the definition of suicide; it is hard to imagine a case sitting more astride the boundaries between suicide and nonsuicide.

Although the analysis proposed above does not differ in some respects from that of Joseph Margolis', the point at which we part company is now evident, for he argues as follows:

> The Buddhist monk who sets fire to himself in order to protest the war that he might have resisted in another way will not be said to have committed suicide if the *overriding* characterization of what he did fixes on the ulterior objective of influencing his countrymen. . . . [If there is] some further purpose that he serves instrumentally, then we normally refuse to say he has suicided; . . . [3]

Margolis thinks there is a decisive difference between whether one's overriding reason is some sacrificial objective or the objective of ending one's life. In my view the matter is more complicated and has little to do with the notions of sacrifice, martyrdom, and patriotism. It has rather to do with whether death is caused by one's own arrangement of the life-threatening conditions causing death for the purpose of bringing about death (whether this purpose be the overriding reason or not). Since the monk arranges the conditions, precisely for this purpose (though for others as well), he is a suicide.

Conclusion

We have arrived, then, at an understanding of suicide that is fairly simple, even if somewhat more complicated than the definitions with which we began: An act is a suicide if a person intentionally brings about his own death in circumstances where others do not coerce him to the action, except in those cases where death occurs through an agent's intentional decision but is caused by conditions not specifically arranged by the agent for the purpose of bringing about his own death. However, in concluding, we should ask whether anything useful has been accomplished by this analysis, and especially whether such a definition of the ordinary language meaning of "suicide" is a proper one for moral philosophy. Terms in their ordinary meaning often contain evaluative accretions due to social attitudes that render them difficult for purposes of moral analysis; and the meaning we have located for "suicide" appears to be a premiere instance of this problem: Because self-caused deaths are often revolting and inexplicable, an emotive meaning of disapproval has been incorporated into our use of "suicide." More importantly, because of this already attached disapproval we find it hard to accept as "suicides" acts of which we approve, or at least do not disapprove. We thus by the very logic of the term prejudice any pending moral analysis of the action of a suicide as being right or wrong, let alone praiseworthy or blameworthy.

Notes

1. See *Scott's Last Expedition* (London: 1935), 1: 462.
2. "Suicide," in J. Rachels, ed., *Moral Problems* (New York: Harper and Row, 1971), pp. 352–353.
3. Joseph Margolis, "Suicide," in *Negativities* (Columbus, Ohio: Charles E. Merrill, 1975), pp. 27–28.

32

The Morality and Rationality of Suicide

RICHARD B. BRANDT, Ph.D.

From the point of view of contemporary philosophy, suicide raises the following distinct questions: whether a person who commits suicide (assuming that there is suicide if and only if there is intentional termination of one's own life) is morally blameworthy, reprehensible, sinful in all circumstances; whether suicide is objectively right or wrong, and in what circumstances it is right or wrong, from a moral point of view; and whether, or in which circumstances, suicide is the best or the rational thing to do from the point of view of the agent's personal welfare.

The Moral Blameworthiness of Suicide

In former times the question of whether suicide is sinful was of great interest because the answer to it was considered relevant to how the agent would spend eternity. At present the practical

Reprinted from Seymour Perlin, ed., *A Handbook for the Study of Suicide*, pp. 61–75, with the permission of Oxford University Press.

issue is not as great, although a normal funeral service may be denied a person judged to have committed suicide sinfully. The chief practical issue now seems to be that persons may disapprove of a decedent for having committed suicide, and his friends or relatives may wish to defend his memory against moral charges.

The question of whether an act of suicide was sinful or morally blameworthy is not apt to arise unless it is already believed that the agent morally ought not to have done it: for instance, if he really had very poor reasons for doing so, and his act foreseeably had catastrophic consequences for his wife and children. But, even if a given suicide is morally wrong, it does not follow that it is morally reprehensible. For, while asserting that a given act of suicide was wrong, we may still think that the act was hardly morally blameworthy or sinful if, say, the agent was in a state of great emotional turmoil at the time. We might then say that, although what he did was wrong, his action is *excusable,* just as in the criminal law it may be decided that, although a person broke the law, he should not be punished because he was *not responsible,* that is, was temporarily insane, and did what he did inadvertently, and so on.

The foregoing remarks assume that to be morally blameworthy (or sinful) on account of an act is one thing, and for the act to be wrong is another. But, if we say this, what after all does it *mean* to say that a person is morally blameworthy on account of an action? We cannot say there is agreement among philosophers on this matter, but I suggest the following account as being safe from serious objection: "X is morally blameworthy on account of an action A" may be taken to mean "X did A, and X would not have done A had not his character been in some respect below standard; and in view of this it is fitting or justified for X to have some disapproving attitudes including remorse toward himself, and for some other persons Y to have some disapproving attitudes toward X and to express them in behavior." Traditional thought would include God as one of the "other persons" who might have and express disapproving attitudes.

In case the foregoing definition does not seem obviously correct, it is worthwhile pointing out that it is usually thought that an agent is not blameworthy or sinful for an action unless it is a *reflection on him;* the definition brings this fact out and makes clear why.

If someone charges that a suicide was sinful, we may not properly ask, "What defect of character did it show?" Some writers have claimed that suicide is blameworthy because it is *cowardly,* and since being cowardly is generally conceded to be a defect of character, if an act of suicide is admitted to be both objectively wrong and also cowardly, the claim to blameworthiness might be warranted in terms of the above definition. Of course, many people would hesitate to call taking one's own life a cowardly act, and there will certainly be controversy about which acts are cowardly and which are not. But at least we can see part of what has to be done to make a charge of blameworthiness valid.

The most interesting question is the general one: which types of suicide in general are ones that, even if objectively wrong (in a sense to be explained below), are not sinful or blameworthy? Or, in other words, when is a suicide *morally excused* even if it is objectively wrong? We can at least identify some types that are morally excusable.

1. Suppose I *think* I am morally bound to commit suicide because I have a terminal illness and continued medical care will ruin my family financially. Suppose, however, that I am mistaken in this belief, and that suicide in such circumstances is not right. But surely I am not morally blameworthy; for I may be doing, out of a sense of duty to my family, what I would personally prefer not to do and is hard for me to do. What defect of character might my action show? Suicide from a genuine sense of duty is not blameworthy, even when the moral conviction in question is mistaken.

2. Suppose that I commit suicide when I am temporarily of unsound mind, either in the sense of the M'Naghten rule that I do not know that what I am doing is wrong, or of the Durham rule that, owing to a mental defect, I am substantially unable to do what is right. Surely, any suicide in an unsound state of mind is morally excused.

3. Suppose I commit suicide when I could not be said to be temporarily of unsound mind, but simply because I am not myself. For instance, I may be in an extremely depressed mood.

Now a person may be in a very depressed mood, and commit suicide on account of being in that mood, when there is nothing the matter with his character—or, in other words, his character is not in any relevant way below standard. What are other examples of being "not myself," of emotional states that might be responsible for a person's committing suicide, and that might render the suicide excusable even if wrong? Being frightened; being distraught; being in almost any highly emotional frame of mind (anger, frustration, disappointment in love); perhaps just being terribly fatigued.

So there are at least three types of suicide which can be morally excused even if they are objectively wrong. The main point is this: Mr. X may commit suicide and it may be conceded that he ought not to have done so, but it is another step to show that he is sinful, or morally blameworthy, for having done so. To make out that further point, it must be shown that his act is attributable to some substandard trait of character. So, Mrs. X after the suicide can concede that her husband ought not to have done what he did, but she can also point out that it is no reflection on his character. The distinction, unfortunately, is often overlooked. St. Thomas Aquinas, who recognizes the distinction in other places, seems blind to it in his discussion of suicide.

The Moral Reasons for and Against Suicide

Persons who say suicide is morally wrong must be asked which of two positions they are affirming: Are they saying that *every* act of suicide is wrong, *everything considered;* or are they merely saying that there is always *some* moral obligation—doubtless of serious weight—not to commit suicide, so that very often suicide is wrong, although it is possible that there are *countervailing considerations* which in particular situations make it right or even a moral duty? It is quite evident that the first position is absurd; only the second has a chance of being defensible.

In order to make clear what is wrong with the first view, we may begin with an example. Suppose an army pilot's single-seater plane goes out of control over a heavily populated area; he has the choice of staying in the plane and bringing it down where it will do little damage but at the cost of certain death for himself, and of bailing out and letting the plane fall where it will, very possibly killing a good many civilians. Suppose he chooses to do the former, and so, by our definition, commits suicide. Does anyone want to say that his action is morally wrong? Even Immanuel Kant, who opposed suicide in all circumstances, apparently would not wish to say that it is; he would, in fact, judge that this act is not one of suicide, for he says, "It is no suicide to risk one's life against one's enemies, and even to sacrifice it, in order to preserve one's duties toward oneself."[1] St. Thomas Aquinas, in his discussion of suicide, may seem to take the position that such an act would be wrong, for he says, "It is altogether unlawful to kill oneself," admitting as an exception only the case of being under special command of God. But I believe St. Thomas would, in fact, have concluded that the act is right because the basic intention of the pilot was to save the lives of civilians, and whether an act is right or wrong is a matter of basic intention.[2]

In general, we have to admit that there are things with some moral obligation to avoid which, on account of other morally relevant considerations, it is sometimes right or even morally obligatory to do. There may be some obligation to tell the truth on every occasion, but surely in many cases the consequences of telling the truth would be so dire that one is obligated to lie. The same goes for promises. There is some moral obligation to do what one has promised (with a few exceptions); but, if one can keep a trivial promise only at serious cost to another person (i.e., keep an appointment only by failing to give aid to someone injured in an accident), it is surely obligatory to break the promise.

The most that the moral critic of suicide could hold, then, is that there is *some* moral obligation not to do what one knows will cause one's death; but he surely cannot deny that circumstances exist in which there are obligations to do things which, in fact, will result in one's death. If so, then in principle it would be possible to argue, for instance, that in order to meet my obligation to my family, it might be right for me to take my own life as the only way to avoid catastrophic hospital expenses in a terminal illness. Possibly the main point that critics of suicide on moral grounds would wish to make is that it is never right to take one's own life *for reasons of one's own personal welfare,* of any kind whatsoever. Some of the arguments used to support the immorality of suicide, however, are so framed that if they were supportable at all, they would prove that suicide is *never* moral.

One well-known type of argument against suicide may be classified as *theological.* St. Augustine and others urged that the Sixth Commandment ("Thou shalt not kill") prohibits suicide, and that we are bound to obey a divine commandment. To this reasoning one might first reply that it is arbitrary exegesis of the Sixth Commandment to assert that it was intended to prohibit suicide. The second reply is that if there is not some consideration which shows on the merits of the case that suicide is morally wrong, God had no business prohibiting it. It is true that some will object to this point, and I must refer them elsewhere for my detailed comments on the divine-will theory of morality.[3]

Another theological argument with wide support was accepted by John Locke, who wrote: "Men being all the workmanship of one omnipotent and infinitely wise Maker; all the servants of one sovereign Master, sent into the world by His order and about His business; they are His property, whose workmanship they are made to last during His, not one another's pleasure. . . . Every one . . . is bound to preserve himself, and not to quit his station wilfully."[4] And Kant: "We have been placed in this world under certain conditions and for specific purposes. But a suicide opposes the purpose of his Creator; he arrives in the other world as one who has deserted his post; he must be looked upon as a rebel against God. So long as we remember the truth that it is God's intention to preserve life, we are bound to regulate our activities in conformity with it. This duty is upon us until the time comes when God expressly commands us to leave this life. Human beings are sentinels on earth and may not leave their posts until relieved by another beneficent hand."[5] Unfortunately, however, even if we grant that it is the duty of human beings to do what God commands or intends them to do, more argument is required to show that God does *not* permit human beings to quit this life when their own personal welfare would be maximized by so doing. How does one draw the requisite inference about the intentions of God? The difficulties and contradictions in arguments to reach such a conclusion are discussed at length and perspicaciously by David Hume in his essay "On Suicide," and in view of the unlikelihood that readers will need to be persuaded about these, I shall merely refer those interested to that essay.[6]

A second group of arguments may be classed as arguments *from natural law*. St. Thomas says: "It is altogether unlawful to kill oneself, for three reasons. First, because everything naturally loves itself, the result being that everything naturally keeps itself in being, and resists corruptions so far as it can. Wherefore suicide is contrary to the inclination of nature, and to charity whereby every man should love himself. Hence suicide is always a mortal sin, as being contrary to the natural law and to charity."[7] Here St. Thomas ignores two obvious points. First, it is not obvious why a human being is morally bound to do what he or she has some inclination to do. (St. Thomas did not criticize chastity.) Second, while it is true that most human beings do feel a strong urge to live, the human being who commits suicide obviously feels a stronger inclination to do something else. It is as natural for a human being to dislike, and to take steps to avoid, say, great pain, as it is to cling to life.

A somewhat similar argument by Immanuel Kant may seem better. In a famous passage Kant writes that the maxim of a person who commits suicide is "From self-love I make it my principle to shorten my life if its continuance threatens more evil than it promises pleasure. The only further question to ask is whether this principle of self-love can become a universal law of nature. It is then seen at once that a system of nature by whose law the very same feeling whose function is to stimulate the furtherance of life should actually destroy life would contradict itself and consequently could not subsist as a system of nature. Hence this maxim cannot possibly hold as a universal law of nature and is therefore entirely opposed to the supreme principle of all duty."[8] What Kant finds contradictory is that the motive of self-love (interest in one's own long-range welfare) should sometimes lead one to struggle to preserve one's life, but at other times to end it. But where is the contradiction? One's circumstances change, and, if the argument of the following section in this chapter is correct, one sometimes maximizes one's own long-range welfare by trying to stay alive, but at other times by bringing about one's demise.

A third group of arguments, a form of which goes back at least to Aristotle, has a more modern and convincing ring. These are arguments to show that, in one way or another, a suicide necessarily does harm to other persons, or to society at large. Aristotle says that the suicide treats the *state* unjustly.[9] Partly following Aristotle, St. Thomas says: "Every man is part of the community, and so, as such, he belongs to the community. Hence by killing himself he injures the community."[10] Blackstone held that a suicide is an offense against the king "who hath an interest in the preservation of all his subjects," perhaps following Judge Brown in 1563, who argued that suicide cost the king a subject—"he being the head has lost one of his mystical members."[11] The premise of such arguments is, as Hume pointed out, obviously mistaken in many instances. It is true that Freud would perhaps have injured society had he, instead of finishing his last book, committed suicide to escape the pain of throat cancer. But surely there have been many suicides whose demise was not a noticeable loss to society; an honest man could only say that in some instances society was better off without them.

It need not be denied that suicide is often injurious to other persons, especially the family of a suicide. Clearly it sometimes is. But, we should notice what this fact establishes. Suppose we admit, as generally would be done, that there is some obligation not to perform any action which will probably or certainly be injurious to other people, the strength of the obligation being dependent on various factors, notably the seriousness of the expected injury. Then there is *some* obligation not to commit suicide, when that act would probably or certainly be injurious to other people. But, as we have already seen, many cases of *some* obligation to do something nevertheless are *not* cases of a duty to do that thing, *everything considered*. So it could sometimes be morally justified to commit suicide, even if the act will harm someone. Must a man with a terminal illness undergo excruciating pain because his death will cause his wife sorrow—when she will be caused sorrow a month later anyway, when he is dead of natural causes? Moreover, to repeat, the fact that an individual has some obligation not to commit suicide when that act will probably injure other persons does not imply that, everything considered, it is wrong for him to do it, namely, that in all circumstances suicide *as such* is something there is some obligation to avoid.

Is there any sound argument, convincing to the modern mind, to establish that there is (or is not) *some moral obligation* to avoid suicide *as such,* an obligation, of course, which might be overriden by other obligations in some or many cases? (Captain Oates may have had a moral obligation not to commit suicide as such, but his obligation not to stand in the way of his comrades' getting to safety might have been so strong that, everything considered, he was justified in leaving the polar camp and allowing himself to freeze to death.)

To present all the arguments necessary to answer this question convincingly would take a great deal of space. I shall, therefore, simply state one answer to it which seems plausible to some contemporary philosophers. Suppose it could be shown that it would maximize the long-run welfare of everybody affected if people were taught that there is a moral obligation to avoid suicide—so that people would be motivated to avoid suicide just because they thought it wrong (would have anticipatory guilt feelings at the very idea), and so that other people would be inclined to disapprove of persons who commit suicide unless there were some excuse (such as those mentioned in the first section). One might ask: how could it maximize utility to mold the conceptual and motivational structure of persons in this way? To which the answer might be: feeling in this way might make persons who are impulsively inclined to commit suicide in a bad mood, or a fit of anger or jealousy, take more time to deliberate; hence, some suicides that have bad effects generally might be prevented. In other words, it might be a good thing in its effects for people to feel about suicide in the way they feel about breach of promise or injuring others, just as it might be a good thing for people to feel a moral obligation not to smoke, or to wear seat belts. However, it might be that negative moral feelings about suicide as such would stand in the way of action by those persons whose welfare really is best served by suicide and whose suicide is the best thing for everybody concerned.

When a Decision to Commit Suicide Is Rational from the Person's Point of View

The person who is contemplating suicide is obviously making a choice between future world-courses; the world-course that includes his demise, say, an hour from now, and several possible ones that contain his demise at a later point. One cannot have precise knowledge about many features of the latter group of world-courses, but it is certain that they will all end with death some (possibly short) finite time from now.

Why do I say the choice is between *world*-courses and not just a choice between future life-courses of the prospective suicide, the one shorter than the other? The reason is that one's suicide has some impact on the world (and one's continued life has some impact on the world), and that conditions in the rest of the world will often make a difference in one's evaluation of the possibilities. One *is* interested in things in the world other than just oneself and one's own happiness.

The basic question a person must answer, in order to determine which world-course is best or rational for him to choose, is which he *would* choose under conditions of optimal use of information, when *all* of his desires are taken into account. It is not just a question of what we prefer *now,* with some clarification of all the possibilities being considered. Our preferences change, and the preferences of tomorrow (assuming we can know something about them) are just as legitimately taken into account in deciding what to do now as the preferences of today. Since any reason that can be given today for weighting heavily today's preference can be given tomorrow for weighting heavily tomorrow's preference, the preferences of any time-stretch have a rational claim to an equal vote. Now the importance of that fact is this: we often know quite well that our desires, aversions, and preferences may change after a short while. When a person is in a state of despair—perhaps brought about by a rejection in love or a discharge from a long-held position—nothing but the thing he cannot have seems desirable; everything else is turned to ashes. Yet we know quite well that the passage of time is likely to reverse all this; replacements may be found or other types of things that are available to us may begin to look attractive. So, if we were to act on the preferences of today alone, when the emotion of despair seems more than we can stand, we might find death preferable to life; but if we allow for the preferences of the weeks and years ahead, when many goals will be enjoyable and attractive, we might find life much preferable to death. So, if a choice of what is best is to be determined by what we want not only now but later (and later desires on an equal basis with the present ones)—as it should be—then what is the best or preferable world-course will often be quite different from what it would be if the choice, or what is best for one, were fixed by one's desires and preferences now.

Of course, if one commits suicide there are no future desires or aversions that may be compared with present ones and that should be allowed an equal vote in deciding what is best. In that respect the course of action that results in death is different from any other course of action we may undertake. I do not wish to suggest the rosy possibility that it is often or always reasonable to believe that next week "I shall be more interested in living than I am today, if today I take a dim view of continued existence." On the contrary, when a person is seriously ill, for instance, he may have no reason to think that the preference-order will be reversed—it may be that tomorrow he will prefer death to life more strongly.

The argument is often used that one can never be *certain* what is going to happen, and hence one is never rationally justified in doing anything as drastic as committing suicide. But we always have to live by probabilities and make our estimates as best we can. As soon as it is clear beyond reasonable doubt not only that death is now preferable to life, but also that it will be every day from now until the end, the rational thing is to act promptly.

Let us not pursue the question of whether it is rational for a person with a painful terminal illness to commit suicide; it is. However, the issue seldom arises, and few terminally ill patients do commit suicide. With such patients matters usually get worse slowly so that no particular time seems to call for action. They are often so heavily sedated that it is impossible for the mental processes of decision leading to action to occur; or else they are incapacitated in a hospital and the very physical possibility of ending their lives is not available. Let us leave this grim topic and turn to a practically more important problem: whether it is rational for persons to commit suicide for some reason other than painful terminal physical illness. Most persons who commit suicide do so, apparently, because they face a non-physical problem that depresses them beyond their ability to bear.

Among the problems that have been regarded as good and sufficient reasons for ending life, we find (in addition to serious illness) the following: some event that has made a person feel ashamed or lose his prestige and status; reduction from affluence to poverty; the loss of a limb or of physical beauty; the loss of sexual capacity; some event that makes it seem impossible to achieve things by which one sets store; the loss of a loved one; disappointment in love; the infirmities of increasing age. It is not to be denied that such things can be serious blows to a person's prospects of happiness.

Whatever the nature of an individual's problem, there are various plain errors to be avoided—errors to which a person is especially prone when he is depressed—in deciding whether, everything considered, he prefers a world-course containing his early demise to one in which his life continues to its natural terminus. Let us forget for a moment the relevance to the decision of preferences that he may have tomorrow, and concentrate on some errors that may infect his preference as of today, and for which correction or allowance must be made.

In the first place, depression, like any severe emotional experience, tends to primitivize one's intellectual processes. It restricts the range of one's survey of the possibilities. One thing that a rational person would do is compare the world-course containing his suicide with his *best* alternative. But his best alternative is precisely a possibility he may overlook if, in a depressed mood, he thinks only of how badly off he is and cannot imagine any way of improving his situation. If a person is disappointed in love, it is possible to adopt a vigorous plan of action that carries a good chance of acquainting him with someone he likes at least as well; and if old age prevents a person from continuing the tennis game with his favorite partner, it is possible to learn some other game that provides the joys of competition without the physical demands.

Depression has another insidious influence on one's planning; it seriously affects one's judgment about probabilities. A person disappointed in love is very likely to take a dim view of himself, his prospects, and his attractiveness; he thinks that because he has been rejected by one person he will probably be rejected by anyone who looks desirable to him. In a less gloomy frame of mind he would make different estimates. Part of the reason for such gloomy probability estimates is that depression tends to repress one's memory of evidence that supports a non-gloomy prediction. Thus, a rejected lover tends to forget any cases in which he has elicited enthusiastic response from ladies in relation to whom he has been the one who has done the rejecting. Thus his pessimistic self-image is based upon a highly selected, and pessimistically selected, set of data. Even when he is reminded of the data, moreover, he is apt to resist an optimistic inference.

Another kind of distortion of the look of future prospects is not a result of depression, but is quite normal. Events distant in the future feel small, just as objects distant in space look small. Their prospect does not have the effect on motivational processes that it would have if it were of an event in the immediate future. Psychologists call this the "goal-gradient" phenomenon; a rat, for instance, will run faster toward a perceived food box than a distant unseen one. In the case of a person who has suffered some misfortune, and whose situation now is an unpleasant one, this reduction of the motivational influence of events distant in time has the effect that present unpleasant states weigh far more heavily than probable future pleasant ones in any choice of world-courses.

If we are trying to determine whether we now prefer, or shall later prefer, the outcome of one world-course to that of another (and this is leaving aside the questions of the weight of the votes of preferences at a later date), we must take into account these and other infirmities of our "sensing" machinery. Since knowing that the machinery is out of order will not tell us what results it would give if it were working, the best recourse might be to refrain from making any decision in a stressful frame of mind. If decisions have to be made, one must recall past reactions, in a normal frame of mind, to outcomes like those under assessment. But many suicides seem to occur in moments of despair. What should be clear from the above is that a moment of despair, if one is seriously contemplating suicide, ought to be a moment of reassessment of one's goals and values, a reassessment which the individual must realize is very difficult to make objectively, because of the very quality of his depressed frame of mind.

A decision to commit suicide may in certain circumstances be a rational one. But a person who wants to act rationally must take into account the various possible "errors" and make appropriate rectification of his initial evaluations.

Notes

1. Immanuel Kant, *Lectures on Ethics* (New York: Harper Torchbook, 1963), p. 150.

2. See St. Thomas Aquinas, *Summa Theologica*, Second Part of the Second Part, Q. 64, Art. 5. In article 7, he says: "Nothing hinders one act from having two effects, only one of which is intended, while the other is beside the intention. Now moral acts take their species according to what is intended, and not according to what is beside the intention, since this is accidental as explained above" (Q. 43, Art. 3: I-II, Q. 1, Art. 3, as 3). Mr. Norman St. John-Stevas, the most articulate contemporary defender of the Catholic view, writes as follows: "Christian thought allows certain exceptions to its general condemnation of suicide. That covered by a particular divine inspiration has already been noted. Another exception arises where suicide is the method imposed by the State for the execution of a just death penalty. A third exception is *altruistic* suicide, of which the best known example is Captain Oates. Such suicides are justified by invoking the principle of double effect. The act from which death results must be good or at least morally indifferent; some other good effect must result; The death must not be directly intended or the real means to the good effect; and a grave reason must exist for adopting the course of action." [*Life, Death, and the Law* (Bloomington: Indiana University Press, 1961), pp. 250–251] Presumably the Catholic doctrine is intended to allow suicide when this is required for meeting strong moral obligations; whether it can do so consistently depends partly on the interpretation given to "real means to the good effect." Readers interested in pursuing further the Catholic doctrine of double effect and its implications for our problem should read Philippa Foot, "The Problem of Abortion and the Doctrine of Double Effect," *The Oxford Review* (Trinity 1967), 5: 5–15.

3. R. B. Brandt, *Ethical Theory* (Englewood Cliffs, N.J.: Prentice-Hall, 1959), pp. 61–82.

4. John Locke, *The Second Treatise on Civil Government*, ch. 2.

5. Kant, *Lectures on Ethics*, p. 154.

6. This essay appears in collections of Hume's works.

7. For an argument similar to Kant's, see also St. Thomas Aquinas, *Summa Theologica*, II, II, Q, 65, Art. 5.

8. Immanuel Kant, *The Fundamental Principles of the Metaphysic of Morals*, H. J. Paton, tr. (London: The Hutchinson Group, 1948), ch. 2.

9. Aristotle, *Nicomachaean Ethics*, bk. 5, ch. 10, p. 1138a.

10. St. Thomas Aquinas, *Summa Theologica*, II, II, Q. 64, Art. 5.

11. Sir William Blackstone, *Commentaries*, 4:189; Brown in *Hales v. Petit*, I Plow. 253, 75 E.R. 387 (C.B. 1563). Both cited by Norman St. John-Stevas, *Life, Death and the Law*, p. 235.

33

Suicide and Covenant

KAREN LEBACQZ, Ph.D.
AND H. TRISTRAM ENGLEHARDT, Jr. M.D., Ph.D.

A t a fundamental level, questions of the ethical acceptability of suicide are questions of the value of life and the dignity of freedom. The authors have already indicated their bias toward a fundamental libertarian principle that puts the burden of proof on those who would deprive persons of freedom over their bodies and lives.

Our argument is simply this: that which gives humans their unique worth is the fact that they can be respected, blamed, or praised for their actions because they are rational free agents.[1] Respect for persons as free moral agents should entail that they be allowed to choose that which endows their lives with meaning as long as such choice will not seriously affect the freedoms of others or violate prior agreements between persons. That is, persons have a *prima facie* right to seek out their own values. The right is a "prima facie" one in this sense: persons are to be held to have that right until there is evidence to the contrary—e.g., covenants by which they cede some liberty.

Reprinted from "Suicide," in Dennis J. Horan and David Mall, eds., *Death, Dying and Euthanasia,* pp. 688–696, 703–705, with the permission of the publisher. Copyright © 1977 by University Publications of America. Footnotes renumbered.

With respect to suicide, therefore, we hold that persons are the best judges of the proper balance of values in their lives. An element of respecting others is respecting their right to take their lives in the absence of any contravening duties. Persons should be permitted to take their own lives when they have chosen to do so freely and rationally and when there are no other duties which would override this freedom.

There is thus nothing in principle morally wrong with suicide. But to say that one has a *prima facie* right to take one's own life is not to say that it is always morally justifiable to do so. It means rather that one has a right to take one's life until a contravening moral obligation obtains. The question of suicide is therefore at root a question of distributive justice—of the proper distribution of benefits and burdens, the proper balancing of personal good and social obligation.

As human beings, we exist in mutual relationships of responsibility. Perhaps the strongest reason that can be given in opposition to suicide is that it violates our covenantal obligations to others. It breaks through the faithfulness we owe to those around us. A critic might agree with us, therefore, that there is a *prima facie* right to kill oneself, but might argue that the right to suicide is nonetheless always defeated by the claims of others.

This argument does not turn on whether bad consequences follow from the act of suicide. It is not a consequentialist or teleological argument. . . . Rather, the argument is that suicide is wrong because it violates certain *prima facie* duties of covenant-fidelity—such as gratitude, promise-keeping, and reparations. For example, parents choosing to have children make an implicit promise to provide for them, just as children who are provided for have obligations of gratitude to their parents. Suicide destroys the possibility of keeping the promise to care or the obligation of showing gratitude. Insofar as it violates these duties the right to suicide is overridden.[2] Suicide is wrong when it violates obligations of covenant-fidelity.

If suicide is wrong when it violates obligations of covenant-fidelity, then it may be right when it does not violate such obligations. We propose that there are at least three circumstances in which suicide might be right.

1. Voluntary Euthanasia. There are circumstances in

which normal obligations of covenant-fidelity cease because their fulfillment is impossible.[3] Under certain life circumstances, such as terminal illness accompanied by great pain, it may be impossible to fulfill normal covenant obligations to one's family and friends. If so, these obligations cease and thus the right to dispose of one's own life is not contravened by any restraining duties. In these circumstances, the right to suicide cannot be defeated because the circumstances themselves defeat the possibility of fulfilling any obligation to others.[4]

2. "Covenantal" Suicide. If the first instance in which suicide is morally justifiable is that in which convenantal obligations cease to exist, the second is that where the suicide itself fosters rather than violates covenantal obligations. Suicide need not be covenant-breaking; it can be covenant-affirming.

There are two types of covenant-affirming suicide. The first is the "suicide pact" or joint suicide in which marriage partners, close friends, or others who live in covenantal relationship bind themselves "even unto death." The second is the "self-sacrificial" suicide of one who chooses to die rather than to burden her family or friends.[5] (For example, one who kills herself rather than deplete family resources with expensive medical treatment affirms the covenant with her family in so doing.)

Whether any particular instance of "covenantal" suicide is justifiable depends on the extent to which it fulfills rather than violates other covenantal obligations. An act of suicide which fosters some covenants at the expense of others might still be wrong. But in cases where the act does not violate the *prima facie* duty of covenant-fidelity, it is not *prima facie* wrong.

3. "Symbolic Protest." In the first two instances of justifiable suicide, the suicide was not judged to be wrong either because the duty of covenant-fidelity ceased or because it was supported by suicide. But are there any cases where the suicide appears to violate covenants but may yet be justifiable? We propose that there is at least one such case: that of suicide as "symbolic protest." Suicide is occasionally used as an act of symbolic protest againt great evil and injustice—e.g., against war or imprisonment—and is meant to support in a radical fashion respect for persons generally.[6]

In such cases, suicide appears to violate one's immediate

obligations of covenant-fidelity, since family and friends may be abandoned in order to make symbolic protest. However, the intention of the act is to protest those institutions and structures which undermine the very conditions that make human life and covenant-fidelity possible. When suicide as symbolic protest provides a significant contribution to the struggle against forces which would destroy the freedom of others, taking one's own life can be at root an affirmation of the dignity of persons.[7] We might say that in this form of suicide, the individual aligns herself with more basic loyalties than those to family and friends— namely the community of moral agents. The need to struggle for justice may in circumstances be more compelling than obligations to one's immediate family and friends.[8]

Viewed within the perspective of justice, therefore, there are at least three instances in which suicide may be right: Those in which *prima facie* obligations of covenant-fidelity cease to exist, those in which the suicide fulfills *prima facie* obligations of covenant-fidelity, and those in which obligations of covenant-fidelity are superseded by demands of justice on a larger scale.

Suicide and Society

If suicide is not always wrong but may be right on occasion, then we must ask what are the obligations of others to one who attempts or desires suicide.

The "rightness" of suicide depends upon two balances required by justice: the balancing of values for the individual, and the balancing of that individual's free choice against the legitimate claims of others. Each of these balances has ramifications for the rights of others to interfere or to assist in the suicide.

We have argued that only the individual can decide what balance of freedom and life constitutes the best choices for her. Clearly, in making this argument, we have assumed that the individual is competent to decide—that is, that she is a rational adult capable of exercising free choice. If the individual is not competent by reason of age or insanity, then she may be presumed not to be able to choose freely the proper balance of values in her life. In this case others have a right and may indeed have a duty to interfere in order to protect her interests.

A difficulty arises, of course, in deciding what constitutes insanity or sufficient impairment of rational choice so as to justify interference. We suggest that in general certain safeguards such as the requirement of a waiting period are acceptable in order to ensure that the individual is indeed rational.[9] However, we also caution against *assuming* that a person is irrational just because she has chosen to kill herself: the intention to die is not *per se* irrational. A person must be shown not to be competent, or there must be good evidence that she is incompetent, before intervention is justified on grounds of protecting her interests.[10]

Where a person is competent and has freely chosen to kill herself, the rights and obligations of others depend upon the balance of justice claims between that individual and those around her. Many if not most of the persons in the last stages of dying from a debilitating disease are not only unable to fulfill their covenant obligations but are also often in great pain and suffering. In such cases, suicide not only does not violate the demands of justice, it may be that we may say that she "needs" suicide. If a person who needs suicide is unable to effect it herself, although she would choose freely to do so if she could, we may have a duty to assist her based on our general duty to assist those in need if no one else is available to give assistance. It would surely be an obligation in cases where the person in need of assistance and the person who can render assistance are bound by covenantal relationships of mutual support. However, we note that this obligation holds only where the decision for suicide is "right"—that is, where the demands of justice are not violated, as in cases of illness in which pain and debility prevents the discharge of any duties on the part of the person needing suicide.

Finally, we must ask about those cases in which a competent adult chooses to die, but others have reason to think that the demands of justice would be violated by the suicide (i.e., that it is wrong and that the person seeking suicide is not relieved of her obligations because illness prevents their discharge). In such circumstances, persons have a right to intervene to prevent the act in order to protect their rights or the rights of others. It is important to keep clear here the distinction between this case and the one above in which the individual is judged not competent to decide her own best interests; in this case, the individual is judged competent, but the claims of others are assessed to be sufficiently strong to override her interests. It is also important to note that this does not mean that others may interfere simply because they disagree with the decisions made; rather, they must have reason to think that it is a wrong decision.

In short, where the individual contemplating suicide is competent and the demands of justice would not be violated by the suicide, others have no right to intervene.[11] The right to intervene to prevent suicide grows out of the demands of justice in one of two circumstances: first, when the individual *cannot* make a rational choice regarding her own life values; or second, when there are legitimate overriding claims of others. The duty to assist in effecting suicide grows out of the "rightness" of the act (i.e., it does not violate the requirements of justice) coupled with the *need* for assistance and one's covenantal relations with the person in need.

This analysis suggests that a legal framework must allow for the possibility of justifiable suicide. Neither suicide nor assisted suicide (voluntary euthanasia) should be illegal in cases such as those described above.[12] Safeguards may be needed to ensure that the decision for suicide is rational; the presumption should be given to saving life when there is doubt (e.g., when someone is found lying in a coma). Nonetheless, room must be made for cases of justifiable suicide.

While suicide should be legal and there may even be instances in which it is the *duty* of others to assist in the suicide, there are also broader responsibilities incumbent upon all persons to work for the conditions which would make the inclination towards suicide less frequent by supporting conditions of justice. The high rate of suicide attempts by women and blacks is a sign that the present conditions of society are not just and do not foster conditions in which life, liberty and happiness are mutually supportive for all persons. Suicide is often symbolic of unresolved racism and sexism. To view suicide under the rubric of the demands of justice is to remind us that these basic problems of society are the responsibility of all.

Suicide, therefore, is not simply a matter of individual

responsibility; it is a matter of social responsibility. The choice of freedom over life is a choice made in the context of social demands and expectations. While we have argued above that limited cases of suicide such as those involved in voluntary euthanasia are justifiable, we are also concerned lest there be coercion of vulnerable persons in pain and distress. Those who do not want to, should never be coerced to take their lives. Towards this end, a euthanasia bill introduced in Britain requires a request in writing thirty days in advance and the certification by two physicians that the patient is indeed suffering from a terminal condition. Such provisions are intended to restrict "assisted suicide" to considered action in the limited case of terminal illness where it is clear that obligations of covenant-fidelity cannot be fulfilled. There are other and serious procedural issues of providing for sufficient safeguards to assure the ability of the person or patient to change her mind any time after an initial decision for suicide.

But the issues concerning coercion are difficult, for how are patients and others in distress to be prevented from being bullied into taking their lives or requesting assistance to do so? When overwhelmed by illness and pain and confronted by the "duty" not to burden one's family with costly, nonproductive continued existence, a pattern of coercion may emerge. Further, the pattern of coercion could be substantial apart from any ambiguous cases where either the physician or the family might have vested interests in the expeditious departure of the patient. Thus, procedural safeguards must convincingly protect against complex patterns of forces which may be brought to bear upon patients and others contemplating suicide.

Conclusions

Conclusions with regard to suicide are difficult. On the one hand, a general argument in principle against suicide does not hold. The accent of this essay has been upon general arguments. Yet these general arguments must be tempered by the realities of covert coercion and the need for convincing procedural safeguards, particularly in the realm of voluntary euthanasia.

Our conclusions are thus in the end somewhat muted. Although (1) arguments in principle against suicide do not succeed and (2) persons have a *prima facie* right to take their own lives, still (3) the duties persons have to others will often override their right to take their own lives, and (4) procedural safeguards are in order to protect vulnerable persons from coercion. We have found three sets of circumstances when it would be morally permissible to take one's own life: (1) when it is impossible to discharge one's duties, (2) when suicide supports rather than violates obligations of covenant-fidelity, and (3) when the intention of the suicide is to support the general good of persons and the conditions which make covenant-fidelity possible. This way of viewing suicide leads us to hold that persons have a right to intervene when another intends suicide (1) if that person is not able to choose freely and rationally, or (2) if that person is defaulting on obligations to others. But persons have no right to intervene, absent these two circumstances, and may have a duty in some cases to assist. How these general conclusions can be worked out in particular circumstances depends on the respect and support given to freedom and to covenant-fidelity in society at large.

Notes

1. To say this is not to deny the value of human life *per se* but to suggest that the meaning of human life goes beyond mere physical existence. We take moral agency and covenant-fidelity as central to the meaning of human life. Cf. Paul Ramsey, *The Patient as Person* (New Haven, Conn.: Yale University Press, 1970), p. xii: "covenant-fidelity is the inner meaning and purpose of our creation as human beings."

2. It is for this reason that Brandt ("The Morality and Rationality of Suicide") suggests that suicide is not simply a choice of one's own future, but a choice of "world" futures. In choosing to foreclose certain future states for oneself, one also chooses to alter the nature of one's covenantal relationships. Suicide therefore points to the nature of human relationships. The central theological problem raised by suicide is not death *per se*, but abandonment, or breach of covenant-fidelity.

3. W. D. Ross, *Foundations of Ethics* (London: Oxford University Press, 1939), p. 109.

4. Our position here stands in sharp contradistinction to that of Eike-Henner Kluge in *The Practice of Death* (New Haven, Yale University Press, 1975), p. 121, who claims that suicide is morally justifiable only when the life of the individual is, in her own eyes, "unwanted and unliveable." To say, as we do here, that one's situation is such that one cannot fulfill covenant obligations is not to say that life has ceased altogether to have value or that the remaining life of the individual is "not worth living." An individual may affirm the value of her life and yet choose freely to end it provided that there are no restraining duties.

5. Because of the importance of covenant-fidelity, however, we would agree with Michael Walzer that the concurrence of friends and others with whom one stands in covenantal relationship ought to be sought. ["Consenting to One's Own Death: The Case of Brutus," in Marvin Kohl, ed., *Beneficent Euthanasia* (New York: Prometheus, 1975), p. 104.]

6. Such acts of symbolic protest should not be labelled irrational: "The broad evidence suggests that those who go on hunger strikes [in jail] are well aware of what they are doing and in fact pursue their course even to the point of death in order to exert pressure on their captors and to bear witness to something they believe to be important." T. Beeson, "Sacrificial Suicides," *Christian Century* (September 18, 1974), 91: 836.

7. J. D. McCaughey, in "Suicide: Some Theological Considerations," *Theology* (Feb. 1967), 70:68, argues that Christians should be cautious about suicide because as Christians they are called to affirm life and resurrection over death and destruction. The kind of suicide described here is precisely such an affirmation. Not all suicide, therefore, is a denial of faith. Cf. L. V. Stein, "Faith, Hope and Suicide," *Journal of Religion and Health* (July 1971), 10:216.

8. Though it may be permissible to take one's life in such circumstances, it does not follow that it is obligatory. It is one thing to hold that one always has a right to contribute to the general good of moral agents, but it is not obligatory to give one's life as a contribution. Giving one's life is generally regarded as an act of supererogation, not of obligation.

9. For example, when a person chooses not to continue renal dialysis, the precaution of one more cleansing of the blood "to make sure that it is the person and not the uremia talking" is an acceptable precaution against irrational suicide.

10. There is of course a presumption that children are incompetent and thus that intervention is justified. A difficult question is that of deciding when a child or young adult may be considered competent for purposes of making such a decision.

11. It is important to stress here that general beneficence does not constitute a demand of justice for purposes of making this decision. The general welfare of society does not present a claim which can legitimately override the individual's free choice. Just as the needs of society are not sufficient to require that one kill herself, so they are not sufficient to prevent one from doing so.

12. We would like to emphasize that this moral obligation is in direct conflict with legal statutes of every state in the United States. American law makes aiding and abetting suicide a felony. It is worth noting that until recently aiding and abetting suicide was not a crime in the state of Texas, see *Sanders v. State,* 112 S.W. 68 (Cr App 1908). The authors, after some search, have not been able to find any case indicating an abuse of this freedom. The conflict between moral obligation to at times assist others in committing suicide versus the legal proscription of giving such assistance, indicates the need for the reform of such laws.

34

Preventing Suicide

EDWIN S. SHNEIDMAN, Ph.D.

In almost every case of suicide, there are hints of the act to come, and physicians and nurses are in a special position to pick up the hints and to prevent the act. They come into contact, in many different settings, with many human beings at especially stressful times in their lives.

A suicide is an especially unhappy event for helping personnel. Although one can, in part, train and inure oneself to deal with the sick and even the dying patient, the abruptness and needlessness of a suicidal act leaves the nurse, the physician, and other survivors with many unanswered questions, many deeply troubling thoughts and feelings.

Currently, the major bottleneck in suicide prevention is not remediation, for there are fairly well-known and effective treatment procedures for many types of suicidal states; rather it is in diagnosis and identification.[1]

Reprinted from the *American Journal of Nursing* (May 1965), 65:111–16, with the permission of the publisher. Copyright © 1965 by the American Journal of Nursing Company.

Assumptions

A few straightforward assumptions are necessary in suicide prevention. Some of them:

Individuals who are intent on killing themselves still wish very much to be rescued or to have their deaths prevented. Suicide prevention consists essentially in recognizing that the potential victim is "in balance" between his wishes to live and his wishes to die, then throwing one's efforts on the side of life.

Suicide prevention depends on the active and forthright behavior of the potential rescuer.

Most individuals who are about to commit suicide are acutely conscious of their intention to do so. They may, of course, be very secretive and not communicate their intentions directly. On the other hand, the suicidally inclined person may actually be unaware of his own lethal potentialities, but nonetheless may give many indirect hints of his unconscious intentions.

Practically all suicidal behaviors stem from a sense of isolation and from feelings of some intolerable emotion on the part of the victim. By and large, suicide is an act to stop an intolerable existence. But each individual defines "intolerable" in his own way. Difficulties, stresses, or disappointments that might be easy for one individual to handle might very well be intolerable for someone else—in *his* frame of mind. In order to anticipate and prevent suicide one must understand what "intolerable" means to the other person. Thus, any "precipitating cause"—being neglected, fearing or having cancer (the fear and actuality can be equally lethal), feeling helpless or hopeless, feeling "boxed-in"— may be intolerable for *that* person.

Although committing suicide is certainly an all-or-none action, thinking about the act ahead of time is a complicated, undecided, internal debate. Many a black-or-white action is taken on a barely pass vote. Professor Henry Murray of Harvard University has written that "a personality is a full Congress" of the mind. In preventing suicide, one looks for any indications in the individual representing the dark side of his internal life-and-death debate. We are so often surprised at "unexpected" suicides because we fail to take into account just this principle that the suicidal action is a decision resulting from an internal debate of many voices, some for life and some for death. Thus we hear all sorts of postmortem statements like "He seemed in good spirits" or "He was looking forward to some event next week," not recognizing that these, in themselves, represent only one aspect of the total picture.

In almost every case, there are precursors to suicide, which are called "prodromal clues." In the "psychological autopsies" that have been done at the Suicide Prevention Center in Los Angeles—in which, by interview with survivors of questionable accident or suicide deaths, they attempt to reconstruct the intention of the deceased in relation to death—it was found that very few suicides occur without casting some shadows before them. The concept of prodromal clues for suicide is certainly an old idea; it is really not very different from what Robert Burton, over 300 years ago in 1652, in his famous *Anatomy of Melancholy,* called "the prognostics of melancholy, or signs of things to come." These prodromal clues typically exist for a few days to some weeks before the actual suicide. Recognition of these clues is a necessary first step to lifesaving.

Suicide prevention is like fire prevention. It is not the main mission of any hospital, nursing home, or other institution, but it is the minimum everpresent peripheral responsibility of each professional; and when the minimal signs of possible fire or suicide are seen, then there are no excuses for holding back on lifesaving measures. The difference between fire prevention and suicide prevention is that the prodromal clues for fire prevention have become an acceptable part of our commonsense folk knowledge; we must also make the clues for suicide a part of our general knowledge.

Clues to Potential Suicide

In general, the prodromal clues to suicide may be classified in terms of four broad types: verbal, behavioral, situational, and syndromatic.

VERBAL

Among the verbal clues we can distinguish between the direct and the indirect. Examples of direct verbal communications would be such statements as "I'm going to commit suicide," "If such and such happens, I'll kill myself," "I'm going to end it all," "I want to die," and so on. Examples of indirect verbal communications would be such statements as "Goodbye," "Farewell," "I've had it," "I can't stand it any longer," "It's too much to put up with," "You'd be better off without me," and, in general, any statements that mirror the individual's intention to stop his intolerable existence.

Some indirect verbal communications can be somewhat more subtle. We all know that in human communication, our words tell only part of the story, and often the main "message" has to be decoded. Every parent or spouse learns to decode the language of loved ones and to understand what they really mean. In a similar vein, many presuicidal communications have to be decoded. An example might be a patient who says to a nurse who is leaving on her vacation, "Goodbye, Miss Jones, I won't be here when you come back." If some time afterward she, knowing that the patient is not scheduled to be transferred or discharged prior to her return, thinks about that conversation, she might do well to telephone her hospital.

Other examples are such statements as "I won't be around much longer for you to put up with," "This is the last shot you'll ever give me," or "This is the last time I'll ever be here," a statement which reflects the patient's private knowledge of his decision to kill himself. Another example is, "How does one leave her body to the medical school?" The latter should never be answered with factual information until after one has found out why the question is being asked, and whose body is being talked about. Individuals often ask for suicide-prevention information for a "friend" or "relative" when they are actually inquiring about themselves.

BEHAVIORAL

Among the behavioral clues, we can distinguish the direct and the indirect. The clearest examples of direct behavioral communications of the intention to kill oneself is a "practice run,"an actual suicide attempt of whatever seriousness. Any action which uses instruments which are conventionally associated with suicide (such as razors, ropes, pills, and the like), regardless of whether or not it could have any lethal outcome, must be interpreted as a direct behavioral "cry for help" and an indication that the person is putting us on our alert. Often, the nonlethal suicide attempt is meant to communicate deeper suicidal intentions. By and large, suicide attempts must be taken seriously as indications of personal crisis and of more severe suicide potentiality.

In general, indirect behavioral communications are such actions as taking a lengthy trip or putting affairs into order. Thus the making of a will under certain peculiar and special circumstances can be an indirect clue to suicidal intention. Buying a casket at the time of another's funeral should always be inquired after most carefully and, if necessary, prompt action (like hospitalization) taken. Giving away prized possessions like a watch, earrings, golf clubs, or heirlooms should be looked on as a possible prodromal clue to suicide.

SITUATIONAL

On occasion the situation itself cries out for attention, especially when there is a variety of stresses. For example, when a patient is extremely anxious about surgery, or when he has been notified that he has a malignancy, when he is scheduled for mutilative surgery, when he is frightened by hospitalization itself, or when outside factors (like family discord, for example, or finances) are a problem—all these are situational. If the doctor or nurse is sensitive to the fact that the situation constitutes a "psychological emergency" for that patient, then he is in a key position to perform lifesaving work. His actions might take the form of sympathetic conversation, or special surveillance of that patient by keeping him with some specially assigned person, or by requesting consultation, or by moving him so that he does not have access to windows at lethal heights. At the least, the nurse should make notations of her behavioral observations in the chart.

To be a suicide diagnostician, one must combine separate symptoms and recognize *and label* a suicidal syndrome in a situation where no one symptom by itself would necessarily lead one to think of a possible suicide.

In this [essay] we shall highlight syndromatic clues for suicide in a medical and surgical hospital setting, although these clues may also be used in other settings. First, it can be said that patient status is stressful for many persons. Everyone who has ever been a patient knows the fantasies of anxiety, fear, and regression that are attendant on illness or surgery. For some in the patient role (especially in a hospital), as the outer world recedes, the fantasy life becomes more active; conflicts and inadequacies and fears may then begin to play a larger and disproportionate role. The point for suicide prevention is that one must try to be aware especially of those patients who are prone to be psychologically overreactive and, being so, are more apt to explode irrationally into suicidal behavior.

SYNDROMATIC

What are the syndromes—the constellations of symptoms—for suicide? Labels for four of them could be: depressed, disoriented, defiant, and dependent-dissatisfied.

1. Depressed: The syndrome of depression is, by and large, made up of symptoms which reflect the shifting of the individual's psychological interests from aspects of his interpersonal life to aspects of his private psychological life, to some intrapsychic crisis within himself. For example, the individual is less interested in food, he loses his appetite, and thus loses weight. Or, his regular patterns of sleeping and waking become disrupted, so that he suffers from lack of energy in the daytime and then sleeplessness and early awakening. The habitual or regular patterns of social and sexual response also tend to change, and the individual loses interest in others. His rate or pace or speed of talking, walking, and doing the activities of his everyday life slows down. At the same time, there is increased preoccupation with internal (intrapsychic) conflicts and problems. The individual is withdrawn, apathetic, apprehensive and anxious, often "blue" and even tearful, somewhat unreachable and seemingly uncaring.

Depression can be seen too in an individual's decreased willingness to communicate. Talking comes harder, there are fewer spontaneous remarks, answers are shorter or even mono-syllabic, the facial expressions are less lively, the posture is more drooped, gestures are less animated, the gait is less springy, and the individual's mind seems occupied and elsewhere.

An additional symptom of the syndrome of depression is detachment, or withdrawing from life. This might be evidenced by behavior which would reflect attitudes, such as "I don't care," "What does it matter," "It's no use anyway." If an individual feels helpless he is certainly frightened, although he may fight for some control or safety; but if he feels hopeless, then the heart is out of him, and life is a burden, and he is only a spectator to a dreary life which does not involve him.

First aid in suicide prevention is directed to counteracting the individual's feelings of hopelessness. Robert E. Litman, chief psychiatrist of the Los Angeles Suicide Prevention Center, has said that "psychological support is transmitted by firm and hope-ful attitude. We convey the impression that the problem which seems to the patient to be overwhelming, dominating his entire personality, and completely insidious, is commonplace and quite familiar to us and we have seen many people make a complete recovery. Hope is a commodity of which we have plenty and we dispense it freely."[2]

It is of course pointless to say "Cheer up" to a depressed person, inasmuch as the problem is that he simply cannot. On the other hand, the effectiveness of the "self-fulfilling prophecy" should never be overestimated. Often an integral part of anyone's climb out of a depression is his faith and the faith of individuals around him that he is going to make it. Just as hopelessness breeds hopelessness, hope—to some extent—breeds hope.

Oftentimes, the syndrome of depression does not seem especially difficult to diagnose. What may be more difficult—and very much related to suicide—is the apparent improvement after a severe depession, when the individual's pace of speech and action picks up a little. The tendency then is for everyone to think that he is cured and to relax vigilance. In reality the situa-tion may be much more dangerous; the individual now has the psychic energy with which to kill himself that he may not have had when he was in the depths of his depression. By far, most suicides relating to depression occur within a short period (a few days to 3 months) after the individual has made an apparent turn for the better. A good rule is that any significant change in behavior, even if it looks like improvement, should be assessed as a possible prodromal index for suicide.

Although depression is the most important single prodromal syndrome for suicide—occurring to some degree in approximately one-third of all suicides—it is not the only one.

2. Disoriented: Disoriented people are apt to be delusional or hallucinatory, and the suicidal danger is that they may respond to commands or voices or experiences that other people cannot share. When a disoriented person expresses any suicidal notions, it is important to take him as a most serious suicidal risk, for he may be in constant danger of taking his own life, not only to cut out those parts of himself that he finds intolerable, but also to respond to the commands of hallucinated voices to kill himself. What makes such a person potentially explosive and particularly hard to predict is that the trigger mechanism may depend on a crazed thought, a hallucinated command, or a fleeting intense fear within a delusional system.

Disoriented states may be clearly organic, such as delirium tremens, certain toxic states, certain drug withdrawal states. Individuals with chronic brain syndromes and cerebral arteriosclerosis may become disoriented. On the other hand, there is the whole spectrum of schizophrenic and schizoaffective disorders, in which the role of organic factors is neither clearly established nor completely accepted. Nonetheless, professional personnel should especially note individuals who manifest some degree of nocturnal disorientation, but who have relative diurnal lucidity. Those physicians who see the patients only during the daytime are apt to miss these cases, particularly if they do not read nurses' notes.

Suicides in general hospitals have occurred among nonpsychiatric patients with subtle organic syndromes, especially those in which symptoms of disorientation are manifested. One should look, too, for the presence of bizarre behavior, fear of death, and clouding of the patient's understanding and awareness. The nurse might well be especially alert to any general hospital patient who has any previous neuropsychiatric history, especially where there are the signs of an acute brain syndrome. Although dyspnea is not a symptom in the syndrome related to disorientation, the presence of severe dyspnea, especially if it is unimproved by treatment in the hospital, has been found to correlate with suicide in hospitals.

When an individual is labeled psychotic, he is almost always disoriented in one sphere or another. Even if he knows where he is and what the date is, he may be off base about who he is, especially if one asks him more or less "philosophic" questions, like "What is the meaning of life?" His thinking processes will seem peculiar, and the words of his speech will have some special or idiosyncratic characteristics. In general, whether or not such patients are transferred to psychiatric wards or psychiatric hospitals, they should—in terms of suicide prevention—be given special care and surveillance, including consultation. Special physical arrangements should be made for them, such as removal of access to operable screens and windows, removal of objects of self-destruction, and the like.

3. Defiant: The Welsh poet, Dylan Thomas, wrote: "Do not go gentle into that good night/. . . . rage, rage against the dying of the light." Many of us remember, usually from high school literature, Henley's "Invictus," "I am master of my fate/ I am the captain of my soul." The point is that many individuals, no matter how miserable their circumstances or how painful their lives, attempt to retain some shred of control over their own fate. Thus a man dying of cancer may, rather than passively capitulate to the disease, choose to play one last active role in his own life by picking the time of his death; so that even in a terminal state (when the staff may believe that he doesn't have the energy to get out of bed), he lifts a heavy window and throws himself out to his death. In this sense, he is willful or defiant.

This kind of individual is an "implementer."[3] Such a person is described as one who has an active need to control his environment. Typically, he would never be fired from any job; he would quit. In a hospital he would attempt to control his environment by refusing some treatments, demanding others, requesting changes, insisting on privileges, and indulging in many other activities indicating some inner need to direct and control his life situation. These individuals are often seen as having low frustration tolerance, being fairly set and rigid in their ways, being somewhat arbitrary and, in general, showing a great oversensitivity to outside control. The last is probably a reflection of their own inability to handle their inner stresses.

Certainly, not every individual who poses ward-management problems needs to be seen as suicidal, but what personnel should look for is the somewhat agitated concern of a patient with controlling his own fate. Suicide is one way of "calling the shot." The nurse can play a lifesaving role with such a person by recognizing his psychological problems and by enduring his controlling (and irritating) behavior—indeed, by being the willing target of his berating or demanding behavior and thus permitting him to expend his energies in this way, rather than in suicidal activities. Her willingness to be a permissible target for these feelings and, more, her sympathetic behavior in giving attention and reassurance even in the face of difficult behavior are in the tradition of the nurturing nurse, even though this can be a difficult role continually to fulfill.

4. Dependent-dissatisfied: Imagine being married to someone on whom you are deeply emotionally dependent, in a situation in which you are terribly dissatisfied with your being dependent. It would be in many ways like being "painted into a corner"—there is no place to go.

This is the pattern we have labeled "dependent-dissatisfied."[4] Such an individual is very dependent on the hospital, realizing he is ill and depending on the hospital to help him; however, he is dissatisfied with being dependent and comes to feel that the hospital is not giving him the help he thinks he needs. Such patients become increasingly tense and depressed, with frequent expressions of guilt and inadequacy. They have emotional disturbances in relation to their illnesses and to their hospital care. Like the "implementer," they make demands and have great need for attention and reassurance. They have a number of somatic complaints, as well as complaints about the hospital. They threaten to leave the hospital against medical advice. They ask to see the doctor, the chaplain, the chief nurse. They request additional therapies of various kinds. They make statements like, "Nothing is being done for me" or "The doctors think I am making this up."

The reactions of irritability on the part of busy staff are not too surprising in view of the difficult behavior of such patients. Tensions in these patients may go up especially at the time of pending discharge from the hospital. Suicide prevention by hospital staff consists of responding to the emotional needs and giving emotional support to these individuals. With such patients the patience of Job is required. Any suicide threats or attempts on the part of such patients, no matter how "mild" or attention-getting, should be taken seriously. Their demand for attention may lead them to suicide. Hospital staff can often, by instituting some sort of new treatment procedure or medication, give this type of patient temporary relief or a feeling of improvement. But most of all, the sympathetic recognition on the part of hospital staff that the complaining, demanding, exasperating behavior of the dependent-dissatisfied patient is an expression of his own inner feelings of desperation may be the best route to preventing his suicide.

Co-workers, Family, Friends

Suicide is "democratic." It touches both patients and staff, unlettered and educated, rich and poor—almost proportionately. As for sex ratio, the statistics are interesting: Most studies have shown that in Western countries more men than women commit suicide, but a recent study indicates that in certain kinds of hospital settings like neuropsychiatric hospitals, a proportionately larger percentage of women kill themselves.[5] The information in this paper is meant to apply not only to patients, but to colleagues, and even to members of our families as well. The point is that only by being free to see the possibility of suicidal potential in everybody can suicide prevention of anybody really become effective.

In our society, we are especially loath to suspect suicide in individuals of some stature or status. For example, of the physicians who commit suicide, some could easily be saved if they would be treated (hospitalized, for example) like ordinary citizens in distress. Needless to say, the point of view that appropriate treatment might cause him professional embarrassment should never be invoked in such a way so as to risk a life being lost.

In general, we should not "run scared" about suicide. In

the last analysis, suicides are, fortunately, infrequent events. On the other hand, if we have even unclear suspicions of suicidal potential in another person, we do well to have "the courage of our own confusions" and take the appropriate steps.

These appropriate steps may include notifying others, obtaining consultation, alerting those concerned with the potentially suicidal person (including relatives and friends), getting the person to a sanctuary in a psychiatric ward or hospital. Certainly, we don't want to holler "Fire" unnecessarily, but we should be able to interpret the clues, erring, if necessary, on the "liberal" side. We may feel chagrined if we turn in a false alarm, but we would feel very much worse if we were too timid to pull that switch that might have prevented a real tragedy.

Earlier in this [essay] the role of the potential rescuer was mentioned. One implication of this is that professionals must be aware of their own reactions and their own personalities, especially in relation to certain patients. For example, does he have the insight to recognize his tendency to be irritated at a querulous and demanding patient and thus to ignore his presuicidal communications? Every rescue operation is a dialogue: Someone cries for help and someone else must be willing to hear him and be capable of responding to him. Otherwise the victim may die because of the potential rescuer's unresponsiveness.

We must develop in ourselves a special attitude for suicide prevention. Each individual can be a lifesaver, a one-person committee to prevent suicide. Happily, elaborate pieces of mechanical equipment are not needed; "all" that is required are sharp eyes and ears, good intuition, a pinch of wisdom, an ability to act appropriately, and a deep resolve.

Notes

1. N. L. Farberow and Edwin Shneidman, eds., *The Cry for Help* (New York: McGraw-Hill, 1961).

2. Robert Litman, "Emergency Response to Potential Suicide," *Journal of the Michigan Medical Society* (1963), 62: 68–72.

3. Norman L. Farberow, Edwin Shneidman, and Leonard Calista, *Suicide among General Medical and Surgical Hospital Patients with Malignant Neoplasms* (Washington, D.C.: Veterans' Administration, 1963).

4. Edwin Shneidman and Norman Farberow, *Evaluation and Treatment of Suicidal Risk among Schizophrenic Patients in Psychiatric Hospitals* (Washington, D.C.: Veterans' Administration, 1962).

5. Sherman Eisenthal, N. L. Farberow, and Edwin Shneidman, "Follow-up of Neuropsychiatric Hospital Patients on Suicide Observation Status," *Public Health Reports* (November 1966), 81:977–990.

35

The Ethics of Suicide

THOMAS S. SZASZ, M.D.

An editorial in the *Journal of the American Medical Association* (March 6, 1967) declared that "the contemporary physician sees suicide as a manifestation of emotional illness. Rarely does he view it in a context other than that of psychiatry." It was thus implied, the emphasis being the stronger for not being articulated, that to view suicide in this way is at once scientifically accurate and morally uplifting. I submit that it is neither; that, instead, this perspective on suicide is both erroneous and evil: erroneous because it treats an act as if it were a happening; and evil, because it serves to legitimize psychiatric force and fraud by justifying it as medical care and treatment.

Before going further, I should like to distinguish three fundamentally different concepts and categories that are combined and confused in most discussions of suicide. They are: (1) suicide proper, or so-called successful suicide; (2) attempted, threatened, or so-called unsuccessful suicide; and (3) the attribution by someone (typically a psychiatrist) to someone else (now called a "pa-

Reprinted from *The Antioch Review* (Spring 1971), 31:7–17, with the permission of the author and publisher. Copyright © 1971 by Thomas Szasz.

tient") of serious (that is, probably successful) suicidal intent. The first two concepts refer to acts by an actually or ostensibly suicidal person; the third refers to the claim of an ostensibly normal person about someone else's suicide-proneness.

I believe that, generally speaking, the person who commits suicide intends to die; whereas the one who threatens suicide or makes an unsuccessful attempt at it intends to improve his life, not to terminate it. (The person who makes claims about someone else's suicidal intent does so usually in order to justify his efforts to control that person.)

Put differently, successful suicide is generally an expression of an individual's desire for greater autonomy—in particular, for self-control over his own death; whereas unsuccessful suicide is generally an expression of an individual's desire for more control over others—in particular, for compelling persons close to him to comply with his wishes. Although in some cases there may be legitimate doubt about which of these conditions obtains, in the majority of instances where people speak of "suicide" or "attempted suicide," the act falls clearly into one or the other group.

In short, I believe that successful and unsuccessful suicide constitute radically different acts or categories, and hence cannot be discussed together. Accordingly, I have limited the scope of this essay to suicide proper, with occasional references to attributions of suicidal intent. (The ascription of suicidal intent is, of course, a very different sort of thing from either successful or unsuccessful suicide. Since psychiatrists use it as if it designated a potentially or probably fatal "condition," it is sometimes necessary to consider this concept together with the phenomenon of suicide proper.)

I

It is difficult to find "responsible" medical or psychiatric authority today that does not regard suicide as a medical, and specifically as a mental health, problem.

For example, Ilza Veith, the noted medical historian, writing in *Modern Medicine* (August 11, 1969), asserts that "the act [of suicide] clearly represents an illness. . . . "

Bernard R. Shochet, a psychiatrist at the University of Maryland, offers a precise description of the kind of illness it is. "Depression," he writes, "is a serious systemic disease, with both physiological and psychological concomitants, and suicide is a part of this syndrome." And he articulates the intervention he feels is implicit in this view: "If the patient's safety is in doubt, psychiatric hospitalization should be insisted on."[1]

Harvey M. Schein and Alan A. Stone, both psychiatrists at the Harvard Medical School, are even more explicit about the psychiatric coercion justified, in their judgment, by the threat of suicide. "Once the patient's suicidal thoughts are shared," they write,

the therapist must take pains to make clear to the patient that he, the therapist, considers suicide to be a maladaptive action, irreversibly counter to the patient's sane interests and goals; that he, the therapist, will do *everything* he can do to prevent it; and that the potential for such an action arises from the patient's illness. It is equally essential that the therapist believe in the professional stance; if he does not he should not be treating the patient within the delicate human framework of psychotherapy.[2]

Schein and Stone do not explain why the patient's confiding in his therapist to the extent of communicating his suicidal thoughts to him should *ipso facto* deprive the patient from being the arbiter of his own best interests. The thrust of their argument is prescriptive rather than logical. They seek to justify depriving the patient of a basic human freedom—the freedom to grant or withhold consent for treatment: "The therapist must insist that patient and physician—*together*—communicate the suicidal potential to important figures in the environment, both professional and family. . . . Suicidal intent must not be part of therapeutic confidentiality." And further on they write: "Obviously this kind of patient must be hospitalized. . . . The therapist must be prepared to step in with hospitalization, with security measures, and with medication."

Schein and Stone thus suggest that the "suicidal" patient should have the right to choose his therapist; and that he should have the right to agree with his therapist and follow the latter's therapeutic recommendation (say, for hospitalization). At the same time, they insist that if "suicidal" patient and therapist disagree on therapy, then the patient should *not* have the right to disengage himself from the first therapist and choose a second— say, one who would consider suicidal intent a part of therapeutic confidentiality.

Many other psychiatric authorities could be cited to illustrate the current unanimity on this view of suicide.

Lawyers and jurists have eagerly accepted the psychiatric perspective on suicide, as they have on nearly everything else. An article in the *American Bar Association Journal* (September 1968) by R. E. Schulman, who is both a lawyer and a psychologist, is illustrative.

Schulman begins with the premise that "No one in contemporary Western society would suggest that people be allowed to commit suicide as they please without some attempt to intervene or prevent such suicides. Even if a person does not value his own life, Western society does value everyone's life."

But I should like to suggest, as others have suggested before me, precisely what Schulman claims no one would suggest. Furthermore, if Schulman chooses to believe that Western society—which includes the United States with its history of slavery, Germany with its history of National Socialism, and Russia with its history of Communism—really "values everyone's life," so be it. But to accept this assertion as true is to fly in the face of the most obvious and brutal facts of history.

II

When a person decides to take his life, and when a physician decides to frustrate him in this action, the question arises: Why should the physician do so?

Conventional psychiatric wisdom answers: Because the suicidal person (now called "patient" for proper emphasis) suffers from a mental illness whose symptom is his desire to kill himself; it is the physician's duty to diagnose and treat illness: *ergo,* he must prevent the "patient" from killing himself and, at the same time, must "treat" the underlying "disease" that "causes" the "patient" to wish doing away with himself. This looks like an ordinary medical diagnosis and intervention. But it is not. What is missing? Everything. This hypothetical, suicidal "patient" is not ill: he has no demonstrable bodily disorder (or if he does, it does not "cause" his suicide); he does not assume the sick role: he does not seek medical help. In short, the physician uses the rhetoric of illness and treatment to justify his forcible intervention in the life of a fellow human being—often in the face of explicit opposition from his so-called "patient."

I do not doubt that attempted or successful suicide may be exceedingly *disturbing* for persons related to, acquainted with, or caring for the ostensible "patient." But I reject the conclusion that the suicidal person is, *ipso facto,* disturbed, that being disturbed equals being *mentally ill,* and that being mentally ill *justifies* psychiatric hospitalization or treatment. I have developed my reasons for this elsewhere, and need not repeat them here.[3] For the sake of emphasis, however, let me state that I consider counseling, persuasion, psychotherapy, or any other *voluntary measure,* especially for persons troubled by their own suicidal inclinations and seeking such help, unobjectionable, and indeed generally desirable, interventions. However, physicians and psychiatrists are usually not satisfied with limiting their help to such measures—and with good reason: from such assistance the individual may gain not only the desire to live, but also the strength to die.

But we still have not answered the question: Why should a physician frustrate an individual from killing himself? As we saw, some psychiatrists answer: Because the physician values the patient's life, at least when the patient is suicidal, more highly than does the patient himself. Let us examine this claim. Why should the physician, often a complete stranger to the suicidal patient, value the patient's life more highly than does the patient himself? He does not do so in medical practice. Why then should he do so in psychiatric practice, which he himself insists is a form of medical practice? Let us assume that a physician is confronted with an individual suffering from diabetes or heart failure who fails to take the drugs prescribed for his illness. We know that this often happens, and that when it does the patient may become disabled and die prematurely. Yet it would be absurd for a physician to consider, much less attempt, taking over the conduct of such a patient's life, confining him in a hospital against his will in order to treat his disease. Indeed, any attempt to do so would bring the physician into conflict with both the civil and the criminal law.

For, significantly, the law recognizes the medical patient's autonomy despite the fact that, unlike the suicidal individual, he suffers from a real disease; and despite the fact that, unlike the nonexistent disease of the suicidal individual, his illness is often easily controlled by simple and safe therapeutic procedures.

Nevertheless, the threat of alleged or real suicide, or so-called dangerousness to oneself, is everywhere considered a proper ground and justification for involuntary mental hospitalization and treatment. Why should this be so?

Let me suggest what I believe is likely to be the most important reason for the profound antisuicidal bias of the medical profession. Physicians are committed to saving lives. How, then, should they react to people who are committed to throwing away their lives? It is natural for people to dislike, indeed to hate, those who challenge their basic values. The physician thus reacts, perhaps "unconsciously" (in the sense that he does not articulate the problem in these terms), to the suicidal patient as if the patient had affronted, insulted, or attacked him: The physician strives valiantly, often at the cost of his own well-being, to save lives; and here comes a person who not only does not let the physician save him, but, *horrible dictu,* makes the physician an unwilling witness to that person's deliberate self-destruction. This is more than most physicians can take. Feeling assaulted in the very center of their spiritual identity, some take to flight, while others fight back.

Some nonpsychiatric physicians will thus have nothing to do with suicidal patients. This explains why many people who end up killing themselves have a record of having consulted a physician, often on the very day of their suicide. I surmise that these persons go in search of help, only to discover that the physician wants nothing to do with them. And, in a sense, it is right that it should be so. I do not blame the doctors. Nor do I advocate teaching them suicide prevention—whatever that might be. I contend that because physicians have a relatively blind faith in their life-saving ideology—which, moreover, they often need to carry them through their daily work—they are the wrong people for listening and talking to individuals, intelligently and calmly, about suicide. So much for those physicians who, in the face of the existential attack which they feel the suicidal patient launches on them, run for *their* lives. Let us now look at those who stand and fight back.

Some physicians (and other mental health professionals) declare themselves not only ready and willing to help suicidal patients who seek assistance, but all persons who are, or are alleged to be, suicidal. Since they, too, seem to perceive suicide as a threat, not just to the suicidal person's physical survival but to their own value system, they strike back and strike back hard. This explains why psychiatrists and suicidologists resort, apparently with a perfectly clear conscience, to the vilest methods: they must believe that their lofty ends justify the basest means. Hence the prevalent use of force and fraud in suicide prevention. The consequence of this kind of interaction between physician and "patient" is a struggle for power. The patient is at least honest about what he wants: to gain control over his life *and* death—by being the agent of his own demise. But the (suicide-preventing) psychiatrist is completely dishonest about what he wants: he claims that he only wants to help his patient, while actually he wants to gain control over the patient's life in order to save himself from having to confront his doubts about the value of his own life. Suicide is medical heresy. Commitment and electroshock are the appropriate psychiatric-inquisitorial remedies for it.

III

In the West, opposition to suicide, like opposition to contraception and abortion, rests on religious grounds. According to both the Jewish and Christian religions, God created man, and man can use himself only in the ways permitted by God. Preventing conception, aborting a pregnancy, or killing oneself are, in this imagery, all sins: each is a violation of the laws laid down by God, or by theological authorities claiming to speak in His name.

But modern man is a revolutionary. Like all revolutionaries, he likes to take away from those who have and to give to those who have not, especially himself. He has thus taken Man from God and given him to the State (with which he often identifies more than he knows). This is why the State gives and takes away so many of our rights, and why we consider this arrangement so "natural."

But this arrangement leaves suicide in a peculiar moral and philosophical limbo. For if a man's life belongs to the State (as it formerly belonged to God), then surely suicide is the taking of a life that belongs not to the taker but to everyone else.

The dilemma of this simplistic transfer of body-ownership from God to State derives from the fundamental difference between a religious and secular world view, especially when the former entails a vivid conception of a life after death, whereas the latter does not (or even emphatically repudiates it). More particularly, the dilemma derives from the problem of how to punish successful suicide? Traditionally, the Roman Catholic Church punished it by depriving the suicide of burial in consecrated ground. As far as I know, this practice is now so rare in the United States as to be practically nonexistent. Suicides are given a Catholic burial, as they are routinely considered having taken their lives while insane.

The modern State, with psychiatry as its secular-religious ally, has no comparable sanction to offer. Could this be one of the reasons why it punishes so severely—so very much more severely than did the Church—the *unsuccessful* suicide? For I consider the psychiatric stigmatization of people as "suicidal risks" and their incarceration in psychiatric institutions a form of punishment, and a very severe one at that. Indeed, although I cannot support this claim with statistics, I believe that accepted psychiatric methods of suicide prevention often aggravate rather than ameliorate the suicidal person's problems. As one reads of the tragic encounters with psychiatry of people like James Forrestal, Marilyn Monroe, or Ernest Hemingway, one gains the impression that they felt demeaned and deeply hurt by the psychiatric indignities inflicted on them, and that, as a result of these experiences, they were even more desperately driven to suicide. In short, I am suggesting that coerced psychiatric interventions may increase, rather than diminish, the suicidal person's desire for self-destruction.

But there is another aspect of the moral and philosophical dimensions of suicide that must be mentioned here. I refer to the growing influence of the resurgent idea of self-determination, especially the conviction that men have certain inalienable rights. Some men have thus come to believe (or perhaps only to believe that they believe) that they have a right to life, liberty, and property. This makes for some interesting complications for the modern legal and psychiatric stand on suicide.

This individualistic position on suicide might be put thus: A man's life belongs to himself. Hence, he has a right to take his own life, that is, to commit suicide. To be sure, this view recognizes that a man may also have a moral responsibility to his family and others, and that, by killing himself, he reneges on these responsibilities. But these are moral wrongs that society, in its corporate capacity as the State, cannot properly punish. Hence the State must eschew attempts to regulate such behavior by means of formal sanctions, such as criminal or mental hygiene laws.

The analogy between life and other types of property lends further support to this line of argument. Having a right to property means that a person can dispose of it even if in so doing he injures himself and his family. A man may give away, or gamble away, his money. But significantly, he cannot—our linguistic conventions do not allow it—be said to *steal from himself.* The concept of theft requires at least two parties: one who steals and another from whom is stolen. There is no such thing as "self-theft." The term "suicide" blurs this very distinction. The etymology of this term implies that suicide is a type of homicide, one in which criminal and victim are one and the same person. Indeed, when a person wants to condemn suicide he calls it "self-murder." Schulman, for example, writes: "Surely, self-murder falls within the province of the law."

History does repeat itself. Until recently, psychiatrists castigated as sick and persecuted those who engaged in self-abuse (that is, masturbation); now they castigate as sick and persecute those who engage in self-murder (that is, suicide).

The suicidologist has a literally schizophrenic view of the suicidal person: He sees him as two persons in one, each at war with the other. One-half of the patient wants to die; the other half wants to live. The former, says the suicidologist, is wrong; the latter is right. And he proceeds to protect the latter by restraining the former. However, since these two people are, like

Siamese twins, one, he can restrain the suicidal half only by restraining the whole person.

The absurdity of this medical-psychiatric position on suicide does not end here. It ends in extolling mental health and physical survival over every other value, particularly individual liberty.

In regarding the desire to live as a legitimate human aspiration, but not the desire to die, the suicidologist stands Patrick Henry's famous exclamation, "Give me liberty, or give me death!" on its head. In effect, he says: "*Give him* commitment, *give him* electroshock, *give him* lobotomy, *give him* life-long slavery, but *do not let him choose* death!" By so radically invalidating another person's (not his own!) wish to die, the suicide-preventer redefines the aspiration of the Other as not an aspiration at all: The wish to die thus becomes something an irrational, mentally diseased being displays, or something that happens to a lower form of life. The result is a far-reaching infantilization and dehumanization of the suicidal person.

For example, Phillip Solomon writes in the *Journal of the American Medical Association* (January 30, 1967), that "We [physicians] must protect the patient from his own [suicidal] wishes." While to Edwin Shneidman, "Suicide prevention is like fire prevention."[4] Solomon thus reduces the would-be suicide to the level of an unruly child, while Shneidman reduces him to the level of a tree! In short, the suicidologist uses his professional stance to illegitimize and punish the wish to die.

There is, of course, nothing new about any of this. Do-gooders have always opposed autonomy or self-determination. In "Amok," written in 1931, Stefan Zweig put these words into the mouth of his protagonist: "Ah, yes, 'It's one's duty to help.' That's your favorite maxim, isn't it? . . . Thank you for your good intentions, but I'd rather be left to myself. . . . So I won't trouble you to call, if you don't mind. Among the 'rights of man' there is a right which no one can take away, the right to croak when and where and how one pleases, without a 'helping hand.' "

But this is not the way the scientific psychiatrist and suicidologist sees the problem. He might agree (I suppose) that, in the abstract, man has the right Zweig claimed for him. But, in practice, suicide (so he says) is the result of insanity, madness, mental illness. Furthermore, it makes no sense to say that one has a right to be mentally ill, especially if the illness is one that, like typhoid fever, threatens the health of other people as well. In short, the suicidologist's job is to try to convince people that wanting to die is a disease.

This is how Ari Kiev, director of the Cornell Program in Social Psychiatry and its suicide-prevention clinic, does it: "We say [to the patient], look, you have a disease, just like the Hong Kong flu. Maybe you've got the Hong Kong depression. First, you've got to realize you are emotionally ill. . . . Most of the patients have never admitted to themselves that they are sick . . . ." (*New York Times,* February 9, 1969).

This pseudomedical perspective is then used to justify psychiatric deception and coercion of the crudest sort.

Here is how, according to the *Wall Street Journal* (March 6, 1969), the Los Angeles Suicide Prevention Center operates. A man calls and says he is about to shoot himself. The worker asks for his address. The man refuses to give it.

"If I pull it [the trigger] now I'll be dead," he [the caller] said in a muffled voice. "And that's what I want." Silently but urgently, Mrs. Whitbook [the worker] has signalled a co-worker to begin tracing the call. And now she worked to keep the man talking. . . . An agonizing 40 minutes passed. Then she heard the voice of a policeman come on the phone to say the man was safe.

But surely, if this man was able to call the Suicide Prevention Center, he could have, had he wanted, called for a policeman himself. But he did not. He was thus deceived by the Center in the "service" he got.

I understand that this kind of deception is standard practice in suicide prevention centers, though it is often denied that it is. A report (*Medical World News,* July 28, 1967) about the Nassau County Suicide Prevention Service corroborates the impression that when the would-be suicide does not cooperate with the suicide-prevention authorities, he is confined involuntarily. "When a caller is obviously suicidal," we are told, "a Meadowbrook ambulance is sent out immediately to pick him up."

One more example of the sort of thing that goes on in the name of suicide prevention should suffice. It is a routine story from a Syracuse newspaper (Syracuse *Post Standard,* September 29, 1969). The gist of it is all in one sentence: "A 28-year-old Minoa [a Syracuse suburb] man was arrested last night on a charge of violation of the Mental Hygiene Law, after police authorities said they spent two hours looking for him in the Minoa woods." But this man has harmed no one; his only "offense" was that someone claimed he might harm himself. Why, then, should the police look for, much less arrest, him? Why not wait until he returns? Or why not look, offer help, but avoid arrest and coerced psychiatry?

These are rhetorical questions. For our answers to them depend on and reflect our concepts of what it means to be a human being.

IV

I submit, then, that the crucial contradiction about suicide viewed as an illness whose treatment is a medical responsibility is that suicide is an action but is treated as if it were a happening. As I showed elsewhere, this contradiction lies at the heart of all so-called mental illnessses or psychiatric problems.[5] However, it poses a particularly acute dilemma for suicide, because suicide is the only fatal "mental illness."

Before concluding, I should like to restate briefly my views on the differences between diseases and desires, and show that by persisting in treating desires as diseases, we only end up treating man as a slave.

Let us take, as our paradigm case of illness, a skier who takes a bad spill and fractures an ankle. This fracture is something that has happened to him. He has not intended it to happen. (To be sure, he may have intended it; but that is another case.) Once it has happened, he will seek medical help and will cooperate with medical efforts to mend his broken bones. In short, the person and his fractured ankle are, as it were, two separate entities, the former acting on the latter.

Let us now consider the case of the suicidal person. Such a person may also look upon his own suicidal inclination as an undesired, almost alien, impulse and seek help to combat it. If so, the ensuing arrangement between him and his psychiatrist is readily assimilated to the standard medical model of treatment: the patient actively seeks and cooperates with professional efforts to remedy his "condition."

But as we have seen this is not the only way, nor perhaps the most important way, that the game of suicide prevention is played. It is accepted medical and psychiatric practice to treat persons for their suicidal desires against their will. And what exactly does this mean? Something quite different from that to which it is often analogized, namely the involuntary (or nonvoluntary) treatment of a bodily illness. For a fractured ankle can be set whether or not a patient consents to its being set. That is because setting a fracture is a *mechanical act on the body*. But a threatened suicide cannot be prevented whether or not the "patient" consents to its being prevented. That is because, suicide being the result of human desire and action, suicide prevention is a *political act on the person*. In other words, since suicide is an exercise and expression of human freedom, it can be prevented only by curtailing human freedom. This is why deprivation of liberty becomes, in institutional psychiatry, a form of treatment.

In the final analysis, the would-be suicide is like the would-be emigrant: both want to leave where they are and move elsewhere. The suicide wants to leave life and embrace death. The emigrant wants to leave his homeland and settle in another country.

Let us take this analogy seriously. It is much more faithful to the facts than is the analogy between suicide and illness. A crucial characteristic that distinguishes open from closed societies is that people are free to leave the former but not the latter. The medical profession's stance toward suicide is thus like the Communists' toward emigration: the doctors insist that the would-be suicide survive, just as the Russians insist that the would-be emigrant stay home.

Whether those who so curtail other people's liberties act with complete sincerity, or with utter cynicism, hardly matters. What matters is what happens: the abridgement of individual liberty, justified, in the case of suicide prevention, by psychiatric rhetoric; and, in the case of emigration prevention, by political rhetoric.

In language and logic we are the prisoners of our premises, just as in politics and law we are the prisoners of our rulers. Hence we had better pick them well. For if suicide is an illness because it terminates in death, and if the prevention of death by any means necessary is the physician's therapeutic mandate, then the proper remedy for suicide is indeed liberticide.

Notes

1. Bernard Shochet, "Recognizing the Suicidal Patient," *Modern Medicine* (May 1970), 38:114–23.

2. Harvey M. Schein and Alan A. Stone, "Psychotherapy Designed to Detect and Treat Suicidal Potential," *American Journal of Psychiatry* (March 1969), 125:1247–51 (emphasis added).

3. Thomas S. Szasz, *Law, Liberty and Psychiatry* (New York: Macmillan, 1963); and *Ideology and Insanity* (Garden City, N.Y.: Doubleday, 1970).

4. Edwin Shneidman, "Preventing Suicide," *Bulletin of Suicidology* (July 1968), pp. 19–25.

5. Thomas S. Szasz, *The Myth of Mental Illness* (New York: Harper and Row, 1961).

36

Bouvia v. County of Riverside

Riverside Superior Court,
No. 159780 (December 16, 1983)

HEWS, Judge:
The plaintiff, Elizabeth Bouvia, an articulate, severely handicapped young woman, asserts in this application for a permanent
injunction, that the defendants County of Riverside, Riverside
General Hospital and its staff, will, unless restrained and enjoined
by order of this court, administer health care against her will or
will cause her transfer or discharge from Riverside General Hospital. She contends that this will cause her great and irreparable
injury and will violate her rights of privacy and self-determination
under the laws and the Constitutions of the United States and the
State of California.

She further asks the court specifically to enjoin the defendants from administering any health care without her consent. She
does not wish to accept any fluid, food or other nutrients or
sustenance. There is to be no installation by insertion, cannula-
tion or surgical operation of any intravenous, nasogastric or gastrostomy tubation or tubing to sustain her. She has stated that
civil and criminal actions will follow if forced feeding is com-
menced. She asks for pain medication and hygienic care until her
ultimate death occurs. In essence, the plaintiff claims that she has

the right to determine when and how her life shall end and that society has the obligation to honor and to assist her in achieving that individual right.

The defendants assert that the plaintiff does not have this right to end her life by virtue of any statutory, constitutional, ethical or moral theory. In the alternative, defendants assert that if the plaintiff has this right, it may be abridged and overcome by compelling state interests.

The defendants further assert that the order sought by plaintiff would have a devastating effect on the medical staff, administration and patients at Riverside General Hospital. It would violate medical ethics. It would constitute participation in the crimes of murder, conspiracy, and aiding and abetting suicide. It would subject the county to civil liability. It would evoke the wrath of the licensing authority of the hospital, its doctors, and its nurses.

Intervenor, Richard Bouvia, plaintiff's estranged husband, claims that the plaintiff is either mentally incompetent or that her judgment is impaired. He asserts that her decision amounts to suicide or self-euthanasia. He further states that criminal prosecution will result and civil actions will be filed if the defendants are ordered to, and do allow the plaintiff to expire. . . .

From the evidence presented, the court finds that the following facts have been established:

That plaintiff, Elizabeth Bouvia, has since birth suffered from cerebral palsy, which has left her with virtually no motor function in any of her limbs or other skeletal muscles. That she retains some slight control of her right hand sufficient to operate the mechanical control of an electrically-powered wheelchair. That she maintains enough voluntary control of the muscles of her mouth, face and throat structures so that she can eat a normal diet, when essentially fed by someone else, and that she can talk with only a very slight speech impediment;

That the cerebral palsy which afflicts plaintiff has left intact her sensory nerves so that she experiences a fairly constant degree of pain and discomfort from her inability to change her own position, from the muscle contractures and increased spasticity which afflict her withered limbs, and from the arthritis which her bodily distortions have caused;

That the plaintiff is physically unable to take her own life;

That though afflicted in her body, plaintiff's mind and intellect are totally unaffected and are quite normal. . . .

On September 3, plaintiff directed her father to take her to the Emergency Department at Riverside General Hospital. There she arranged for a voluntary psychiatric admission. She disclosed her intent to discontinue sufficient caloric intake so that she would eventually succumb to starvation following her admission.

The plaintiff's life is not in a terminal state and her death is not imminent as a result of her disability. . . .

The court is convinced that plaintiff has made her own decision to forego further feedings, and will vigorously resist any feedings forced upon her. This decision was made by her after careful and mature deliberation of the alternatives, consequences and irreversibility of her decision.

The court further finds that her decision was rational and that plaintiff is mentally competent to make decisions affecting her life. . . .

The court is convinced that the plaintiff is sincere in her desire to terminate her life, and that she no longer desires to live. The court is also convinced that all counsel want her to live and they hope that she might change her mind. . . . All her bodily systems are fully functional and she is not on any life-support system. . . .

The court has determined that the ultimate issue is whether or not a severely handicapped, mentally competent person who is otherwise physically healthy and not terminally ill has the right to end her life with the assistance of society. The court concludes that she does not. The equitable powers of this court may not be invoked for such a purpose. . . .

The court concludes that the plaintiff in this instance does have a "fundamental or preferred" right to terminate her own life and to terminate medical intervention but that this right has been overcome by the strong interests of the State and society.

Preservation of life is the strongest state interest involved . . . None of the parties has cited any legal precedent which approves the proposition that a non-terminal person with a life expectancy of 15 to 20 years who has a disabling but non-progressive physical condition should be allowed to terminate life because of a sincere desire to do so by reason of the disability.

Next are the interests of third parties involved in this case. Third parties here include other patients in the hospital, other persons similarly situated who suffer from chronic disabling diseases, and health care professionals employed at Riverside General Hospital who would have to assist in the plaintiff's demise.

The next interest of society the court has considered is the prevention of suicide. . . . Cerebral palsy is not terminal—self-starvation is terminal. . . . By not issuing the requested order, the state will be protecting the plaintiff from suicide. . . .

Lastly, the court has considered the state's interest in the maintenance of the integrity of the medical profession. Prevailing medical ethical standards do not, without exception, demand that all efforts toward life prolongation be made in all circumstances. It is recognized that the dying are more often in need of comfort than treatment. However . . . the court comes back to the established fact that plaintiff in this case is not dying and is not terminal. The established ethics of the medical profession clearly outweigh and overcome her own right of self-determination. . . .

What are we now faced with? If the medical staff . . . determines that plaintiff should receive further care and treatment within the confines of the hospital setting and if the plaintiff voluntarily agrees to stay but declines nutrients necessary to sustain her life, the defendants now will face the problem of forcing nutrients upon her. . . . Forced feeding, however invasive, would be administered for the purpose of saving the life of an otherwise non-terminal patient and should be permitted. There is no other reasonable option. Saving her life would be paramount.

Where does this leave the plaintiff, Elizabeth Bouvia? None of us can fully appreciate what her life has been—to suffer the pain and the frustrations of full dependency on others every day for all the things that most of us consider significantly contribute to the quality of one's life. . . . However, the court cannot allow her to end her life in this manner. She does have the right to terminate her existence, but not while she is non-terminal with the assistance of society. An injunction should not be granted where the harm which will occur via the injunction is greater than the harm it is designed to avoid. . . .

Index